sex &
SINGLE GIRLS
STRAIGHT AND QUEER WOMEN ON SEXUALITY
EDITED BY LEE DAMSKY

SEAL PRESS

Cover design by Kathleen Kincaid
Typeset by Maren Costa

Library of Congress Cataloging-in-Publication Data

Sex & single girls : straight and queer women on sexuality / edited by Lee Damsky.
    p. cm.
  ISBN 1-58005-038-7 (paper)
   1. Women—Sexual behavior—Case studies. 2. Single women—Sexual behavior—Case studies. 3. Generation X—Sexual behavior—Case studies. I. Title: Sex and single girls. II. Damsky, Lee.

HQ29 .S486 2000
306.7'082—dc21
                                       00-063515

Printed in Canada
First printing, October 2000
10   9   8   7   6   5   4   3   2   1

"The High Holy Days Are Not Sexy" was originally published in *2SexE: Urban Tales of Love, Liberty, and the Pursuit of Gettin' It On,* edited by Antonio Cuevas and Jennifer Lee. Published by Frog Ltd. Reprinted by permission of the author.

Distributed to the trade by Publishers Group West
In Canada: PGW Canada, Toronto, Ontario
In the U.K. and Europe: Airlift Book Distributors, Middlesex, England
In Australia: Banyan Tree Book Distributors, Kent Town, South Australia

To my parents, for coming out

Acknowledgments

My deepest gratitude to my editor Jennie Goode for her wonderful editorial advice and help envisioning this book; and to Seal Press publisher Faith Conlon, for her belief in me and this project, and for her patience during its completion.

Special thanks to the staff and former staff of Seal Press: Patricia Ann, Rosemary Caperton, Ingrid Emerick, Laura Gronewold, Kate Loeb, Anne Mathews, Leslie Miller, Lucie Ocenas, Lisa Okey, Alison Rogalsky and Lynn Siniscalchi for all their help producing this book, their editorial suggestions and their friendship in my years at Seal Press.

To copyeditor extraordinaire Annie Decker, cover designer Kathleen Kincaid and typesetter Maren Costa. And to Clare Conrad for her help with production.

To Kate Ledger, whose collaboration at the start of this project helped give it shape. And to Kristin Pula for kindly reading and sharing her thoughts on portions of the manuscript.

Most of all to Robert Kaplan, whom I can never thank enough for his love and support, and for always giving me a reason to look forward to the finish.

Contents

⊛ INTRODUCTION

In Search of the Single Girl

In 1962 Helen Gurley Brown published *Sex and the Single Girl,* an advice book for young women on life, love and sex, declaring, "Nice, single girls *do* have affairs, and they do not necessarily die of them!" a shocking revelation that kept the book on the *New York Times* bestseller list for sixteen weeks. Although the phrase "Sex and the Single Girl" has since become ingrained in the popular consciousness, few of us born in the baby bust of the sexual revolution know where it actually comes from. Our first sex book was more likely our parents' copy of *The Joy of Sex,* and we probably felt more pressure to be sexually active than to guard our virginity or its public facade. Even so, public titillation has a long half-life. A few years ago, I had never heard of Brown's book, but the immediately recognizable catchphrase "Sex and the Single Girl" had the intriguing ring of either a Cold War–era mental-hygiene tract on the importance of virginity, or a dirty movie, circa 1972, featuring the debauched sex life of a ponytailed coed.

Since I am adapting her title for my own use, I want to say that I appreciate Brown speaking out for the right of young, white, heterosexual, "good" girls—women more or less like me—to have independent sex lives. While Brown's single girl may have been confined to the rather limited and traditional role of the aspiring seductress (it's no coincidence that Brown was the longtime editor of *Cosmopolitan* magazine) and while her book had little to say to lesbians or anyone else who didn't have access to the "good girl" role to begin with, it was a start. It didn't take much to be sex-positive in 1962: No one else was giving us permission to get laid. The overwhelming success of the book, one suspects, stemmed from its proclamation of a social truth about women's expanded sexual possibilities that, in the years leading up to the sexual revolution, many of its readers were already putting into practice, albeit with varying degrees of guilt and secrecy. Someone was finally admitting, in print, that what they were doing was okay.

If anything definitively dates *Sex and the Single Girl*—both the book and its title—to 1962, it is its conception of "the single girl." *The* single girl. Granted, the concept was as misleading in 1962 as it is today, but because of the social gains of feminism and the civil rights and queer movements, it's now clear there are many ways to be a girl, many ways to be single and many, many ways to have sex. While media culture may continue to trot out one formulaic single girl after the next—the *Cosmo* girl, Ally McBeal, Bridget Jones, even the lipstick lesbian—we can recognize any monolithic conception of "the single girl" (along with the ever-popular "What do women want?") as absurdly flat and reductive. When it comes to our sex lives, we are all living with a lot of freedom, a lot of complexity and many more choices.

Navigating this relatively new sexual landscape, the last thing we need is another advice book. But with so many possibilities and so few role models, I couldn't help being curious about what other women are doing with their sex lives these days. *Sex and Single Girls* is an attempt to fill this void—not with "the girl" but with girls: women with a range of backgrounds, both straight and queer, telling their own stories about sexual experiences, desires and identity.

What Rules?
A lot has changed since 1962, when the social expectations for sexual behavior were at least relatively clear (if constraining, at best). The society we live in now has embraced a perverse combination of sexual repression, fear and the overhyped sexualization of everything from food to morality to politics. Women in my generation were born in the '60s and '70s with the sexual revolution and the feminist movement, but we grew up with a mix of socio-sexual contradictions: the

conservative backlash and the AIDS epidemic, the queer movement and genderfuck. We got divorced parents and "family values," homophobia and lesbian chic, "Just Say No" and "Ten Ways to Drive Him Wild." We were raised with a gluttony of freedoms, fed on visions of egalitarianism and suckled on MTV. We also got hit with our share of sexual violence and discovered that the sexual and racial double standards our mothers grew up with, however criticized in liberal discourse, were alive and well in our high schools and college dorms. Growing up in the '70s, our earliest knowledge of sex was likely to come from porn. When we first discovered feminism, porn became anathema, and by the time we got to college-level women's studies it was part of the curriculum. More than anything else, we simply grew up surrounded by sex, where the old rules were not so much overthrown as internalized, displaced, contradicted.

Because sex has traditionally been tied to marriage, or at least to long-term monogamous partnership, sexual choices are inseparable from life choices. We are still pressured to marry by eager family members, a billion-dollar bridal industry and a society organized around and for nuclear families. Yet more women are choosing to stay single for longer periods of time, gaining more freedom to explore sexual relationships.

The traditional concept of "singlehood," identifying people by their unmarried status, suggests a before-and-after scenario, in which the point of being single—even if that singlehood is prolonged—is finding someone to marry; and being married means that one's sex life is a done deal. This notion of singlehood, its obvious heterosexism in a society that does not recognize gay marriage (nor the variety of different partnerships that defy easy categorization) aside, glosses over what for many women, queer and straight, is a central experience of autonomous, single life: having sex. Being single can have as much—or much more—to do with experimenting with sex and finding our sexual selves than finding the perfect partner.

Most women I know personally take for granted a range of options for their sexual behavior, whether or not they are interested in or comfortable with all of the alternatives: serial monogamy (plus or minus cohabitation), recreational sex with dates or fuckbuddies, abstinence, using sex toys or porn, trying S/M, having children, getting married, experimenting with open relationships. Many of these possibilities for sexual experimentation came to straight culture through queer culture. With the successes of the gay movement and the creation of a highly visible queer community, people have been more free to come out, and straight people have benefited from queer alternatives to patriarchal institutions, relationships and gender roles. The concept of exploring or experimenting with one's sexuality is first and foremost a queer one, for it implies that one's interests or desires may diverge from the dominant heterosexual model we all learned as the norm and the ideal. But everyone goes through a sexual coming-of-age, sometimes more than one. Understanding sexuality as a distinct part of who we are, independent of (though wrapped up with) our romantic relationships, simply gives us the freedom to explore our sexuality—our turn-ons, inhibitions, fantasies, defining experiences, partnering preferences, quirks and definite dislikes—as its own semiautonomous force in our lives.

This freedom is hardly simple. Sex can be empowering, exhilarating and pleasurable, or it can be a source of violence, alienation or shame. Standing in the rubble of three generations of sexual politics, we all have to write our own rules.

Everything You Always Wanted to Know About Sex?
Let me say up front that I am not a "sexpert." That's why I started looking for some good reading material to inspire me. But I soon realized the sex book I most wanted to read didn't exist. I wanted to read personal stories about how other women in their twenties and thirties are having sex: how they explore sexuality, how sex fits into their lives, how they understand their own desires, how they've screwed up, how they weather the emotional and physical hazards of a sexually active life, what sex means to them, how they choose to get laid. Maybe I wanted a vicarious thrill, maybe I wanted to learn something about myself, maybe I wanted a sense of the possibilities, maybe I was curious about other women's private lives, maybe I wanted to crack up, maybe I just wanted something I could relate to. I couldn't find it. Even as a layperson (so to speak), I thought this constituted a significant gap in the literature.

In the sexuality section of one of the few remaining independent bookstores where I live, I find a lot of advice books: orgasm tips, dating tips, sex tips for straight women from gay men, how-to books on everything from anal sex to S/M. Certainly these have their uses—particularly for specific sexual interests one might want to explore—but am I the only average practitioner who considers technique the least challenging aspect of getting into bed? I find collections of breezy sex columns from lifestyle magazines, which provide welcome comic relief with their madcap game of "sex in the '90s"—without much depth or complexity to get in the way. I find monographs by professional sex writers and activists: While their experiences and insights make for fascinating reading, the very fact that their lives revolve so much around sex—having it, writing about it and making their livings as sex-positive poster girls—means that as someone with a non–sex related full-time job, I usually can't relate to them. I find New Age books on sex and spirituality (I think I'd rather read *Cosmo*). I find shelf after shelf of women's erotica, which, since my sex life bears no resemblance to a series of fantasy encounters, feels like part of the problem rather than part of the solution.

I shift over to the gay and lesbian section just a few feet down the shelf. Here I can find examples of the kind of writing I am looking for: honest, personal, adventurous, feminist, telling it like it is. (For the most part, this genre of sex writing does not exist by and for heterosexual women, and *Bridget Jones' Diary* isn't doing it for me.) But even the queer section doesn't have what I most want to read. Many of these writers are baby boomers, which means that as much as I have to learn from them they are not always describing the world I live in now. Increasingly, collections seem to be getting narrower and more focused. If I want to read *only* coming-out stories or fetish stories or writings about butch/femme or S/M, I can find them. Obviously such collections are good, necessary, important things—and they are the best means of exploring specific sexual desires and identities in real depth. But what if I also want to think about sexuality in a way that isn't constrained to a particular sexual orientation or identity?

As a bisexual woman I am used to cross-identifying. Sometimes I find myself identifying with another person's experience in ways I would not have expected, and only rarely do I come up against the limits of my own sexual preferences on the page. But most of all it is because what I am drawn to in a personal story about sex does not hinge on whether the writer is queer or straight, bottom or top, vanilla or kinky, promiscuous or celibate. I am reading for stories of pleasure, desire, survival, risk, weirdness and all-too-human foibles. I am reading more for how the writer experiences her own sexuality and where her desire takes her than the mechanics of what she does to get off.

Of course, when it comes to what other women do in bed, I admit that I'm interested in variety—in actual sexual experiences, in the ways other women experience desire and in the social and personal obstacles they experience on the way to full sexual expression. True, sex is a highly personal, private matter; it only makes sense, I think, to question the value of sex stories in an exhibitionistic and seemingly oversexed culture. As much as we are surrounded by sex and sold sex, exploring and understanding our own sexualities is a solo journey. But this does not mean that we cannot connect with others' stories in a humorous, strange and life-changing process.

The Morning After: Sexuality and Feminism
The only sex books I found specifically aimed at both queer and straight women were in the women's studies section. In fact I didn't exactly "find" them, I rediscovered them: *Pleasure and Danger* and *Powers of Desire,* both books with a mix

of academic feminist criticism and personal essays, stories and poems that I read in my first women's studies classes, circa 1990. The books themselves dated back even further, to the feminist "sex wars" of the early 1980s, when "sex-positive" and "anti-porn" feminists made the relationship between sex and feminism a matter of heated debate. Back then, sexuality was fundamentally a political issue for feminists—sometimes even more than a personal one.

Politicizing our sexuality was essential to the progress of second-wave feminism. In conceptualizing the personal as political, feminists were able to fight rape and domestic violence, leave unfulfilling and limiting marriages, come out as lesbians, and discard narrow, socially enforced expectations of traditional femininity in behavior and appearance. Sexuality is the very site of women's oppression in a patriarchal culture, and part of the feminist coming-to-consciousness was the recognition of how our own sexualities were tied up with some of our most painful, limiting experiences. It is not surprising then that in this formative period of the feminist movement, expressions of women's sexuality that appeared to contradict a utopian vision of feminism seemed threatening to feminist ideals. In retrospect, the sex wars can be seen as a struggle over what the relationship between the personal and the political should be, when attempts to reshape our vision of women's sexuality in relation to feminist politics were confronted with the utter resistance of sexual desire to external political or social agendas. What mainstream feminism eventually learned from the radical sex movement was the importance of letting our sexuality—and the importance of its liberation and full consensual expression—inform our politics, rather than somehow trying to separate what is "feminist" from what is "oppressive" in our own deepest desires.

But does that mean that sex should be detached from social issues altogether? What I took from those anthologies compiled in the early '80s was a feminist examination of sexuality that included personal experiences of sex by women of diverse backgrounds and sexual interests and that also seriously addressed the questions of women's sexual oppression. Now that the sex wars are over, this unified feminist approach to the subject of sexuality has faded into the background. And in the hustle and bustle of sex-positivity that now surrounds the subject of women's sexuality, it is easy to gloss over the ways our experience of sex can be weighed down—by sexual assault or a history of sexual abuse, by racism, by unplanned pregnancies or STDs, by sexual double standards, by the absence of a sense of entitlement or privilege, by homophobia, by ableism, by the ingrained dislike of our own bodies that is so easy to deconstruct but still so hard to shed, by intolerance for our choice of gender expression, or by the sexual harassment that is still a mundane part of women's lives. Many of these experiences are shared by straight women and queer women alike.

As a collection of personal essays, the purpose of this anthology is not to make a political statement about women's sexuality. But it is an attempt to begin to explore women's sexuality in an open, inclusive, feminist way that recognizes the centrality of sexuality in women's lives. Understanding and expressing our sexuality has something to do with life, something to do with power, something to do with self-realization. And the way we experience sex goes a long way toward teaching us who we are and what we can do in the world.

Sex and Single Girls

As I thought more about the kind of sex book that I wanted to read, I decided (perhaps as a fantasy of my own) to edit this collection myself. The process of working with these writers and reading their work has inspired, educated and entertained me.

Throughout the process of editing this collection I struggled with the desire to explore in a single volume a truly wide range of sexual interests and choices; to incorporate feminist perspectives on all of the experiences that separate women from our sexuality or attempt to usurp our control of it; to bring to light writers whose untrammeled appetite for both sex and life can be an inspiration to us all; to show women going against the grain of social expectations and making their own sexual choices; to get a glimpse of the individual meaning of sex for a diverse group of women; and to resist the overwhelming social pressure, both in mainstream culture and at times in sex-positive feminism, to make our sexuality the measure of our womanhood—all without losing sight of the quirky humor that often goes hand in hand with sex. Clearly no anthology can do all of the above in a comprehensive way; indeed, the illusion of comprehensiveness is one danger of a large anthology on a much larger subject. As an editor I cannot help but be aware of the stories and issues not represented in this book, which can only scratch the surface of women's sexual experiences. But I hope this collection reflects all of these concerns in some form.

The range of experiences included here means that pieces speak to each other and contradict each other in informative and sometimes surprising ways. Something as simple as sexual autonomy can take on a range of meanings for different writers. In "Armed and Satisfied," by Black Artemis, a virgin who prides herself on her independence explores her sexuality with sex toys; in "The Allure of the One-Night Stand," by Meg Daly, sexual autonomy is the freedom to play out private fantasies in sexual encounters with both sexes; in "On the Altar," by Cecilia Tan, it is the ability to express different sides of herself in ongoing polyamorous relationships. And for Carla Richmond, writing on a long-term lesbian relationship, it is "realizing that I don't need her, that I can talk and breathe and flourish without her—but that I'd rather not."

Several writers explore the kinks of their individual sexual proclivities and the adventures and conflicts these inspire: In "Confessions of an Unrepentant Cocktease," Hanne Blank describes the tantalizing thrill of unconsummated desire. In "Sight Unseen," Christy Damio—who is legally blind—describes her "fascination with secretive public sex acts" that are hidden in plain view. In "Confusion Is Sex," magdalen seeks "the strange bliss of submission" but recounts the frustration of looking for partners with whom she is compatible both sexually and in "real life." Both queer and straight writers describe fantasies that cross over gender and sexual orientation to create a sexual charge: In "Blowjob Queen," Lisa Johnson, a straight woman, fantasizes about having a penis and coming in the mouth of a girl. In "Better Living Through Porn," Abby Levine finds a powerful turn-on in gay male pornography. In "Watching You Watching Me," Kary Barrett Wayson appropriates the stereotypical straight male fantasy of lesbian sex—a soft-focus vision of "naked women in a porn orgy scene"—as both performer and observer. And in "Seductions of a Bordertown Boy," Karleen Pendleton Jiménez, an S/M boydyke, plays with power, race and revenge in her fantasy of topping President Clinton.

Yet alongside this playful and empowered approach to sex and desire, several writers describe how deeply sexual violence and intimidation have colored their sexual experience. Both Siobhan Brooks ("A Blackgirl Taking Control of Her Sexuality") and Karen Rosenberg ("The Seventeen Year Twitch") describe how harassment affected their sexual development as teenagers. Recounting the aftermath of her rape in relation to concepts of "safe" and "unsafe" sex, J. Keiko Lane shows why "for some of us, sex was never safe." In "Dreaming of a Color-Blind Affair," E. René Parker recounts the experience of being consistently exoticized—and at one point sexually assaulted—by whites in some of her first sexual explorations as a college student.

The significance of claiming, owning and acting on sexual desire—often in the face of cultural forces that keep women sexually passive, focused on others' desires rather than their own, sexually invisible or desexualized—is central in many essays. In "Silence and the Word," Mary Anne Mohanraj works to express her sexual desires to her partners without embarrassment, in spite of being a prolific writer of erotica. In "The Not-SoFizgig Affair," @nonymous, a fat woman, dives into online sex only to discover that most men's responses to her female alias overlook her virtual performance and roleplay in favor of their fantasies of a physical ideal—and seeks a twisted revenge. In "From Here to Eternity," Annie Koh explores how social scripts and expectations have shaped her sexual experiences (both positively and negatively) to the point that she questions where her own desire begins and ends. Siobhan Brooks brings her sexuality out of hiding while working as an exotic dancer. And in "The Virgin and the Fuckdoll," Augusta Moore is able to freely explore her sexuality when she sheds her expectations of love, commitment and stability in relationships and instead takes on the roles of the "initiator, the deflowerer and the user."

Finding (or lacking) role models for our sexuality can have a powerful effect on our experience of sex and our sense of entitlement to sexual fulfillment. In "How Do You Do That Thing You Do?" Mary Martone describes how a stint at the National Gay and Lesbian Task Force straight out of college finally gave her the role models she needed to "sharpen the images in [her] head, spell it out in [her] ear, and ultimately, to kick [her] ass out the door"—into her first lesbian experience. For some writers, finding empowering images and stories is less simple. Geraldine Mitchell writes that she "must take her sexual cues from some Punany Diva whose acquaintance [she] has not yet officially made." Searching for cultural images of black women's sexuality, she identifies most with Star Trek's Lieutenant Commander Uhuru, who is "much too busy trying to prove herself, run the whole goddamn ship and represent the race to busy herself with . . . pleasure." E. René Parker is open to interracial relationships but is often confronted with racist stereotypes: "I never wanted the rape story between white men and Black women to be mine . . . [But] coming up with a new story is more challenging than deconstructing old myths." And Diana Courvant confronts the assumption that disabled women are asexual and finds little to counter this stereotype, even in progressive communities.

It is primarily queer writers who take on issues of sexual identity and community—indeed, sexual identity is something most straight women never need to question. Both Adrien-Alice Hansel and Daisy Hernández describe how their sexuality separated them from their families and the cultures in which they were raised, and both seek ways to bridge the gap. For Hernández it is a gap of culture and language, and for Hansel one of culture and class. Cecilia Tan describes the importance of belonging to her own community of sexual outlaws. And Sara Johnston and Tara Hardy explore the connection between gender expression, identity and sexuality. Johnston writes, "My recent exploration of masculinity progressively has closed off parts of my body to you . . . fucking with a strap-on is a gendered act for me: my body feels different, it feels male, I feel right." Hardy describes how embracing her working-class femme identity and "loud" femininity has been sexually empowering—in spite of the dominant assumption that to be liberated is to be "as far as possible from female."

Perhaps most of all, these essays demonstrate how the meaning of a sexual encounter is bound up in the idiosyncratic amalgam of experiences, desires and fantasies each partner brings to the scene. Underlying all of these threads is power: the power to seek pleasure, to explore sexuality, to express our desires, to find sexual fulfillment—as well as all the ways our power may be constrained. Nothing could be more intimate, more gratuitous or more unproductive than sexual pleasure; yet there is little else that connects so strongly to our self-expression and self-determination. If there is an overarching theme in this collection, then, it is that our sexuality is connected to every other part of our lives.

Lee Damsky
Seattle, Washington
July 2000

sex &
SINGLE GIRLS

Confessions of an Unrepentant Cocktease

 Hanne Blank

I love being a cocktease. Whenever I admit my passion for teasing men until they moan in a delicious combination of agony and pure sensuality, the first reaction I get from other women is usually shock. "But I thought you were a feminist!" they protest. "That's so . . . *fifties*."

For me, being a cocktease isn't about being some man's coy little sex kitten. It's about manipulating raw sexual power, not giving men what they want and making them love it anyway. (And yes, you can be a cocktease to women as well.) Even more than that, it's about getting off on it myself.

I'm a top, no question about it. I love seeing a man's lips red with arousal, his eyes and nostrils dilated with lust, and reminding him that there's no way in hell he's going to get to fuck me. Hearing a whispered plea in my ear, in a voice guttural with desire and a tone that verges on outright begging, brings a jaunty smile to my lips and a definite dampness between my thighs. When a man's eyes are following my every move, drinking in each deliberately sexualized gesture, already hard as steel when I haven't even so much as touched his arm, I'm in high-voltage heaven. I have a treasure trove of letters from admirers that I sometimes read while I masturbate, each of them sizzling with desire. They tell me how badly they want to strip for me, how badly they want to taste my pussy or suck my nipples for hours—anything I want, they say, "but God I just want you, I want to please you, so bad." If that's "fifties," I'm Mamie Eisenhower.

The truth must be told, though: I wasn't always a cocktease. I would never even have dreamed of it as a teenager or in my early twenties when I believed, first of all, that good girls didn't do things like that, and that, secondly, any woman who wanted an egalitarian relationship with the man in her life would never pull the cocktease trump card. It just didn't seem fair. Besides, I figured that only centerfold-gorgeous types with constant throngs of suitors really had enough latitude and arrogance about their own attractiveness to pull the cocktease routine anyway. That left me out of the running.

A couple years later, though, it was an entirely different story. In a strange and bleak period when I was having utterly inappropriate affairs with a half-dozen people at any given time, it began to dawn on me that the part of the affairs I'd been enjoying most (which is to say the only part I'd been truly enjoying at all) was the buildup, the chance to flex my seductress muscles while enjoying the give and take of erotic play on the way toward actual sex.

I started to deliberately prolong that part of my affairs, slipping purringly into the role of cocktease without even really knowing it. I was a much more callous soul then—partly because of my own unhealed wounds and partly, I think, out of sheer stupid youth—and would even go so far as to ditch a partner once the teasing, buildup and foreplay seemed to be reaching their logical limit. I didn't really care so much about the fucking. It was getting there that was getting me off. It was selfish, sure, and I paid for it in messy breakups. But while it lasted, it had its moments.

Around the same time, I encountered BDSM for the first time. Bottoming, as I discovered, was just not my cup of Lapsang Souchong. Topping, on the other hand, made me purr. It was everything I liked about sex, with the added advantage that, as a top, I could also fuck my partner if I decided I wanted to. Suddenly it all clicked. It no longer mattered whether being a cocktease was fair or not. It was deliciously unfair, subversively inegalitarian, teeteringly unbalanced when it came to who really had the upper hand, and blessedly devoid of the staginess I disliked about the leather scene. In one elegant step, cockteasing was transformed from guilty pleasure into art form.

I can't resist the look in the eyes of a man who clearly wants me, and just as clearly understands that he can't actually have me. The sexual tension gets so thick it's almost visible, the way air above the road shimmers on a hot summer day. Friends of mine have suggested that perhaps my penchant for being a cocktease is a result of my own insecurities, but I don't think so. Though it might seem hard to believe, the amazing electricity of a really intense cockteasing session is as good in its own way as any fuck I've ever had. Keeping a man poised, almost breathless, giddy with anticipation and hoping against hope for a yes even though he knows I've already said no is a kind of sex on its own. I love the art of the tease, the almost-but-not-quite, the so-far-but-no-further.

I'm not the kind of cocktease who shimmies her ass in front of a man, then pulls an ice princess routine when he shows interest. I'm a cocktease for selfish reasons, and I don't try to hide it. My own sexual response goes through the roof when I'm feeding off a man's pent-up lust. Letting my partners—or should I say victims?—know just how aroused I am is, of course, part of the tease. It never fails to elicit a moan, which, of course, makes me all the wetter. It's an ever-so-delectably vicious cycle.

Occasionally, friends seem rather horrified at my cockteasing tales. I've been called a manipulative bitch by those who don't understand the attraction. What they don't understand is that as much as I love being a cocktease, there are quite a few men who love to take it just as much as I love to dish it out. How else can you explain the man who followed up an exquisite evening of necking and petting above the waist—yes, Virginia, some of us do occasionally orgasm from having our nipples played with the right way—by sending me an enormous bouquet of stargazer lilies and a thank-you note?

The men whom I tease seem to come into my life much in the way I've been known to come in their arms—more or less by accident. We tend to become friends first, and only later do things move into deeper waters. They know I'm in a non-monogamous relationship and am thus open to the notion of other lovers in my life. So it's not particularly shocking that I permit an advance or two. Just the same, I don't think that most of the men I end up teasing think it's going to be that way when things begin. I don't exactly initiate conversations with a sprightly, "Hi, I'm Hanne and I'll be your cocktease tonight."

Still, they have an astonishing tendency to stick around and come back for more, even once it's been made completely clear what the score is going to be. No one looks quite as pleased with himself as a man who's just spent several hours with a purring, wriggling, teasing woman with a dirty mind and a mouth full of double-entendres. A woman who finds him sexy, lets him tease her and, while steadfastly refusing to fuck him, makes no bones about the fact that she'd be a voluptuous fireball in bed if she did.

The men I tease tell me that it's a wild combination of desire, intense pleasure and an agonizing, but also strangely satisfying, physical frustration. It reminds them of high school, of being fifteen again. It lets both of us wallow in the luxuriousness of raw desire without any performance anxiety. I suspect these things, plus possibly the simple triumph of hope over experience, are a large part of why they keep coming back for more.

My zest for seeing them tremble, however, is what really seems to do the trick. I'm no beauty, and I have been warned all my life that I'm "too fat and too mouthy" for men to find me attractive. However, one needn't be a supermodel to be a stunningly successful tease. Shortly after I began to acknowledge my femme bitch top side—without consciously advertising it—my dance card was suddenly full of men who were more than happy to suffer the exquisite pleasure-pain of languishing, rock-hard and no place to go, in my presence.

It does, of course, help if you like men, which I genuinely do. This seems to put me in the minority among my women friends, many of whom subscribe wholeheartedly to the "men are dogs" theory, if not to something even more Dworkinesque. If I'm going to dislike someone, it'll be on the basis of something more interesting and specific than gender.

No, I like men, and the ones I tease hold a special place in my heart. My relationships with the men I tease are intimate friendships, like the best of my friendships with women. I challenge them, I support them, I kick their butts. I've been able to encourage some of them to get into therapy and save their marriages. I've held their hands as they've negotiated the rocks on the far side of a divorce, or helped them negotiate relationships with women they adore. I've had their support while I've ranted and cried, their back rubs when I've been stressed, their company, warmth and compassion mine for the asking.

The owners of the cocks I tease are men I not only like and trust, but even, in my own thoroughly polyamorous and strangely unromantic way, men I love. I think the unconventional bond I share with my admirers protects us in the treacherous territory of the cocktease: We are intimate, and yet we accept that there are places in one another's lives where we simply do not go. Fortunately for all of us, maintaining boundaries doesn't have to mean forgoing lust.

Last week I met with Rob, one of my oldest and dearest admirers, for lunch. Like several but by no means all of the men I tease, he is married. Rob and his wife have an eleven-year-old son and a six-year-old daughter. He's a dedicated husband and a devoted and intensely loving father. Graying handsomely, with a broad chest I find particularly satisfying to lay my head upon or gently claw at depending on my whim, he's knowledgeable and an engaging raconteur. He's got energy, heart and talent, and he loves both his wife and me.

I say this precisely because I refuse to trot out the tired old mistress's excuse that "he and his wife just don't love each other anymore." For one thing, I'm not his mistress, and for another, he does love his wife but is a bit frustrated by how their love in his marriage has changed over time. The lust and heat have gone, leaving him with a familial love that satisfies his head and heart. His marriage no longer answers his longing to be caught up in the excited intimacy of reciprocal desire, but otherwise Rob is a happily married man.

Over lunch that day, we chatted and flirted, the sexual energy slowly bubbling up through our conversation as I reveled in his sweet handsome smile and the way he so willingly spread his legs for me as I gently stroked the inside of his calf with my toe. We talked about work, about the changes since his new division head came in, about the plans he has been making to take a vacation to Washington, D.C., to show his kids the sights. As he spoke, I dipped a celery stick from my salad into the dressing, then brought it to my mouth, tongue tip swooping the ranch dressing off the light-green stalk before I suggestively pursed my lips around its end. His eyes never left my mouth. Like many men, he's a sucker for a blowjob pucker.

Picking a cherry tomato from his salad, I held it out for him to take it from my fingers with his teeth, and refused to let go when he did. Holding firm to the plump little fruit, I waited, forcing him to bite down enough to penetrate the taut red skin, making him close his lips around my fingers to avoid having the sweet jelly of the seeds explode from his mouth. He murmured appreciatively, and closed his eyes as I let him suck my fingertips for the barest moment before pulling them away. Pleased, enjoying the chance to watch him and appreciate his momentarily unselfconscious sensuality, I told him that he had a lovely mouth.

He blushed, but he always blushes when I tell him he's beautiful. Most men do. They never know how to take it. "You're the one with the lush lips," he told me. Realizing that he was just sitting there, defenseless, ready for me to reduce him to jelly, I took the makeup case from my bag to let him watch me repair my lipstick. Out of the corner of my eye, I saw his jaw go slack for a moment while I outlined my lips in dark purplish red, then filled them in, dabbing a small bit of iridescent gloss in the center of my lower lip. He licked his lips, then discreetly uncrossed and recrossed his legs. As if I had a phantom limb, I had the distinct sensation that I knew what it must feel like as his cock swelled in his boxers. I blew him a kiss across the table, freshly painted lips pursing in a gesture as unmistakable as a whore's wink. Shaking his head as if in disbelief, he reached out for my hand, just barely letting me hear a sweet low whispery moan.

"You like it when I'm a tart for you, don't you?" I asked, letting him take my hand. He nodded, watching me speak and swallowing with some difficulty. "You like to watch my lips," I said, carefully enunciating each word.

He nodded again. "I love watching you be sexy. When you buckle the strap on your shoe, when you wind a scarf around your neck, when you run your hands through your hair, when you look at yourself in your compact and dab just a little more lipstick on. That thing you do when you suck your finger to make sure you won't get lipstick on your teeth. I love that. You have no idea how sexy it is to watch you do that."

I had a very good idea, actually, but I didn't say so. "Maybe I'll let you watch later," I continued, slipping my foot out of my shoe again and fondling the inside of his ankle with my stockinged toes, "when I straighten my garters. I bet you'd like that, too." He squeezed my hand and watched me pick up my soda again, nodding at me and turning a slow and definite pink. He knew I was playing with him, batting at him like a cat with a cornered lizard. What's more, he loved it.

I love the moment when it's perfectly clear that the man I'm teasing knows that I'm just playing with him, reveling in his sexual hunger, manipulating him, all because it makes me wet. It's an exercise, calculated and cool, but at the same time it's a genuinely sexual act, dangerous and full of the weight of mutual desire. Being a cocktease is filled with the emotional, intellectual and very, very physical awareness that sex is about desire, not completion, and that the biggest sexual organ is between your ears, not your legs.

Calling it "teasing" might suggest that it isn't really sex, but I can assure you that it most definitely is. The desire I share with my admirers is mutual, raw and honest, a ripe, enigmatic, and shatteringly effective aphrodisiac. Often I'll leave an admirer panting, almost sobbing with frustration, to go home and masturbate, my mind swimming with images and sensory memories, more excited still because I know that, most likely, the man I was with is doing the same thing at the same time. Other times I'll rush home, panties soaked and nipples stiff, to the bed I share with my lover, nostrils still flaring from the scent of another man's arousal. My lover, a sweet submissive who has been known to enjoy my teasing quite a bit himself, doesn't complain a bit. I've even told a couple of the other men in my life that I would be doing just that after I left them, and it only inflamed them more. The boundaries that we have in place make it possible for them to enjoy the phantom image of me fucking, even though they don't get to experience it for themselves.

I tease them, and their lust and need make my clit throb and my nipples ache. As my arousal rises, so does theirs, the ache for release palpable in the air around us. When I leave, I take that electricity with me and unleash it on myself or on another, lust and desire becoimng transmutable, transferable, transformative. Hovering in a space of "so much and no more," memorably long-lasting gratification can emerge out of nothing more than a few moments of physical contact as they kiss me good-bye.

That was all I had intended when I asked Rob to take me back to my car after lunch. He parked illegally rather than make me walk up the garage stairwell alone, and he put his arm around my shoulders as we walked across the concrete expanse of the garage floor. Stopping just before we got to my car, I curled against his chest, pressing into him for our usual farewell embrace, letting him encircle me in his arms.

Nuzzling against his neck, I heard him whisper, "You make me want you so much, Hanne. I wonder what it would be like to be with you. You have no idea."

I took his hand in mine and pressed his knuckles to my lips.

"Do you think of me?" I asked, my voice as low a rumble as I could make it, my lips brushing his fingers.

"Often enough," Rob admitted. "When I'm lying awake at night."

"Do you ever touch yourself and think of me?"

He paused for a moment. I slid my other hand to his hip and gently forced my tonguetip between his middle finger and his ring finger, teasing the crease between his knuckles. He shuddered hard. "All the time," he rasped, "all the time."

"Do you ever imagine what it might feel like to have my mouth on your cock?"

He looked at me, not sure how to answer, perhaps not quite knowing whether I was asking him a simple question or making a proposition. Gripping his hips with both hands, I sank to my knees in front of him. He cast a quick glance around the parking garage to see if we were indeed alone, and stroked my hair.

"Hanne, Hanne . . . God, what if we get caught?" His voice was eager, frantic, afraid, half remembering that he knew full well that I was only going to tease him mercilessly, half remembering that that was exactly what he wanted.

"Hush. Let me." Holding him firmly by the hips, my fingers rippling rhythmically, I nuzzled his crotch until I found the fly of his pants with my lips. Listening to him whimper quietly, fretfully, feeling the tension making his hands shake as he stroked my hair and tried desperately not to make noise, I began to unzip his fly. Slowly, slowly, I tugged his zipper down with my teeth, one notch at a time. His cock was hard as a spike and I could smell his arousal. The scent made me swoon, my cunt slippery, hot and clenching. I heard his breath rasping in the echoey space of the garage when I took the little metal tag in my mouth. He moaned out loud, feeling my breath on his cock through his boxers, and I rose to my feet.

He stood there staring at me, an expression of tenderness and tremendous want on his face. I kissed him on the cheek, got into my car and shut the door.

He stepped aside, and I pulled out of the space, backing up alongside him. I could see the tip of his cock protruding from his fly, the fabric of his boxers pulled taut over the head. He was so aroused that he didn't even care.

The urge to just grab him, and find some secluded corner where I could suck him in earnest, was almost overwhelming. I rolled down the window and beckoned to him. He bent over to the window and I kissed him hard. "Go and finish for me," I whispered. "I want to feel you coming for me. Tell me about it later. Come for me."

He nodded, and began to turn away, then stopped and caught my gaze again. "I love you, you know," he blurted out.

"Yes, I know."

"I want you, Hanne."

I wanted to tell Rob to get in the car. I wanted to drag him into a cheap hotel room and suck him, to make him stroke his own cock while I watched. I imagined how he'd look bent over the edge of some Holiday Inn mattress while I fingerfucked his ass until he screamed. I wanted to straddle his face, his cock, to ride and writhe and claw his chest and shoulders until I couldn't hold myself upright. Hoping that my face didn't betray my lust, I looked him dead in the eye, and slowly and deliberately shook my head no.

"I know," he said softly, "I know." His eyes were locked on mine and I felt little tremors threatening to spill over deep inside my pussy. He smiled drunkenly, shaking his head in amusement at his own besotted arousal.

"Go finish for me," I whispered, and pulled away, blowing him a last kiss. In my rearview mirror, I could see him nodding, holding his hand and my flying kiss to his lips.

I drove home, almost oblivious to the traffic. Even before I got home, there was a gasping, moaning, breathless message from Rob on my voice mail, letting me hear him as he ecstatically, desperately did as I had told him. I replayed the message three times as I masturbated, my fingers sliding frantically through the thick wetness that had been building since I began to tease him that afternoon, orgasm after orgasm washing over me as I remembered the smell of him and the look in his eyes. I can still hear the last words he spoke into the receiver, after he calmed down from orgasm and before he hung up: "Thank you, Hanne, you cocktease, you wonderful bitch, thank you so much. Thank you, thank you for *everything*."

MO SEX MO PROBLEMS

● Notorious M.E.G.

I'm not gonna get into stories like the one explaining why my ex-boss carried a pair of my underwear to work in a small paper bag after I'd dog-sat for him and his family—well, maybe a few. Who among us has never been so sick with love—or lust—that she does something stupid? Obsessing over a crush, stalking an ex, sleeping with co-workers . . . most of us have done all this and more. Love or lust. Truth or dare. In the early stages, who can tell one from the other? Lust is the pursuit of love, sometimes—or it can morph into love at a moment's notice. How can anyone turn away from a budding relationship or sexual affair before exploring it fully to see if there's more than just hope? Maybe some of us explore a little too deeply, sometimes. Or maybe not deeply enough. That's the part I'm still trying to figure out. Love is a logic-threatening force, and logic has never been my strong suit.

I wouldn't call myself desperate, though some might. Instead, I like to think of all the little "desperate" choices I make as those of just another soldier of love, taking everyday reconnaissance

11

trips into mine-riddled fields. Things do seem to blow up in my face, though, whether because of a lack of action, a physically painful realization of way too much or the futility of trying to tackle safe sex with a vat of Vaseline and a family-sized roll of Saran Wrap. That's just with the girls, and "relations" with boys haven't been any more successful. I know I'm not breaking new ground when I reminisce about the condom that disappeared "somewhere" up inside me; a whopping case of body lice; a heroin junkie boyfriend; permanent scars on my back from indoor/outdoor carpeting; or con artists like the nameless Boy Wonder who seduced me before bolting with cash and a truckload of cantaloupes that belonged to our boss, bouncing checks on his merry way out of town.

I like sex too much to adopt an "Oh, shit, I'm always getting screwed-over" attitude. It's more of an "Oh, cool, I'm getting screwed!" attitude, at which point I realize the relationship in question is over. Not exactly the same thing but, at times, alarmingly close. The choices are even more complicated when you're bi and have to discover your inner dyke after growing up with the assumption that you're straight. Not only are you on the outside looking in at the whole world of queer girls, you're also prone to unfortunate dating decisions, multiplying the threat of confusion, mixed signals, bad sex and sudden death. Am I looking for love in all the wrong places? Is it just that, under the delusionary effects of lust, I don't know how to pick 'em? Or am I really just a pathetic loser outside the scope of normal human relationships?

I saw the first girl I desired when she walked across a campus green at the University of New Hampshire. It was her walk: the dull, resistant tough-girl butch stride. Long and heavy and cocky and vulnerable. Her fuck-you-for-staring-at-me attitude made my body buzz and my mind wonder. I continued to wonder for the next three years until we ended up in an English class together: Was she gay? She sure looked it but I had no idea. Other than my flaming, closeted male cousin, I didn't know anyone who was gay. Definitely no dykes. (I must have had my head buried in the sand because I'd lived with the women's rugby team the year prior.) I approached her after class one day, sweating.

"Hey, uh . . . do you wanna get coffee or something after class some time?"

She had hazel eyes and lolled in her chair like a guy, her knees spread way the fuck apart and her feet splayed out. Her hair hung over her face, and she looked out at me from underneath it. Suspiciously. She flickered her eyelashes at me, the cosmos crashed together and I saw stars. There was an interminable wait.

"Okay . . . Yeah, sure."

We arranged to meet at the house of a mutual friend, and coffee turned into a plan for Rolling Rocks at Erik's house, then dinner. Sam sat across from me on the couch, laughing and smoking and sucking down beers. Erik and I talked about a class we had taken together, and I was stunned to learn that he was coming to dinner with us. I was at sea. Was she not gay? Was she trying to avoid embarrassing me because I'd been horribly wrong and this was an easy way to get both of us out of that conversation? Did she not want me? Did she not realize I wanted her? (Fuck, how could she not know?) Did she hate me? She was laughing and her laugh was deep and throaty and it made me feel like I was falling. I started to wonder if she was trying to set me up with Erik and felt a little nauseous. I already had a boyfriend, and he didn't know anything about this. Everything was fuzzy and confusing and getting fuzzier with every beer.

We went to a shitty little bar on the main street of town. The locals glared at us briefly and then went back to their beers. Karaoke was starting and someone began wailing a country tune. Sam grabbed a chair, and the three of us sat at a small table, settled in and ordered Rolling Rocks and chicken wings. I couldn't concentrate. She was magnetic: tall and loose. Her thick brown hair was unkempt and kinda went everywhere, spilling into her face and down her shoulders. Her eyes changed color from blue to green, and she kept her head down and looked out at me from the corner of her eye, which killed me. Her glance shot through my eyes and trickled down to the back of my throat, making it wet and thick. The warmth spread through every limb.

Behind us a man in a flannel shirt, jeans and boots had set down his beer and was belting out "Margaritaville" to a handful of customers in the bar. When I turned, I could see the TV monitor with the words flashing across the bottom of the screen. Erik's mouth was moving, but I couldn't tell what he was saying over the wailing. Everything felt underwater. Suddenly something, a hand, was on my thigh, right above my knee. Holy shit. I shot a glance at Erik, terrified, but he was too far away. It was her.

I couldn't look at her but I couldn't not. I looked at her and we smiled into each other's eyes, drowning, and then I turned to Erik to say something but I couldn't think of anything to say so I just smiled like a freak. It was far too loud now to talk anyway; the Jimmy Buffett fan was going off.

"Some people say that there's a wooooomaaaan to blame . . . "

Sam leaned back and took a slug of beer, her arm still under the table. Erik looked at her and back at me. Her hand was burning into my thigh, but I tried to ignore it so he wouldn't catch on. Erik stopped speaking; his eyes were fixed on Sam's arm. He grinned nervously with his little dimples, reached into his back pocket, got out his wallet, slammed a ten on the table and stood up, weaving slightly.

"Think I'm gonna head." He paused. "You staying, Sam?" He knew she wasn't going anywhere.

"Yeah. Think I'll just finish my beer," she said.

Erik walked out of the bar, and we turned to look at one another, utterly giddy. Sam took another swig and leaned in toward me. I put my elbows on the table and we were kissing and oh my god we were kissing and my lips were touching hers and it was all beerbreath and wetlips and her eyes and her hand was moving up my knee and my eyes were closed and then shit! We were in a bar. In New Hampshire. I pulled away, breathing heavily. Sam's eyes were cloudy. Over her shoulder I saw a guy in a flannel shirt and wool hat staring at us over his lifted Bud. I looked around the bar, and two women in their mid-forties were drinking margaritas at the bar and glancing over, their pink-lipped mouths gaping open like little blowfish. One of them saw me looking and shut her mouth like a trap, whispered something in her friend's ear. Sam was grinning wildly, and she kept her hand on my knee. She was wasted.

"I think we better get out of here," I said.

We grabbed our jackets, slugged the rest of our beers and slapped some money on the table, running out into the night. It was March, and it had just begun to snow.

The snowflakes came down on our faces and coats, and we ran back to my apartment, holding hands and laughing drunkenly, and with relief. We stopped to kiss in front of Marrelli's Fruit and Real Estate and then again across the street under a lamp post along the Lamprey River, and she tasted like stale smoke and beer and warmth and . . . love. Lust? I dunno. She tasted wet. She tasted like food that was too spicy but that I couldn't stop eating. I might be sick later but I couldn't stop, couldn't stop, didn't want to stop. The snow muffled every sound except some faint music from an apartment nearby, Dusty Springfield singing "Windmills of Your Mind." We kissed and one of us was shivering but I wasn't sure who. I could hear Dusty's voice and the music and wetness shot photons of light into my heart and I felt like I was going to explode right there. We headed back to my place and proceeded to kiss and rub against each other, fully clothed, for hours. Even with clothes on, the surface of my skin was a million mouths, permanently open to receive her: the moisture and warmth of her body, her gaze. She was the fixed point in my sky, my Polaris. I couldn't see around her, couldn't see anything but her.

Thus began our series of midnight rendezvous. I broke up with my boyfriend after he told me that it was okay if I slept with a girl. ("If it was a guy, yeah, I'd be jealous! Are you kidding me?!?") Sam was an alcoholic reaching her nadir, and she was in serious denial about being gay. I was a pothead so stunned by her beauty and toughness and the rough rasp of her voice I barely finished my thesis (a collection of poems about her, natch). No one could know about our relationship since Sam was so paranoid about it. She'd drive over to my place in the middle of the night, knock on my window, and I'd let her in the back porch door. After a few nights she let me pull off her shirt, unhook her bra and yank down her jeans. But her underwear was superglued to her ass—there was no way I was getting it off. She didn't say as much, but I knew she thought that by unlocking her chastity belt to me she'd be admitting to herself that she was gay. So she didn't let me near the forest between her legs.

"No, no . . . " she said vaguely, as I dug my fingers into her thighs and licked her stomach, ran my tongue along the length of her legs. Her eyes were lost with wanting, her knees parting even as she spoke the words. We kissed endlessly, glued together. I lay my head between her breasts and suckled her nipples and she moaned and writhed, but I wanted Down There and she'd have none of it. I was in love and ecstatic but pent-up. I felt like Charlie Brown staring down the pants of the red-headed girl—paralyzed. Was I always to be frustrated like this? The affair continued this way until we graduated. She cut all ties when her AA group told her she had to stop talking to the people she used to drink with. At this point I lived a continent away from her so I didn't understand how could I be a threat to her sobriety, but whatever.

I was living in a new, unfamiliar city, my heart in tatters, waiting tables at a tourist trap when Seneca, another waitress, had her Halloween party. We had to dress up for work anyway, so everyone planned just to get drunk after work and walk over to her place. Serving tourists chicken burgers and lumpy clam chowder while wearing a mandatory costume would be a lesson in humility, but at least I wasn't a temporary Christmas elf at a local department store, like my roommate.

I was broke and couldn't afford a nice costume so I smoked a bowl and stayed up all night cutting cardboard into star shapes and covering them with aluminum foil. I happened to have this freaky pair of black tights with silver stars, and I wore a black skirt and shirt and safety-pinned the stars all over me: I was the night sky. Natalie at least made me invisible in this lame-ass costume. Natalie was a waitress with a daughter in France and had taken peyote and carried special herbs around in her apron that were supposed to bring money her way. She'd pull her tips out at the end of the day and all these little leaves would mix in with the change and crumpled dollar bills. She swore she could see the color of people's auras. That Halloween, she whipped out some makeup and glitter and drew a bunch of stars on my face so at least you couldn't really tell it was me. By mid-afternoon, though, I was sweating, running back and forth with BLTs and watery Greyhounds on my little tray, and the makeup started to run down my face in black and white streaks.

Seneca was the devil at her party, dressed in the requisite sexy black outfit with horns rubber-cemented to her head, wearing a bowler hat.

"Jesus Christ, why'd you use rubber cement?" She was already tipsy, someone was wearing her hat, and she had her arm around my shoulder for support as we stood in the corner.

"Well, I tried Elmer's Glue but they kept falling off when I moved my head even the tiniest bit, so I just used the rubber cement. It was under the sink."

I put my hand up and touched the horns. They didn't budge.

My tinfoil stars kept coming unpinned and falling off as the night wore on. It was a full moon, and I could feel the earth spinning, felt something looming—disaster or an emergency. Sirens sex by outside the window. I began to deputize everyone with my fallen stars, in case a posse was needed.

After everyone went home, I stayed. Seneca wanted me to. Not that she said it in words; she just tipped her bowler at me and I knew. We sat there struggling with her horns, like tiny spurs of darkness, scratching at them, arms entangled, trying to get them off. Finally they broke off, the nubs still stuck fast to her skull. We slept on her dirty futon on the floor and it was winebreath and darkness and breasts and lips and blankets. I could feel the small nubs of cracked plastic rubbing against my belly and thighs. For the first time, I saw and tasted another woman. Going down on her was like diving into a dark cave of earthly delights: The muskiness of her smell, the salt and the cream—were intoxicating. The delicious brine, the wrinkled folds of sweet flesh between my teeth and the taste of her: Every strange part of her seemed made for pleasure. I slipped a finger closer and closer to her tight, wet anus, wanting to go inside but not daring. At last she moaned and came, and the folds of skin funneled streams of white liquid I could put my wet tongue into and lap up, swallowing, swallowing. I drowned myself in the wetness, the hairs that inevitably caught in my teeth and throat. I'd washed the streaks of glitter and moonscape off my face, but she told me I was beautiful, stroking my hair from my cheeks and pressing her lips to my eyelids. I felt hopeful for the first time in a long time.

The next morning I woke up still wildly optimistic. My jaw ached like nobody's business and I was miserably hungover, but I was full of joy. I dressed silently but didn't want to leave without saying goodbye. She slept, or pretended to be asleep, for a long time, then finally opened her eyes.

"Can you grab me a cigarette?"

I got her one from the bureau. She rustled around on the ground and came up with a lighter, lit it and took a long, slow drag. She glanced over at me quickly, then away.

"David's coming over here," she said.

"Now? This morning? Didn't you guys break up?"

"Yeah, well, you know how that goes," she said, looking out the window. "He said he'd come over to help me clean up. It might be a little weird if you're here."

"Yeah, I guess," I said, and left.

When I got home that day, I couldn't eat. I could only open my jaw a third of the normal way. That afternoon I had my roommate drive me to the emergency room. I'd told her what had happened, and she was in hysterics, laughing so hard she peed in her pants and said she'd wait in the car.

The doc told me I had TMD—temporomandibular joint disorder. Brilliant— my first time going down on a girl, and I'd fucked up my jaw.

"When did this come on?" He asked me. He was leaning over me and had his hands on my jaw, feeling the muscles on the sides.

"Um. This morning." I avoided his eyes; he looked like my uncle.

"Were you eating something hard—an apple or a bagel—when it locked? Usually something triggers this type of thing—especially if you haven't experienced it before . . . "

"No . . . I just woke up and it was . . . like this." It was getting more difficult to speak.

He looked at me and I felt like his eyes could see right through me.

"Well, you must have been grinding your teeth in your sleep. Your muscles are pretty clenched in here but they'll relax . . . eventually. Just take it easy; try a hot compress."

It was weeks before I could eat anything other than soup.

When I could eat again, I craved sandwiches. I started eating lunch alone at the only lesbian bar in town, a weekly jaunt that continued for a few years. I guess I figured maybe I'd meet someone, but I never thought of it as desperation. Even though I had to drive clear across town to eat there, the service was lousy and the food mediocre, I found ways to rationalize it. "They have good BLTs," I reminded myself. "And nobody looks at me funny for being a woman eating alone." I allowed myself to forget about the embarrassing notes and generous tips I left the servers there. It wasn't until a waitress decided to play matchmaker for me and another dyke eating by herself—we were too incompatible even for a fifteen-minute conversation—that I realized it was *possible* I looked desperate.

I began to think I lived in the netherworld of dykedom, some tiny, remote corner of the country where bi-curious girls are allowed to flit in and out without having to worry about a passport, but far removed from the world of real women-loving-women. It had been years since I'd come out to my family as bisexual but despite that rather giant step I still floated in the ether. I also had lost all ability to get myself off, and just got some mileage out of stroking my underarms in the shower (somewhat satisfying with all the nerve endings). I needed action.

In search of dykes, I joined a women's chorus. I figured I had to meet some-body—or at least make some friends. I had dreams of being swept up into a warm, loving lesbian community that would educate me on how to do everything gay: dress, date, talk, walk, shop, protest, go veggie, pee in the wild at Michigan, give good head—whatever! Somehow, though, that didn't happen. The average age of the gals in the choir hovered around forty-five and the singles scene was nothing if not lean. These were women who had been in relationships for de-cades, old-school dykes who'd somehow—miraculously—hooked up with their partners when they were twenty-one years old and living in San Francisco. They were encouraging, these long-term lesbian relationships—but also dishearten-ing. It was a different gay world we lived in today: less bra-burning, leg hair or unplugged women's music; more confusion, genderbending and STDs. Also, though the group was 90 percent lezbo, I feared falling for a straight girl.

M was twenty-two and the youngest person in the ensemble. She had legally changed her first and last name, which gave her a certain cachet, although the fact that she'd changed her first name to an initial I found truly bizarre and rather rock-star-like. M carried a construction worker's black lunchbox with a rainbow sticker on it, so I had to conclude she wasn't a ten-percenter. We were both geeky sopranos, so we sang together and started dating. She was rather an odd duck—a computer programmer who was fanatical about ballroom dance, the Lindy Hop in particular. Weird, yes, but she was a good sport too, which counts for a lot: At a party my housemates and I had, M took over the role of hostess after I passed out well before midnight. She was the last one up, attempting to get the drunken revelers to Lindy Hop with her and breaking up a fight between two buttrocker guys who were arguing about the name of the drummer in Def Leppard; she also calmed down an anonymous woman no one seemed to know who'd leaned back into a candle and set her hair on fire, singeing a substantial chunk.

M and I wandered the city on public transportation, saw a few movies. She asked me to be her date for her work's holiday party. Maybe the party was a sign; if it was, I was blind enough not to recognize it. She had presented herself, I think, as "straight but not narrow" to people at work, and she didn't speak to me the entire time. I made conversation with a few techies, but no one was that friendly so I took advantage of the free bar and hung out with the DJ the whole night, making idiotic requests and asking the name of every other song he put on. He had an excellent music collection but was annoyed by me. He started ignoring me, DJ-style. (Headphones on, music blaring, one finger up in an I'll-be-right-with-you-but-right-now-I'm-incredibly-busy-keeping-the-party-going pose, and then he'd turn around and start going through his bins and never turn back to me.) "Asshole," I hissed.

I was still in exploratory mode, though, and other than the party, things with M seemed to be going okay—except that whenever we went back to her apartment she just wanted to sleep. We'd kiss for a while on her bed, and if she was in a good mood she'd get up and put some music on, try to show me a few dance moves, but it was like she was stalling. Once back in bed, she was passive and nearly unresponsive. She'd kiss for a while and seem to be getting aroused, but when I tried to advance the troops, moving my hand down between her legs, she'd grab my wrist in a viselike grip and say, "Not tonight, Lester." (She liked to call me Lester. I didn't get it and she didn't explain, but whatever.)

Finally I asked her what the problem was. She said she was concerned about the two of us touching "beneath the waist." We were both totally unfamiliar with girl-on-girl safe sex, having heard of dental dams but never using them. I think I may have protested weakly—"I don't know how to do it. I'm clean, I swear!"— but ever the resourceful gal, M sighed, went into her kitchen and brought out a roll of plastic film.

"What about this? I've heard Saran Wrap can work," she said.

I was doubtful, but we tried it. She cut a square the size of Nebraska and rested it against my little girl. Have you ever tried to make a piece of Saran Wrap stick to something that completely resists its stickiness? What if the plastic were smeared with petroleum jelly? Total fucking disaster. You can't feel a damn thing through two layers of Saran Wrap—she insisted on two layers—and a thick coating of Vaseline. Sitting on a moving bus provides more friction. (Note: Regular lube is entirely different.) Naturally, I slipped on the discarded little slimy thing the next morning after crawling out of bed, and it took weeks for the bruises to go away. Like all the others, this relationship soon met its maker, and not long after, I heard she was dating the DJ.

For some reason, that made me furious. I took a hammer and smashed the only thing she had given me, a glass picture frame. It made me feel really powerful and wild. I wanted to smash the whole house up, I wanted to be so pissed I didn't care about the consequences, but I tore out of the house and walked around the neighborhood, making dents in street signs with the hammer and telling myself that I was a juvie in a past life. This helped.

I decided I had to figure out how to attract some girls who knew what they were doing. I'm pretty femme-y (have longish hair, like to wear makeup, don't have a problem with skirts), and dykes never seemed to realize I was one of them. At any rate, that's the justification I made to myself for why they weren't hitting on me. Maybe femmes are just not as popular as butches, or maybe I'm just butt-ugly and never realized it. I'd go to Ladies Night at the local gay club and get hit on by drunk frat boys who didn't even know they were in a gay bar. I wanted to scream. But I didn't want to completely reinvent who I was or how I presented myself simply because I liked women. I'd cut my hair short before, and I didn't like it, didn't like occasionally being mistaken for a boy. I just wanted to be myself and have girls swoon over me—or at least recognize that I was one of them. Was that too much to ask?

The lezbo bar that had been the site of many BLTs and the failed, pseudo-blind date was the only dyke bar in town, and I ended up there again to meet my friend Jo for a beer. It was a Saturday night, and the place was packed and raucous but we found a little table. Jo and I got to talking about sex toys. I'd had a few more moderately successful encounters at this point, but nothing mind-blowing. And, most significant, I'd never used toys. It seemed symbolic. I wanted to try all these things, and despite my best efforts nothing was getting crossed off the list.

"I want to use a dildo but no girl I've been with has ever wanted to. They all say they don't like the idea of something unnatural being inside them." I paused, thinking about it. "Is it the same for you?"

Jo's eyes grew huge behind her beer. "You gotta be kidding me!" she said. "I can't believe that . . . Every girl I've ever been with—we go back to her house and the first thing she does is pull out a huge box of toys."

I looked at her, stunned. I was beginning to feel like Woody Allen in *Everything You Always Wanted to Know About Sex but Were Afraid to Ask* when, after being chased around by a giant breast, he says, "When it comes to sex, there are certain things that should be always left unknown. And, with my luck, they probably will be."

By now I had gay friends and had helped start a queer-grrl zine, but somehow I still felt like a fraud: a fake lesbian and a loser of a straight girl. It was as if I wore an invisible cloak of desperation, and everybody could see it but me. Plus I was dumb enough to date people I worked with on a semi-regular basis. Couples in long-term relationships—like the women in the lezzie-choir and my straight friend who'd met her future husband the first week at college—seemed from another planet.

I was beginning to wonder if I should just stop trying. When all my sexual urges went underground for a spell, I felt a surge of hope. Maybe celibacy was the answer! I'd certainly accomplish more, and it would indicate discipline. Maybe it would even make me wiser. I could reach a new plane of enlightenment. But, naturally, it didn't last long. I had The Dream, and celibacy was kicked back into the corner.

I was working at another restaurant, and Cecilia was a manager and technically my boss. But my desire for her came on like gangbusters, suddenly, out of nowhere. Well, not nowhere. One night I had a dream with her in it, and the next evening I walked into the restaurant where we worked and started folding napkins, and, when she walked into the room, her ass in tight khakis made me cream. I hadn't felt that way in ages. It was as if my sexuality had been switched back on, and the surge was terrifying and electrifying. My knees literally went weak.

I talked about my crush to friends, and my legs would buzz so hard I just couldn't stop laughing. I had to lay down on the floor because they couldn't support me. I was smitten. At work I volunteered to help her carry things, bring in the liquor, anything to keep me near her. I even hung around watching her change her tongue piercing in the bathroom after her shift.

"This is a ten-gauge. The smaller the number, the thicker the bar. I want to get to a four-gauge eventually." My face was close to hers, and I could smell the alcohol on her breath. She flicked her tongue against the back of her top front teeth before she inserted the thicker harder bar through the hole in her red tongue.

"Show me the underside," I demanded.

She lifted her tongue obligingly. The hole was clean and round. I could see the roof of her mouth through it. My underwear was growing wet and heavy; I could feel my whole body buzzing.

"Why go bigger?" I said. We walked out of the bathroom together and into the bustling restaurant.

"I have an oral fixation." She did smoke like a fiend.

"What is it good for?"

"The bar? Oh, you mean for sex? It conducts heat or cold. I can suck on an ice cube and then flick my tongue across a nipple . . . It's amazing."

"I'm afraid," I said. She slung her arm around my waist as we walked. Turned her face through her dark hair and caught my eyes with hers. There were dark circles under her green eyes. She was smiling.

"Don't be afraid. It won't hurt you."

Fuck!

She was a big girl—a first for me—and it was as if I couldn't get enough of her. After I'd hit on her at work and we'd gone out for drinks, we ended up dry humping in the squashed front seat of her Honda, parked right under a streetlight at a busy intersection in a questionably legal spot. The kissing was like liquid fire, wet and mind-blowing and addictive and I clambered on top of her, squeezing my body between her and the steering wheel.

"Shit, this is like fucking high school," she groaned. She put her little hands on my ass and started moving me on her. I couldn't contain myself and got off within seconds. She didn't (the physical limitations of the space were a problem). We sat in the car, breathing heavily. The windows were completely steamed up. I was panting, half-lying in the passenger seat. She banged her head on the steering wheel.

"I just want to fuck you," she hissed.

I couldn't wait to experience the tongue stud. I'm not a huge fan of receiving oral sex—it's just never done that much for me. *Love* to give it, but as far as receiving . . . I'm more of a penetration gal. But kissing her with the stud was fantastic, and I could only imagine how it—how she, with it in—might change my mind for good about cunnilingus. In any case, surely a woman who'd let somebody stick a needle through her tongue would be open to trying a few props. She was, after all, from Vegas.

At work we would rub our breasts and sides into each other's backs while waiting for drinks at the bar. We couldn't keep our hands off each other. I brought up the idea of a strap-on on our second date. We were sitting in this divey bar, and I mentioned it. It just seemed like it might be a nice idea to let her know what was on my mind.

"Eeeuw. I'm not sure," she said.

"Can't you imagine it?" I asked her. I moved in so my lips were closer to her cheek. "Leather straps across a bare ass? Doesn't that sound exciting?" She looked doubtful.

We finally made it back to her house a few dates later. (Our dates consisted of conversations like "This is really really stupid, we work together," "Yeah, I know," followed by wild making-out in the car.) Tipsy, we got naked. I was in awe. Her body did not turn me off—just the opposite—but still I was intimidated by her breasts. The weight of them, the heft and curve. (My own look like the breast buds of a pre-adolescent; some girls have called them "the small ones.") But Cecelia—whoa. Her nipples—almost the size of my palm—were two dark secrets that held the answers to the world's questions. I'd never been into breasts before—have always been very groin-centric—but hers I wanted to devour. I wanted to slide my tongue around the round flesh, the perk of the nipple—kiss it awake. I wanted to feed on her. I would sit at the temp job I held during the day and write about them: how they would become erect upon the slightest touch, and she'd begin breathing heavily, as if she were going to pass out. When she was naked, her head looked small compared to her body. She was like an opera singer: voluptuous with big womanly hips and a big ass and big breasts and plenty to hold on to. Even as I think about it now, my pelvis grows warm. She was a cute, brassy, punky dyke with a husky voice that could be small and girly or rip with a bellowing, craggy laugh.

My whole being just vibrated. Was she more than I could handle? My butt muscles were sore from pumping, thrusting into her. She told me she wouldn't come for a while, but she was wrong. She came our second night together. We listened to Massive Attack and Tricky and mc solaar and stayed up all night fucking and smoking pot. She knew my favorite thing was just to solder myself to her, sex to sex, and rock away until I reached bliss. She liked me to lie on top of her and bang my pelvic bone into her until her head arched back and tears squeezed out of the corners of her eyes. We didn't have much to talk about, but just being near her was enough. I loved that she was addicted to *South Park* even though I found it crass and overdone. I loved that she knew everything about movies and spoke Italian. I loved that she cooked eggplant parmesan when we were at her house, and how, at the restaurant, she always gave the dishwashers a beer after their shift when none of the other bartenders would.

The fact that it was all cloak-and-daggers at work was fun in the beginning, but soon it became tiresome and frustrating. She said she needed time off, and everything started to turn sour. Work was hell because I had no idea what was going through her mind—she wouldn't talk to me. There were weird rules, too. She refused to come over to my house. She never let me kiss her between her legs, or vice versa. It was something to work up to and we never got to it. My tongue stud fantasies were not to be. This had been my one opportunity to experience something close to a sex toy, however small, and it all ended before I got the chance.

Almost unbelievably, I was still an innocent when it came to toys. Well, so what? I'd gotten her off, hadn't I? I'd made her happy . . . for a while. Isn't that the point—or at least a big part of it? Sure, I was a femme in a world of butches and, sure, I still had to do all the asking out. But by this point I was a bona fide queer grrl. No one could dispute that. I mean, how many dykes do I have to hit on? How much lockjaw does a grrl have to suffer through before she's accepted into the real world of dykedom? It was ridiculous for me to think that just because I lived there I'd be Mayor. I was just a newcomer getting to know my way around town. And at this rate, it was probably going to take a while.

Especially if I regressed to high school mentality. Shortly after the breakup with Cecelia I found myself on the highway. I swear I didn't will it to happen— the car just turned right when it should have turned left and suddenly I was cruising at sixty miles per hour, my beater of a car shaking violently and moving of its own free will up the exit ramp nearest her house. Within minutes I was turning onto her dark street. Her car was there; she was home. I turned off the radio and lights as I cruised past the small white cottage she rented. There were other cars around, cars I'd never seen parked on her street before—did one of them belong to a new lover? I kept having to wipe my palms on my jeans, and I could feel my blood rushing in my ears. A sick-giddy feeling was churning in my stomach. I couldn't believe how pathetic I was, but I couldn't help it. I had to know what she was doing, if she was with someone else. I felt desperate with this sudden loss of control—over our relationship and over my emotions and actions.

I couldn't see jack from the street so I drove around the block, parked and started walking back to her house. Her blinds were drawn. I couldn't even go peer in the windows because she had a motion-sensor light. I sat down on the curb and berated myself. There was no glimmer of hope. I had to get out of here soon.

Driving home, I felt the desperation quivering through my body, and tears started sliding down my face. I'd spent all this time and energy meeting grrls and figuring out how to be bi in a straight world, and where did I end up? Creeping around somebody's front lawn in the darkness as if I hadn't learned anything at all. The late Notorious B.I.G.'s "Mo Money Mo Problems" came on the radio, and I cranked it all the way up and let it flood the car with sound, the bass beating through the floor. I had to laugh at the insanity of it all. The music filled me. Diana Ross was singing "I'm Coming Out" underneath the beat and Biggie's voice was rapping and the back-up singers sang "What's going on?" à la Marvin Gaye and I was alive. Alone but alive. And ready for the next round.

Armed and Satisfied

 Black Artemis

T*he Overachiever's Paradise*
I arrive and immediately know that I have entered the eighth
wonder of the world. My first trip to the Bay Area, and I have
little time for sightseeing. There is so much I want to do and
see—visit Alcatraz, ride a cable car, watch my Yanks take on
the Oakland A's—but after business meetings and friendly
visits, I only have time for one pleasure trip on my itinerary.
The choice is obvious. Next stop, Good Vibrations, Berkeley.

If you asked me ten, fifteen years ago if I even fantasized
about finding the courage, let alone seizing the opportunity,
to experience such a marvelous place, I would've scoffed in
disgust. Me, a Catholic girl growing up in a Black and Latino
working-class 'hood in the Bronx, visiting a place like that?
But the second I open the door and feast my eyes on the rows
of books, toys and videos, I embrace the irony. A sex-toy shop
is exactly the kind of place where an overachiever like me is
supposed to be. Especially when she's an unapologetically
lusty, inquisitive, feminist virgin.

For reasons personal and political, I entered my thirties with my virginity technically intact. Of course you want to know why, but that's another essay. For the sake of context and to accommodate the curious, I will say a few words.

No, I'm not shy, frigid or inhibited. Man, am I laughing my ass off at that thought! If you could hear my stand-up routine or see some of the Mariah Carey–wear in my closet . . .

Okay, I'm probably too picky. But dammit, shouldn't we all be just a little more choosy? If not to advance our admirable quests for healthy self-esteem and fulfilling personal relationships, at least to get Ricki Lake off the fuckin' air?

No, I'm not unattractive, and no, that's not just my conceited opinion. Of course, beauty is in the eye of the beholder, is only skin deep, etc. Let's just say that this particular beauty has plenty of beholders eyeing to get skin deep.

Yes, I like men. Well, rarely the ones I want to fuck. I mean, usually all I want to do is fuck them, which means that they're hardly worthy of fucking and . . . See, often the ones I genuinely like I don't find fuckable. Not that I wish I did; it's just that, well, like the majority of heterosexual women, I'm pretty much looking for another woman in a man's body with obvious exceptions. For example, growing his hair longer than mine or saying shit like, "Why don't you try to see it from your mother's perspective?" are grounds for immediate separation.

No, I'm not extremely religious, saving myself to marry Mr. Right or anything like that. For a variety of reasons—personal and political—I'm just trying to avoid Mr. Right Now. Unless, of course, he's Alex Rodriguez. Or Vin Diesel. Or Russell Wong. Or that UPS fox . . .

Oh, yeah, we were discussing my virginity. Well, when I was fifteen and focused on graduating high school with scholarships and sans children, Mr. Right Now was the breakdancer who took three years to get out of the tenth grade and knocked up two classmates in the same period of time. Fine as he was, he didn't even get to sniff it. At the age of twenty-one I concentrated on my personal development while engaging in the dance of approach-avoidance with this shy yet handsome philosophy major trying to bed every sista on campus after being dumped by the class queen. Now him I was quite happy to let lick it, most times thinking, "Oh, yeah . . . no wonder she left."

Now I am thirty years old. A thriving professional. A prolific artist. Blessed with great health, close family and loyal friends. Infinitely more confident in my sexual appeal and abilities. Significantly more comfortable in my economic situation and prospects. Quite more aware of my personal journey toward fulfillment and considerably more capable of maximizing the opportunities that further me on that path, while negotiating the challenges that do not.

In other words, I'm now a radical feminist, and most mere mortal males just can't hang.

Think I can invest all this time and talent into cultivating what spoken-word artist Rha Goddess calls 360 degrees of fly divahood to fall on my back for just any man? While I'm still a work in progress, I'm too spiritually clear to play emotional games with men, too politically conscious to allow games to be played with me and too emotionally aware not to recognize when the threat of either looms. Since my politics took a sharp turn left, a man who's long on cash, looks and influence isn't enough to make me wet anymore and that's usually all the multitude of Mr. Right Nows have to offer.

At minimum, the Chosen One has to offer me more honesty than flattery, more reciprocity than chivalry and more integrity than luxury. Now any man who boasts all these qualities—whether he's my first or my fiftieth—will be offered the privilege of carrying half my load, my moist bottom and my last name.

In the meantime, I have become adept and comfortable in assuming sole responsibility for my own sexual fulfillment. With my Girl Scout training still intact, I decided to follow the motto Always be prepared. Maybe I subscribe to romantic myths and patriarchal socialization, but I still believe that the first time I have sex will have a tremendous influence on the rest of my sex life. Being a decade and a half past my curious and libidinous fifteen-year-old self reinforces that belief. However, still curious and libidinous yet considerably less emotionally naive or insecure, I experience an empowering thrill in being sexually self-reliant until I can find a dude with similar qualities (that is, he won't be intimidated by a virgin with a vibrator). Until then, since I'm not waiting for Prince Charming to buy a home or travel the world, it only makes sense to take my sexual needs into my hands, so to speak. So, like a good Brownie, I got to practicing. My only regret is that I didn't start younger. I would've rather earned a badge for this instead of for selling those damn cookies.

The Sexual Evolution of a Digital Diva

To some extent, my sex-toy collection is based on a preexisting personality trait. Lack of inhibition, desire to know, improve and be at peace with all aspects of myself, desire for self-sufficiency, curiosity, libido? . . .Yeah, yeah, yeah, all that's true, but I'm talking about my penchant for collecting things. Nothing with the promise of financial return like stamps or coins (God no!), but things that only mean something to me: tarot cards, hip-hop memorabilia and electronic appliances.

Yes, I am an unapologetic gadget queen. If it has an electrical cord or battery pack, comes with a warranty card and an instruction manual, I gotta have it. A display window, multiple buttons and a host of accessories on which to squander more of my money are all pluses. The more programming time and storage space it demands from the little I have, the harder it is for me to resist the temptation to pull out the MasterCard. Like many people, I own a pager, a cellular telephone, a digital camera and an electronic organizer. Unlike most, however, I also own a scanner pen, an MP3 player and an acupuncture machine, among other things. Practicality is not a prerequisite—no matter if it'd be quicker to do it by hand or lighter to leave it at home (take that as you will).

My favorite gadgets to collect? Toys, of course. Hand-held versions of classic board games like Monopoly, as well as popular game shows like Jeopardy. What I liked most about these toys is that I could play with them by myself. (In fact, I hoard my toys precisely because I don't want to share.) These were so much fun to own, let alone play with, I decided to indulge in some toys I can't exactly whip out on the subway. (Well, I could, but . . .)

The same criteria I use to assess other technology before purchase applies to sex toys. Do the ease, power and other qualities of the appliance justify the price tag? The answers all should be yes. Will this gadget allow me to multi-task? Not a required feature, but preferred, as is the availability of upgrades and accessories (more on that shortly). Can I become so dependent on this technology that I'll lose the ability to accomplish the task on my own? The answer must be a resounding *hell no*.

As a matter of fact, fears of the loss of sensitivity and the onset of dependency were the final barriers I had to overcome before purchasing my first sex toy. I'm pleased to report that orgasms via gadgetry are no different than by any other means. Their intensity varies widely due to a variety of factors, none of which can ever be orchestrated, duplicated or otherwise controlled. Even after the occasional, puny, I-should've-watched-that-sitcom-rerun-instead orgasm (you know, the feeble kind outdone by its own tremendously delicious buildup that leaves you rolling over and grumbling, "I guess I should be happy I fuckin' came at all"), I say thank the Divine for unpredictability. Like rainy days, missed trains and other sorts of rotten luck, such mishaps help you appreciate how much and how often life goes right—as with a vigorously earned and wonderfully explosive orgasm.

Finally, the most important criterion, the make or break question, the unnegotiable bottom line: Would this be a nifty thing to say I own? But of course!

Dear Customer Service . . . What the Hell Were You Thinking?
Wonder Woman would trade in her invisible jet and golden lasso in a heartbeat for my sex-toy collection. We're talking one helluva garage sale here, except it'd be ludicrous to sell a treasure like this. However, as with many things pertaining

to female sexuality—from birth control to health care—much room for improvement remains. My wonderful collection results from trial and error.

From my very first purchase, I discovered a troubling contradiction in the sex-toy industry. The same mail-order companies that vow to protect your privacy sell products hell-bent on announcing to everyone within a mile radius of your *boudoir* what you're doing. In a few blunt words, these toys are too damn *loud!* What's the point of shipping the Cyber Beaver in a plain brown wrapper, sending the catalog in rosy stationery with the warning "To Be Opened By Addressee Only" and refusing to sell my name to other companies without my expressed permission when it sounds like I've stuffed a food processor under my comforter? Manufacturers, hear my cries! For those of us who live within thin walls barely separating them from conservative parents with no concept of privacy on one side and meddlesome neighbors on the other, pipe that product down. The thrill of being caught does not apply when you're working solo.

Another tip for sex-toy manufacturers: design and sell appropriate—if not downright fashionable—coverings for your products. You'd think with all the dildos and vibrators shaped as kangaroos, medieval knights, dolphins, butterflies and street vendor pretzels (okay, that last one is just another suggestion from yours truly—I'm from New York City), this would be a given. Perhaps I haven't found them yet or the industry is leaving this creative task to its customers, but when are they going to design some nifty covers for sex toys? In all fairness, the latest Good Vibrations catalog boasts what it calls the Natural Contours line because, as one customer lamented, "I take my vibrator everywhere, but I'm tired of having to explain it to those nosy airport security guards." Designed by adult filmmaker Candida Royalle and available in several artsy colors and shapes, these toys, the company insists, "will pass at the airport, your mom's house and between the sheets."

But that doesn't solve the entire problem. One of my favorite toys—the Turbo Tongue—now sports a woody odor and teal spots from being concealed in my bottom drawer beneath my favorite palazzo pants. People, there's got to be a better way. Hey, you don't have to be a fashion slave to appreciate the finishing touch of the perfect handbag. They make dildos that can be concealed in plain view on your dresser as just another tube of lipstick; surely they can make sex-toy wraps to hang unabashedly on your closet door in a fetching tote or swing from your shoulder in an attractive flapover.

Dildo makers also dismiss the notion that less can be more. They seem to assume that any woman in pursuit of pleasure via non-human mechanisms is uninterested in human proportions. Have you seen the size of these things? They almost make me scour through the catalog in search of a chastity belt.

Despite the aesthetic beauty of a smooth Jeff Stryker or a veiny Tom Chase, there's a reason why these folks make movies, y'all! Such gargantuan sizes are the exception, not the rule.

I learned this from my dissatisfying (and first dildo) encounter with Happy Henry. His classified ad read, "Here's a clever little vibrator that's sure to bring a smile to your face. Happy Henry's exclusive shape can take care of any passion, anytime. His big, smooth tip is 2" in diameter tapering to an easy 1-1/2"." However, the suction cup action and the endearing cartoon photo sold me. He bowed his bulbous head toward me in the most chivalrous way, as if to say, "At your pleasure, madame."

On sight of his two-inch diameter, however, I knew that Happy Henry and I were over before we began. So much for those fears of insensitivity and dependency. I'll be the bad guy in this failed relationship. My warped sense of measure—clouded by my libido—misled me to believe that I could handle Henry's dimensions. Or that's what I initially believed.

In retrospect, I realize that the true culprit was my ego. I wanted to believe that I needed all that bulk. Indeed, that I should be able to handle it. I had such high hopes for Henry and me that when I finally accepted that we weren't sexually compatible I went into a serious funk. Okay, so my sexual frustration was further compounded by the prospect of packing up Henry, taking him to the post office and waiting for my credit card charges to be reversed. But my melancholy was due largely to a deep-seated (albeit irrational) belief that I was less than a woman because I couldn't take all that Henry had. I worried that my inner freak would never be free. If I couldn't coax her out in the safety of my own bedroom, how the hell was I going to unleash her on a partner?

I underwent a process not unlike the five stages of death in getting over Henry. First, there was denial. No way could he be too big for me! For several nights I sweated myself into knots trying to make Henry fit. Let it be known that it is possible to frustrate yourself to sleep, even if fitfully. Then came anger. I was furious with the sex-toy industry for violating its own mission by creating a product that made me feel sexually inadequate and inhibited. As I was trying to figure out whether to file my formal complaint with the FDA or the ATF (just who regulates this stuff anyway?), bargaining set in. I told myself, God, Fate— any and all listening to my inner pleas—that if it worked out between Henry and me, I never would never glance at another dildo again. Approximately three minutes later, I moved on to depression. I experienced all the emotions that psychiatrists associate with the disorder—loss, sadness, hopelessness, failure and even rejection.

Finally, I graduated to acceptance. I accepted not only that Henry was just much too large for me but also that nothing was wrong with me because of that. Several things helped. For one, I considered the many virtues of my snugness. Plus, when you fall off the horse (and while Henry's far from stallion proportions, he could make a frisky filly whinny), the best thing to do is to climb back on. Back to the Xandria catalog I went and rediscovered all the other delectable options. I found other uses for Henry. Yes, he's still with me, and no, he's not a doorstop or rolling pin. Thanks to the suction cups that first made me fall for him, the little bastard is a great tease in the shower!

Not all endings are so happy. I speak of my doomed liaison with the Honey Dipper. As its tantalizing name suggests, Honey's a vibrator with a springlike shaft that "thrusts" at your command. Great idea, terrible execution. The little fucker pinches like you wouldn't believe! Unlike Henry, Honey got only one chance with me. Do not pass come and do not collect $34.95 plus shipping and handling. I deeply hope that one day they'll get it right, because I'm still not over this one.

Sometimes the manufacturers do get it right, but in their proud rush to market they skimp on quality. Take Lover Lips. Were it not for the shabby construction, he coulda been a contenda. Oh, the toy itself—an oral sex simulator by virtue of a hand pump (vibrator option included for those times when you need that something extra)—was fine. But after just one use (and given the nature of the exercise, not an unusually vigorous one at that), the battery pack disintegrated. When I should've been sleeping soundly in orgasmic afterglow, I was suffering goosebumps on my bare ass as I crawled and flailed across the linoleum in the dark, searching for whatever went ping when it hit the floor. Turned out to be the tiny slab of metal without which the current cannot transfer from the battery to the appliance.

In fact, I have had at least three toys—all brilliantly conceived sexual tools—rendered powerless due to cheaply made battery packs. Too many pleasure appliances—fragile and sturdy alike—require multiple, large batteries to operate (the few that come with AC adaptors tend to be considerably more pricey). Leave those batteries in for a heartbeat and, *voilà,* you have a rusty nightmare. Of these toys, only Lover Lips remains with me today. The batteries are only necessary for using the vibrator, a rarity when I'm in the mood for cunnilingus imitatus. But I've got to say, if I wanted my stimulant to collapse only after one round, I'd opt for a guy.

And the Cummy Goes To . . .

Nevertheless, the gems I discover on occasion make the trials and tribulations of buying and using sex toys all worthwhile.

Some needn't be experienced to be appreciated. Given my preference for modest dimensions and dildos of color (and I refuse to engage the ridiculous notion that these are contradictory desires. Shame on you for buying that Mandingo nonsense—fantasies are fair game, but stereotypes are foul play), I can't help but admire the lifelike erect replicas they make of porn giants such as Peter North and John Holmes. I have to give it up for . . . uh, I mean give praise to the "RealCast" process by which they mold these erect replicas. It'd better be patented, for such genius warrants protection.

Then there is the Twister, which enjoys the distinction of having delivered my first gadgetgasm. The Twister creates a maddening buildup, frenzied bucking and lasting aftershocks that make you forgive and forget the wuss you had the previous night. This nifty gadget not only vibrates, it rotates. It even has a fraternal twin—Bumpy Twister—should you want to double date. In my humble opinion, this toy succeeds where Honey Dipper failed. Along with the aforementioned Turbo Tongue and Lover Lips, whose names speak for themselves, the Twister holds a special place in my heart (and I'm not talking the center of my circulatory system, although it, too, extends gratitude for the much needed workout). It just goes to show you that sometimes sophistication lies in simplicity, and I raced back to my catalogs looking for more of it.

In fact, my favorite toy of all, the one that I reach for most, is the simplest I own: Manskins. Theoretically, this vibrating dildo feels like a man with foreskin. Since I can't testify yet to the veracity of this claim, my appreciation comes from its no-frills design—although with the right lubricant, the sensation of those latex folds ain't too shabby. Maybe it's because I've experienced so many sex toys that I can value Manskins for the simple Joe he is, but when all is moaned and thrown, it's the most typical of dildos that won me over.

All I Want for Christmas

As impressive as my collection is, I still have quite a wish list. Unfortunately, these desired items are going to have to wait until I buy my own place. I'm seriously thinking of adding the following to my housewarming gift registry:

E-Z Rider Rocker and Dong. Or the Sexagon. Or both. Remember that '70s toy that resembled a giant rubber ball? A kid could just straddle the ball, grab onto a handle (one variation had the handle shaped like an animal head) and bounce to her little heart's content. Well, replace the handle with a dildo, and you have the adult version. The Sexagon has a hands-free base with a flexible dildo. I love the idea of owning my own carnival ride and suspect that I'll mount it more often than the doubly expensive Power Rider, Total Gym and other exercise machines that I already own, which presently are collecting dust.

Microwavable Hot Cock. Fifteen seconds in the ole Sharp Carousel, and this baby heats to body temperature. I haven't given up my cell phone for fear of developing brain cancer, so why not?

Ecstasy Swing. Because this one will require some construction, it has inspired fantasies of converting a room into a sex den. The contraption hangs from an adjustable swing and rotating eyebolt. Slip my feet into the stirrups and my tush in the padded seat and off I come. Granted, the catalog illustration features a couple, but when there's a will, there's a way. Since I expect having a place of my own will boost my libido and my prospects, this will be a great investment. For the blessed fellow I care enough for to go the distance, the Ecstasy Swing should be a rewarding introduction to my sex-toy collection. For the unworthy, I'll reserve Happy Henry and a copy of *Bend Over Boyfriend*. (To the man who can get with both, I'm proposing marriage.)

After having lived with my parents for so long, it's going to be difficult to get worked up about selecting a china pattern or bathroom ensemble. But these items offer quite an incentive to save for that down payment!

Before I Sign Off to Get Off

I can hardly throw "shoulds" at other women if I want my choices respected as healthy and right for me. But girlfriend, you gotta consider! If you're comfortable with or interested in masturbating, by all means spice up the solo love life with a prop or two. Not only do mine allow me to explore my sexuality and satisfy my needs in the absence of worthy partners, but they also support the maintenance of the healthy self-love and sexual confidence critical to great sexual experiences with others. If I can have this much of a blast by my lonesome, imagine the rave when I decide to let someone else in on the fun.

As a matter of fact, my sex-toy collection has raised the bar for potential suitors even as it delivers more sexual liberation. Lucky I'm a fan of irony (so much that it can make me horny). One of my favorite fantasies has become The Test. I'm about to get down and dirty for the first time ever with an Adonis who has all the requirements and a healthy dose of the preferreds. We engage in some heavy caressing and pillow talk that fluctuates between the raw and the romantic. But before I proceed I have to know:

Is this going to mean the same to him as it will to me?

How willing is he to share the vulnerability and trust that go with sexual abandon and emotional intimacy?

Can he give as good as he takes, and vice versa?

There's only one way to find out.

I reach under the bed for—you guessed it—Happy Henry and *Bend Over*

Boyfriend. I nibble on his ears, then whisper, "I promise to be gentle."

His eyes widen with shock, and he laughs nervously. Then he realizes that I'm serious. A first for me for a first for him.

Adonis is both aroused and frightened. He takes a deep breath and swallows hard. "Okay, but go sloooowly." He's passed the test.

You know how it ends.

Until that fantasty comes true—and I wholeheartedly believe it will—all mere mortal men must beware of SuperVirgin; she's armed and satisfied.

Pleasing Alex

 Meg Weber

Meet me at the Cup and Saucer at 7:15 a.m. and be prepared to deliver your apology on your knees. Cup and Saucer is our usual breakfast spot, but this promises to be a meeting outside the ordinary. As I turn the corner onto Hawthorne Street, I see Alex's car parked outside the cafe.

She is all dyked out in tight jeans, black leather jacket, kick-ass motorcycle boots and a perfectly honed icy attitude. Her demeanor is pure top—cool and confident, arrogant as hell. Alex saunters into the Cup as I kill the engine, gather myself and step out of my car. I follow her, unnoticed, catching the door she expects to slam behind her. Sheepishly, I imagine her looking around for me, marveling at my audacity. First I cop this bullshit attitude and then I keep her waiting?

As I enter the cafe, Alex nods briefly to acknowledge my presence and proceeds to sit down, facing me as I walk in. I pull out the chair opposite her and perch on the edge of it. A herd of butterflies wrestles in my stomach. I'm not sure which one of us is supposed to break this crushing silence. She glares at me, arms folded sternly across her chest. "I'm waiting . . . " she says.

The chill of her words adds to my embarrassment as I gulp and mumble, "Do you expect me on my knees?" She nods in response. Rising from my chair without a second thought, I position myself on my knees with my back to the other early morning diners. Speaking words I'd tried to rehearse ("impetuous," that's good, maybe I'll remember to say that), I offer up an eloquent lie of apology. And then . . . I wait.

The apology hovers in the air between us. I gaze at her, seeking some hint from those steely blue eyes of what happens next. Finally, her hand moves to the side of my face, caressing me so gently I almost cry, and she whispers, "Get up." At her touch I am liquid, certain that any shame I had about kneeling in public was eradicated by the tenderness of her caress. In that moment, on my knees in a public cafe, melting under the white hot intensity of her calculated gaze, something started to make sense.

I imagine you're wondering how this all came about. For what would I owe this woman such a grandiose apology? Why would I agree to be humiliated in public? Have I not a shred of self-respect? I'd best start from the beginning . . .

The personals in *Willamette Week* drew me in; week after week I scanned them for entertainment, not intending ever to answer one. The entire subculture of the "Wild Encounters" personals seemed out of my league somehow. I was a recovering Catholic dyke from suburbia trapped behind one-way glass, peering in hungrily at a world entirely unattainable to me. Or so I thought. Then I found his ad . . .

> No euphemisms, no B.S. I'm a single, intelligent, honest, experienced, creative male top seeking a compatible erotically submissive woman. I like to bind, bite, spank, command, tease and much more. Limits negotiated and respected. Novice welcome. Safe, sane and consensual.

"Erotically submissive woman" . . . Is that what I was? What I aspired to? Did I really want to take part in his laundry list of desires? Was I willing to be this involved with a man? Curiosity was the true catalyst. At the time, I thought there was magic in his language. But his words were merely colored by my aching desire to experiment. My interest in S/M had blossomed from a naive wonder to a gnawing need to explore. In previous sexual relationships I'd blurred the line between vanilla and kinky sex. My first lover had introduced me to basic elements of S/M, including subtle power and submission games, blindfolds and light bondage with scarves and handcuffs. With my latest lover, I'd taken the dominant role, adding spanking to the repertoire once used on me. Whichever role I played, I was only dabbling and didn't know what the hell I was doing. I craved experience under a trained hand. Besides, I'd wanted to have sex with a man since before I came out as a dyke. So here, in forty words or less, was my chance at both.

While my mind pondered the threat of danger, my cunt pulsed at the perversions he'd strung into an invitation. For once, the physical response of my body overcame caution. I would not ignore these cravings for sensation. I didn't understand the compulsion—sometimes I still don't. It isn't founded in logic, reason or emotion, it's a bodily hunger.

The first time I played with Sheldon, we spent two hours negotiating prior to any real action taking place. (Negotiating is to S/M as processing is to lesbian relationships.) We sat on the futon in the living room of his sparsely furnished apartment discussing limits and boundaries. "This is where you pull out a menu and I just get to pick what I want, right?" I asked hopefully. He laughed; it didn't work that way. Sheldon rattled off a list of things, including bondage, name calling, biting and various hitting implements like paddles, whips and canes. My facial expressions told the story of my reactions: eyes lit up and sparkling, a faint blush at ideas that intrigued me; scrunched up nose and head shaking an emphatic No to those that frightened me in all the wrong ways. I found myself tongue-tied, wanting to impress him by speaking clearly and decisively. But I had no clue what my limits were. I couldn't translate the jumbled mess in my head into coherent language. It's one thing to dream, in the privacy of my imagination, of how I want to be teased, controlled and fucked. Admitting those perversions out loud is terrifying. This was lesson number one in blunt communication.

Eventually our negotiations wound their way around to safe sex and the ever important bodily fluids talk. When I answered Sheldon's ad, I stated that my primary attraction was to women. Apparently I'd neglected to mention that I'd never had sex with a man, a minor omission that led him to believe I'd been around that block. As he casually asked what I expected in terms of safer sex, I began to panic. Maybe he won't want me if I've never been with a man . . . is he willing to be my first? Do I really want to lose my heterosexual virginity to this guy? Flustered, I did my best to clear up the misunderstanding. "Well, you see, that's a good question . . . I mean, I've never really done this part before . . ." My voice trailed off, silenced by the look of surprised consternation on his face. "No, I mean I've just never had sex with a man before. The whole bodily fluids issue is different between men and women." A long awkward moment followed. Sheldon asked if that meant I didn't want our play relationship to be overtly sexual. I quickly explained that I'd answered his ad to satisfy two curiosities in one shot—hardcore S/M and sex with men. The fact that I wanted sex in this experience was irrefutable. (Not because I was desperately attracted to Sheldon, per se, but because I'd always wanted to be fucked by a man and I saw this as a surefire chance.)

In fact, the sex part turned out fantastic, better than a devout lesbian could ever expect from a guy. Sheldon knew precisely how to fuck me—deep, hard and long enough to feel like it just might last forever. But our S/M interactions never qualified as hardcore. He was safe to a fault. A huge part of my impetus to do S/M was to feel danger, taste fear in this daring encounter. Not too much fear, just enough to know it was present and believable. Make-believe had never been my strong suit; even as a young child, I was too pragmatic to bother dreaming of imaginary stories. If this willing suspension of disbelief was going to succeed, Sheldon would have to be damn convincing.

He wasn't.

Playing with Sheldon was like learning to ride a bike with training wheels. I felt the thrill of a new experience without any real threat of danger. It rings hollow to say I was never afraid—that first time we played I knelt to him, stripped bare on the floor of his one-bedroom apartment. When Sheldon locked his collar around my neck, a shivering thrill ran through my body. He pushed me forward onto my hands and knees, inspecting me like a thoroughbred racehorse. I knelt there motionless, hoping to please him without the faintest idea what that might entail. Holding my breath, wanting to savor this anticipation, I was wholly exposed, poised on the edge of a brilliant, potentially terrifying experience. Even then, it wasn't fear I tasted in the back of my throat. Curiosity, more sweet than bitter, dripped from my lips as I waited for the unknown adventure.

At Sheldon's command I sat back on my heels, hands clasped behind my back. Every move he made was calculated, each ounce of tension drawn out to its fullest measure. He pulled me to standing by my hair, and directed me into his bedroom to lie face down on the bed. I had already suspected that Sheldon was the epitome of beige. His room was proof. It had bare walls, off-white sheets on the bed and nothing for decoration but a computer system and bookshelves full of information technology texts. My wrists and ankles were placed in thick leather cuffs that locked, like the collar, with tiny padlocks. Anticipation tortured me. Lengths of thick chain soon bound me to the four corners of the bed. "I decided to be nice and not freeze these first," he commented wryly. "Since it's your first time and all." I was grateful. As it was, they were cold to the touch. I relaxed into this bondage, still uncertain of what he might do to me, but feeling surprisingly free in this confinement. Is this when fear ought to have seized me—caught spread-eagle under the control of this scrawny computer geek I'd met only twice? Perhaps in that moment I should have been afraid.

But there was no compelling reason to fear Sheldon. My instincts had already decided he wouldn't harm me, ruling out a reaction of genuine terror. And his authority over me was a facade, not believable enough to offer me a glimpse at the erotic charge I knew fear could carry. It circled back to my ineptitude at make-believe. Authentic fear began to seem nonexistent in S/M, as if sifted out somehow in the process of negotiation. Really then, we were only playing with surprise and perceived threat. It's a mind-fuck. We're taught to fear pain and violence, so we respond to S/M with fear. Or do we? I desperately wanted to play along, to see if I could coax myself into believing, allow myself to feel danger and experience pain as a way of coming home to my body. My doubt was the product of an overactive rational mind. I wanted to silence my intellect and allow the sensations at hand to carry me somewhere my mind couldn't take me.

As he locked the final padlock, fastening the chain to eyebolts on the bed frame, I heard him mutter, "Now where did I put that axe . . . " My mind tried to induce panic; after all, I was now securely chained to the bed of a near stranger, utterly powerless. But my gut knew I was safe, which allowed me to laugh it off and play along. Sheldon's humor endeared me to him in ways the rest of his demeanor never could; he surprised me and I liked that.

During the six months that we played together, he gave me a thorough introduction to the S/M scene. As with any subculture, there was a lot to learn before I could mingle in a crowd of S/M folks without offending anyone or making a fool of myself. Sheldon taught me the things I needed to know to get by, for which I am quite thankful. And I very actively enjoyed being sexual with him. I began to wonder if I had to alter my identity now that I liked fucking men. And who got to decide that anyway? A jury of my peers was ready to snatch away my lesbian credentials for sleeping with one man, but I held fast to what felt most true. I was just a dyke who liked sex with men. It was a contradiction I could live with.

Although I enjoyed my relationship with Sheldon, he never once scared me as I wanted. Not for a moment did I feel threatened, controlled or submissive to him. And for a myriad of reasons that I hadn't fully defined, that is what I craved—my cunt begged for it, my mind turned itself inside out and backwards to create a place where I could be, do and want all the things I feared most and still respect myself in the morning. I was tired of training wheels, craving something faster, more dangerous . . .

Which brings me to Alex. Sheldon had given me Alex's name as a reference, someone he had played with who could vouch for his integrity. Her assurance of his safety was the identical twin to my gut instinct that predicted that the risk was negligible. Alex invited me to call her when I needed to process my experiences with Sheldon. She'd been in my shoes, and knew that my vanilla friends weren't likely to understand. I eagerly accepted her offer. After playing with Sheldon a few times, I called Alex, bursting with insights, questions and stories that no one else in my life could fathom. We met for lunch and she listened attentively as I told the tales of what I'd done with Sheldon and how it was affecting me. Relief sank in as she shared her own experiences. Not only did Alex comprehend my situation as one kinky dyke with another; she had bottomed to Sheldon and fully understood the particular quirks of his personality. Hers was the wise voice of experience that the rest of my life completely lacked. Every couple weeks Alex and I met over breakfast to explore our common experiences. These intellectually intimate conversations unknowingly laid the groundwork for my next adventure. You never know who someone might become.

Alex became the object of my obsession. The standard by which I measured my worth, the fire that fueled my lust. She was goddess-slut-mother-whore-madam-sir-now-faster-harder-more-pain-sex-love-lust-loss. I didn't intend for it to go all those places—never wanted to subject either of us to that horror of idolatry so worthless for each, so destined to fail. Long before I'd discovered S/M, I went through a series of relationships with women whom I worshiped. I made them into larger-than-life deities and reduced myself to nothing. With Alex this potential existed again, which made playing with her both highly intriguing and undoubtedly edgy. Everything I'd learned thus far about safe, sane and consensual S/M warned that the interaction had to occur between two people of equal influence choosing to play with a power dynamic. While I saw the logic in that, I couldn't deny the urge to play out my issues of self-worth and obsession in this sexy new arena. I desperately wanted to bottom to Alex, but feared my motivation relied too heavily on the self-deprecating pattern of my past.

I was determined to avoid that trap in favor of a mentoring friendship. Still a novice in the scene, I reasoned that having a friend who knew the ropes would be wise. So, with my lust for Alex running rampant, I limited myself to casual, platonic interactions with her. But Alex was a smart, sexy, literate, polyamorous dyke with plenty of experience in the S/M scene, and the more I got to know her, the more I wanted her. The last shred of hope for curbing my crush on Alex was obliterated when she propositioned me at my first play party.

Alex was scolding me from across the room—her eye caught mine as a lazy yawn escaped my mouth. "You could punish her for that," someone joked. "That's not my job," she replied, grinning. So I figured I'd say farewell and head home to begin processing everything I'd seen and heard that night. Instead, Alex sauntered across the room, sat down beside me and bluntly inquired, "So, are you too tired to get spanked?" My exhaustion was instantly replaced by arousal. I accepted her offer, regardless of my prior resolve.

As we made our way to the basement dungeon, I was nervous and awkward in my excitement. In the spoken equivalent of tripping down the stairs, I asked how to address her during this scene. It wasn't a wholly ridiculous question; plenty of tops demand the title "sir" or "madam" while playing. "You can call me Alex," she smirked. She was confidently tender as we discussed boundaries and expectations. With that finished, she instructed me to remove my jeans. "Turn around," she ordered. "Let me see my canvas." As I leaned forward on my hands and knees, she drew in her breath and pronounced me beautiful. A brilliant, shy smile crossed my face. She hadn't even laid a hand on me yet and already I was flying. Pulling me onto her lap, she laid me across her knee and began to spank me. Her touch was electrifying and I savored the comfort of her body beneath mine. Whether I like sex with men or not, nothing compares to the sheer eroticism of two women's curves fitting together like long-separated puzzle pieces reunited. With each stroke of Alex's hand on my ass I was more aroused. It wasn't the sheer physicality of being spanked by her that captured me but the sensual, erotic tone of her voice. Ultimately, I'm a language slut. Her words engaged my mind as well as my body, making the scene even hotter. The physical sensation of being spanked drowned in the sweetness of Alex's voice as she praised me, "You're being so good . . . " That paradox itself was exciting to me—being praised for doing something taboo. Guilt and shame, pleasure and pain . . . the lines blurred into oblivion.

This contradiction was precisely what I craved. As much as I longed for physical sensation to ground me in my body, I needed praise for how I handled pain. Sheldon never once showed appreciation for how I took the pain and humiliation he doled out, as if my reactions didn't matter at all. The indifference stung more than any blow he dealt, but left me cold. Alex's adulation nourished me in ways I still can't fathom. Maybe it reassured me that doing S/M was a viable form of sexual pleasure. Or perhaps it was the mother issues that sneak their way into my intense relationships with older women—Alex's praise soothing unhealed mother/daughter wounds. I was inherently able to be more vulnerable with Alex. It wasn't intentional; I found myself literally unable to resist her.

My connection with women stems from a deeply visceral place. No one has hurt me more than the women I've loved—starting with my mother and including most of my female lovers. And yet, with unshakable desire, it is communion with women that I seek. My attractions to men have never run as deeply, resulting most often in a sense of emotional indifference mingled with sexual lust. With Sheldon, for example, my attraction was primarily sexual; I could take it or leave it. But Alex captivated my entire being—mind, heart, body, soul, cunt. I wanted to fold myself into the comfort of her arms and sob, surrender myself to her unequivocally. Unlike with Sheldon, there was no need to invent a power differential between Alex and me. It already existed, erotically compelling in its intensity.

Spilled across her lap in that basement dungeon, I was drunk on Alex's touch and the melody of her words. She reined me back in by stating there would be ten more spankings and that I was to thank her after each one. Internally I cringed, reluctant for it to end. Did she feel the pleasure too? Or was I merely caught in her spell, encompassed by an erotic, sensual spirituality that defied definition? In her arms I was whole and sexy, sacred and safe. One by one, the last ten spankings were delivered and I confessed my gratitude for them, as required. All too soon it was over, reality interrupting like an impatient child. I slowly put my jeans back on and we made our way upstairs.

It didn't take long, following that evening, for my obsession to fully take root. I resigned myself to the least painful method of confessing my desire. I turned to writing, hoping my affinity for language would ease the trauma of spilling my guts. In my journal I composed an entry entitled *If I weren't afraid, this is what I would say to Alex*. I declared: "I would admit my desire to play with her. I would own up to and find words for my detailed fantasies regarding her, submission, sex and tenderness. I would learn to trust and not be afraid. I would be more present with her. Alex, I'm not trying to hide from you . . . but I'm afraid . . . afraid of rejection, afraid of wanting more than you will give me, afraid of not being able to give sufficiently in return . . . afraid of being too much and of simultaneously not being enough."

That entire journal entry became my written confession, sent to Alex via email three weeks after playing with her. She received it well, praising my courage and thanking me for my honesty. She proposed we discuss the situation in person. When we met later that week, I no longer had the luxury of hiding behind the written word. I had to face her and my admission of desire. Alex was flattered by my frank declaration. She had sensed my attraction to her, and clearly had some interest in me, judging by her proposition at the play party. She said she would like to explore a play relationship with me, but could not commit the required time and energy. She was already overbooked with work and other relationships. Polyamory does have a way of complicating one's schedule. But Alex was intrigued by the attraction between us. We needed a compromise—a decision I willingly deferred to her.

Her solution was to craft an email correspondence, conducted in role as dominant and submissive, wherein Alex would pose questions that I was to answer by a deadline of her choosing. This created for us the playing field on which to explore our mutual attraction without the time commitment inherent to an ongoing, physical S/M relationship. From within the cloud of my obsession, I was willing to accept any scrap of attention she offered. The language slut in me was thrilled by the literary aspect of this relationship. Alex hinted that perhaps this would develop into a real-life play relationship. Harboring that longing, I readily agreed to an online correspondence.

The first few assignments established our power dynamic and allowed Alex to get to know me better. I answered questions about my sexual history, early fantasies about S/M, power relationships in my house growing up and my first orgasm. With the help of a sexuality questionnaire she provided, I compiled lists of kinky things I'd done, things I wanted to experience and activities I refused to try under any circumstances. Bottoming to Alex online elicited more genuine submission from me than anything I ever did with Sheldon. Her authority over me felt authentic—I cared what she thought of me, craved her attention. I would have given myself over to her completely if she had allowed such idiocy. Her questions were blunt and pointed, demanding complete honesty on my part. My responses, dripping with candor and deference to her, were crafted in language as polished as I could manage in order to please her. I held nothing back . . . until the fourth assignment.

Alex ordered me to write an erotic account of the sexiest S/M scene I'd ever done. I balked. Since my hottest scene consisted of Alex spanking me at the play party, writing that story for her felt incredibly daunting. Besides, behaving at every turn hadn't generated sufficient attention from Alex. I figured acting out a little might do the trick. Part of why I wanted to do S/M in the first place had been to alter my relationship to authority, to push against established limits and have them hold strong. All along, I'd been a good girl who did what she was told; this time I decided to challenge her. In a brief email, after explaining that her spanking me was the hottest scene I'd had, I flat out refused to write about it. Ask me a different question, I dared her. Alex's reply claimed that "I don't feel like it" was not an acceptable response. My options at that point were to end the correspondence, contact her out of role to explain why I was acting out or get over myself and complete the assignment.

Thinking I'd had my fun, I wrote back explaining my motives. I promised that the assignment would be finished as scheduled. Her next email shocked me by continuing this exchange. I may have had my fun, but Alex apparently had a point to make. She asserted that she was waiting for my apology and that it had better be good to justify my blatant disrespect. Trembling with excitement, I drafted an eloquent apology that was ultimately false. I felt no remorse for finally getting the focused attention Alex continually withheld. Nonetheless, I sent off my apology under the subject heading of *abject, humble plea for forgiveness.* "Alex, my behavior has been deplorable. In an attempt to selfishly gain your attention I have offended, disrespected and angered you. I surrender to your mercy and pledge to do anything necessary to regain your favor. Anything. Please forgive me." Once again, I figured that would be the end of the issue. Then I received her summons. "Not good enough. Meet me at the Cup and Saucer at 7:15 a.m. and be prepared to deliver your apology on your knees."

That morning, apologizing to Alex on my knees, I was completely on the edge, exposed and vulnerable. Pleasing Alex was all that mattered; it wasn't that I had no self-respect, or even that I respected her more than myself. It was a game to me, one that engaged my mind as well as my lust. I had become the erotically submissive woman I'd once doubted I could be, willing to suffer humiliation in exchange for the places it could take me. In subjecting myself to the whim and direction of Alex, I invited her punishment. But I also created the opportunity to earn her attention and praise. Through this loan of my power, I became infused with a personal strength that exceeded my previous imaginings. One layer of this strength is the very knowledge that I have power to concede. Beneath that lies the certainty that loaning my power does not mean it is lost to me. It returns to me, increased. Communicating my desire in excruciatingly blunt language teaches me to listen to the voice deep within, to satisfy her cravings and needs. As we left the cafe that morning, Alex whispered in my ear, "You pleased me this morning . . . " Blushing furiously, I thanked her, claiming that as my goal all along.

Although I desperately wanted to submit to Alex sexually, I thrived in this intellectual, emotional submission that challenged my established patterns of idolatry. Interacting with Alex also stirred up lingering threads of power issues with my own mother, leading me down a path towards potential resolution. All that aside, it turned me on. Language holds intense erotic potential when used deliberately in the context of a mind-fuck. Especially to a word slut like me. Alex's eloquence and unshakable authority sent me on a rollercoaster ride to the edges of submission, turning my ideas about sex, power, and pain inside out along the way.

Through the lens of S/M I began to recognize danger and safety, pain and pleasure, submission and power, not as static polar-opposite entities, but as intricate amalgams of experience. Pain is pain is pain doesn't hold true in this realm. What is perceived as pain translates into erotic pleasure in the context of submission. Submission as a powerless stance doesn't exist under the pretext of willful consent. Bending my mind around this counterintuitive logic parallels the ways in which my body contorts to accommodate the demands of physical S/M play.

The equation I had emotionally with Alex translates easily to the physical realm. I offer my body to be used in ways that may be demeaning, physically painful or unpleasant in exchange for sexual pleasure. It's a corporeal system of barter. As Sheldon once remarked, "Oh good, here's the part where I get to hit you with things." It was true . . . he got to hit me with things, and I got to be fucked. That was the deal we struck. But sexual gratification is not my sole motivation for exploring S/M. The freedom to examine my relationships with power, desire, pain and submission on a physical level far outweighs the thrill of a good fuck.

Doing S/M brings me home to my body in a way nothing else ever has. I consciously obliterate the boundaries of my sexuality to experience this lust, this wholeness, this peace. I savor the smell of lust as it rises to meet my lover. I taste the delicious truth that I am sexy in this body. I dance inside the pain inflicted, feel my muscles and my spirit yielding in their quest for catharsis. I willingly abdicate my power, grateful for the experience of emotional release through physical sensation. Silencing the chaos of my conscious mind, I allow my physical senses to take over and celebrate the ability to feel, this gift of sentience.

The Not-SoFizgig Affair

 @nonymous

It certainly wasn't a love affair. It wasn't even a sex affair. It is perhaps most appropriate to think of it as a bit of well-lubricated tactical psychodrama. On one level it was a (r)e-venge fuck plain and simple. On another, it was a revealing bit of feminist adventure gaming.

A couple of years ago, I golemed up a barely legal, eighteen-year-old high school student and performed her in a very deceptive "affair" conducted in the sex underground of America's Biggest On-Line Service. I called her SoFizgig as a sideways nod to my own "failed" southern girl adolescence.

"Fizgig" means "flirty young woman" or "small firecracker," and, though archaic, the word is still in use as a term of endearment in some parts of the South. It is one of my very favorite words. Firecracker girls are those graceful, un-innocent, funny, tomboy/femme fuck-you girls who have the verve and the smarts and the looks to do pretty much as they will and get away with anything, sometimes up to a tragic point. *Seventeen, Cosmo* and *Playboy* all attempt to appropriate her, but never quite manage it. She's that good girl simply bursting with secret knowledge of her own potential to be as bad as she wants to be.

Now I can joke that I have always been more sheela-na-gig than fizgig, but as a teenager, my failure to be SoFizgig (or at least be able to play her in the halls of my high school) was the primal shame of my life. I was that most culturally despised type of teenage girl. I yo-yoed back and forth between chubby and fat. I could not tan evenly to save my life. I always had at least one prominent zit. I wore braces. I was a geek and a smart-mouthed "smart girl." If I had been a cartoon character, I would have resembled a cross between *South Park's* Shelly (Stan's lumpy, headgear-wearing sister) and MTV's Daria. I was my own squat little package of TNT: tremendous explosive capacity, only no one wanted to touch it, no one knew where to begin.

That I was growing up fairly affluent in the South only threw my anti-fizgigness into higher cultural relief. By the time I was fourteen, I'd been subjected to two commercial diet plans, was bulimic, and, although I remained—outwardly at least—somewhat spunky and outspoken, I felt totally undesirable and just plain culturally invisible. I deflected and dodged a lot of harassment and bit back on a lot of rage. As a little sister of the women's movement, I fronted all the self-esteem in the world and was patted on the head for my not-infrequent boldness, but I had no self-esteem whatsoever.

The pop culture of the late '70s and early '80s was the other mirror against which I measured myself. I absorbed, mainly from television and magazines, a sexualized version of The Girl I Was Supposed to Be, while my world offered no validation of my own girl geek sexuality. This was a problem, because from the time I had my first utterly surprising immature orgasm rocking in the crotch of a dogwood tree in my grandmother's front yard, I'd been an avid masturbator and was extremely curious about sex. At a very tender age, a cousin and I discovered a male relative's cache of porn mags and were fascinated. Around this time, my more precocious friends and I began playing a warped version of the Playboy Club. Every little girl has a dream, right? Mine was to dance in a cage in a nightclub wearing a gold lamé bikini.

In middle school, i.e., as the girlsap was starting to rise in a serious way, my best friend was a smart, slender and conventionally sexy blonde girl named Mary Kathryn. We were at such different ends of the teen desirability continuum that we actually had a lot in common. Our favorite movies were *Little Darlings* and *Endless Love*. We read Lisa Alther, Nancy Friday, Anaïs Nin. We were big fans of Anonymous. By the time we finished seventh grade, Mary Kathryn and I had virtually memorized not just the prurient sections of the infamous Judy Blume novel *Forever,* but the "Playing the Pink Piccolo" section of the first Happy

Hooker book as well. It was easy for us to amass quite a library of smut on our weekly forays to the neighborhood used-paperback store.

Now that I'm a mature and picky consumer, I realize how profoundly some extremely dubious smut colonized my sexual imagination before I had any critical skills whatsoever—writing any possibility of my own, not-so-fizgig sexuality out of the scene, usually in extremely demeaning ways. In spite of its questionable effects on my sexual self-image, my adolescent familiarity with generic het pornography and literary erotica served me well in my eventual exploration of feminist pornotica during my grad school angry-grrrl phase. Talking with friends, I was fascinated to discover that in this community, *all* of our adolescent sexual fantasy lives were shaped by our early fascination with porn. In grad school, as we began to explore sex beyond the boundaries of vanilla heterosexuality, we went through a kind of second adolescence together. Queer, straight and in between, we pored over the Good Vibrations catalog, read Susie Bright, and hosted girl-porn video slumber parties. Girl sex as resistance was in the air. With no exposure to the feminist sex wars of the early '80s, we proudly, if mostly naively, defined ourselves as "pro-sex feminists."

Flash forward to the present. Compared to my zipless-fuckey girlhood fantasies and compared to most of my friends, many of whom consider me a total sexual enigma, I lead a fairly conservative sex life. I've never been a promiscuous person, partly because of my body/weight issues, partly because I came of age just after the advent of the AIDS and herpes epidemics, partly because that's just not how I play. I'm not casual about sex as a mode of communication. Still, over time I have become comfortable with and taken ownership of *my* sexuality— in large part thanks to the sex-positive feminist movement's championing of female masturbation. I have a deep toy chest and the imaginative capacity to amuse myself endlessly, or at least until passing out. As my dear old dad likes to remind me, a single lady must be self-reliant in all areas of life!

Discreet gal that I am, I probably wouldn't have taken my love to cybertown if I had not found myself all alone in a big new city. Being the new feminist in town is a weird gig, especially if you are Camryn Manheim–esque. When you're fat, the lesbians assume you are a dyke and introduce you to their adorable chubdyke friends; the straight girls smile and pretend they think you're not fat while secretly comparing the size of your ass to theirs; and most of the het men who don't simply dismiss or harass you are confused, shy or terrified. Or they just don't want to offend, or are conflicted about their desire for a fat woman, or want a mother (which I decidedly am not), or want a woman on whom they can lay a *Pygmalion* fantasy. What's a nice chubby wild girl who mostly likes boys to do?

After my move, I was between Internet service providers. That is, I was horny *and* Net-jonesing. One Sunday afternoon, I broke down and found myself scrounging around in my laptop case for that shiny silver disc promising hours upon hours of free infotainment from America's Biggest Online Service. I set up the software and logged on. Hmm. Community Connection. Wonder what they do in there. *Click click.*

Imagine, please, the broad, screen-illuminated grin that spread across my face as I discovered that, just beneath the bright, happy, depthless infoveneer of the biggest online service, there pulses a heavily anonymous subculture whose entire *raison d'être* is the computer-mediated sexual hookup. Virtual and/or real. All flavors, all the time.

This was titillating. Actually, it was *nasty.* But it gave me pause. Except for a little flirting on mail lists, I'd never gone looking for sex-proper online. Still, there I was: on a Sunday afternoon sitting in my naked new apartment, strangely horny and tired of unpacking. I might not have known which box held my finer kitchen implements, but I knew where the sex toys were. Besides, my very favorite thing at that particular moment was my brand new, heavily customized PowerBook. Not a problem to reconceptualize it as a sex toy, too. Since childhood, a part of me always *had* wanted to be both anonymously and unabashedly promiscuous. Here was my chance. Bring on the disembodied interactive fantasy, the smuttier the better!

I came up with a provocative alias (my first of maybe twenty-five or thirty), logged back on to the service and clicked and pointed my way down the corridors of the chat channel, through the mirror of official, service-sanctioned "community" chats into the member-defined spaces: bif4bif, f4Marine, BarelyLegalF4olderM, verybarelylegalf4f, heels and stockings, Truckers do Look, I'm A Bad Girl, submissive men, PANTYHOSE, CUTE FAT CHICKS, Military M4M, Gang Rape, romantic attorneys, female sock fetish, Nicest Lesbians Ever, f sub to degrade, jbr chat [yes, that's jbr as in "JonBenet Ramsey"; no, they weren't discussing the murder case], Texas Ladies, unhappily married, BLKMENWHTWOMEN, et cetera, et cetera—screen upon screen of chatrooms, just press the "more" button for additional options.

The chatrooms themselves are just gathering places; hookups happen via the system's internal messaging system. My trolling MO evolved and soon became quite efficient: My game was to keep moving, darting in and out of groups, like I'd clicked by accident out of "F investors chat" or "Friendly Talk" and into "M working late 4F" or "gang rape dungeon." The intensity of the attention I attracted was funny at first: all I had to do was show up. A minute later at the most, messages would cluster on the screen: "Hey, baby. What's up?" "How are you today?" "Mmmm . . . You sound sexy." "Want to chat?" "Offline?" "Pic?" "Phone?" "8 throbbing inches for you right now!"

I went into this whole thing feeling very open and generous. Of course, I got burned. Some of the guys I engaged turned out to be assholes who wanked off during what I would consider the preliminaries, then disappeared as soon as they, er, "came." No fun for me there. I became ruthless in dispatching men who didn't meet certain grammatical, keyboarding, or conversational standards. As soon as I adopted a system of triage, the cybersex became much more interesting.

Once the interpersonal connection clicks, the source from which all good cybersex flows is fourfold: at-least-intermediate keyboarding skill, a well-tempered smutpuppy vocabulary, a certain literary sophistication and shame-lessness and the ability to choose and time one's words to arouse. As a word person well-versed in erotica, I was good at this. Cybersex is largely a matter of careful pauses and leavening: what you would do, what you would do right now and what you would do only if. What you would want your partner to do right now. Are you wet yet? Tell me, how hard are you for me? It's arousing to caress a kind, if strange, man (or woman) with words, to share stories and desires, even if you know that some or all of it is likely to be bullshit. I had only three rules: no photographs; no real names; and, if it proceeds to phone, I *67 and call first.

Of the hundreds of entities I engaged, I hooked up with exactly three men of whom I became genuinely fond: a gentlemanly Deadhead high school English teacher; a producer of travel and entertainment documentaries; and a lonely young translator and consultant who traveled extensively in Asia and now suf-fers for wealth in a particularly miserable corner of corporate America. All are masters of the mindblowing remote mojo; all are very much into experimenting with language, mind and flesh. Over a period of some months, these guys and I revealed ourselves to one another right up to those security measures every anony-mous cybersexer should keep in place, right up to that tenuous sliver of ano-nymity that functions like a whole new erogenous zone.

For all the jokes about one-handed typing, I think it's different for girls. I would become very aroused during cybersex, then masturbate offline, or later, with toys or on the phone with one of those special guys. I find phone sex with strangers an enormous turn-on. It's always a crapshoot, but if you get lucky and connect with an imaginative and articulate partner with a sexy voice, ahhh, there's nothing like it in the world of anonymous interactive sex without secretions.

I didn't stop trolling the chatrooms, though. I enjoyed the thrill of the new pickup and of "safe" promiscuity. But even with advanced triage in place, the abruptness and coldness started to grate on my soul. The boundaries of feeling started to blur. Who was I again? More often than not, at the end of these anonymous chat or phone sessions, I logged off angry and disgusted, not even in the mood to masturbate. I had never before spent quite so much time in any sort of pornographic mindscape. I began to suspect that what lived inside the whole compulsion was hollowness. And then there was the matter of how I was coded in this space: generic female.

Even as a willing and active partner cloaked in an alias, "I" or "she" or whatever online persona I adopted was subjected to one probe after another that made me feel used and objectified. (Example: "You don't want to do pics? So are you really a man?") Even when I was being flattered or "pleasured," it was usually according to some favorite sex loop running through "his" head. I/she/whoever might as well not exist, even as a totally fictional being. "My" performances didn't even have an audience. For the most part it didn't matter if I was witty or clever. I quit even expecting to get off with most of these guys online, but I kept showing up, letting them interact with me/her/whoever while I had a virtual, out-of-body experience. (I also realized that what was so good about my Deadhead, my producer, and my corporate whore buddy was that they each responded to me/her, that we were equally engaged.) My inner, text-only slut was not exactly surprised by how most men reacted to the female alias, but still found it demoralizing to be addressed and manipulated as if they were paying for it by the minute. I may have wanted anonymity, but I also wanted engagement.

I re-thought, too, all my opinions about those prurient packets of "feminist" pornflakes marketed to the women of my generation and subcultural affiliations. The whole commercial feminist porn scene was and is so confusing, because it is supposed to be about nothing less than female desire unbound. Right on! Right? Never mind that much of the appeal of feminist porn is the fantasy of feminist porn, the carefully marketed promise of subversive or empowering porn that is more than porn. But nobody in my experimental literature class really got off on that femmerotica stuff. Once we got over the adolescent flashback naughtiness of it all, those women's porn vids we watched were boring (though not as utterly mind-numbing as the provocatively scrambled fuck signal that runs 24/7 on my local cable pay-per-view channel). And with the revolution in the accessibility of pornography and virtual sexual interaction created by sex-video mills, 1-900 lines, and the Internet, "feminist porn" is only a boutique niche in a multi-billion dollar growth industry. Maybe that is the impossibility of "liberatory" porn: Once you bottle and sell "sex," no matter who is doing the packaging and distribution, you've always already pithed the frog.

Once my analytical sense intruded, I needed a new drug. I figured that some novelty might refocus the experience. Maybe what I wanted was a real fantasy *challenge,* preferably with an edge that would offset the depersonalization that was grinding on me so. I wanted some remove, some illusion of control. Out of the recesses of my psyche—and grounded in my one real sexual prejudice (old guys who fetishize and/or fuck teenagers)—it came to me. I decided that I would play out one of the most heavily patriarchal and popular fantasies of all: the "barely legal" girl/much older man fantasy. The sheer number of "olderM4youngF" chats suggested that this would be a snap. It was a fantasy that I'd never explored in real-life, and that (thankfully) had never come looking for me.

I will allow that there is some possibility that respectful, loving and thoroughly uncoerced sexual partnerships of this kind do exist, even though I've never encountered one. I *have* heard plenty of women's stories that contradict our culture's para-incestuous, consumerist, utterly immature fantasy of what such a relationship is like. Plus, all the old dude/young chick action I've seen on the Net is not even of the exquisitely tortured and Lolitan "most beautiful butterfly, oh, tragic butterfly" variety. On web sites and in chats, the same imagery comes up over and over again: the pleasure of being "first in," the busted innocence of the "hot, tight, teen slut who wants it," the lure of the forbidden ("If only her parents knew how nasty she is!"), and an explicit focus on humiliation ("cum dripping from her soft young face"). Given the prevalence of sexual assault by men on adolescent and even prepubescent girls, I find these sites chilling, even if, at least on the American sites, all the glassy-eyed girls are supposed to be between eighteen and twenty.

This was the plan: I'd create a most provocative, "desirable" character—an affluent, "barely legal," all-American, college-bound WASP girl, a real fizgig—and take her out on a chatroom fishing expedition. Here, finally, was my chance to Be Her, never mind that the context was maybe a little fucked up. Why hadn't I thought of this before?

Username: SoFizgig

Name: Not until I get to know you better

DOB: 10/10

Location: Houston, TX

Occupation: Student

Computer: Macintosh

Hobbies: Listening to music, guitar, rollerblading, reading, Internet, riding horses

Quote: "Words are hotter than flame/Words are wetter than water" —Ani DiFranco

By the time I had breathed this much life into her, I had an agenda. Yes, this was going to be a performance of a full-on feminist revenge fantasy. This was going to be three three three pleasures in one. As SoFizgig, I was going to fuck one of these Humbert Humbert/Rod Stewart wannabes right back—on behalf of the girls they fetishized and the girls they didn't. I was going to (disem)bodysnatch this Girl Ideal that had always found me wanting and deploy it to my own ends. What was it going to be like to "play" The Girl in a real-life virtual setting that I could manipulate so no one would know the difference, up to the point at which I revealed "myself"? I wondered. And, of course, I was going to enjoy road-testing this fantasy, mapping this guy, getting off both on the cyber/phone sex and on my own deception. Generally, I don't go looking to mete out karmic justice, but I was totally into this. Take that, you sleazy patriarchal enforcer! Let me make you feel unpretty, too, you Viagra target-market man, Viagra target-market man, you!

I was so into my own cleverness—and later, into the experience—that I never planned how I was going to reveal myself to maximum effect. I also never forebrained the possibility that this experience might fuck me up a little. I was too motivated. I remembered how my old friend Mary Kathryn woke up one summer morning when she was sixteen to find her mother's naked boyfriend crawling into bed with her after her mother had left for work. And I thought about all the similar stories—and the parallel stories about rejection and sexual erasure that echoed my own—I'd heard from classmates and friends and the riot grrrl zines stacked in one of my still-unpacked boxes. I thought that I was on a mission. ("Wait! Aren't you negating the possibility of 'her' desire?" a little voice inside me demanded. "Let's see if 'her' desire is even an issue," I countered.)

There SoFizgig and I went, hot as a firecracker, wafting through the chats, responding like a proper little lust beacon whenever anyone made a sex/age call: SoFizgig, 18F here.

An entity calling itself Drogulus[1] jumped on the hook almost immediately:
Drogulus: Hello there.
SoFizgig: Hi.
Drogulus: I saw your profile. Care to chat?
I looked him up.
Screen name: Drogulus
Name: Richard
DOB: I'm 48
Sex: M
Location: St. Louis, MO[2]

---

1. Drogulus: an entity whose presence is unverifiable because it has no physical effects.
2. Good citizens of St. Louis, don't go looking among yourselves. Certain details of this story have been altered to protect the fellow's privacy.

Occupation: A very profitable one

Computer: Pentium III

Hobbies: Sex, collecting antique watches, sex, golf, sex

Ah, a likely suspect.

SoFizgig: Sure.

Drogulus: What are you up to this afternoon?

SoFizgig: Taking a break from calculus homework. I HATE calculus.

Drogulus: College student?

SoFizgig: Homework sucks.

SoFizgig: High school student, actually.

Drogulus: You are eighteen, right?

SoFizgig: Yep. As of two weeks ago.

Drogulus: I don't remember where I caught up to you now. Unusual name.

Drogulus: What's it mean?

SoFizgig: Fizgig means flirty girl.

Drogulus: =)

Drogulus: Do you visit chatrooms a lot?

SoFizgig: Sometimes, when I'm bored.

Drogulus: Where did I catch up to you?

SoFizgig: Don't know. I just sort of flit around.

Drogulus: "I like to watch"? Maybe?

SoFizgig: Maybe *blush* ha ha.

Drogulus: Do you have a picture? I'll send you one of me.

SoFizgig: I don't have a picture. Sorry.

Drogulus: It's nice to have a picture so you can show people what you look like.

Drogulus: Look in your mailbox.

SoFizgig: brb

To the mailbox: balding, middle-aged, blondish guy in a tuxedo against a background that was, best as I could tell, the living room of one of those subdivision mini-mansions. Hunting prints on the wall behind him. He sort of looked like Jimmy Buffett, only taller, and not quite so bald. Well groomed. Obviously affluent. From the looks of the fancy waistcoat, he was some sort of hipster. Well, damn. That was easy.

SoFizgig: You're cute.

Drogulus: You're sweet. That was taken a couple of years ago, my girlfriend took it before some thing we went to.

SoFizgig: Girlfriend, huh? Are you divorced?

Drogulus: Yes.

SoFizgig: Kids?

Drogulus: One son. Seventeen. He lives with me part time.

SoFizgig: Hmmmmm . . . weird. He's my age.

SoFizgig: So do you ever hit on his girlfriends? lol

Drogulus: Well, my girlfriend just turned twenty-two, laugh.

SoFizgig: Uh, okay. That's funny.

Drogulus: She's asleep in the next room.

It looked like I'd found my man.

We talked about school and more family stuff. SoFizgig was an only child, her father a partner in an accounting firm, her mother a hospital administrator. We talked about what she looked like. She told him she'd just found out she'd been accepted at Brown and Smith. He warned her about all the lesbians at Smith. He tried to talk about golf. She changed the subject.

SoFizgig: So what do you do anyway when you're not chatting up girls on here? Or playing golf? ;)

Drogulus: Investment consultant.

SoFizgig: Is that like a stockbroker?

Drogulus: Yeah.

Drogulus: Why, you got some money you want to invest? ;)

SoFizgig: Not yet. Just lots of potential.

Drogulus: lol

Drogulus: I'm a typical 6'2" male.

SoFizgig: I'm 5'10". I get shit for being tall. Everybody seems to think I should play basketball.

Drogulus: Now I won't bore you with penis size .

Here we go.

SoFizgig: That's okay. You can bore me ;) I find penises fas-cin-ating.

Drogulus: You sound like a perfect height for me.

SoFizgig: We'd be good dancing together.

Drogulus: 4 inches soft, 7 hard.

Drogulus: That is true, do you like kissing? I do.

SoFizgig: Yes.

Drogulus: I have a gif of it but do not know if you would really want it .

Drogulus: Are you a virgin?

SoFizgig: Well, it would be my first explicit gif. I guess I'm up for it if you are.

Drogulus: What would your parents say?

SoFizgig: No. Disappointed? But I've only been with one guy.

Drogulus: I'm not either. lol

SoFizgig: I'll delete it after I look at it.

Drogulus: I will send it, but please keep it to yourself.

SoFizgig: My mother only fakes computer illiteracy.

Drogulus: Okay. You have it.

Drogulus: I have a scanner and we had fun with a graphics program.

Drogulus: It will give you the idea.

Drogulus: If you keep it put it on a disk and not for everyone to see.

Drogulus: If you ever want me to scan for you I will. They do not have to be nude.

Drogulus: And email it back, it's nice to show people what you look like.

Indeed, in my mailbox was a collage of five high-saturation living-color shots of his cock in various stages of tumescence. Holy Exhibitionist Andy Warhol! We moved off into a private chatroom called SoFizgig.

SoFizgig: Got it. Ha. That was cool. I like the flare around the tip. It looks like it would feel good.

Drogulus: By the way, my name's Richard.

SoFizgig: Hi Richard. My name's Claire.

Drogulus: I have had no complaints. If you lived closer we could try it.

Drogulus: I hope we can be friends and someday lovers.

SoFizgig: I've never met anyone from chats.

Drogulus: Do you enjoy oral sex?

SoFizgig: I . . . guess I need to learn more about it.

Drogulus: Has anyone made love to you that way?

SoFizgig: Incompetently, yeah. Like a lick so I'd suck his cock.

Drogulus: Do you enjoy sucking a penis?

SoFizgig: Sometimes. Limited experience, I guess.

SoFizgig: Cocks are so funny and alive.

Drogulus: The female clit is the same. It grows and pulses.

Drogulus: And the vaginal juices are delicious . . .

We chatted a while longer, then, just as he worked up to the "So what are you wearing?" line, I begged off, saying I had to finish my homework. We agreed to "meet" again the next evening since SoFizgig's parents would be working late. He claimed that he was a cybervirgin, that he had never done this before. He assured me that he was HIV-negative, that he'd had a vasectomy and that I "didn't have to worry." When I logged off, I found a couple more gifs in my mailbox. There was Richard, lounging naked on a big bed, shot from the front and the rear. "Enjoy!" the attached note read. "I'll be looking for you online. You're wonderful. Hugs, Richard."

This was the quickest I'd ever gone from "Hello" to "Someday we really must get together in real life and fuck." I was going to have to come up with a pic.

He had given me his (fairly unusual) last name. I hopped on the Web and did a search. He was either a Net neophyte or liked to live on the edge of privacy. I found the site for his investment firm, which included his photo, business phone, fax and email. I found his home phone and home address. This guy was real. Very real.

The next evening I logged on, did some other work and waited. The message alert went "Eeep!"

Drogulus: Hi there sweetie.

SoFizgig: Hi.

Drogulus: How was your day?

SoFizgig: You know. School and stuff.

SoFizgig: How was your day?

Drogulus: Oh, money and stuff. lol

Drogulus: Driving home, I was thinking I should just jump on a plane and come to Houston. LOL

Yow.

SoFizgig: Uh . . .

Drogulus: That might not be such a good idea, huh?

Drogulus: I don't want to make you feel uncomfortable.

SoFizgig: It's just, you do know I live with my parents, don't you?

Drogulus: Don't worry. I promise not to show up at your door.

Drogulus: If I ever come to town, we could stay at a hotel.

Drogulus: I was just getting so hot thinking about your tight little body.

SoFizgig: Well, look, you're nice and everything, but I hardly KNOW you.

Shit. What the hell had happened here? SoFizgig was getting boxed in. "Tight little body"? This was much different from playing me/her/whomever more or less as "me." I began to feel a little claustrophobic. I was in control of the situation, finally, but to make SoFizgig at all believable, she couldn't be. The more he pressed, the more restricted I/she was by the codes of behavior he expected her to follow. I decided to throw myself more deeply into the performance, and that was uncomfortable. (During the particularly torrid phase of this affair, I was SoFizgigging for two or three hours per night.)

I waited a couple of minutes.

SoFizgig: Hey. Sorry. I had to let the dog out.

Drogulus: Want to continue?

SoFizgig: Sure, I guess.

Drogulus: Let's go to SoFizgig.

SoFizgig: Okay.

Drogulus: Do you use vibrators?

SoFizgig: Just my fingers. Where would I get a vibrator?

Drogulus: You should try a vib just below the clit.

SoFizgig: I guess once I get out of my parents' house sex toys are a priority. lol

Drogulus: Would you like to make love to an older man?

SoFizgig: I think so . . . sort of . . . I mean I like my boyfriend and my guy friends.

SoFizgig: But I think/hope an older guy would know more and have more of a sense of humor or something. I don't know.

Drogulus: You saw what I look like.

Drogulus: Down to the penis.

Drogulus: Sex should be fun.

Drogulus: Older men take longer to cum too.

Drogulus: We like to build to an orgasm and make love all nite.

SoFizgig: Hmmmm. This is making me horny. ;)

Drogulus: I have had a vasectomy, just to let you know.

Drogulus: That's okay.

SoFizgig: I have a pierced tongue, just to let you know.

Drogulus: Please enjoy my pics.

Drogulus: I am visualizing you.

It was time.

SoFizgig: Do you want to fantasize together?

Drogulus: Yes.

SoFizgig: What are you wearing?

Drogulus: Nothing.

SoFizgig: Really?

Drogulus: Really.

Drogulus: What are you wearing?

SoFizgig: A T-shirt and sweatpants.

Drogulus: Bra? Panties?

SoFizgig: Panties.

Drogulus: Are you wet?

SoFizgig: Yes.

Drogulus: Have you been touching yourself?

SoFizgig: No.

SoFizgig: Let me lock the door, brb.

Drogulus: I sent you a new pic.

Drogulus: Here's what I have for you someday.

It was a picture of his hand wrapped around his erect cock.

Drogulus: Imagine you were here on my big bed with me.

SoFizgig: *Snuggle*

Drogulus: Did you like the pic?

Drogulus: It's for you, sweetie.

SoFizgig: Yes. Very much.

Drogulus: Imagine it deep within you.

No preliminaries.

SoFizgig: I imagine it sliding in me.

Drogulus: I would love to taste your moist clit.

Drogulus: The head of it gently parts your lips.

Drogulus: Slowly I slide it into your warm tunnel of love.

Tunnel of love? Oh, dear. Had I not been SoFizgig, this would have been cause to disconnect, log back on and block any further messages from him.

Drogulus: Can you feel it?

SoFizgig: Mmmmmmmm . . . I can feel every rock-hard inch.

Drogulus: Teasing your warm vagina.

Drogulus: Slowly I slide all seven inches in to the base of my balls.

Drogulus: Can you feel my balls against your butt?

SoFizgig: I arch my back against you, grab your shoulders, hold you there.

SoFizgig: Yes.

Drogulus: Take it baby.

SoFizgig: I'm so full.

Drogulus: I slide out and slam it back into your hot pussy.

SoFizgig: Oh.

Drogulus: I am getting bigger.

Drogulus: Your sexy body turns me on so.

SoFizgig: I feel you swelling in me.

Drogulus: I gently suck your nipples as I move my hips to your movements.

SoFizgig: Stroking your head, head thrown back, moaning.

Drogulus: Let me give it all to you, baby.

SoFizgig: My pussy gripping your cock.

SoFizgig: Can you feel it.

Drogulus: Oh God yes.

Drogulus: God you are good.

SoFizgig: I love you inside me, your shaft rubbing against my clit as you fuck me.

Drogulus: Take me sweetie.

Drogulus: I want you to cum so hard all over me.

Drogulus: I enter and pull back.

Drogulus: Slamming into you.

Drogulus: Slamming into you.

SoFizgig: Oh yeah.

Drogulus: I am so hard.

SoFizgig: Oh yeah.

This became pretty typical: First he was on top, then we did it from behind, then she was on top, and about a hundred lines later he came. And she said she came. And then he went down on her. Et cetera. My cunt was usually pounding by the end of each session. Consciously manipulating Drogulus took a lot of concentration and made me feel sexually powerful—and that was quite a turn-on. It was a novel way to become aroused. Usually I'd masturbate after to re-center and ground myself. It was a kind of meditative space in which I let the Drogulus version of her/me/whomever go.

Drogulus: You are so great.

Drogulus: Maybe next time we should try phone.

SoFizgig: It's hard to do that and type.

Drogulus: I'd like to hear you cum.

Drogulus: God you are good if you are half that good in person, wow.

SoFizgig: Sweaty. lol

We negotiated the phone number thing. I didn't give him my number. I told him I'd use the phone card of a cousin at Southern Methodist University, whose parents always just gave her money to pay the bill because her boyfriend was in med school in Florida. In reality, I'd long since worked out a deal so that all these long distance calls didn't cost me anything. He begged and reasoned and I promised I'd try to scan a pic to send him, that I was pretty sure I could do that at school.

I needed a picture. I phoned a college friend who was working for a much-sought-after portrait and headshot photographer. Sure enough, before midnight SoFizgig's high-school graduation portfolio was sitting in my mailbox. Perfection. I remember apologizing to the shy, willowy, beautiful girl on the screen for what I was about to do with her pictures. Then I ignored Drogulus's solicitous emails for two whole days.

At the end of the third day, I logged on briefly and emailed him: "Hey, sweetie! I've got to run to orchestra rehearsal, but here's a present for you! I used the scanner in the art department. Sorry they're not better. Smoochies, Claire." Attached were the pics. I went to see a band that night. When I got home, I logged on and found: "Sweetie—You're beautiful. Your pics made me so hard I had to jerk off in the office before I could go home. Where have you been? I miss you. I can work late tomorrow if you want to talk on the phone. Love, Richard."

The next night, we cybered again. That Sunday afternoon while SoFizgig's parents were out shopping, phone. I gave a great performance, if I do say so myself. Any tickles of guilt I had about taking this guy for a ride totally disappeared. On chat, he'd seemed more or less extremely arduous, exhibitionistic and almost mechanically eager to please. On the phone, his arrogance and pomposity really shone. Her/my/whomever's desire was utterly irrelevant to the exchange, and he was a condescending instructor. Whatever. I moaned a lot and came three or four times, anyway, the first times I'd actually orgasmed as SoFizgig. My eyes closed, fingers freed from the keyboard, I went much further into it.

"I'm coming to Houston to find you and bring you back here with me," he moaned.

"I don't think so," SoFizgig giggled. This was maybe the most difficult part of being SoFizgig. I had to pitch my voice up, and giggle and equivocate, preferably at the same time. I missed my own voice.

I was in a heady, complicated feedback loop. It felt jarring to look in the mirror after doing phone sex. SoFizgig was taking on a life of her own. I started giving "her" a lot more slack, adding layers and layers to the lie.

I started torturing Drogulus with prattling stories about disagreements among SoFizgig's group of friends, about clothes she'd bought that day. I gave her deep insecurities and adolescent, self-important smart-girl views on current events. He had to sit through a lot of that before I'd tell him the stories he really wanted to hear, all about what SoFizgig and her on-again/off-again boyfriend did when they were alone. I kept teasing him with lines like "and then, like, fifteen minutes later he was hard again. But he still won't go down on me!" As Drogulus counseled her, he kept working that same "Older men are better lovers, let me show you" line. I made him explain how SoFizgig could teach her boyfriend to control his ejaculations. He got exasperated, but hung in there and kept building this fantasy about the first time we would "make love" in person. I kept reminding myself that I was the prey who was the hunter, but this was slippery. SoFizgig's swings into self-absorption lent us a little traction, respite.

We went on like this for a couple of fairly intense weeks during which I learned all about his failed marriage (she "let herself go" and "didn't like sex"— how classic is that? I thought), his son (whom he feared his wife had "turned gay") and his girlfriend (who had been working in his office when they met, and whom "I took to get a tongue stud last weekend because yours was such a turn-on"). Wait a minute. *What!?* Actual woman gets hole in body based on boyfriend being turned on by what I thought hipster old guys might find arousing in young women? Long pause. "She'd been wanting one," he offered. "Cool," SoFizgig typed, as my jaw dropped.

As part of SoFizgig's "education," he began to bombard her mailbox with all sorts of hardcore porno stills. Anything—and I do mean anything—in which she had indicated passing interest would simply show up in the mail. "Every girl should be as open as you," he once typed to her, "and lucky enough to find a teacher like me. lol."

As we talked more on the phone, his voice got inside my head. Condescending, certainly. Arrogant, hurried. Never warm or supportive, in spite of all that robotic blather about how "I only get off on giving a woman pleasure." When he wasn't enjoying listening to himself drone on about his family history or his money or his dick dick dick, always his dick . . . Well, frankly, he was a bore and a bad conversationalist. I didn't know how much more I could take. SoFizgig was not having fun either. Every time I got really pissed off at him, I'd pause and take a deep breath, and SoFizgig would purr empathetically like the best little kitten in the world, and more and more hesitantly tell him what he wanted to hear. When it became apparent that she was contorting herself to get his approval, things really disintegrated. He thought he had her then.

He put the big kibosh on SoFizgig's tendency to prattle. SoFizgig almost never got to finish a sentence except if she was describing how she'd like to minister to his cock with her mouth or her pussy. It was shocking how quickly this happened, and I suspected for a little while that he suspected something. He quit even *acting* interested in any observation or idea—or concern or problem—she laid on him, even as he continued working her to gain her "confidence" so that he could fuck her in real life. Suddenly it was all "You're so beautiful," "You're so hot," "You're so mature. I know you will make the right decision," "Oh, I'm so sorry, I wish I could be there to 'comfort' you. Lol," or the ever popular "Say the word and I'm on a plane. I love you. I'm so glad you're mine." Then, in the throes of our, er, "passion," he started saying stuff like, "What a filthy little slut, dirty little slut. How can somebody look like you and be such a whore? Wanna fuck that hot little body, fuck that hot little body." That sounded familiar enough, and it turned me cold.

SoFizgig and I had seen and heard enough. In retrospect, I should have stopped it in the middle of being called "filthy little slut" or some variant thereof, and revealed the con while I had him pumping it and panting. Instead, for about a week, SoFizgig was much less available and responsive. "Schoolwork," she said. "No, for the hundredth time, I can't tell you my last name. My parents would kill me." He began to elaborate on serious plans to come to Houston for a weekend, and actually emailed me web pages of various expensive hotels. "Please don't," she said. "I'm not sure," she said. "I'm too nervous." His reply: "You're an adult. If we meet and you change your mind, you don't have to do anything you don't want to. I want you baby. I want you so much. Don't you want me? You don't have to do ANYTHING you don't want to."

That was it. I mailed him and suggested we meet online.

Drogulus: Hi Sexy. How are you tonight?

Sigh. "I have something to tell you," I typed. There was a pause. "And you're really not going to like it." Long pause on his end.

Drogulus: Are you going to tell me that you're not really eighteen?

I let the pause stretch out. How to reply?

Drogulus: Well? What is it?

Options:

1) Yeah. I'm really fifteen. (And that would be that?)

2) This is Claire's mother and she's only sixteen and you're in big trouble, mister, if you ever contact her again.

3) Actually, I'm a way-full-grown agent of Feminism, Incorporated, on a deep-cover fact-finding mission, and I've been making this all up. You have not failed to disappoint. How sexy am I now, fucker?

Tell the truth, my little voice said.

SoFizgig: No. I'm really twenty-seven. And I've been making all of this up.

Drogulus: Are you kidding?

SoFizgig: Nope. No kidding.

Drogulus: Are you sure you're not kidding?

SoFizgig: Yep.

Drogulus: That's not your picture?

SoFizgig: Nope.

Drogulus: You're not kidding are you?

SoFizgig: No. I'm not.

Drogulus: Really.

SoFizgig: Really.

There was a long pause on the other end.

And he must have been thinking, "That bitch!" And he also may have been thinking, "Christ! She knows my name, where I live, what I look like, the name of my business, my office phone, my home phone." I imagined him pacing in his office, cursing around, feeling violated and humiliated and just plain pranked. I had been an eighteen-year-old high school student listening to his heavy breathing bouncing off the walls of his paneled office on the thirty-first floor, his pants around his ankles. I'd had him. A few intense, heavily fraught seconds passed.

Drogulus: Why?

I didn't reply. Fuck. I didn't know what to say. I was paralyzed, and I didn't have a prepared manifesto at the ready. I couldn't even get it together to type something all angrygrrrl like, "In protest against middle-aged fucks such as yourself who get off on sexual/status powertripping/mindfucking emotionally malleable Teenage Pussy (tm)! I hex your dick!" I had contemplated sending him on a booty run to some very expensive hotel in SoFizgig's vicinity, but I didn't want to take this thing real world in any way that might make him more likely to be even uglier or more manipulative than he was already likely to be with the next curious and/or willing, quite probably "real" teenage girl he encountered in a chatroom.

The words "I've got to go now, but let's talk later" popped up on the screen, and he was gone.

I remained online composing an email update to my photographer friend. Ten minutes later he was back.

Drogulus: WHY?

SoFizgig: What?

Drogulus: You're really not kidding? Is your name even Claire?

SoFizgig: No, it's not.

Drogulus: I'll bet you're still really hot. Come on. What's your name?

SoFizgig: SoFizgig.

Drogulus: Don't be like that.

SoFizgig: I'm a little old for you, aren't I?

Drogulus: How old did you say you were?

Drogulus: You think I'm a dirty old man? That didn't bother you before.

SoFizgig: Twenty-seven. I was doing research.

Drogulus: Come on. Send me a pic. I want to know what you look like.

SoFizgig: I don't do pics.

Drogulus: Oh, bullshit. What kind of research?

Drogulus: What do you look like, then?

SoFizgig: Honestly?

Drogulus: That would be a nice change.

Drogulus: I ought to report you to the service cops.

SoFizgig: From where I'm sitting, it looks to me like you ought to be relieved that I'm of age.

SoFizgig: Don't threaten me, Richard. What would you allege, anyway? Cybersex fraud? There are no package guarantees in cybersex. Big lol.

SoFizgig: Besides, I've been logging all this.

Drogulus: I'm sick of playing games with you.

SoFizgig: Live by the scam, die by the scam, sweetie. And you're a master.

It was past time to disappear SoFizgig. I wiped her from the service.

This certainly hadn't turned out to be the feminist prank of my initial enthused conceptualization. After I thought about it for a day or so, I even kicked myself for being so egotistical as to need to reveal myself. I did not want to just disappear as SoFizgig, as if she had simply stopped returning his emails. As it was, he was probably just pissed off and confused, and didn't feel even the least bit spanked. I certainly wasn't about to attempt to engage him in some sort of dialogue. Finally, it didn't matter if he "got it" or not. This hadn't been about him personally, anyway.

My fantasy assumption of "barely legal" fizgigness was in part intended to offset my frustration with the difficulty of finding partners with any sense of how to approach sexual disembodiment. Performing SoFizgig, complete with a photographic portfolio and elaborate backstory, was, indeed, a leap to the other extreme of online sex play. It was very strange to be "representing" in that space as this hot commodity, to know that this old guy in St. Louis with whom I'd been having what I consider sub-par cybersex was jerking off over hard copies of "my" pics, the proof of SoFizgig's pudding, as it were. How ridiculous it seemed.

At the same time, from the moment that I decided to drop bait, I had been absolutely sure I could flesh out SoFizgig convincingly, having already imagined and fetishized her from the other side of the mirror. For far too many years, it had been Her I saw when I looked with adolescent longing straight through my own despised reflection and into the realm of culturally constructed fantasy. Everybody—female and male—has to want the fizgig (or one of her sisters), or "she" fails as a status-invested sexual object, and therefore as a mechanism of the desirability police. This, too, seems utterly ridiculous.

As I was thinking about all of this, I happened upon this insightful passage in Shelly Bovey's book *The Forbidden Body: Why Being Fat Is Not a Sin:* "The fat woman . . . whose body is objectively perceived as unacceptable, occupies only an empty space [in culture] . . . To see oneself absent, outside the boundaries of human life, causes a feeling of unreality, and of annihilation. It endangers the soul." Even though the attention I attracted in the chats was novel and unsatisfying at best, I was so intrigued by the disembodied promise of anonymous cyberpromiscuity for reasons identical to why I found "feminist" porn so intriguing—because I have never truly experienced the privilege of culturally acceptable or desirable sexual embodiment in real life, not even when I have been relatively thin. It *was* thrilling to open a magazine and see two beautiful pear-shaped dykes fisting one another. It *was* thrilling to shed my body in the chats. Up to a point, it *was* fun to play SoFizgig behind those stolen photographs.

Yet there was no room here for my body. My bold experiment in low-risk virtual promiscuity had culminated in a disorienting auto-erotic dive into the very tenderest spongy part of my psyche. Not only was "I" not present as a fat woman in heterosexual cybersexland, I had found it impossible to be present as a woman, period. It wasn't *just* about my fat body, even though it is the specter of possibly even fantasizing sexually with a mind attached to a body like mine that drives the increasingly widespread (if easily circumvented) male-enforced convention of "no live pic, no cybersex." If I have a gripe with the porn industry (beyond my strong objection to its seedy and slaughterhouse-like industrial practices) it is that, in my experience, the successive porn explosions of the '80s and '90s and '00s—combined with the way porn and fascination with porn has overflowed into other popular genres—have undermined the capacity of far too many women to see themselves as individual, desiring, sexual subjects. They have also diminished the capacity of far too many men to see women at all, except as pale reflections of the women cached in private collections on their hard drives or featured in their favorite videos.

My extremely oppressive experience coming of age under sexual erasure didn't destroy me, but pushed me early into a life of critical cultural outlawry. In defiance of the big mindfuck, I have filled that "empty space" for myself, with myself. I struggle to make it a habit to remind myself of that in all situations, perhaps especially sexual ones. It's not easy. See, this is the key to this whole conundrum of fizgigness: Almost every woman is deeply invested in her own version of "SoFizgig," some "better," "perfected," "infinitely more desirable" fantasy version of herself. Her desire never ever can matter, because she is a projection, a consensual hallucination of feminine sexual desirability. The fizgig is *never* real. The fizgig is the mirror image in the mirror image in the mirror image who keeps the cosmetics, "aesthetic" surgery and diet industries afloat along with the porn industry.

Finally, the SoFizgig Affair marked my release of a two decades–long negative obsession with fizgigness, as well as the end of my brief career as a chatroom-trolling cyberslut. I spent almost a quarter century vacillating between pretending that I didn't even have a body, and telling myself that this wasn't my "real" body. No more. I live here now, even when I'm online and some totally unsolicited guy with an intriguing profile pops up in a message window: "Fascinating profile. Want to chat?" He may just want to talk about stuff, may not even be looking for cybersex, but I never dissemble about what I look like when it comes down to it, nor do I *ever* underplay my charms. The rare and truly cool ones get it. The rest? Who cares? This is a great exercise in self-esteem. It comes down to this: I insist on defining the terms of my own desirability, just as I define my desire.

WATCHING YOU WATCHING ME

 Kary Barrett Wayson

When my ex-girlfriend left me after four years together for another (much younger) woman, I was devastated. At the same time, I was also absolutely aroused by my tortured, visual nightmare-fantasies of the two of them having sex. For months I visualized my ex running her big hands up under the skirt of her new lover's loose, blue dress and spreading her inconceivable, imaginary, buttery thighs. They were so beautiful! I wrote a poem about it, about me watching them having sex, and left it on my ex's answering machine. The only thing sexier than the two of them together was me watching them together. I masturbated while I invented their sex in my head and cried.

I've been having sex with women since the fifth grade, when I first initiated what was to become a years-long series of furtive "kissing practice" sessions with best girlfriends. I've been sleeping with women ever since I became sexual—at age ten, with SuAnne Jones in her parents' basement—and I am still amazed by how incredibly aroused I get with just the thought of women having sex with women. The combination of soft bodies, the marshy, wonderful, wet bare thighs and puffy mouths turns me on like nothing else. There's a decadence in both the idea and the act of women pleasuring women that feels like a falling and a falling and then more falling back into the twenty pillows of a low bed, and I am absolutely breathless, whether I'm in the bed or watching it. Usually I'm doing both—I'm fully aware of myself and my lover having sex as if I were both inside and outside of the experience. Most of me is in the bed (or in the car—I like the car) while a sliver of my vision watches from across the room and loves the tangle of women's arms and legs. There is nothing more beautiful to me than a woman's body, nothing more gorgeous than her face while she's coming, nothing more touchable than her perfect ass, and I often can't help but get distracted by the sexiness of sex between two women even while I'm right in the middle of it.

I've always identified with straight male sexuality, which is often described in terms such as "objectifying" or "responding to visual cues." Straight male desire becomes the stage where my own fantasies play out. Indeed, my basest sexual fantasies arise from my idea of the fantasies of a horny straight boy. Just being a lesbian (through the eyes of a male) is one of my biggest turn-ons. When I am most aroused, I'm aware of myself having sex with a woman as if I were a man watching porn, except that I get to live inside the scene while it is actually going on. I am a curvy, blonde, big-breasted woman. I wear tight T-shirts and messy, architectural hairdos. I present myself as sexy and I get a lot of sexual attention from strangers, mostly men, who assume that I'm straight until I show them or tell them otherwise. That is exactly where it all begins for me: I'm watching a man watch me with desire and I show him that I'm a dyke, that I'm actually with the woman beside me. He wants me, he thinks I'm sexy, so he's already undressed me, and then he realizes that I'm a lesbian, so he has to put me with my lover, which makes for an even sexier fantasy, which is the same fantasy as mine: a soft-focus vision of beautiful, naked women kissing and coming and sucking and fucking in a sort of porn-orgy scene with a lot of red velvet. His fantasy lets me into my fantasy, which is real. He knows that I know what he knows, which is that the idea of women together is just sexy as hell. That's where my sense of sexuality lives: at the crossroads of have and can't have, at the intersection of audience and actor, inside my own version of the stereotypical male fantasy of lesbian sex. I'm watching you watch me (and hoping you'll want me) while I wait tables in my knee-high black spacegirl boots with zippers up the sides.

So yes, I am a tease. I love the power of riveting someone's eyes, especially when I have nothing at stake in the exchange, when the pleasure of seeing someone (male or female) who can't take their eyes off me is magnified by my own surprise or indifference. When it comes to acting on my own desire, however, I become the pursuer, the voyeur. There is a certain absolutely liberating power that comes for me when I flip from the self-consciousness and effort of exhibitionism to the dark quietude and self-containment of voyeurism. It is the cool detachment of just watching rather than acting or reacting, of consuming from a distance, of anticipation, of preparing to make a move.

Maybe even more than the bare shoulders of sex (the sweaty, wet woman in my bed, white cotton panties cuffing her ankles), maybe even more than the full thighs (both hands holding them open at the knees), the swollen clit (the swollen breasts, the swollen mouth), maybe almost as much as the deep fuck, I love the *prospect* of the deep fuck (combined with my own sense of "Goddamn, girl, if you only knew what I want to do to you, you'd be begging for it right now"). This is how my desire to watch takes over. I am sitting in a cafe and I watch the woman across from me rub the handle of her coffee cup while she reads the paper. She's dressed for work and I am mentally unbuttoning her blouse and dipping both my hands into the cups of her bra. She's grabbing her bag to catch the bus and I am sitting in the seat next to her, running my hand up the inside of her close thigh. On my favorite days, I watch women like a man watches women: with pure sexual desire. I do not measure my own face and body against the hotties I see walking up and down Pine Street because I'm too busy admiring them: the tank tops and the business suits; the pantylines and bra straps; the beautiful, leathery-faced, raspy-voiced motorcycle dyke holding one hand in the small of her girlfriend's back while they walk down the street; the nearly naked woman speaking French on her cell phone at the beach, the milk-fed skateboard chick playing pinball at the arcade.

On my favorite days, I dress more butch. I wear baggy clothes and my hair in a low ponytail. I don't need or want any male sexual attention in order to gain access to my own private girl-porn-movie scenes because I am the male: virile, powerful and potent, with piercing eyes and a bigger, better dick than his. I approach the straight couple sitting at table six. I watch the woman watch her boyfriend look at my breasts. I could give a shit about the boy by now. I keep my eyes on the woman. I watch her warm up. I watch her blush spread across her chest while I give her my best attention. I imagine the soft sounds she'd make if I kissed her mouth, one of my knees wedged between her two bare thighs. I watch her while I say, "Can I bring you something besides water to drink?" I take her order, then his, and walk away from the table like I own it.

In my romantic/sexual pursuits with women, the prospect of sex, particularly the prospect of first sex, seems to always begin with one long, unwavering stare. It goes like this: I'm at the company Christmas party with my ex-girlfriend (who's not actually my ex yet because I'm still sleeping with her, still trying to convince her to get back together with me even though I know it won't work). I'm at the Christmas party and I'm doing my sexy look-at-me/showgirl thing and I go to get myself a glass of wine and while I'm pouring, I'm watching a woman walk into the room. She's wearing men's trousers and a beautifully tailored, tight-fitting blouse with the sleeves rolled high enough to show a glimpse of a black band tattooed high on one of her brown biceps. She turns her head and our eyes lock. I see her like I've never laid eyes on a single goddamn woman before. I see her and I know her like the right answer to a question I didn't know I'd asked. All of a sudden I could care less about who's watching me (or who's watching me watch her). Her eyes are navy blue. She's got gold in her black hair. I sit back down and I watch and I can't wait.

The next day my seduction begins, which means that I find a way to find her again so I can situate myself where I can watch her again. Weeks, months, maybe more time goes by. I'm not exactly stalking, but I am watching. I am definitely aware of where she might be while I make my way through the city. Usually by the time I take the opportunity to talk to her, I'm nearly ready to confess my crush on her. Usually I do—too soon. But on my favorite days, she already knows I want her and she wants me too. I get to talk to her, which means I'm close to kissing her, which is just the beginning of what I've been wanting while I've been memorizing the exact inch where her blue sleeves brush on her biceps, high on her beautiful brown arms. I want the girl and I know I'll get her. I am the man—but even better. I am stealthy and strong with capable hands. I am driving my red car, steering with my one arm draped over the wheel while I watch that beautiful woman in my rearview mirror.

Overall I feel pretty damn lucky. I'm traditionally pretty enough to get the attention I want from the majority of straight men, but at the same time I get to experience the rush of power that comes from the act of rejecting that attention: Nope, you can't have me, but yes, isn't she sexy sitting here so near my lap? I can take over straight male desire and make it my own: I am the man and I am what he can never be, which is a beautiful woman. And I have what he can never have, which is the girl/girl sex without him: my face buried in my lover's cunt at the head of the bed, her face in mine at the foot. I am watching the movie while I'm also inside the movie. I'm the object and the viewer, and I have enough of what it takes to work the scene that I both watch and perform.

SIGHT UNSEEN

Christy Damio

On an Amtrak Metro Liner from New York to Baltimore, my boyfriend is reading Raymond Chandler's *The Long Goodbye* to me in between sips of steaming coffee. I lean my head against his shoulder, inhaling the coffee, the unsmoked tobacco in his shirt pocket, and his sweet, clean scent. His voice is serious as he reads, conveying every linguistic nuance (Chandler's a favorite), and—as is often the case—I'm distracted from the mystery by a sudden urge to shock him. My hand slowly snakes its way down into his lap, fingers pressing into his jeans.

He stops reading. He is embarrassed. "Christy," he reminds me gently, trying not to sound too uninterested, "there are other people here." I know. I'm exhilarated.

I think my fascination with secretive public sex acts has to do with being legally blind. Since so much of the world seems hidden from me, I have an odd desire to create my own private excitement and hide it from the world—and as an added twist, to hide it in plain view. To my boyfriend's amusement (and sometimes his horror), this desire all too often manifests itself in attempts at under-the-family-dinner-table hanky-panky or oral sex on a Greyhound bus. Since he is such a good citizen, though, these molestation missions are usually aborted.

I don't know why he's so concerned about getting caught. I've never suggested full-on sex in the park or anything (I lost my virginity that way, and once is enough). All I really want is to play under a blanket. Like little kids in a fort. Remember how much fun that was? If someone does notice us—say, the jittery old guy in the seat in front of ours pretending to read *People* magazine but really eavesdropping (you know the type)—well, what's the harm? If someone is that captivated by our private little performance, I say let 'em watch. I'd ogle people all the time if I could.

But I'm legally blind. Which is a whole damn gold star better than being completely blind. Which I know all about. The summer before I started high school, one girl from my eighth-grade homeroom lost her virginity and I lost my eyesight. We were the two big stories in the lunchroom that fall. I still don't know why it all happened. Okay, I can guess why she lost her virginity. But I don't know why, after having 20/20 vision for almost fourteen years, I woke up one morning and couldn't see my hand, with its dated glitter nail polish, in front of my face.

The umpteen doctors my mother and I consulted that summer didn't know either. They could only say that my optic nerves were in pretty bad shape. Some claimed to know what caused it, but when pressed they had to admit that they couldn't be certain. They guessed everything from heavy drug use (I don't remember doing any drugs as a kid, but maybe that's a sign that I did) to a genetic disease (no one in my family had ever gone blind like that) to a parasite (my mother made me get colonics—blech—for weeks to rule that out).

After a few doctors said I'd never see again (one real winner put his face up to mine and said, "Learn Braille"), my mother started carting me around to natural healers. Within a year, I'd tried Reiki, acupuncture, acupressure, nutritional supplements, and a full complement of other treatments too numerous to list. Something worked, though I'm not sure which. I like to think it was the acupuncture, since that one was the most unpleasant and I'd hate to think I suffered through it for nothing.

By the end of the year, I could see well enough to look "normal" and walk around without a cane or a dog or any other fun blind tools. I rarely fell down stairs or crashed into glass doors. But my vision was still severely impaired—and my other senses were heightened. My sense of touch became especially sensitive. I could count change without looking at it and dress in the dark, knowing every article of clothing—even underwear—by its weight and weave.

Some unwashed barfly once said to me, "Blind people must be so sensual," while placing his sweaty hand on my knee. (Such an insightful remark from a braying jackass on the make.) I never learned Braille, but my fingers replaced my eyes in many ways. I think that's why I got to like the idea of secretive sex and touching so much; it was something I could "see" that others couldn't. After years with me, my boyfriend's sense of touch has improved too. We've developed a semiconscious touch language and can convey a wide range of sentiments to each other without making eye contact or speaking. By just tapping a shoulder or squeezing a hand, we can say, "Don't worry," "Thank you," or the ever-important "Shut up before you get into trouble." I need that squeeze a lot.

I first discovered my love of public-but-secretive seduction at high school parties. I learned something about myself in those years—that I found it far sexier not to flirt verbally or even make eye contact, but instead to entice and be enticed through small physical contact. This was a logical choice, since I couldn't look up and seduce someone with my smile from across a crowded room (what supermarket romance novel did that image crawl out of?). But even though the idea probably came to me out of shyness and a fear that I'd try to make eye contact with a guy and end up staring at his collar, I soon discovered that I found it far more erotic to brush gently against a guy without a glance than to flirt actively in the conventional, expected ways.

So all the stories about smoldering gazes leading to passion that my friends told me (many of which, I'm positive, were pilfered from the copies of *Penthouse* they slipped out from under their parents' beds) were lost on me. I preferred to go to a party, find a good-smelling guy with a voice I liked, take the seat next to him and begin touching his arm lightly with my fingers—trying to look unaware—while talking to a friend on my other side. Often the guys seemed to enjoy it; they returned my little caresses and eventually started talking to me. Sometimes they got up and left, quite possibly annoyed. One guy asked me, very politely, to keep my hands to myself. (I'm not saying it always worked; it's just what I did.)

My first sexual experience was neither a kiss nor anything more romantic, but it was secretive, and that was all I needed. I was about fifteen. I was taking the subway home from school, and I'd had the lack of foresight to sit in one of those two-seater sections—you know, where you find yourself squashed in between a metal bar and someone carrying fifteen shopping bags.

When the train stopped at City Hall, a man slid in beside me. He was youngish, tall and dressed all in black. He opened his trench coat, and one side of it flopped onto my lap. Then, without a word or even a glance, the man slid a furtive hand between my obscured thighs and began to squeeze and massage them.

I sat very still, too stunned to speak. I was scared, but what could I do? Yell out for help? No. Since I was sure he was crazy, that might make him dangerous. Get up and move? No, he might follow me. So I stayed where I was, staring straight ahead and trying to avoid acknowledging that—to my profound dismay—I was actually beginning to find the whole thing exciting. The fast motion of the train, the closeness of his body and the tense, shivering certainty that none of the strap-hangers had an inkling of what was happening between us made my breath come faster. When the man got off at his stop a few minutes later—without so much as a backwards glance—I missed him.

Ever since high school, I've found that kind of sexual encounter—right out in front of people, yet entirely private—the most stimulating. Whether it's the darkness of a movie theater, the anonymity of a strange city or the dark water of a swimming pool at night, the chance for a little discreet, daring decadence is one of my greatest joys. Maybe I feel it levels the playing field a little; I'm not sure. But I'd recommend it to anyone.

I'd especially recommend the rush of copping a feel in a crowded elevator, which I do to my boyfriend every chance I get. Crowded elevators are so uncomfortable; you might as well have a little fun. Also, since people try so hard not to look at one another in an elevator, it's the perfect setting to grope your partner's goodies blatantly without anyone being the wiser. And hey, if someone does notice you, it's on him or her. They shouldn't have been looking.

Part of me hopes we've been caught. If we have, my boyfriend hasn't said anything (since he can see well, it's his job to make sure we're discreet). But I'd like to think we've given someone a thrill in those suffocating little boxes. Maybe someone was aroused by our—my—boldness. Maybe they were disgusted. Either way, anyone who's seen us in action came away with a story.

Another great venue for a little touch-too-much activity is a show. Performances at small clubs are fine as long as the audience is packed and no one can see your hands, but I'm really thinking of big concerts where everyone's standing and cheering the whole time. This past Fourth of July, we went to Baltimore to catch a Metallica concert (I'm a sucker for Jason Newsted). We were standing in the middle of a football field, surrounded by beer-guzzling rock fans out for a good time, and the sultry weather and the opening bands (Kid Rock and Korn—the price you pay to see Metallica these days) had jazzed the audience up to a fever pitch. While we were waiting for the main act to come on stage, a woman in the throng got up on a guy's shoulders and slowly began to peel off her tube top. The guys went nuts, chanting, "Show your tits! Show your tits!"

Behavior like that is tacky. I don't even like to see couples embracing on the street. Does that sound hypocritical after all I've said here? Well, I may like to fool around in public, but I try to keep it under wraps. Not everyone is interested in my sex life, and I think other people should understand that too. Do us a favor and exercise some self-control.

That said, I have to admit that the bare-breasted chick did me a favor. She monopolized everyone's attention and gave my boyfriend and me a few minutes to be "alone." While all the other guys were staring delightedly at her breasts, my boyfriend slipped his hand under my tank top and gently stroked mine. The guy next to us looked over and grinned for a moment, then went back to eyeballing the topless woman. I leaned back against my boyfriend's chest and thought, We are getting more out of this moment than any of these people.

Of course, you can't just jump up and do it doggie-style in a Burger King booth and not be noticed. But I don't mind that: I'm actually not that big on intercourse. It's not that I don't like it; it's just that it strikes me as a baby-making activity. I don't like babies, so I'm a little wary. No method of birth control is 100 percent guaranteed, and what would I do with a baby? I'd forget about it the way I forget to feed the turtle. I'd leave it on the windowsill to cool like a loaf of banana bread.

The idea of someone else's entire body growing tumor-like inside my own also fills me with dread and revulsion unlike any other sensation I've known. Even as I think about it, I feel an urge to reach in there and snatch (if you'll pardon the pun) it out quickly.

So intercourse is great, but so are the countless (well, I've never tried counting) other ways of exciting and satisfying yourself and your partner. Sex play is something you can do just about anywhere. Whether it's a little footsie under the table at a business brunch or a big ole blowjob under a leather jacket on an airplane (put your head in his lap, cover it with the jacket, and pretend to be sleeping), it can all be done—with a little ingenuity—whenever the mood strikes. Just remember to look straight ahead as if lost in thought. If you make eye contact, people will guess what you're up to. People have such filthy minds.

I think that's my boyfriend's problem; he almost always looks at me if I try to start anything, and then he gets embarrassed. But he'll learn. After all, he's got a great teacher. As a greasy barfly once said, blind people are very sensual.

BLOWJOB QUEEN

 Lisa Johnson

H e likes . . . oral sex," Grandma whispered incriminatingly into the phone. She was talking about President Clinton, but I seized the opportunity to explore this point further, entering a space where granddaughters rarely tread. I'd always wondered about her sex life, debating with cousins and boyfriends whether this mannerly southern lady took on a different personality when she left the drawing room for the bedroom. Everybody liked to think so. Without asking directly, I inquired as to her thoughts on "that subject." "I'm a normal person," she responded, enunciating her words carefully. "I love sex. With my husband. But putting a man's penis in your mouth—that's disgusting." And there I had it. The definitive answer to all my adolescent speculations: Grandma does not go down. Then she posed the deadly return question: "Don't you think so?" I don't exactly think blowjobs are disgusting, but I don't go seeking them out, either. While I wasn't about to examine this area of my life with full disclosure in a conversation with Grandma, our exchange did prompt me to think further about my views on sucking dick.

They are complicated. Growing up in an upper-middle-class family in the South, eager to escape the constraints of traditional femininity, giving blowjobs meant being dirty and bad—sexual, and therefore dangerous and powerful. Over time, however, the rebellious allure of blowjobs wore thin, as my early sexual experiences only seemed to confirm that oral sex was a one-sided proposition. I quickly learned who got on their knees, whose pleasure took priority, around whose genitals the world revolved. My own opportunities for pleasure and power in this patriarchal sexual formula were limited indeed. And only recently has a new, more mutual and sexually satisfying relationship enabled me to truly overcome the anti-blowjob bias these formative experiences inspired.

To complicate my conflicting emotions on this subject, I admit there is another part of me that thinks, "If you had a cock you'd be thrusting it down the throat of every halfway-interested girlie who crossed your path." And it's true. I'd like to pin one down and have my terrible way with her.

Each of these reactions threads through my real-life and fantasy trips in the realm of the Blowjob Queen. It seems I need to say out loud, finally, in one place, all the contradictory things I think about pleasuring the male organ.

My first blowjob memory stars my best friend in elementary school. Jane (not her real name) was the daughter of a factory worker and a truck driver, and the brashness of working-class culture as I encountered it in her home appealed strongly to the part of me that wanted to be loud and wild. We'd leave the skating rink (where we were supposed to be spending the evening) and ride around with "trashy" sixteen-year-old boys, rednecks from across the Alabama state line, drinking tequila from the bottle, Bud Light from cans, smoking cigarettes and blowing perfect circles with our fuck-me lipgloss on bright.

One of these nights, Jane and I were riding in the back seat with a guy we knew from school. As my older cousins used to say, we got "just drunk enough." Giggling like the schoolgirls we were, Jane and I took turns frenching the boy, our stomachs in our throats from knowing what this kind of thing could do to our reputations. We started talking about blowjobs—would we ever do one, that sort of thing. We loved freaking guys out with our sexually aggressive repartee. I dared her to do it. She shrieked and said, "No," and turned her head away. Everything was happening fast. I dared her again, "Do it, do it." And she unzipped his pants and did. I couldn't fathom what she found down there, never having seen an actual penis, but I was thrilled and mortified and sucking dick vicariously for the very first time. I wanted to be sexual in all the prohibited ways, but my church upbringing and socially classed conception of the body as dirty only let me get as far as being a voyeur that night.

I don't remember the first time I gave a blowjob, but I know it was with my first serious boyfriend, and I know I did it to prove two things: how much I loved him, and, maybe more important, how terribly bad and dangerous I was. Both of us were conflicted over having premarital sex and lustful thoughts, and we decided many times to go on the wagon and quit doing it. It was always me trying to lure him back over to the dark side. One night we said we'd only let him put it at the edge of my hole, and we kept it there for a long time and kissed and struggled with desire and eternal damnation. I started pushing my hips forward a little too much, taking in the head of his penis. He'd pull back like I was a viper, only to give in for a minute and let me tantalize him with my juicy crotch. Then he called me the Devil. I liked being thought of as that powerful, and I know that was a big part of why I sucked his dick.

But being a bad girl turned out to be just another side to the good girl persona I was trying to ditch. Over the course of this relationship, sex stopped being something I was doing to break out of my straight-laced family background. Instead, it slipped into the mirror experience of servicing the male body—as boyfriend rather than father, a subordinate position I was loathe to replicate, yet found myself strangely gravitating toward. And in this role, I became a good girl all over again.

This boyfriend—let's call him Junior—was not a good lover. (How could he have been? We were fifteen when we started.) He was selfish and impatient and emotionally manipulative. As our relationship wore on and the sex lost its novelty, we began to fight about it. Somehow the memory of trying to get Junior to stay awake with me one night is tangled with my memories of his responses to my requests for oral sex: "Complain, complain, com*fucking*plain." Looking back, I realize neither of us liked to give face, yet both of us wanted it badly. I became bitter towards him for withholding it. Then bitterness changed to embarrassment: why did I want it so much, why did I take so long to come, why did I have to bargain for sexual favors? Finally, my feelings settled on self-denial. If it was going to be this much trouble to get satisfaction, I would just determine not to want it anymore. I would take pleasure in giving pleasure, performing pleasure. And I would climb up my shower at night with one foot on the soap holder and the other on the glass door's towel rack to bring my clit into contact with the shower head—the non-pulsating variety—and build towards orgasm till both feet fell asleep, my arms shaking from holding up my weight. I lived in terror of somebody walking in, but I slept well.

I left that relationship with complicated feelings about oral sex and a bitterness that infused all my future blowjobs (until recently). When I thought about sucking dick, what came to mind was an image of Junior, standing there with his dick in my mouth like he owned the place. *Deep Throat* is a hard cultural standard to live up to (the premise of this '70s porn flick was that the woman's clit was located in the back of her throat, so the more the guy thrusted, the more Linda Lovelace moaned and sword swallowed). It's not a clit you'll find in the back of my throat; it's a gag reflex. In fact, I often tear up and my nose runs. It looks like I'm crying, and sometimes it's so intense being overfilled with sex organ that I kind of feel like crying for real. I mean, the penis-in-mouth fit asks a bit much of a girl. Beyond the anatomical affront of the blowjob its sexual purposes struck me as redundant. How many holes did a penis need, or merit? Sex seemed designed for men's orgasm: Why give them more? I wondered. It was my clit that got short shrift.

So I admit it: I didn't give many blowjobs as a girlfriend, wife, or one-night stand. This feels like a failure to measure up to my own bad girl image. I didn't think they deserved it (especially not more than me). Male eroticism seemed simplistic (linear), primary (patriarchal, a men-first kind of thing), and unsatisfying (heavy on penetration and a one-shot deal). This last point may be even more important than the others: once men come (most of them, anyway), it's over. Go to sleep. Not only can they not fuck you after they come, they don't even want to. It's like the faucet of desire runs dry, and everything that turned them on just moments before, now repulses. The body they pursued all day suddenly becomes a burden, a question mark left hanging in the semen-scented air. Ten stiff fingers remain able to do the damage, but a wet pussy quickly loses its appeal after they blow their wad. *Blow* them? You must be kidding. I'd have to be a fool as a woman to heighten men's erotic delight and hasten the end—a fool, a martyr, or a woman with more than one lover. Yes, I hear myself sounding like a shrew, but that's what years of pent-up resentment and thwarted pleasures do to a vivacious, orgasmic woman like myself. My point is that I never got enough and when I did I was made to feel guilty for insisting on my own pleasure, nagged by next-day comments of sore jaws and tongues rubbed raw by the backs of their teeth. Fuck 'em, I barked inside my head.

And maybe I'm not so far from Grandma's views on putting a man's penis in your mouth, either. As it happens, I'm a little squeamish about bodies and the viscosity of "private" parts. I hate to admit it; sexual bravado is more my style. The truth is I would fuck a stranger far sooner than I would go down on one. I had a roommate for a while who was the exact opposite. She would blow a guy in order to avoid the pressure to fuck—also to demonstrate her virtuosity and win their hearts (located in their frat-boy khakis). I tried to explain my hesitation to her: your mouth has to taste it; your face smells it. You experience their bodies so much more sensually that way. I don't want to get that close to people just passing through my sexual landscape. I once heard oral sex described as "kissing each other down there," a phrase that gets at the intimacy and perversity of this gesture. And personally, I don't get kinky with just anyone. It's gross—that's what's so great about it—but I only enter into gross bonds with men I mean to love. Like swallowing gold fish, sucking dick is a kind of initiation ceremony, indubitable proof of my commitment to do unto you as I would have you do unto me. There: my very own golden rule.

Sex, however, isn't always about golden rules. I remember Edward, my second serious boyfriend (whom I have since married and divorced). How we laid together on the bed in his room on one end of his mother's trailer, curtains drawn in the half-light of afternoon teenage sex. My feelings and fantasies surrounding oral sex reach back in part to that dim room (the one his mother threatened to put a red light outside of because we had sex there so much).

I remember blowing him. He was on his back; I was on my knees, bending over his crotch and preparing to minister to his adolescent cock. I liked to think this was a great gift I was bestowing on him, one of those scenes like Tom Cruise and Rebecca DeMornay in *Risky Business*—not the train scene but the earlier one on the stairs of his house, before she cared about him. I was skilled, relatively speaking, attractive, and popular (or at least not unpopular) in a sexpot/bookworm sort of way. He wasn't exactly a nerd, but he was scrawny, played in the band (really well, but still), and I remember him carrying a briefcase to science class in eighth grade even though he didn't make good grades. What was that song back then? Something like: "How could a guy like me attract your angel eyes?" That's how I conceived of our relationship at first, to his dismay. I knew he was a virgin, and I took great pleasure in thinking of deflowering him, rubbing blue-jeaned groins together till my clit rubbed raw, our blood moving to the thudding beat of Madonna's "Justify My Love" in the back seat of my car.

I was looking to explore my sexual power by being with someone less experienced. I wanted him to lose control, to know I was the one who took him across the border into manhood. In a sense I entered the space of masculinity vicariously through him. I wanted him to submit to me, offer up his innocence and enter me as if *I* embodied the manhood towards which he aspired. You've got to go through me, I wanted to say. So committed was I to this territorial vision, I cried hysterically the night I discovered he'd been blown before by his—get this—ninth-grade girlfriend (we were seniors), whom he dumped for me. I wept and wept, had one of those crying jags where your eyes are still swollen in the morning. Rebel and doormat rolled up in one skinny eighteen-year-old body, I learned to take pleasure in producing manhood with the motions of my mouth.

But that was later. On this afternoon, I leaned down imperiously and took him in my mouth, licking and sucking, careful to keep my teeth clear of his delicate genital skin, a contortion that means holding your lips out from your teeth like a buck-toothed girl while moving sloppily, steadily, up and down the column. It's a good thing men have such an obstructed view of this procedure, 'cause it cannot be pretty. It certainly doesn't feel pretty. What it can feel is powerful—the power of the Blowjob Queen, bestowing gifts on her favorite peasant boy.

I saw a movie once called *Crystal Palace*. I remember only the basics of the plot: a guy's fiancée had died and he was having trouble getting over her. He met another woman at a diner (played by Susan Sarandon) who kept trying to seduce him, but he was loyal and resisted. One night he was drunk and passed out, and he began to dream about his dead fiancée: beautiful, blond, angelic. She was on top of him, beginning to make love. He became aroused, and also felt relieved to be reunited with her, like it saved him from dealing with strange mouths and cunts. Then he woke up a little and realized Sarandon was sucking his cock. He was horrified, but too close to orgasm to stop. He gave a little cry of protest and she sucked harder, pinning him down by the pelvis as he came in her mouth. He cried and cried.

Oh, how my own pelvis shifted and gathered fluid as that scene played out. I'm so turned on and so disturbed by the betrayal this orgasm represents— turned on because it's so bad, because it screws with his morality by valuing pleasure over emotional bonds. It kills me to think about, tears me up inside; it hurts—and it makes me come.

In my masturbation fantasies, I identify with the man in this movie—the character whose desire overpowers his own morality, the character whose orgasming cock becomes more important, more powerful, than his rational alle- giances and values. I feel this way when I masturbate and imagine someone walking in right as I reach the orgasmic point of no return. I identify with the woman as well. Sarandon's character sucked loyalty, sadness and deep-buried pleasure out from between this guy's legs. I want to suck feelings from men through their cocks, too, to make blowjobs into something besides submission, a performance of sexual and, perhaps more importantly, emotional power—lead- ing a man around by his cock, holding the heterosexual world by the balls. Dangerous equation: He loves me because I fuck so well. The underlying fear is knowing someone will always come along who can fuck better, just by virtue of being new and different from you.

Maybe blowjobs only produce an illusion of female control. The power of pleasing a guy with hand and mouth is an enticing elixir, yet controlling the penis (in a way that extends beyond the bedroom) seems an unlikely turn of events. Ultimately, being on your knees for sexual service doesn't feel tremendously different from being on your knees for a big crying jag after being cast off by the man you love. A feeling of being less than the man permeates both.

These are some of the things I didn't know the day I first blew Edward. His track-tight thighs felt rigid under my one free hand. I could tell he was getting close, but I wasn't sure how close. (Sometimes I had better luck than others producing results with these young cocks.) I warily continued. We had made a deal that he would tell me first, that he wouldn't come in my mouth, but it's hard to trust people moving towards the throes of orgasm. His hand lay softly on the back of my head. We were so in love, so tender and forceful in our young passion. I felt him throb in my mouth, able even at that age to pick up on the variations of tumescence, figuring out they get bigger right before they come. Then his hand clamped down to hold me in place while he came. Surprise! My eyes bulged and I swallowed quickly to get it out of my mouth.

Who was this person? I would have asked had my mouth not been coated with a tingly residue of pearly white mucus. This person I had trusted, this person who was supposed to look up to me as the girl just out of his reach, the one on top? What betrayal. He stepped outside the grammar I had created for our relationship, throwing everything—my sense of myself, of him, of us—off balance. What was this display of power on his part? *And where could I get more of it?* There was something horrifically erotic about the betrayal of trust, the sudden shifting of sexual syntax between lovers, something sexy about the assertion of sovereignty. In this moment of force, I went from giving-the-blowjob-as-domination to giving-the-blowjob-as-submission. And liking it. Sort of.

This was the first time I got off on being coerced, entering a more adult "good girl" role where I was obedient but not oblivious. I created a space between his pleasure and my own, a channel where one blurred into the other, where I could draw on his role as well as my own. I could appreciate the desire to be sucked off and perform in the service of that desire, which was somehow disconnected from any particular man or penis. I learned about being turned on by the other person's desire, power, and orgasm, but more than that, I chased that free-floating desire for a blowjob and caught it by the tail. Every now and then when I was giving head it would seem for a second like I was sucking myself off; I was everywhere. I was desire itself.

The way that small gesture of Edward's hand on the back of my head affected my perspective on blowjobs was hazy at first, but emerged over several years as a landmark moment when my desire was jolted into a more complex form. I would remember it while masturbating, explore and re-explore that instant of surprise, that door into the complicated manipulations of desire in the adult world. As I replayed this moment in my mind, I began to inhabit the memory as a conscious performance of "taking it like a good girl," and submission became less clearly marked as weakness or inferiority. Instead, I glimpsed the possibility of submission as active collaboration in a mutual fantasy of control and being controlled. I was *choosing* this position over and over as I got off on my own. My fantasy life appropriated these blowjob experiences for its own ends, twisting them like after-sex sheets.

As ambivalent as I am about the male orgasm in reality, in fantasy I focus on the parts I love: the insistence, the convulsions, the endurance, how it takes the punishment. With this fantasy cock in mind, I imagine stroking myself like a man while I masturbate, and my frenzy doubles. I'd developed the habit of simulating the gesture of jerking a guy off while masturbating, ever since the time my first boyfriend post-divorce engaged me in mutual masturbation and I found it intensified my own sensations. (He even used to fake orgasm while eating me out—a surefire method of making me come.)

Fantasy is a powerful force: I get sucked into scenes in my head (or movies and books), in a way that makes imagined experiences feel like real life. Sensations flash across my body as if it were a screen of desire. Nothing is sexier to me than the moment right before a man's orgasm, where loss of control tangles with the disciplined codes of masculinity; he is so vulnerable and so powerful all at once. I want to be in this space of taking and giving, this peaking of desire, so I concentrate on escaping the constraints of my own body and learn to inhabit the male orgasm. Like porn, sex becomes a show I watch, and I climax along with the main character, the dick. As they say in sports psychology: Be the ball.

One day while lying in the tub for a cool summer afternoon masturbation session, I tried to imagine the sensation of a penis orgasming. I love how they look like they're being milked by an invisible hand right before they spew, and it occured to me to try connecting the gesture of jerking someone else off with the sensation on my clit from the running water. What would it feel like? With this magnificent mental sleight of hand, I crisscrossed the wires in my head, the neurons or synapses or whatever, or maybe I discovered already crossed wires. Either way, it worked. I tuned into the sensations of my body more deeply and with more focus than ever before as I imagined them coming from my fist moving up and down.

I had tried this move in bed before as my lovers ate me out, making small undetectable motions under the covers. I had even imagined they were sucking my cock—the men! And let me say again—it worked. Flushed with pleasure and guilt, shame and bravado, I came hard as I betrayed them with these "transsexual" fantasies, trading places with them in my head. I never felt able to tell my past lovers what I was doing, fearing it might threaten their manhood, or worse, their sense of my femininity. If they experience fantasy as half as real as I do, the image of me with a set of hairy testicles would be all they could see afterwards. In my mind, the transformation is irreversible—once you go there, that new part of you is forever revealed—erotic play becomes magic, a conjuring. The night my current boyfriend licked a glow-in-the-dark dildo resting between my legs, he fed my deepest fantasies, and I was pretty sure afterwards that I wanted to propose. I did tell one person before him—a lesbian with whom I had a brief affair. Her androgynous wardrobe and hairstyle suggested she would be less unsettled by my sexual fluidity, although I still feared she might think it terribly unfeminist or just plain perverted. To my great relief and excitement, she said not only that she had similar fantasies, but that she would play mine out, talk about sucking my cock while she gave me oral sex. We never did it, I'm sorry to say, but her response went a long way in affirming my unconventional desires.

This conversation rooted around in my psyche for a couple of years before surfacing again, suddenly and powerfully, that day in the tub. You know how when you get close to coming from masturbation, sometimes your mind spins in search of the nastiest, most horrifyingly orgasm-inducing image you can come up with? I turned on the faucet and lay back while water flooded my crotch—instant thrill—shuffling in my mind for the right erotic image. The usual fare appeared: a man eating me out, a woman eating me out. Eden from the long-cancelled soap opera *Santa Barbara*. My mind spun as if scanning a crowded room and my fist kept pace. My clit was pulsing, my hand worked my imaginary penis, and then I hit on it—a girl giving me head (that's right—sucking my dick). The things I said to her. The way I came on her tits. *Quelle horreur!* This was off-limits (where I love to be right before I come). This was me getting off on something sort of anti-woman, because I'm not talking about some pleasantly mutual session of oral sex; I'm talking about force and discipline, self-absorption and sovereignty. When guys talk about being sucked off, they sound like kings, feet planted solidly apart with a wench on her knees, all about pleasing that prick. Imagining myself as one of them, I decided at that moment to become a Blowjob Queen—not the one giving, but the one receiving—embracing my nasty little secret.

She lay beneath me in the tub, my cock sunk deeply into her face—the most vulnerable position possible. I promised her, as Edward had promised me, not to come in her mouth, positioning myself as her protector, her benevolent master. I looked down at her long, dark hair, striking aqua eyes, a teen heroine from one of those novels I read in elementary school about beautiful girls having adventures (tee hee)—and I tried to mask the oncoming orgasm manifesting itself in my quivering forearms and grimacing face, tried to convince her I wasn't nearly there, that it just felt good, that my muscles were merely tired. Then I placed a hand on her forehead like a farmer clamping a cow in place just before the slaughter and held my spasming cock in her mouth. Her eyes grew large, oceans of aqua, and her throat opened to the load.

I had crossed a line. In imagining that other female body servicing me as if I were a man, I feared that I'd bought into the cultural subordination of women. I sensed on some level that I was expanding my sexual imagery, not just resigning myself to the existing options of misogyny, but I found it hard to tell the difference. I worried my fantasy reeked of the old adage: if you can't beat them, join them. The nightmarish concepts of penis envy and female masochism haunted me. Was I fucking women up, so to speak? I wasn't sure. These are the structures of my desire: the eroticization of betrayal, the appropriation of the masculine erotic landscape. These are my truths: I enjoy submitting. And I hate it. And I fantasize about commanding it from others.

My "transgender" fantasy allows me to benefit from the ubiquitous male orgasm, taking over its privileged entitlement to pleasure for my own female body. This was a hard interpretation to come to, but I realize now that I'm not glorifying the cock as such. I'm imagining the cock dimension of my own sexuality—my desire to be submitted to, my desire for sexual scenes that make central my erotic pleasure. When I orgasm to images of thrusting this "cock" into a girl's mouth, I am punishing both of the good girls I've internalized—the one who subordinates her bodily desires to Christian morality in abstinence, as well as the one who foregoes orgasm in the service of male sexuality. I am taking up a new kind of female sexuality—voracious, rough, autonomous—not good at all.

When I lie back and close my eyes, I rise up from the constraints my girl body creates for me in actual heterosexual encounters and become free to enjoy myself without limit and without guilt. The blowjob loses its connection to real-time threats of premature ejaculation (meaning, before I come) and instead becomes my—pardon the Atari imagery—joystick in another dimension of reality. I recently read a book called *Dick for a Day: What Would You Do If You Had One?* Without hesitation, my answer comes: I would go get a blowjob—from a Blowjob Queen. Despite all the qualms I've described, I truly love oral sex, love how nasty it is, having someone put their mouth on my privates (I thought I invented the idea while masturbating when I was eleven). And getting a blowjob would be like being eaten out, all that pleasure without the "where's the spot" bullshit and feelings of general physical troublesomeness. That's what I would love about my penis: the self-evident anatomy. *There it is, baby: suck it.* I do love my clitoris (well and often), but I can't help feeling that a cock gives you more to work with when you're lathering up for an orgasm. The pleasure of wide open motions and external, available organs jibes better with the explosive orgasmic feeling I get that makes me want to knock holes in walls and break shit.

I was fascinated to learn recently that the architecture of the clitoris resembles the penis in miniature: base, shaft, and crown. When I'm alone, I love how my clit gets big and hard, insisting on itself like a dick (all puffed up and red with pride in itself). How exciting—and embarrassing. Here I am marveling at the pleasures of having a big cock, yet I remain unable to utter boy phrases like "lick the length of my shaft" even though, god, how I want him to.

I try to say it and words stick in my throat like cum, my face goes red. I like the idea of exchanging positions of domination and submission, penetration and vulnerability. Pulling all of my dirtiest, most complicated feelings out into the light has taught me that desire is complicated and gender fluid. It also leads me to concede that male eroticism and male "power" may be less straightforward than I thought: If men are anywhere near as complicated as I am (and surely some men are), there must be fascinating sexual twists hidden away like girl parts, waiting to be coaxed out in the open. The problem is, I'm afraid. I'm afraid of what would happen if I let go, even for a moment, of my femininity as I have constructed it all these years, afraid of the masculine part of me, fear it as a failure of femininity. So I bleach my facial hair, pluck my nipples, and stave off my inner man.

But I stop short of censoring my fantasies, because I can't seem to get over equating top with penis and bottom with pussy. Reveling in the aggressive part of my desire, I am ready to become a "man" in this realm. So I fuck my boyfriend, imagine my penis and picture the chick. Blowjob Queens, all three of us.

Seductions of a Bordertown Boy

 Karleen Pendleton Jiménez

I watched the entire Barbara Walters–Monica Lewinsky special. I am tired of intelligent and artsy people telling me that they are above this type of voyeurism. That they avoided the show or turned it off after ten minutes. They announce this all proud of themselves. Maybe for me it's a connection thing. I feel like I gotta know what the rest of the world is watching if I am to have any chance of connecting with other people— even if only over Monica. Myself, I think Monica is important. And the thought of somebody younger than I having that much power over the world through her sexuality is hugely exciting and inspiring.

In polite conversation, I am mostly alone on that thought. Yet the bitterness toward her for messing everything up by sucking cock strikes home. Would anyone believe that Monica and I have anything in common? While I've not become so famous, fucking for power's sake is what I know best. Shortly before she broke up with me, my ex-girlfriend told a woman (my current girlfriend) over lunch that sex to me was only about power. I wanted to defend myself when I heard that. After all, my ex was the one who taught me how to fuck my way through to the top of community politics. (That didn't make me less complicit.) But it saddened me, because I really did love her.

Years ago, my therapist said that most people find some overlap between sex and love. At the time I felt none. I've felt the overlap since then and it *is* all that it's cracked up to be: All the Hollywood romances, the brightest moon in 133 years, every molestation fantasy that ever turned me on, that made me feel at once the most beautiful and the most loved child on earth.

"So I don't get it. I mean, how can you mess around with other people if you're all 'in love' now?" an old friend blurted out, almost surprising herself, during a late-night New Year's conversation. I tried to decide if it was a sincere question or a rhetorical moral moment. I answered, because either way I wanted to keep pretending we were just sharing our philosophies of life over Squirts with tequila. I grinned, a little nervously, shrugged my shoulders and said, "I just use sex for more things than most people."

Simply put, I use sex to fuck with things. I'm possessed by the internal places I feel most hurt and most vulnerable. I used to be ashamed of this. For instance, how could a lady or a fag giving me a blow job turn me on more than any other act? How could this be when this was precisely one of the first acts I performed on a molester? The act that disgusted me. I can still taste it slimy in my mouth. How could I want that given to me when it had hurt me the most?

Then again, that's the point. I can't get the taste out of my mouth. It will come and go over a lifetime. Figuring out the truth of the memory doesn't end anything, though I think it does grant me an opening to mess with that memory, to twist it into something less hurtful. So, while the pictures from my lost childhood flash in my head, I find ways to manipulate them into pleasure, power and even laughter, depending. As a mixed-blood Chicana boydyke, I find that molestation memories are only the iceberg's tip in terms of my vulnerability. People and institutions have spent a lot of time fucking around with me. Bringing these politics into sex is one of my favorite strategies for fucking back.

Consider molester #2—the important one, the one who did it with love. Even this last Christmas he was still at it. He shuttled me in from the airport, bought all my favorite foods, gave me a car to use. He was on his best behavior for three whole days. But he couldn't make it through the last afternoon together.

I asked him to move because I needed to use the phone and he was occupying the only seat next to it. He said, "Well, can you sit on my lap?" My body flamed up immediately with the usual heap of anger. My voice shifted cold. "No, I can't because . . ." I stopped myself. Come on Karleen, it's okay, don't get so mad so quick, don't finish the sentence, he may not have meant anything by it, it has all been real nice for the last few days, and you wouldn't want to leave, wrecking that—

"Yeah, haven't you heard of lap dancing?" he shoots out with a laugh, stopping me from finishing my "because you can't control yourself" sentence.

I keep pretending my dad someday will not desire me. I say to friends, "He's just a weirdo, he can't control himself, he's some kind of extreme social misfit." While all that might be true, it comes down to the fact that he's still in love with me—or the image of my mother in me. After all, it started when she kicked him out of the house. I was nine, and he invited me into his bed. When I was twenty-one years old, I forced him to confess in front of my therapist. I forced him in the only way a lover can: I threatened never to see him again. So he came and spoke, awkwardly but clearly: "I guess I just thought of you as my wife."

"It just has to not be my fault," I tell my therapist. I am excited over my recent discovery that if I can just feel like a little girl with no control over her molestation, I can receive. I finally can let my girlfriend touch me, without physical force or the subsequent bruises. My girlfriend just needs to tell me what she'll take from me, sometimes in my dad's exact words, and I instinctively open up again. It fucks my mind up enough to finally believe it's not my fault and to let my female body be touched.

I can't help wondering if I would feel like a woman at all if my dad hadn't made me one.

"You are a boy, right?" my girlfriend's four-year-old boy asked, frustrated, staring at my naked female body dripping in the shower. Before I could form an answer, he ran off to play with his little sister. I didn't really know how to answer, though. I wanted to tell him that it's not so simple, that not everybody is just one or the other, and then my ideas and words got jumbled and I heard my girlfriend telling me that anything you can't find the words to explain to a four-year-old you probably can't explain to yourself either. I decided I'd wait it out until I could formulate the explanation more clearly. But the situation is getting more drastic. Two weeks ago he ran into the kitchen on a Sunday morning and shouted, "Do you have a penis, or what?"

He's not alone with his assumptions, though he is more open to honestly exploring the matter than others. Grownup reactions are as follows:

1. "Oh, come on now, it wouldn't be a good idea if you came. I mean, you do look too queer for mainstream social engagements."

2. "Son, you're not old enough to play with matches on your own."
3. "Yes, Mr. Pendleton, your departure gate is number 23, on the left and up the escalator."
4. "Ahhh! The men's rest room is over there."
5. "You can't be butch. I mean, you don't look like a man to me."
6. "Look at this. Isn't she the most perfect boy? She's walking around like everyone's sickest molestation fantasy."

I've almost always been proud that I pull off my boyness so well—as long as it wasn't acknowledged around my mom. At my drag king debut, the whole audience clapped and smiled. I was "El Chicano" for five minutes and fifty clapping hands. In LA I would've been a fake, too mixed and pale to pull off even a Spaniard. Here in Canada they're not even sure what a Chicano is. Whisked away, I could be my earliest fantasy—the man my mom was in love with my entire childhood, Julio Iglesias. His was the first concert that I ever went to. I would've been embarrassed about that, except that I saw how my mom's eyes watered when she hummed along with his suave Latino self. Latino men were my butch role models, never my white dad. My dad brought her irritation, while they brought passion and heartache.

Breasts strapped down, in my freshly dry-cleaned tux, with my shiny CD playing, I imagined my mom out there in the audience with her heart moving to my voice, and I sang wildly. Later I checked the NAFTA list for earnings as a male impersonator but couldn't find it, so I have to keep this event quiet.

Passing only has upset me once in the last few years. At a drugstore, a checker got confused for an instant and thought I was the next person in line. The person who was in fact first was a pale, anguished looking woman. I saw the package of menstrual pads in her hand, and I said something like, "Oh, it's cool, just go ahead." She looked at me looking at the pads and gave me a you-nasty-boy-don't-even-think-about-what's-in-my-body-didn't-your-mother-raise-you-better-than-that scowl. She moved the box to the other side of her body so that I couldn't see it and rushed forward. So strange to lose my allegiance over one of the few body experiences that I share.

One day, not long ago, when the snow melted and gushed down into the gutters, I bled heavily into my pad and wanted to cry. I bled over my Calvin Klein butthuggers that I had stolen from my brother. I saw my shadow against the wall, and it looked like a slouched woman with big breasts. My girlfriend had just told me that a male lover fucked her recently. I hadn't asked. I thought about his genitals inside her and how I could never really do that, and I hated being a woman right then. I felt humiliated for myself.

More and more I am hearing about Chicanas transsexualizing their bodies with drugs and operations. Yet even years later, my first reaction is to think that they are doing this because of the corruptive influence of weird white queers. Can you believe this? This is exactly what I thought about Chicano queers initially—that their state was so unnatural that it must have been thought up by white people with too much time on their hands. How ridiculous that initial thought feels to me after a decade of my open dyke lifestyle. How absurd that I apply it to trans stuff now, after I have spent the last few years thinking about all these gender issues. I have to admit, it was different to hear about it firsthand from my brown Chicana buddies. As with the Chicana dykes I first met, they are people whom I love and respect. And their unique flesh and faces mean I cannot believe in any of the indoctrinated bullshit or fears.

I thought about it myself. But I was never so certain about the female, lesbian aspect of myself until I touched an actual hard, boy body. Boys feel like another species. They are harder and hairier; they smell different; their skin and bones don't allow for many openings. I would advise any dyke out there thinking seriously about transitioning to consider finding a nice queer boy to fuck. I mean fuck him, be as male as you want, make him as female as you want. If all the hardness and hairiness is exactly what you want, and in fact makes you want it even more, then go for it. But make sure you smell it out first. Boy sex has been the most clarifying thing for me, even after dozens of conversations, books and panels on the subject.

Fag sex with men feels like a good game of basketball. Sweaty, physical, exhilarating, challenging, hard, disconnected. I want to win, but there is no heart involved. No fear of falling in love or lingering guilt or responsibility. A simple craving for a new game, a date or time to feel that kind of adrenaline pumping.

Let's face it: the world is run by men fucking men. The public world anyway. International politics is men fucking each other with bodies and power. Everyone knows this. When men walk into a room and greet each other, the women with them are barely present.

I know that's not at all what is really important. I mean, the deep shit, the love and jealousy and hunger, the needs that really drive people, are controlled by women. But I've never let go of my craving for male arenas. I could never handle the idea of being excluded from any place, especially those that seemed to house all the young masculine bodies around me.

All I wanted was a piece of that. I wanted another man to feel my dick thrust into him. I wanted him to tremble from the pain I could inflict inside of him. I wanted to be a part of that world. Just an extension of my membership in barbershops and fraternities. I wanted to be a man fucking another man for a moment on a bed just before dawn. I wanted a taste of it. I don't know if a feminine woman understands that impulse. And maybe men don't even notice feeling it. Because it is, after all, so ordinary. For me, it was a joy.

There is no possibility for love in my fag sex. And there is no possibility for me to ever feel female. With women, there is always the very slight possibility that they will flip me and I will feel like a woman for an hour of my life. I can only give this up to women, and only to certain femme top ones. They have to see it in me, and reach for it.

There's more. I have to confess that my girlfriend is white. In the past, I've had very few white lovers and certainly no other serious relationship with a white person. My need for a brown woman lover is deeply embedded. This desire is both colonialist and me missing my mom. It is what every fair-skinned man in my family has done for generations. I am fueled by nothing less than the desperation of a dozen ancestors.

She found me and loved me first, and I was crazy about how good it felt to be loved. It felt amazing to connect with someone intellectually and politically. It was a relief to find someone who participated in dyke drama on a similar level. But I still couldn't love her. I wanted too, but I couldn't. She couldn't be home to me as long as I couldn't fit her into a family I hungered for.

When I look at her, I think she is the whitest person I've ever seen, and I remember how she's told me before that she's not sure how I can keep loving her, considering how precarious it makes my identity. That I wouldn't want her sperm, I wouldn't want to have a baby who looks like her father, because she's known all along my plan to have some young Chicano man sperm. And I think how ironic it is that pinned down here on her bed, my plan falls apart. I think about the hundred years my family married white to become white: the years I've spent hating the women for finding men they never felt passionate about but made babies with nonetheless because of the "future." How ironic that in 2000, after effective social movements, when I finally can choose not to make my baby in my girlfriend's white image, I still would do it. Just so I would never lose her. Maybe it should and must come down to this: loving a white person instead of hating her skin. Maybe that's the only way I can learn to love all of myself.

So I made myself her brown woman, and I made her my white man—even if the moments are infrequent, even while I am still the butch and she the femme. I just needed to know I could fit her into my family to love her.

I'm mixed. One-quarter Mexican, three-quarters white. I tell anyone who asks me if I am white that people are like paint—once color is mixed in, they're never white again. And it was my mother, my grandmother and my Latino community who taught me how to be a person. But nothing in the mirror linked me to that person but dark eyes. There had to be more—an arm, or a leg, or a shade browner to connect me. And then I saw it: Staring back at me from the sex store shelf was the coffee-colored dick, so dark it's almost purple. Of course, I think. I can have my phantom dick and color all in one and strap it tight to me.

Mexican border agents open my suitcase and look suspicious. "These are men's clothes. Who do they belong to?" What is the least dangerous answer?

American border agents stop my mother and me as we try to cross. The big guy with graying hair looks at me, at my mom, and back at me again, and smirks. "What country were you born in, *sir?* What is your nationality, *sir?*" He says it as rudely as possible in front of my mom. I see her eyes look away. My cheeks flush. I answer, "American." I keep my chin high.

People ask me all the time how I could've ever left Southern California for Canada. They don't know how hard it was to live in California. When you're part white, part Mexican, and these are the two major groups in a statewide war, it sucks to live in your body. And I got the light skin, the symbol of who is the destroyer. I could pass as white until it folds my insides into fire. Walking along the street, I could hear Mexicanos talking about me as el gringito, unaware that I would understand our language. I could try my best to avoid all the groups of young men in San Diego, but the five major military bases ensure that they are every-where at every hour. Not to mention all the agents hanging around the world's most heavily militarized border. If they saw me as a boy, I could be their "son" when they spoke to me. If they saw me as a woman, they could rape me. If they saw me as a butch, they could rape and bash me. San Diego felt as if it were in a constant state of battle.

But everyone who has their eyes open knows that America was founded on rape and violence. I was just sick of being the offspring. I wanted vindication there too, but it seemed too huge and intangible. I couldn't see how I could fuck this one out of me. How do you get the entire nation to bend over and feel the thrust of one young mixed-breed dyke? While my mind and body were going crazy over the immensity of this need, an opportunity presented itself.

This power dilemma exploded for me in a single sexual encounter. This encounter electrified me. It put every moment of individual hurt into perspec-tive. It put every bureaucratic, nationally sanctioned act of hate at a temporary standstill. I was thankful for all of my previous sexual encounters, however queer, experimental or simply politically useful, because they made me into a skilled and strong lover for this occasion. And while it wasn't the best of circumstances and led to my eventual exile, the event brought me the most intense sexual dominating moment of my life.

I have chosen this small publication to expose the secret of a lifetime. I could have gone with *People* or *Newsweek* or even *Vanity Fair,* but I wanted to make it clear that it was not about the money. This is not to say that if at some point in my life Barbara Walters decides to pay me millions to speak, I won't accept. I believe in journalism and the world's right to know, the world's right to consume the truth, the world's right to consume me. And I am still very guilty about this event and I believe the moralistic and punishing tone of Ms. Walter's voice could help me with it. And I would donate my rewards to deserving left-wing organizations across the continent and in Cuba.

This is my secret: I was the one who replaced Monica Lewinsky when President Clinton once again could not control his desires.

In the early summer of 1998, when President Clinton visited the San Diego border region to show support for Operation Gatekeeper (i.e., Operation Sick, Twisted, Murderous, Racist Hypocrites), I was simply a protester in the crowd. I didn't think he would even notice us. But as we chanted, he turned and watched our signs move up and down, dancing in the air to our voices beating in the afternoon sky. He whispered something to one of his Secret Service men, and several of them followed him when he approached us.

Growing up in LA, I saw many stars (that guy Winchester from *M*A*S*H*,* Ricky Schroeder at a Hands Across America rally, and Cheech and the handsome Jimmy Smits). They all have this kind of overwhelming star presence that makes your mouth drop open—even when they look regular on TV and even if you don't particularly like them or you are a cynic in general. They all have this glow. That's what I expected to find with Clinton, because I saw Ronald Reagan once and, as much as I hated him, even he had that sparkling thing going. But when Clinton approached, there was nothing starlike about him. He looked like a regular guy, like a neighbor about to mow his lawn wearing worn-out sweats or something. The media has always said that about him, and I don't mean to be cliché, but it was amazing to actually experience it. He uses this feature strategically to disarm you. He began to speak to us impromptu with a soothing, creamy voice. I knew that every word he said to me was a lie. I knew that he had done horrible evil things to me and millions around me; yet, he is the smoothest most charming speaker, and he convinces you all over again that he's a great guy. His effect is that of an incredibly manipulative abuser, or maybe I am just susceptible to abusers because of my own incestuous history.

I went home that afternoon angry with myself for once again not being mad enough at a hurtful person. I cursed my father for beginning this legacy with me. I lay in my office in the dark, listening to the Santa Ana winds creep up on the night. A knock startled me out of the beginnings of dreams. I opened the door to three Secret Service officers, clad in black suits, with those little wires that look like overgrown hearing aids and wearing dark sunglasses. My heart practically burst from my chest. I thought for a moment that my border guard neighbor must have turned me in. But for what exactly? The smuggled mole, or Cuban cigars, or that huge plant that Ana's mother made me carry over from Jalisco, my autograph of Fidel Castro, those moments in Cuba when my diary disappeared under suspicious circumstances . . . ? I panicked. I didn't know what to confess to or not to confess to. I had known that it would be dangerous living next to the border guard, but I couldn't deny the opportunity for so much writing material. I had been thinking in the back of my head about my next book: border-guard secrets and lifestyles exposed by Chicana dyke. But, in my excitement, I forgot to think about what is most important—my own safety!

But the officers only interrogated me about my lifestyle. I thought this must be a San Diego military thing getting out of hand, and so I tried to explain that not every single person in San Diego is military personnel and that there are no homosexual civilian laws left on the books in California that I could be breaking. I confessed to wearing military uniforms on Halloween and at every leather or Imperial Court function I could possibly attend, but that I was definitely not actually enlisted.

They asked about my use of sex toys, my tendency towards topping, and my philosophy underlying my S/M lifestyle. They threatened to imprison me over the cigar smuggling; they actually had a file on me, with some photos of me protesting years before at Berkeley when I still had shaggy hair. So I answered everything they needed to know and even put on my harness and packed my new jelly dildo when I was ordered to do so.

Minutes later, the President himself and several more agents entered my apartment. At that point it was too much for my small home, and my cats ran and hid under the futon in my office. The President motioned to me that we should go alone to my bedroom.

I could hardly breathe. I wanted to scream out that I was a dyke, thinking: Isn't this clear? I mean, I do look pretty obvious and your agents now know every intricate detail about my sexual urges and aren't there already enough straight women in America to take care of this man? As soon as he closed the door, he lunged for my jelly dick, started working it roughly, jerking me off through my jeans. I honestly did not want to feel pleasure. I felt like it would betray every one of my political causes, but I must confess that I am helpless when my dick begins to harden under stroking. I become totally boy. Bill fell to his knees and began rubbing his lips along my crotch. I was in disbelief. While I have let gay boys suck me on occasion, I thought this was a straight man. And it was so surreal and such an incredible turn-on watching the President, mostly seen on television, kneeling on my shaggy gray carpet, urgently needing my cock down his throat, that I almost came before he could even pull my dick out.

But I decided to take back control of my body. If I am to have this singular sexual episode with the President of the United States, I thought, I want and need to be more in control. I told him to slow down; I told him that he was bad for being so greedy and assuming that he could just suck the cock of any dyke protester. I began pushing and kicking him down with my Docs. He whimpered and began panting. I dug with my boots into his soft back and tummy, leaving a red pattern in a trail across his skin. For a moment I felt guilty. Am I disrespecting the feminism I should share with Hillary by doing this with her man? But I couldn't stop, I was honestly way too turned on. I pulled out handcuffs and ankle restraints and tied him down to my bed. My tinted windows began to steam up. I pulled out the riding crop from between my mattresses and began the whipping.

The Secret Service men knocked at the door and inquired as to the President's safety. He assured them in this heavy groaning voice that all was okay. I whipped hard enough to leave long, swollen welts across his ass and thighs. He twisted and shivered. I yelled obscenities at him. I cursed him for every fucked-up, murderous thing he had done. I felt totally high. I felt like clean electricity, making precise, liquid movements with every swing of my arm. He began to sob. I stroked my hand in his silvery peppered hair and then jerked his head up. I released the handcuffs and pulled him to his knees. I undid my fly and told him that I was ready, and that he had better do it good.

The man took me full into his mouth and down his throat. I gave in to my own shivering. It felt so good, and his fleshy, rosy lips looked beautiful around my cock. When I began to squirt, I pulled out just enough to watch it splash over his cheeks and chest, to stick right there in his curly hair. He licked vigorously at my cum, using his fingers to bring it all back into his mouth.

I fell over content and exhausted. There was another knock at the door, and, with this one, he tidied up his clothes, smoothed back down his hair. He came over and caressed my shaven head and then my face. He told me that when he first saw me at the rally, he thought I was a beautiful young boy, and when he looked again and watched my passionate angry chanting, he understood that I was also a dyke who could take him down where he needed to go. He apologized for the threatening tactics his agents imposed upon me. He explained that he no longer had sexual relations with heterosexual women, or men, or anybody else for that matter besides butch dykes. That our sexuality defied any regulation definition of sexual relations thought up by any legal or governmental system. That only with us could he continue to have a healthy, active sex life and not have to lie about anything to the press, to the lawyers, to his family, to the world. He kissed me once and then left my life forever. And I might have been fine and kept silent for years to come, but for the subsequent course of events.

At the end of the summer, within a couple weeks, I mysteriously lost my wife and my paying job and was forced to switch organizations with my volunteer work. I consequently was driven to Canada. While I am loving my life in Toronto, I have discovered that those losses were not coincidental and that employers and girlfriends all over the nation have been paid off to turn away the dykes with whom Clinton has had relations. He is pushing them into exile so that these stories will not be revealed. It has made for an even more queer and exciting Canada, but what will be the consequence to queer politics in the United States? Regardless of Bill's inspirational and tremendous talent for sucking, this question must be addressed. These incidents must be exposed.

How to Be a Slut

⊛ Erika Mikkalo

It started by accident. I was a kid, completely naive, and he was only slightly less so. Aha, I realized, my nose in dark curls as he put his lips on the skin above my first bra: when a boy says, "Want to go for a walk and talk?" it means, "Let's go someplace where I can try to get under your clothing as quickly as possible." I didn't object—I alternated between confusion and astonishment. I was fully apprised of the biology—cross-sections of females with hidden hollow pears and tube stems, tucked away, and males with swollen inflatable bean sprouts—which was supposed to be why we did this. And romance, which was, for girls, supposed to be why we did this. But I could only discern some not unpleasant physical sensations and not much else. Mostly, I was just stunned that someone found me attractive enough to call up, to want to touch. Although I later learned that this is not much of a distinction, at the time it shocked me: I was monstrous, cylindrical, bloated, bespectacled, covered with boils and festooned with greasy, lank hair. Being a tomboy is fine, but it gets complicated once you grow tits. We were years away from vehicles so we couldn't drive someplace secluded. Both of our mothers were annoying June Cleaver anachronisms with the audacity to actually be in our houses sticking forks in pot roasts, polishing furniture until they could see their reflections, or ironing our fathers' business shirts, handkerchiefs, white cotton briefs spritzed with the dark green aerosol can of Niagara spray starch, so that option was limited. The alternatives were quiet and improvised: natural niches of suburbia, fence rows, tall-grassed hollows and the periphery of woods. I stood still out of ignorance and feigned indifference, quietly watching the sky. This was pretense: I locked my heart in an iron box and swallowed the key to keep its wet pounding out of my throat, prevent its galloping escape away over the horizon in a burst of amazed strength that someone, anyone, actually wanted me.

Black fingers of branches spread out over the gray overhead, reminding me of painting childhood forests by blowing ink over construction paper with a straw. It was an obvious jigsaw, combining whatever was warm or wet or particularly, both. Is this what all the fuss is about? I puzzled. Mouths eating each other were supposed to inspire visions of red hearts and full-blown flowers, rosy ruffles, golden rings, lantern-jawed knights, fainting heroines biting their lower lips in confusion, but all I could tell was that he had eaten Cheetos and didn't brush his teeth afterwards. I executed a small-scale investigation of stimulus response, albeit a more interesting one than the mandatory science fair demonstrations: squash seeds in Styrofoam cups; closet-cultivated molds farmed in petri-dishes; a sculpted plasticine volcano with vinegar-scented faux magma; diagrams of photosynthesis—air, water, light, green chlorophyll linked by arrows, responsible for all life on earth. We didn't have much to say. The pictures in my head were my business. My skin was a map for hands. He got grounded for a C in algebra, so things stopped and didn't resume.

Sometimes I wonder if he was a little frightened, if he could tell that there were no limits, that I didn't know enough or care enough to say "No," or "Don't do that." I wasn't too concerned about being a "good" girl because I'd never been one. Molly Blakely's mother had raised her as an eventual Miss America, with dresses and training in stage-worthy skills, piano and comportment. Being a girl the right way appeared to involve an extensive wardrobe, hair maintenance with a wide-tooth comb carried in the back jeans pocket at all times, petitioning to wear lip gloss as soon as possible and spending time with a bunch of other girls giggling without discrimination. I'd rather just read. The last time that I'd had female friends, Rachel and Beth were the cute ones, and Laura and I were the bookish ones. My family moved across the country, and I hadn't found a new group. I was pretty much on my own. With the guy, as long as it felt good and I was getting attention, it was fine by me. But then we quit. He said that he was grounded, but maybe he decided that I was ugly. It was getting too cold outside, anyway.

If I'd been more social, this could have become a pattern: almost anything with anyone I considered comparably attractive in order to get attention, in order to have evidence that I was at least that pretty, maybe, for those minutes. My own isolation kept the numbers down, kept me from getting a "reputation," for a few years, at least. There was no charge like sexual recognition: the stare, the speculative evaluation, the grin of recognition if I smiled back. "I know what you're thinking about," and, "Maybe we could." Most of the time, the ones who looked weren't acceptable: just frown, look away, ignore it. They should only be able to consider me that way if I'd consider them. Later, I learned that certain articles of clothing got more of a response—a low shirt, a dress, a skirt, a tight belt. I didn't wear them that often. There was a sense of power in it, but it was frightening. I could make people want me with a change in costume. A little black lace worked, although I was told that sixteen-year-old girls weren't supposed to wear things like that. Usually, I just stuck to jeans and t-shirts.

But I did expand my research, eventually, or perhaps the laboratories found me. They included: stands of scrub oak, abandoned orchards, broad and practical family cars, desolate parks, poured-concrete stairwells, loading docks, back hallways, store rooms, closets, county fairgrounds, an ice-skating rink, garages, basements, parking lots, churches, alleys, front porches, back yards, pickup trucks, golf courses and hotels. The subjects were remarkably consistent: just some minor variations in form, duration, and pace. And in what they said, although "Oh, God," "Yes," or a vague and general groan appeared to be the most common exclamations. I told myself that I was there for the proximity and the distance that it provided in the same instant, a pleasure that was my right and my prerogative. For the way that the air above froze to a silver pane and then shattered to melting slivers, a school of mercury fish that swam around my head. It was a buzz, a high, a fix. A little drama, a ritual—they almost always seemed to need to tell me their ethnicity, their middle names—and then a most compelling distraction from myself, and a release. Even though I'd stick with a playmate for a few bouts, the illicit nature, the taboo locations, the enforced limitations, were their own charge. "Don't think that this is about you," I wanted these choices to tell them. "This is about what I need, what I can get." With a good one, the physical sensations were electric, a series of explosions, a warm and jagged drug. It was a humiliating thing, bringing this hunger to strangers, but they generally had it, too. Except that I wasn't supposed to, wasn't allowed. It was entirely vulnerable and entirely mammalian: perhaps the only way I knew how to be human, the only acceptable category of need. Now, I just try to remember with compassion, a desperately transparent childish game for approval and acceptance. Do you like it when I do this? I can do it again. And I did.

Apparently I was doing it wrong. Girls are supposed to want attention from boys, but only within a given set of parameters, set exchanges. Your whole being as a girl depends on male attention; but to limit it to sex, to refuse the ritual of flirtation, pursuit, tease, conquest, immediately disqualifies you. Sex as an end in itself isn't in the script—the rules they never gave me a copy of, the codes and regulations of appropriate female behavior, what nice girls do. Girls approached me in the hall and asked earnest questions about birth control. I responded as well as I was able: the pill is good, and so are condoms. You have to take care of yourself, right? Take responsibility. Then they departed, giggling into their hands, notebooks clasped closer to pastel-monogrammed sweaters. I dreamed of emigration, moving to the Netherlands, or Sweden. What was I doing wrong? Was my body not my own? Was it wrong not to follow whomever it was around and cheer for him at ballgames, not to hold out to receive some tawdry piece of drugstore jewelry, some semi-articulate mumbling of a stupid phrase that everyone knows is a lie, anyway? I did go to a hockey game one boy played in, once. We did it in the cold concrete corner of a back hall, with the smell of old mildew and fresh sweat, a refreshing pause even without the amenities. I liked boys: broad shoulders, thick arms, flat chests, narrow hips and high asses. It always seemed to go fast, with a certain programmed inevitability. Some kissing, some groping, some sucking, some licking, some fucking. Occasionally, I tried to count how many thrusts it took them, but fortunately, generally lost track. Traveling as hard as you can in one place. And then the lull. So sweet, even without a context. When I saw him again, we either would or we wouldn't. Ignore one another. Except with the possible pointed stare of inquiry, the even returned look and nod, or just an averted glance if I didn't want to revisit.

I always bathed promptly upon returning home. "I can smell semen a mile away," my mother once warned me. I pictured her led, blindfolded, to a hill-top, clad in perfectly pressed beige linen, and spun around three times, then stopped to point in the direction of an offending little puddle of jizz, upwind, beneath a tree, in order to test this special skill. I may not have had her respect, but I didn't want to be her. "So I may have completely misread the situation," she continued, "but if you're doing anything, I want you to shower the moment that you walk in the door." I got in the habit of showering whenever I got home, so that if she tried to use running to the bathroom as a gauge of activity, her count would be completely skewed. I wished I was getting that much. I knew that I was too far gone for any sort of parental approval—too funny-looking, too strange, too unconcerned with what the neighbors thought—and quickly adapted to taking what I could get, a target of enthusiastic attention, albeit for a limited interval. It was exhilarating. I could put on the girl outfit and wear it well, or at least well enough. The look of appraisal, simultaneously frank and sly. "Yeah, so I'm one of those girls," I'd reply with a silent leveling of eyes. "Are you going to try to do something about it?"

The first one was an All-American. He looked like he'd run for Congress in twenty years, encased in a navy suit and smiling too broadly from behind a podium. Even his teeth were blonde. The golden boy really had a calisthenic aspect, like someone doing push-ups over me. Maybe he could do them one-handed. "Oh my, God," he said afterwards. "This is the best that I've ever felt in my life." I resisted the temptation to respond, "No shit." At least he was appreciative. Later, some seemed to want to cultivate seamyness, to get off on an element of sleaze. This struck me as unnecessary. If you're getting lucky, play nice. Maybe to them there had to be something dirty about it, about them wanting me, and they put the dirtiness back on me. But I was doing the same thing that they were, right? Why should I be made to feel like a public toilet? I was no more or less wrong. Golden boy tried to play with my hair, but there was too much goo in it, minutes of each morning dedicated to teasing it to a nest of rats and spikes. The freak gets the pretty boy. Of course, I'd never be publicly acknowledged, except for occasional stares and hisses, but I told myself that I didn't want that, anyway. It wasn't my fault that the rules were different for girls. Why should I have to play by them? In the elevator, he wanted to give me a wallet-sized photograph of himself but couldn't find any. I smiled and assured him that it was okay. Did he expect me to take it home and build a shrine, folding mahogany panels with lit candles, smoldering incense in a brass holder, orange marigolds and fragrant frangipani in wreaths? Would he have signed it if I asked him? "Thanks!"

Then there was a boyfriend. Imagine that: I had a boyfriend. It was nice—an arm to curl up under, a familiar couch, bowling outings, movies and ice cream. I felt like a tourist in Teen-land. We listened to the radio riding in the car, my head propped on his leg, the sun on my cheek. "They're playing our song," he said, turning up the volume. David Bowie sang, "You've torn your dress. Your face is a mess . . . " Boyfriend was better—it wasn't bad getting to know someone. In fact, having access to the "right" role was amazing, the possibility that I might be special, that it might mean something. But the security was clearly conditional. What was the transformation that suddenly made me okay? That made people smile with approval when they saw us. Wasn't I the same? Half an hour in the back of a car, and he told me, "You're a beautiful person." I wanted nothing more than to believe him, but harbored suspicions that "beautiful person" meant, "girl who lets me do these things." I'd done those things before, and would again, but apparently doing them with the same individual, from the same educational and class background, is closer to okay.

When boyfriend went away to college, I hooked up with this loser he'd introduced me to—a nice change from the skinny honor-society cohort. (I wasn't going to try maintaining the image.) His tattoos were complete trash: bats and spider webs lacing his thick upper arms, his left hand an alphabet soup of supposed women's initials. The hand made me, but I didn't make it. New Year's Eve found me cleaning coagulated cum off a coat in Susan's family room at 3 a.m.

Earlier he'd come up to me at the party. This one knew boyfriend, or could just guess how to entertain me when he asked how I was doing and I responded, with a shrug and a pull at my beer, "Bored." If it wasn't a possibility, I wouldn't have told him the truth. Sometimes it was just something to do.

"Still bored?" he asked. We went into the underbrush but stopped when two girls came out of the house. They saw our shapes and elbowed each other, sloshing keg beer out of plastic cups.

"Look, it's somebody passed out," the one with the white Mohawk snickered to her companion.

"They think that it's somebody passed out," he slurred, chin on my navel.

"Shut up," I hissed at him. He was thoughtful enough to eat before prodding and possessed a healthy lack of squeamishness around the menstrual taboo. "It's extra lube," he once shrugged, wiping off two fingers, painting a horizontal line on my underbelly. Quite chivalrous and considerate for the frightening sociopath he pretended at. Once he reminded me about the prophylactic before starting. His affectations met mine in comfortable symbiosis: Want to be a bad girl? Find a bad boy. If girls are supposed to package themselves and trade up, I ignored that aspect, denigrated it, traded down, made the boy into a fetish. Our symbiosis was very time-efficient: I could pursue my requisite interests, pad my little high school résumé, and convince myself that I was an obvious bad-ass in less than a hour a week. Plus, it was fun. This bad boy wasn't bad to me, but I didn't go visit him in juvie. I forget what he was in for. We weren't that close. But he didn't get busted until spring.

I was on another level now, I went after them: "bad boys" became a category. "Specimen" was another sub-set: these were the ones who were only supposed to consider girly girls, perfectly powdered pastel females with empty heads and 'O' mouths and big hair, boys who were notably athletic or more conventionally attractive than myself. "Travelers" composed the third group: boys just passing through, so I wouldn't have to be concerned with seeing them again. Acquiring the boys was fine. The act itself was enjoyable. The aftermath was always awkward. The kiss and pet is beforehand: then, you just right yourself and your clothing and face the light of day with an attempt at discretion and walk off in opposite directions, eyes away, or a defiant stare. So you live as the target of the smirk and snicker. What of it? Fuck them. They wouldn't respond if they didn't want to, too.

That New Year's Eve was spring-like in warmth. Once the chicks tripped back into the house, we moved to a more secluded location, temporarily replacing clothing to step through brambles. He held down the barbed wire of a fence so that I could climb over. He was drunk, an antiseptic whiff of gin over my head, but it didn't take long either way. Whipped the rubber off, and there was a white splotch on the black wool coat that served double-duty as a blanket. I spat on a paper towel in the family room and scraped it off. The band in the video was wearing magenta satin jackets. Probably singing some love song, but I don't remember.

I tried to convince myself that I had enlisted in some army against the double standard, a foot soldier for equal opportunity endorphins, new recruit for the fuck infantry, proof positive that girls can play as hard as boys, take as much and give as little. But why did it never seem to play out that way? I considered some of my colleagues. Petra Lawrence had hickeys on the insides of her thighs and had recently been woken up from a dream of sex, by sex: a male friend had climbed in the window. "Hey, guess what?" she said one Thursday, between swigs of tequila in the parking lot of the Sherwood Boys' and Girls' Club, "The band wants me to go to Detroit with them." What a surprise. That was thirteen years ago, and now I wonder how she's doing, if she's okay. I was blessed with a healthy portion of fear, an innate interest in self-preservation despite my lapses. I knew how good I had it with a safe suburban home, some structure, the hoops to jump through and the eventual reward of college. No need to blow it just because the folks didn't want the libido in the house. Keep It Out of the House.

Only certain options for sexual activity were available to a girl like me. There weren't many males I liked to talk to, who were attractive, who would talk to me. Celibacy did not appeal. Nor did I want to deal with sex like a girl, pretending to ignore it, having no power, no control. This is the Catch-22 of femininity: If you stand still long enough, someone will try to do you. And while the self-nominated suitors are frequently repulsive, the only more insulting possibility is that no one tries at all.

Instead, it was taking care of business. There was a kind of touch I needed: rough, sexual, wanting—one that went on me and through me at the same time—and I went out to get it. Help scratching the itch that I couldn't quite reach. Just like one of the guys—but inverted, with tits. I had to pick them: by taking the initiative, I masculinized myself. Granted, taking the initiative didn't entail much. To put myself in the line of fire, I generally just had to sidle up and say "Hello," respond pleasantly to whatever inanities ensued—"I like your earrings"—and then stumble off to the assignation. I was not a pink spandex–encased, banana comb–wearing, peroxide-abusing Barbie wannabe. They were my experiment: I could control it. But if I used them, then the inverse obviously applied, and in what should logically be an equal exchange, I got the stigma.

Being easy is easy. If they're going to call you a freak, anyway, why not give them something to talk about? If you're not one of the girls, why worry about being a good one? I never wanted to make rally squad. We're still taught that some all-encompassing male will actualize us, define us, make us whole. To reject that, and be active, is to have your gender make you a pariah. Even years later, there was the odd harassing phone call at the university.

"I guess they were right when they called you a bitch, you whore."

"I guess they were right when they called you a slut, you bitch."

And as long as I'm willing to stand alone and get mine, I guess they're right.

THE SEVENTEEN YEAR TWITCH

 Karen Rosenberg

S andy asked the three of us to drip the grease from our pizza onto hers—she liked it extra greasy. As I pointed my slice over hers (at just the right angle so as not to lose the cheese), Erica said, "It was *incredible*. Fantastic. Incredible. I don't know what to say." Erica rubbed her fingers under her eyes to smudge her teal eyeliner just so, then checked her work in a small mirror.

"I've been waiting all day," Liz said. "I thought the lunch bell would never ring."

Erica took a long sip of grape soda and sighed.

"Erica, you promised you'd tell me. You promised."

Erica finally put down her soda and leaned in to whisper to Liz.

The four of us sat on a stoop near our junior high school. The way we sat—Erica and Liz on one step and Sandy and I below—I couldn't hear a thing. Except for Liz's "Oh my God, oh my *God,* oh my *fucking* God."

"No fair!" Sandy held her pizza carefully, so that the extra grease wouldn't run down her forearm.

Erica continued whispering.

Two years before, in fifth grade, Erica had been a large and awkward girl. We all felt bad for her during limbo when her breast nubs grazed the broom handle (though she didn't have a chance—I saw Jed and Sam lower the broom onto her breasts once, and that wasn't very nice, but who was going to tell the teacher?). But now, Erica was practically one of Them—the popular girls who leaned against cars and smoked cigarettes after school, the girls who swapped strawberry lip gloss and friendship pins. Erica had ten friendship pins—safety pins strung with beads and fastened around a shoelace—and I only had one.

Erica looked down at Sandy and me. "Derek says that springtime brings the most wonderful smells."

I smelled car exhaust, old piss and Erica's hair spray. Maybe springtime brings the most wonderful smells to *Little House on the Prairie,* I thought, but not Manhattan.

Erica took a deep breath and smiled. "Does either of you girls know what finger fucking is?"

"What?" Sandy's eyes grew wide.

Erica leaned down close. I smelled her grape soda. "It's when he puts his fingers inside of you, you know . . . "

I didn't know. Back in fifth grade, Andi Benjamin's mother came to talk to the girls about feeling ourselves *inside.* She brought diagrams and talked about taking extra time in the shower for the task. We laughed at her behind her back; the information was absurdly early and I at least had no intention of searching out anything so gross. But we were used to getting information early—and laughing. We all read *Are You There God? It's Me, Margaret* in second grade and *Forever* (with the penis named Ralph) in fourth. But Erica telling us about finger fucking in seventh grade wasn't funny.

Erica studied her nails. "Derek says he needs to do that to prepare me . . . "

"I bet it hurt." Sandy picked at her crust.

"Sure it hurt, but it was worth it. No pain, no gain . . . right, girls?"

The springtime sunshine suddenly seemed too bright. Three homeless men sat on a stoop across the street. I heard an ambulance rush down 8th Avenue.

I tapped Sandy on the shoulder. "Do you want the rest of my pizza? I'm not hungry anymore."

After school, I walked home trying to imagine Erica and Derek. Were they sitting or lying down? Did they keep the light on? If not, how could he see? Which finger did he use? Did he put it in quick like a toothpick in a baking cake, or did he wiggle it around? I was curious, but I couldn't shake that nauseous feeling that got me at lunch.

I hated the thirteen-block walk home from school. My mother had gotten Section 8 housing the year before, so we moved from a sleepy, residential street in Brooklyn to a nameless neighborhood in Manhattan. South of Hell's Kitchen, north of Chelsea, this new neighborhood stunned me with the number of men on the street. Lingering in doorways, pushing racks of fur down the street, ripping down old buildings, putting up new ones. They always had something to say.

Sexy Mama.

You've got a fine ass.

You know you want it.

You know what I could do to you?

I imagined what they could do to me. I hated their comments; they terrified me. But they became as natural as traffic lights and newspaper stands. I walked quickly, trying not to draw attention to myself.

A few months before Erica told us about finger fucking, I left the apartment to go to the subway station. Two men sucked air through their teeth as I passed. I kept walking. I crossed 8th Avenue and headed down a long block of crumbling office buildings and fur wholesalers. I saw a man watching me at the other end of the block. He bobbed his head up and down as if he were listening to music. It was only as I approached that I noticed he bobbed his head to the rhythm of my walk. It took twenty paces more to see that he was laughing at me. His gaze steady on my chest . . . my chest! His head following my breasts. As I passed him, he leaned in and whispered, "Baby, let me tame those titties for you." I was twelve years old.

And so it was that I got my first bra: not because Erica or Sandy or Liz had one, not out of excitement or because I wanted to act like a woman. It was because the men on the street let me know it was time. When I went with my mother to Macy's to buy my first bra—Warner's size 34A—I wasn't looking for something satiny or soft. I was looking for armor.

After I got my bra, I learned that if I walked fast and hard, with a stern face, that some of the men shut up. Other ones said,

Hey baby, give me a smile.

Honey, what's up your ass?

Bitch.

But the skills I learned to feel safe on the walk to school didn't serve me well once I got there. The popular girls were all boy crazy, experimenting with Wet N' Wild makeup, glitter nail polish and Sun-In hair lightener. Even though I went with Sandy and Liz to steal purple eyeliners from Woolworth's, I felt ambivalent about making myself up. I wanted friendship pins, popularity. But I also wanted to rush back to flat-chested fifth grade.

When I walked with my friends—safety in numbers—we routinely chorused "fuck you" to men who cat-called us, barely missing a beat in conversation. But we never talked about how they made us feel. Now that I live far from that Manhattan neighborhood, I see that it was a peculiar environment, heavy with the threat of violence. The wrong place to get breasts. At the time, though, I assumed it was all my fault. The comments, the lascivious stares, the butt pinches. I acted as if everything were perfectly fine, and, just like Erica, things would be *incredible* once I found a guy, the right guy.

My junior year in high school, I met Joey. He had soft curly hair and a lopsided grin. He talked about playing football, writing and his mother. He was leaving for college in a few weeks, and we said from the outset that we didn't want anything "serious." The first time he kissed me, in front of a Korean grocery, I hoped he wouldn't know that I had never kissed anyone before. He tasted like Crest and French fries. If he noticed my inexperience, he didn't mention it. I thought he was kind.

A week later we went for a walk through Washington Square Park. "Do you want to come over for a while? My mom will be away for hours." He drew out the word "hours," made it sound long as a day.

He had been telling me about his shoulder injury, how he had to give up football and everything. I knew that if I went to his apartment we wouldn't be talking about torn ligaments and Ace bandages anymore. I hesitated, then said, "Uh, sure."

"Great." He kissed me on the cheek.

In his apartment, we sat on a white couch. He leaned over to kiss me. *I've got to remember every detail,* I thought, *I can't wait to tell Marcy.* His cheek was rough with stubble. The couch smelled like dogs. The whir of the air conditioner covered the street noise.

"You're really beautiful, you know that?" Joey eased my shirt over my head. *Marcy's not going to believe this . . .*

He reached around to unclasp my bra. "Is this okay?" he asked. I nodded and smiled. A closed-lip smile that I hoped was both seductive and relaxed at the same time. A smile that said, "Sure, no big deal."

But then things started going wrong.

First, Joey's fingers got caught in my bra straps and he scratched me. Hard. Then I kicked the coffee table and spilled a glass of soda on the floor.

But I'm sure those small fumbles would have faded away in the rosy memories of that afternoon if it hadn't been for the biggest problem; the one for which neither Joey nor I was prepared.

I twitched.

Not graceful shudders or feminine shivers. No, these were full-on fish-out-of-water jerks. It happened the first time Joey leaned down to kiss my breast. Without warning, I felt a strong tickle in my lower back, then my body lurched forward. My breast slapped him in the mouth.

"Oh my god, I'm so sorry." I felt my face redden.

"Wow." Joey rubbed his lips. He tried touching my breasts, but after a moment I felt that same tickle in my back, and then I twitched. "Maybe you'd be more comfortable lying down." He put a pillow under my head and another under my knees. He kneeled down on the floor beside me. I tried to distract myself by looking at the irregular bumps on his stucco ceiling. Joey moved his hands around my neck and chest. Every time he touched my breasts, I twitched.

Joey, as I have mentioned, was a kind person, and I thought it was really wonderful that he didn't mention the obvious. That I had a very, very serious problem. Probably some sort of rare nervous disorder. Judy Blume never mentioned this, neither did Erica. In all of her movies, Molly Ringwald didn't twitch once.

"Here, let me help you on with your shirt," Joey said later. We drank Dr Pepper and he talked about the differences between college and high school football. I sat on the couch and he sat on the floor, with his legs crossed. Then I left his apartment. We saw each other a few times after that, always outside. Even though Joey never mentioned my problem, I was relieved when he left for college a few weeks later.

The next year, when I was seventeen, I fell in love. Christopher and I met in ceramics class. At first I thought he was a freak. He was the only one who interrupted the teacher as he droned on about coil pots, raku and underglazes. In our first conversations, Christopher gestured wildly with his hands full of clay, making bad jokes. I rolled my eyes and said, "Ha, ha" in as much of a monotone as I could muster. But outside school he calmed down. He told me that he hated school and that he spent his time studying China and Chinese. While the rest of my schoolmates prepared to go to college, he prepared to move to Taiwan. This made him something of a rebel. He intrigued me.

When we eventually kissed, I prayed my twitch had gone away. We sat on the edge of Sheep's Meadow in Central Park. Kids played frisbee and hackeysack in the middle of the field. I made it through the first kiss without incident. But as soon as he edged his hands near my chest, I felt the tickle in my lower back, like a thousand icy feathers. It gathered strength like a sneeze. The next moment, I twitched. The more I tried to stop it, the more spastic my movements became.

I felt more comfortable with Christopher than with Joey, so we eventually talked about it. We were housesitting in Brooklyn for a married couple who lived in an old funeral home and sat on the roof one night, looking at rows of brownstones and wooden water towers. We'd been kissing; my back and chest had been twitching and jerking as usual. I finally leaned back on my hands.

"It's interesting," Christopher said.

"Interesting? What if it gets worse? Maybe I'll start convulsing when you just look at me."

"I might like that." He grinned.

"I'm not kidding. I think it's a disease or something."

"Yeah, probably. I give you another six months."

I gave him my best *this is serious* look and he stopped smiling. Taking my hand, he said, "I'm sure it's totally normal, really." He took a sip of root beer. "Totally normal," he repeated. "I bet there's even a name for it. I've got it—The Seventeen Year Twitch!" He burst out laughing.

His laughter was contagious, so I looked away. He didn't understand. Twitching wasn't a joke. I wanted to sigh into sex, with romantic, heavy-lidded eyes and a pliant, cooperative body. Wasn't that what I was supposed to do?

This conversation was one of the last we had before he moved to Taiwan. A few weeks after he left, I entered my own foreign country: college. The campus was small and green. I spent the first few months feeling like I lived in the middle of Central Park. Suddenly, everything I had taken for granted had disappeared. No great city, no neighborhoods, no babble of languages and foods. No men lingering on street corners. Students all seemed to walk in a daze from the dining hall to the library, from dorms to classrooms.

"You walk so fast," people told me.

"I'm from New York," became my stock answer.

"People move fast in the big city, right?"

"Yeah . . . I guess so." I didn't tell them that I moved fast by instinct, to stay safe. My hypervigilence was misplaced here. For the first time since I'd gotten breasts, no strange men yelled about them. In the absence of constant harassment, I had the space to think about it.

I realized that I had learned to view harassment as an annoyance, to be dismissed with a swat of the hand, a roll of the eyes. When a man yelled, "Nice titties," or "Fine ass," my mother told me to ignore him. When men catcalled her, she quickened her pace and grabbed my hand. She drilled me in safety rules: Walk down the center of the sidewalk, so no one can snatch you into a building or car. Never ask a man for help. Ride next to the conductor in the subway . . . the list went on. I thought harassment wasn't supposed to affect me any more than smog, traffic or garbage in the gutters. But of course it did. I began to struggle consciously with the contradiction between my intense attraction to individual guys and my distrust of men in general.

Meanwhile, I had come to accept my twitch, to some extent. In what felt like a tremendous bout of maturity, I understood that many people had, well, quirks. I had read "Dear Abby" throughout childhood and could draw solace from the husband who wrote in, complaining that his wife farted like a fiend every time they had sex. Or the woman who pulled out her eyebrow hairs, one by one, as she slept. My nervous miswiring wasn't any worse than those. I mapped my twitching trigger points and firmly guided guys' hands away from them. I noted that the twitch lost its edge when the rest of my body was focused on pleasure.

But I still felt dramatically behind. I also knew the twitch lurked just under my skin, like a temporarily dormant virus. Things would have been easier for me if I had ignored the pressure to catch up to the other girls (or *women,* as we had mysteriously yet emphatically become in the summer between high school and college). Though I knew I wasn't ready for sex, I didn't feel confident enough in myself or my body's timeline to hear sex talk without feeling worried that there was something wrong with me.

We seemed to separate ourselves into two camps, those who had done it and those who hadn't. Those who stood firmly in the first spoke to us virgins with an authoritative nonchalance that both impressed and intimidated me. One evening, Becky studied her beer bottle and tried to make an accurate comparison between its size and the size of her boyfriend's penis. She pointed high on the neck of the bottle and grinned. "You know," she said, leaning back in her chair. "It got a lot better after about the hundredth time or so."

A hundred times! It felt like junior high school all over again. Except the conversations had come so disturbingly far from fingers. To swallow or not to swallow? Sponge versus diaphragm? Was he good? Was he big? Becky told me not to stress about it, that one day it would happen to me too. Her tone, confident and patronizing as a babysitter's, did little to settle my anxieties. Elaine didn't help, either. My sophomore year she taped a few sheets of notebook paper into a large square and charted everyone who had gotten together. Intercourse wasn't required to make the chart, so my name appeared on a couple of dead-end offshoots. Some people were like suns, with rays pointing out in all directions. At the end, Elaine discovered that practically everyone at our small college was connected sexually. "Even me and you," she announced cheerfully.

Secret flings didn't exist on our thimble-sized campus—someone was bound to spot you stumbling back to your dorm room in the gray pre-dawn hours, and people gossiped as freely as if they were talking about the weather. My freshman dorm had a room in the basement dubbed the Fuck Room, complete with a stained twin mattress, heavy beige curtains and a stale, vaguely sweet odor. I'm not sure how the information got disseminated, but we all knew who visited that room as sure as if a sign-up sheet were tacked to the door.

My junior year I took a semester off and moved to Ecuador. I decided I wanted to do "real work," in the "real world." I didn't have a firm idea what either one of those things meant, but I knew for certain that college had begun to feel decidedly unreal.

I moved to Cuenca, a small Andean city where I found volunteer work on a drinking water and latrine project. The center of town had narrow cobblestoned streets and old buildings with ornate facades and wrought iron balconies. An enormous cathedral flanked the main plaza. Indigenous women with strands of golden beads circling their necks sold everything from avocados to hats to richly dyed sweaters. Men appeared suddenly by my side and seemed ready to follow me for hours if I wanted. I never relaxed with these instant companions, though I often enjoyed their conversation. One of the rare times men yelled after me was at the public university in Quito. I was walking with another foreigner, a woman with pale skin and bright red hair. We heard the men behind us and quickened our step. But we soon realized that they yelled not about our breasts or butts. "Capitalist! Imperialist! Yankee Go Home!" were their slogans.

The one man I was interested in didn't try to talk to me at all. He stood by himself, leaning against the side of a building and looking up at the sky. We were at a party for a tiny museum on the banks of the Tomebamba River, in Cuenca. Ribbons of white lights laced the trees outside, casting windy shadows on the guests. Girls carried trays with small plastic cups filled with hot drinks that smelled like rubbing alcohol and cinnamon. I coughed each time I took a sip.

He stared at the sky and I stared at him. He had pale, flawless skin and raven black hair. He wore jeans, a white T-shirt and a black leather jacket. He absentmindedly ran his hand through his thick hair. I downed a second drink (coughing less this time) and walked up to him. I don't remember what I said— my pick-ups were awkward enough in English, let alone Spanish. His name was Rodrigo and he was a student a year older than I. We talked for a long time, leaning against the building. I listened to the rush of the river under the chatter of the other guests. It was a cool night and soon Rodrigo offered me his jacket. It smelled like leather and incense. I was giddy.

By the time he kissed me, two extremely long weeks after I met him, my entire body ached for him. We stood at a street corner and he reached over and brushed his lips across mine. I took his hand. Instead of walking me home, he led me to a small, deserted shrine on a hillside. We found a dark spot and started making out in earnest. Every so often, Rodrigo would draw my attention to the sky, pointing out constellations I pretended I could pick out from the dazzling pinpricks of light. It was only when we quietly stood up and brushed the dirt off our clothes that I realized I hadn't twitched at all.

Although Rodrigo didn't stand out physically (except for his good looks), he was different from anyone I had met in Ecuador. It wasn't only that he didn't try to charm me with awful metaphors comparing my body parts to tropical fruits. He didn't have a strong need to assert his masculinity, which I found shocking and incredibly attractive. He saw himself like a bird, perched on a branch high above the cultural world of his peers.

I was completely smitten. If the cliché "love is blind" is too extreme, something less catchy like "love is visually impaired" or even "love needs glasses" works. Because if my love had had glasses, I would have realized from the outset that he was a bit odd. And I wouldn't have been so crushed when we finally admitted that we weren't going to ride off into the sunset together. But that's a different story. Suffice it to say that when we met, I felt like I had finally found the true love that I had heard so much about. The kind of love that knocks you down like a strong wave.

"Wow, it still feels strange," Rodrigo said one afternoon, running his hand through his hair as we sat on the banks of the river.

"Strange?"

"To have all this hair. I shaved my head for all the years I was with Krishna."

I had a vision of orange-robed young men trying to press thin books into my hands outside the New York subway. "You don't mean Hare Krishna, do you?"

Rodrigo smiled, obviously pleased. "Exactly." He was one of the very few Ecuadorians to reject Catholicism and join the Krishnas. He used to wake at 4:00 a.m. to meditate, work in their restaurant and read the Bhagavad Gita. He eventually left because he found out that the local Krishna leadership was corrupt. "But I still subscribe to many of the concepts and ideas," he said.

We walked from the river to the hillside shrine where we first kissed. "I don't want to scare you," he told me in his slow and even Spanish. "But we were destined to meet."

"Destined?"

"That's right. Because we knew each other in another lifetime."

My eyebrows inched up my forehead and I bit my lip to keep from laughing. I must have inadvertently conveyed a look of deep interest because he launched into a long explanation, most of which I don't remember. Then we started making out. I wanted to press my entire body against his. When he finally whispered, "You believe me, don't you?" I nodded without hesitation.

My twitch sometimes reappeared, but Rodrigo didn't pay much attention. "The body is merely a temporary home," he reassured me. Though I wasn't sure what I thought about reincarnation, I appreciated his way of thinking about things. He never took mainstream culture too seriously. His concerns rested with genderless souls. This made him an ideal companion in a male dominated society.

A couple months into the relationship, we took a twelve-hour bus ride from Cuenca to Quito. A brightly colored statue of the Virgin Mary stood on the wall above the bus driver. Pasted next to the Virgin was a silver glitter decal of a bikini-clad woman with breasts hanging down like water balloons. Two bumper stickers lay next to her. One decried the evils of mothers-in-law. The second showed a picture of a large screw attached to a pair of hairy male legs. The screw chased a donut-shaped nut, attached to a pair of skinny women's legs. The text read, "Please, please, not without oil!"

After about six hours of staring at the display, I was furious. "This is sick!" I told Rodrigo. He didn't disagree. I went on about the conflicting messages about sex and soon I was telling him about my experiences with harassment as a girl in New York City. He responded with an incredulity that I have seen in "good men" many times since then and now find annoying. But on that bus ride I appreciated his respectful shock. I told him how growing up I thought harassment was a permanent part of the landscape and that changing the environment was out of my control.

It was the first time I had told this to a man. I felt so grateful for his support that I overlooked his bizarre comments. He explained that he coped with an insane society by practicing astral projection. He tried to fly his soul, kite-like, on the edge of the universe. But, he confessed, so far his soul had only made it as far as his kitchen: and only on a few occasions, in the dead of night.

We had another few hours on the bus, and the promise of launching my soul skyward did little to temper my agitation. So Rodrigo asked me to close my eyes, and he gently led me in a guided meditation, telling me to allow the roar of the ocean to carry my anger and unrest away.

The anger and unrest didn't stay away for long. When I returned to college, I started learning about feminism. I began to gather words to describe my physical reality growing up. For the first time, I labeled harassment as a form of sexual violence. I began to draw connections between the men who hissed "nice titties" and my friends who had been raped. I realized that my experiences were on a continuum with sexual assault. With this perspective, I finally began to confront my fears directly.

During this time, my fantasy was to ice men from my sexuality altogether. I secretly envied friends who came out as lesbians, figuring that the anguish of telling mom and dad was a small price to pay for the rewards of ignoring men and prescribed gender roles. But the frustrating reality was that I wasn't attracted to women. It took me quite a while to realize that I didn't need to sleep with women in order to learn from women who did.

I remember a late-night conversation with my friend Lucinda. We whispered in a dorm lounge, sprawled on old couches. "The first time Mary and I kissed, it was like our bodies fit together perfectly," she said. "There were no rules and no expectations. We just made it up as we went along." She talked about playing with masculine and feminine roles, changing and exploring. While I wrote obtuse papers about the social construction of gender, she actually understood the concepts well enough to integrate them into her life. Eventually, in time, I found the same giddy sense of adventure that Lucinda described. I got there fastest when I stopped thinking about how I was supposed to act when I was with men.

Then, without warning or fanfare, the twitch disappeared for good. Along with acne, braces and teal eyeliner, it passed with adolescence. Seventeen year twitch indeed. Was it merely an odd neurological quirk that randomly righted itself, or something more?

Maybe I just have to console myself that all of those lurches, jerks and tremors happened for a reason. That those teenage humiliations, when I was as smooth and as svelte as a carp on land, had a higher meaning. It's a strong possibility. But I do believe that bodies are strange, wonderful, awkward machines. Mine manufactured an electric fence in an effort to protect me from harm, until I felt safe and firmly in control with men. My twitch was trying to keep me in charge. In its own weird way.

How Do You Do That Thing You Do?

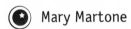 Mary Martone

Names have not been changed, because I'd like to consider this a thank-you letter.

In my fourth-grade Girl Scout troop, I knew more dirty jokes than anyone else did, and I worked at my craft. I made a careful list, and kept it tucked in my uniform pocket—which is where my mother found it one day as I was heading out the door to Saint Bridget's. In a move both embarrassing and devastating to that day's performance, she kept it.

Despite my early facility with words about sex, I had no idea how to make it happen. Some people are thrust by their bodies into the wild unknown, and discover truths to which they must later put words. Other folks need a little more than the faint sirens lilting in the distance. I desperately needed role models to sharpen the pictures in my head, to spell them out into my ear and, ultimately, to kick my ass out the door.

I didn't understand how I was supposed to get someone else interested in doing it with me (and secretly, why anybody bothered). Having read *A Tree Grows in Brooklyn,* I knew that some strange men with pale penises attacked girls in dark hallways, some married men liked women with rouged nipples and sometimes people had sex on the job. Judy Blume's *Forever* informed me that boys name their penises. We had fun passing these tidbits around in study hall, but had anyone I'd known done such things? Nancy Drew was more my kind of gal. She went off by herself and drove her own car. Ned might have ridden next to her and lent her his jacket, but he never tried anything. I found that to be a comforting reflection of my reality.

By the time I started high school, I was pretty sure I would never be having sex. I spent my nubile adolescence volunteering at the library or with my church youth group. My friends and I did the usual sneaky teen drinking, but we were mystified about what you did when you got to the "I might just do something crazy" stage. So we talked. And talked. Held apart by fear, self-consciousness and raw awkwardness, we whirled in discrete orbits, never touching. The sun of this anxious, wobbling universe was Maggie.

Maggie was one of the only girls less popular than I. After devoting my freshman year to keeping her down (to ensure my enviable status as second lowest on the totem pole), I realized how great she was. She was smart and funny, but best of all she didn't give a good goddamn about what other people thought about her. Scrawny and pale, she didn't play down either quality by wearing an enormous down coat most of the year. She peered out at the world through heavy glasses and wore Mary Janes before they were the order of the day. She was the Anti-Slut. Her house was the vortex of our social circle, despite her schizophrenic mother who with no particular instigation would occasionally explode into screams and throw us all out.

Maggie and I would lie still in our beds, whispering endlessly across the darkness about The Topic: whether or not she should have sex with her boyfriend. She wasn't worried about whether or not she wanted to, or if her parents would approve, but whether or not it was a sin. And if so, at what point it technically became one. I assured her that I couldn't imagine that god cared, and that for all the hell-time a person could earn, having sex seemed like an unlikely way to rack up points. She came to the same conclusion herself, headed off into the unknown, and I got to hear the stories. Her boyfriend went down on her before they had intercourse: I was impressed, and thought that sounded pretty cool. They did it on a leather couch: I thought that would be a very nice thing to do. She told me he had an uncut dick, and that she cried when she first saw it because it looked weird and scary: I concurred that dicks seemed a little weird and scary. I learned about going down on a guy, and liked hearing about the elaborate machinations required to find suitable places for sex. Pete would ride his bike thirty miles from the next town over to be with her, and I made a mental note that I'd appreciate that brand of enthusiasm. I was proud of Maggie. I admired her. Most of all, the fact that someone I knew was getting some meant it was in the realm of the conceivable for me.

By the time I started college, I was wordlessly sure I was a homo. Over the previous few years I'd occasionally found myself thinking, "I should sleep with a boy first." I never wondered who came next. In September, a high-school friend called me in a panic because she saw her two roommates making out. I thought, "Well, that shows how much you know about me." I was officially out to myself. By October, I was disgusted with each weekend's identical routine: have "cocktails," spend hours putting on makeup and trading outfits, wander around looking for a party, drink too much and watch the girls I came with make out with guys. I'd inevitably wake up to an incoherent, sobbing roommate puking in the trash can.

I started spending more and more time at the studio, where I discovered my salvation in Carmine. He read me *Metopolitan Life,* showed me David Hockney and played me Laurie Anderson. He taught me to dance, and showed me what a great thing drinking could be if you did it just the right amount. He told me that if you could dance well, you'd be good in bed. He told me that it was worth driving to New York for sex. He did that a lot. He was my first friend who just happened to be a big fag. I couldn't fathom being so at ease with my words and my body, but imagined that if I ever were, I might make a pretty good gay man.

I slept in his room, in his pajamas, and enjoyed the confusion it created. I liked wearing his clothing. I felt comforted by his smell, and the protection that being chosen by someone so odd and powerful conferred upon me. Curled against a gay man's back, this was as close as I'd been to another person's body. I liked it, and was relieved by the mandatory boundary. I was close to where sex happened, but comfortably free of obligation. In the safety of this warm limbo, I began to feel like a potentially sexual person.

The next year I transferred, and found myself compulsively writing *I'm a lesbian* on scraps of paper, then balling them up and throwing them out. I couldn't imagine that there were no other lesbians at my women's college, but damned if I could meet any. I followed a woman home from class one day because she sat in front of me and smelled mysterious and looked nasty in a way that made the tops of my thighs shiver. As I stood behind an oak tree and watched her disappear into her house, the spell broke and I felt ridiculous. I waited a minute, then, embarrassed, walked home.

Marianne, the sexiest straight girl I'd ever met, lent me a copy of *Rubyfruit Jungle.* It was full of facts. Apparently, sometimes cheerleaders were lesbians.

Who knew? I learned about role-playing, and cheating, and women who slept on mattresses on the floor (which was very lesbian). To augment what I'd learned about men from my junior-high reading, it was made apparent to me that lesbians occasionally enjoyed having grapefruits thrown at their naked bodies until they came.

I felt like a doll with painted-on underwear. Logically, I would have been a prime candidate for some serious digital self-love, but I just couldn't care long enough to make it work. *Our Bodies, Ourselves* instructed me amply on every aspect of masturbation except why I'd want to do it. There seemed to be no sex in me. I approached my body with all the knowledge and interest I had in, say, a Volkswagon.

Then it all got blown around. Chester transferred in my junior year and set the whole campus on end. "Whose brother is that?" I knew she wasn't anyone's brother. In fact, she was the kind of not-brother I had a pretty deep longing to hang out with, though I hadn't known it until right then. We got on famously, and she was able to worm it out of me in about two seconds that I was some sort of queer. Meeting more people in a week than I'd met in a year, she was as out as it got, and inspired that level of honesty in everyone she was near. So in pretty short order I was out too.

Chester was incredibly kind to me, and let me into the secret corners of her life. At two in the morning there would be a knock on my door, and she'd stumble in giggling, fucked up, with that month's or evening's girl, and they'd sit on the end of the bed and tell me where they'd been, and where they were off to next. The next day occasionally featured remorse, but I envied the life she was devouring. I read her books. She told me stories about the music festivals with nothing but wall-to-wall women, golf carts and tempeh, whatever that was. Women visited her: women who had that same mysterious smell, who came from a place I ached to live.

The door had been flung open, but I was still on the porch. The proximity of sex slapped me so hard my head spun around. I wanted it. For the first time ever I was jealous. I had never seen anyone having sex I wanted to be having. Now people I knew were doing it, a lot, with other people that I wouldn't mind having sex with. I saw real live lesbians in bed, and I knew what they were going to do when I left.

At this point, sexual opportunity presented itself. There was someone, dangling ripe from the girl tree, and Chester coached me. I wasn't particularly attracted to this girl. That didn't matter, she said: You need to do it with somebody the first time. I was attracted to someone else. So what? I was never going to have a shot at her. I made the honorable and cowardly choice: I didn't do it. I wasn't interested in her, which meant it wouldn't be fair or nice. Frankly, the thought of getting up close and personal with someone I didn't want made me feel a little sick. Another woman asked me out soon afterwards, and again I said no, stepping over the invisible line between "late bloomer" and "socially retarded."

Fortunately, the Fates, in utter disgust, threw me into the roiling stew of steamy homosexuality that was the National Gay and Lesbian Task Force. No one could have been luckier than I was to get a job like this right out of college. I said the word "sodomy" for money. I got to correspond, longhand, with mentally ill people and prisoners. I learned how to identify a letter bomb. But best of all, I got to work with the most pro-sex people I've ever known.

I was twenty-one, and sopped it up like a sponge. These people, not much older than I, were strong and smart and sexy. They were desirable and desired. Sometimes they had lovers. Sometimes they just got lucky. The best? They talked details. Each weekly staff meeting started with a go around to see who was getting it, with whom and how it was going. I begged off week after week until they noticed and extracted the appalling truth from me. I was humiliated, but no longer afraid of being discovered. And they were full of useful information and encouraged me to go get some. Some encouraged me to get some with them. I politely declined, pleading observance of good work boundaries. That proved wise: one of my first lessons at work was that no one wants to see footsie at the staff meeting.

They seemed so sure of themselves, but I never felt patronized. I tried to strike a graceful balance between blathering idiot and tongue-tied idiot, and usually ended up being kind of, well, an idiot. I was young, and they were patient. I learned how to craft an argument without histrionics. I learned to brave finding and disposing of the dead rats in the store room. I learned to check with Sue before I told any woman on the phone whether or not she was "in."

Sue was the master of laid-back appraisal and incisive approach. She was also a bottomless font of information on technique. I learned about strapping on a dildo from an article she wrote. I tried not to think about the fact that the illustrations were photos of her personal ass. She was not the only teacher, of course. A bunch of us once spent a good twenty minutes huddled together, folding and curling our fingers in on themselves, practicing the best way to get a fist into a woman. I made a mental note to myself to do that a lot when presented with the opportunity. I learned that handcuffs were crappy for bondage, and scarves were hard to untie quickly. And, in a brief conversation that has stuck with me to this day, it was impressed upon me that it was lazy to just do a little perfunctory breast sucking, then go down on someone. Sex had a million more flavors than that, and you should rise to the challenge. I promised myself I'd get right on that as soon as I conquered the basics.

Sue and Urv were pals from long before they'd started this stint together, and in an endless conversation that had been going on for years, they hashed out the probable particulars of who was butch and who was femme and what that meant, particularly in relation to who could do what with whom. When I said I didn't think I was either, they laughed. When I said, well then, I'm probably butch, they laughed even harder. Fortunately, they were there to clarify the mitigating qualities of being a top or a bottom, which supposedly further elucidated how I'd interact with the ladies. I was leery of this pigeonholing. How could they tell what I'd be like in bed? Over time, infuriatingly, their prediction turned out to be right on. I'm a femme top, like I'm a Virgo: both completely baseless and eerily accurate descriptors.

Once Sue and Urv clipped on tit clamps in a staff meeting, strung together like they were jumping a battery. Urv was always doing three things at once, and one of them was frequently explaining to a girlfriend that she was busy but she'd be right there. She would describe her dates, and seemed so good at choosing restaurants and clubs and wine and girls. I watched and planned on being smooth and treating the ladies right.

The boys, echoing Chester's earlier wisdom, encouraged me to just shut up and fuck someone. I read *Drummer* and *Blueboy,* and realized that sex wasn't really that mysterious. It was just two people showing each other a good time, frequently in a bunkhouse with chaps, but no pants. As everyone in the office scrambled to grab the mail first on the days that they arrived, I learned that dirty could be good. And that you didn't have to fall in love to have sex, especially if you were already Wessoned up and on a wrestling mat.

I loved hanging out with the guys. Once again, it was easier because I never felt like I was failing to perform some obligatory cruise. In one particularly illuminating friendship, one of the loveliest, sexiest men I've ever known showed me that what you perceived yourself to be is not necessarily who you are— sometimes you are so much better. He was handsome, brilliant, talented, charming, hysterical and incredibly gracious, and saw none of that in himself. I realized that I needed to look more deeply at what I was really presenting to the world.

Kimberly and Ivy and PJ were fat and sexy, and made it clear that some women preferred it that way. They teased me and flirted with me and as I said no, and no, and no, I became able to imagine myself being desired. PJ could (and did) spend quite a bit of time vividly describing the substantial circumference of her girlfriend's nipples, and grilling everyone else on size-based details. The bigger, the better. And that went for what went in, too. I saw PJ go from someone who joked about lobbying to pass *more* laws against anal sex to someone who regaled me with more details than I needed on her training series of buttplugs, affectionately known as Number One, Number Two and Number Three. Apparently all it had taken was the introduction of a partner that she was willing to let near her butt. We would come in on a Monday morning to her cheerful announcement that she had conquered Number Two. There would be congratulations all around. We were all stretching ourselves.

Because I had a queer job, I had to come out to my family posthaste. In the bloody aftermath, I realized that they were revolted and horrified not just by the idea of me following an unsanctioned path, but by the admission of anything sexual. We never talked about sex. No one in my family ever visibly dated. The fact that I was *any*sexual was disgusting and inappropriate. I was made to suffer. The most pathetic part was that I was being punished for something I wasn't even getting to enjoy.

I went on and I weathered incompatible housemates, bad pornography and several terrible haircuts. I lived alone. I took better care of my body, and finally figured out "petting the bunny." (Solution? Lube, fantasy and more than ten seconds of nonchalant poking. Go figure.) I felt as peaceful and comfortable with myself as any twenty-five-year-old virgin could. Of course, the swollen strain of simultaneously being and not being something was no longer just embarrassing: it was suffocating. So I decided to make it happen.

I'd been asking girls out with no tangible success. I'd been quite confident that Tonight Was the Night several times, only to find out that 1) we really *were* just housesitting, 2) she didn't think of me that way, and, of course, 3) "That's so flattering! No." I finally listened to everyone who said I needed to weigh the odds of imminent blinding mutual love against the importance of my continued mental health. So I identified a cutie I liked who might be up for a romp. I propositioned her, and she said yes.

After a mere week of anxiety-ridden dicking around, I scrubbed up with some rosemary soap, went home from a party with her and that was that. A mind-blowing, time-blurring that. I wasn't thinking about everything I'd learned, but I couldn't help benefiting from all of the time I'd had for the lessons to soak in. I felt happy and relaxed with my body and hers, and not mystified about how it all worked. Everything was better than I could have imagined, largely due to the discovery of something no one had mentioned. One of the most righteous things was how you felt when you did someone right. That rocked my ass off.

And then she said the sweetest thing: "I thought you said you'd never done that before." If that was a lie, Annie P., god love you for saying it.

Some advice didn't come in time. After I gingerly extricated myself from that first relationship as it got way too intense, far too quickly, Sue told me, "Martone! Never, ever, sleep with a girl two days in a row unless you want her to think you're serious." What did I know? I was just happy getting it 24/7. Why stop? I discovered why as I squirmed out of the situation and saw how capable I was of hurting someone. I started learning my own lessons.

Maggie and Chester are still two of my best friends, and they still stretch my ideas of what I should expect from myself. This spring Chester flew to Africa to find out if someone still loved her. She said she had no idea what she'd find, but she knew that if she didn't go, she would never know what could have happened.

Maggie has filled out into a rose of a woman, who still deeply loves her best friend, Pete, even as she rests, a continent away, in bed with her girlfriend. Sex vines itself through her adventures, and now I have something to say back to her. We live far apart, but when we have the luxury of time together, again we lie in our beds, whispering endlessly across the darkness about all of it—sex and love and getting it, and having gotten it, and where it all has gotten us.

My Punany Diva

 Geraldine Mitchell

Cocks and my black experience do not make for a very sensual combination. When it's me and him, those moments that should count as afterglow give way to an interminable, inescapable uneasiness. Nearing thirty, a high-yellow half-Jamaican middle-class girl, I am conscious of every thrust's potential consequence. I must take my sexual cues from some Punany Diva whose acquaintance I have not yet officially made. I call her PD for short and we're supposed to meet up sometime soon—soon in terms of a lifetime, that is. I have some ground to cover before I catch up with her.

She's the girl who has all the men she wants. Black, white, Latin, Israeli, Pakistani, Asian, other. She owns and loves her own body, knows herself. She gets down on her knees, opens her thick mouth for any man who happens to make her tingle, never feeling subservient. She puts her hand down her ample blue jeans whenever wherever she wants to. She gives herself up to that wonderful coital shudder with abandon, with or without a partner.

Her form falls somewhere between Angela Bassett and Jennifer Lopez, all curves and muscle and strength and lusciousness. PD's a tough cookie. She can be serious as a Peek Frean, but when she laughs, it feels like an earthquake is getting underway, about to swallow her whole.

She relaxes in a post-penetration stupor never giving a rat's ass about her imaginary first child's identity crisis. Or about the past hour of frivolity that could have been spent making her way in this world. Or about . . . or about . . . or about . . . anything other than pleasure for the sake of pleasure.

No. I don't know that girl yet. But when I do, we'll be tight. I can tell.

I do know a lot of other ladies.

I know Audre Lorde. But I like boys and have never been much of a poet myself. I know Ntozake Shange. But I don't know above 125th Street hardly at all and I can't hardly dance. I'm well acquainted with Terry McMillan. Yes, TM and I hang out every now and again, mostly during the summer when I have time alone on the beach and I don't mind getting those small grains of sand between the pages as the wind starts up. However, I'm not a Buppie.

At least not yet. And frankly, I'm not much of a reader.

I am good in bed. I used to date, and I use the term loosely, a dark chocolate baldy who should have been perfect for me. We were too the same, whatever that means.

Our sex was comprised of two modes. The first was stumbly fumbles, where his onetime-football-player's body would nearly crush mine and I would come after him or not at all. We had our own little rituals that would approximate those feelings they emote on the big or small screens.

Mostly, the model we followed came from something we caught on television or at the movies. When it got dull, we followed the map set out by the "dream factories" out West. But, for the most part, in their world, sex happened between two malnourished blondes in an apartment the size of the Met. The female of the media species is twig thin with tiny little thighs and enormous breasts. The male has sinewy arms and a stomach that ripples. The two trade pleasantries, tell each other how in love they are or use their own existential crises as pillow talk. They have the time for this, you see, because they don't have to pull down cash, don't have bosses and never seem to need to use a restroom.

Infrequently, in the blue glow, or on the silver screen, he and I would find black people to mimic. They had dark purple lips like ours and more familiar shapes and moves. It was difficult to locate them.

So me and him, my chocolatey never-meant-to-be, we mostly had to improvise. We did. Poorly.

His heft added to the weight of those Afro-American legends that danced in my head as I thought of something, anything other than the moment at hand. It got so heavy, I made Atlas look arthritic.

Then there was the second mode: all that scary shit that he pulled somewhere from the porno section of his mind, the kind of stuff that would leave me checking to see if he had secretly installed a Camcorder under the damn night table it hurt so much. My throat had his fingerprints all over it, my upper thighs felt bruised and I would do a lot of gasping.

His head could be stubbly if he didn't take good care of it and it would scratch between the insides of my legs while his tongue poked around looking for the spot I had showed him so many times before with my own fingers. Smart as a whip he was, but damn if he could ever coordinate his mind and his mouth. The two were as separate as black from white or good girl from bad girl.

Yeah, I faked it a lot. So? That's not a crime. When he put himself inside of me, I would cringe or cry and pass it off as orgasm. Not good . . . not good.

But I stayed for years. I wanted that hint of beauteous in-and-out so badly. And besides, I had a job to do. Populate the world with smart beautiful black children and maybe someday be a good upstanding—yet perennially hip—wife.

I don't see PD out there yet. I see other women.

Lieutenant Commander Uhuru wore short skirts, a Supremes bob and knee-high leather boots. She kissed the captain of the *Starship Enterprise* but only under coercion by an alien force. Uhuru, God bless her Klingon-fightin' heart, didn't have a chance to flirt and tease Kirk like the other out-of-this-world women who came across the twenty-fourth century. But she was on almost every episode of that sci-fi show. Unlike the white ephemera.

I didn't know it at the time, but as I watched that first forced interracial smooch—thanks to the miracle of syndication—I inadvertently learned something. Uhuru couldn't have sex with the strapped-in captain because she was like me. Black and much too busy trying to prove herself, run the whole goddamn ship and represent the race to busy herself with—that word again—pleasure. She was beautiful and sexy, but she didn't know it.

I picked up somewhere that beautiful sexiness is linked to luxury. Uhuru didn't have that. I don't have that. The time, the means, the confidence to say I want that climax sheerly for the splendor, the shudder, the big O-ness of it. The pleasure of it.

Pleasure. Leisure. They're linked by that four letter word, "sure." I'm not cocksure or cuntsure because that takes an undeniable certitude that is reserved for sorts who can wear pasties on top of their handfuls of breasts and feel just fine.

I see Lil' Kim with her pants unzipped almost to the furry garden that you *know* she has down there and a big tattoo circling her navel. She gets what she wants and she has no fear, that Kim of ours. No fear that when she gets what she wants—after a few gyrations and a mouth full of sex talk—people will say she's whoring. The girl's body, her mind, her voice point toward that one thing: the act. But she's not worried about her self, her soul as currency. She shouldn't be.

Because there is nothing wrong with getting something in return, right? As long as it's not cash money but in another form. Dinner, a movie, an ear to chew on, companionship, a compliment. Those are legal in exchange for an hour or two of your own time, and they're necessities, not luxuries. I have to make it on my own somehow and I have to use what I have. I have a face that can make men smile and a body that begs for strong man hands to manhandle it. I need to make my way in this world and I need to do it with what God gave me. By any means necessary.

Waaay back, I can spy Erykah Badu with her pristine African queen outfit, smiling with ankhs dangling from her ears and her neck. She is the epitome of confidence, telling Tyrone where to get off and shuttling back and forth between the Ivory Coast and Brooklyn. Her head's on straight, straighter than mine even under the weight of that humongous head wrap. How does she do it? I don't know and were I to meet her, I'd be afraid to ask.

She'd be angry if I told her that every time a man catches my eye at the supermarket, the laundry, on the subway, crossing the street, I case him out for his fatherhood potential. This is even before I've judged the look he may throw. You know, the look you get when someone's looking at your ass or trying to figure out if that's a weave or just taking stock of your almond eyes.

Before I check between his legs, or into his face, I make little notes. Glasses? Poor eyesight for the kid. Books in his hand? Ahhh, yes. An intelligent man. Scholarship for junior. Long fingers? Athletic progeny and even a side benefit for me, the girl who will lie underneath him as he runs those things all over my body.

Instead, I have three men that I sleep with on occasion and if you put them all together they would probably make one pretty good boyfriend. One colorless, amorphous lump of guydom. But for the most part I satisfy myself and wonder while I try to drift off to sleep if I wasted one of my precious eggs.

Where is that girl, PD? I told her to meet me around the corner from my apartment at about half past thirty-seven years old. Oh . . . okay. I see her now. PD's got some man on her arm, just like she said she would. No . . . I can't quite make out his face or the shape of his body or the texture of his hair from this distance.

From here, it looks like he's fondling her fingers with one hand and trying to cop a feel with the other. I can tell she likes it 'cuz she's laughing and they're heading into the park. That's just how she likes it. If I hurry, maybe I can catch up with her. Oops. I lost her. She and he disappeared behind the trees. But I'm not going to call the cops just yet. She looked as if she only had one thing on her mind. That's a good thing.

The Long Walk Home

⊛ Adrien-Alice Hansel

I was going to be a virgin forever. Fifth grade, small room, girls only. Sex ed. It's hot (or maybe that's my face) as we go around the room, reading the vocabulary words aloud. Funny, I think, counting down the word list to prepare for my turn, that I'll end up reading both "penis" and "vagina." My discomfort is obvious and very, very funny, because I'm the one the teacher calls on when something needs to be read. I'm that girl: long hair, bad skin, thick books. I'll get glasses in two years and complete the picture, but right now my arms are around my stomach and we're talking about "penetration" or something else clinical and mildly smutty. The hygienist, or whatever she is, notices and is sympathetic. "Don't worry, Adrien," she says. "You'll be a virgin until you're twenty-three."

The other girls laughed, anonymous in their relative sophistication, but I remember it as a kindness. I certainly cultivated the image, clothed myself in corduroy and wit and shunned the boys with the same ferocity they used to shun me. I found her prediction comforting. I was who I thought I

130

was, and who I was meant I didn't have to care about hair or boys or the countless betrayals and aspirations found on the cusp of adolescence. My concerns centered on rereading *The Lord of the Rings* and finding the area of a circle—not the circumference of my inarticulate hunger.

My childhood had been one of confusion, shame and retreat into an internal intellectual landscape. My mother's people were down country, two hours away, and every summer and most weekends, I slapped against the life I should be living, the life that could be mine. My father spent summers with us here, organic farming, when he was east on break from his professorial life in the Midwest. My mother came down weekends from the city. My parents chose this life when it fit them, raised my brother and me with our cousins to give us values, continuity. They didn't live together during the year, and finally divorced when I was in sixth grade. My father was secure, emotionally and financially. But I lived with my mother more, and her needs were less predictable. When I was in seventh grade, she married a man who lived half a mile from my grandparents' trailer, and visited him every weekend until his suicide two years later. She worked at a nonprofit company up in the city, dressed better than she earned and was always buying things we couldn't really afford. Or maybe we could, but she'd tell me we couldn't and I believed her. I tried to want less, to shrink myself to my perception of our world, hemmed as it was by a lack I was told was not mine, but that I had absorbed nonetheless.

What were mine were the jumble of memories, a fear of exclusion found in belonging to and in rejecting this world and middle-class expectations in a world that couldn't always follow through. My parents' assumption that I would go to college, the second woman in my family to do so. The Christmas my uncle gave his wife a doll, telling her it was the only child they'd be able to afford. The summer smell of their gas station: oil, dust, gasoline, candy bars melting against their wrappers and exhaust, sweet and lethal. Venison and Genny Light. Reading books my grandparents hadn't heard of. Never asking for food in anyone's house because what would they think about my home? The fear that ran through me every time my mother brought home something new, that we would grow to regret that decision. Everything we had represented something else we would not have. I knew too much, I knew the wrong things. Fearless to spiders, I gained a witch's reputation at my elementary school, where others' home lives were as desperate and government-subsidized as my own, though defined by a particularly urban poverty that was not mine.

I did not expect to belong to either world, rural or urban. I would shuttle between them with my culture of arrival and departure. I would be caught in transition, belong neither to the fifth-grade girls or the farm-raised cousins. We were just visiting, and I would always be the rich cousin, even when my mother was too unstable to work and we were living on Social Security from my stepfather's suicide. I split myself and my understanding, tried not to think too much about why I didn't fit anywhere. I escaped into books, into schoolwork, trying to forge another world which would be my success and revenge on the kids who mocked and hit me, took my books and gym clothes, laughed with an understanding that was foreign and exclusive.

So I wrapped myself in virgin's clothes, mute to my own desire, and found the words for everything but longing. There was the sixth-grade girl when I was in third grade. She was a dancer, and I watched her devotedly: front row at assemblies, harsh to my restless classmates; silent behind her on the bus, her hair slightly sweaty from rehearsal. I wrote her elaborate and anonymous poems, slipped them into her backpack while she talked with the bus driver. Because she was a dancer, because she was good. My fifth-grade teacher, Mrs. Fisher. Tall and beautiful, dark skin against darker hair. I thought she knew everything. She demanded more of me than anyone had and I never understood why I was surprised to meet her husband. My terrifying crush on my best friend, spinning huge strange worlds for her through junior high, staying up all night at group sleepovers, staring at the back of her hair and imagining ways to bridge the charged and casual distance between us. I could exhale, move closer and sleep all night within the scent of her shampoo, turn over and we'd touch knees—my hunger was specific and unknowing. There was Sara Forrest, a senior my first year of high school, who smelled of fresh bread and kale soup. She was the smartest girl I'd ever met and charmed me with talk of Vonnegut and Cubism. I humiliated myself for her every day, bringing her books and poems, sharing rides to protest the Gulf War, treasuring every story (she was afraid she'd mistake her pump soap for her pump toothpaste; I was afraid she would never mistake me for anyone), finding excuses to touch her hair, her arm, oblivious to my appetite for her friendship above anyone else's.

I met the girl who would be my first lover at the end of my first year of high school, the last week of school, leaving midday from the Earth Science Regents exam. So quotidian, our first meeting, at a friend's house where she was frying cheese sandwiches and coiling copper wire around and around itself. I remember the taste of the metal in the air, bloodlike, my hair smelling of grease as I left, aware of my body through space and not curious why. She happened to get my phone number and remembered to call me three months later when I returned from a summer spent with my father and friends from junior high. We talked for two hours, guarded but insatiable, and she called back. Five months and several excruciating sleepovers later, my lips moved to hers. It was a light turned on, my past snapping into perspective. It was the obvious end of my sentence, the word I had missed. It was desire.

I've been told that everything you will ever learn about a relationship can be read in the first time that you have sex—a microcosm of approach and consent, power and hesitation; I believe this. Her hands on me were desperate, searching. My body beneath hers, yielding and responsive. We entered the world of so many early-career lesbians, intense and self-contained, desperate for the recognition and radical wonder we found in the other's eyes and breath and flesh. Sixteen years of desert, and only her to slake me. Sex was new, dangerous in its intensity and range. Like walking on ice, I told her. A pleasure both daring and exquisite. She discovered my body, almost shameless, so new under her hands, and nothing like anyone mentioned in fifth grade. We were a delicate balance of hunger and fear—her eyes on mine in the library as she smelled her hands just in me; school vacations at her mother's apartment, leaving her bedroom to shower or eat; her fierce appropriation of my life, my time, my secrets.

The next three years were danger and desire, entwined with my hands in her hair. We barely touched in public. We went to movies, hungry hands in the dark, drunk as much with our deviance as with desire. She ran electric beneath my skin and caught my hand in the girls' bathroom, pushed my back against the door, breathless between bells. Holding our breath as we moved over and under each other, my mother in the kitchen below us, starting another renovation project that would never be finished—the door to the patio she would never build, the kitchen wall in piles of plaster and thwarted ambition. Her mouth swallowing my sound as her mother got ready to leave for the bar where she waitressed. Our bodies naked in a tent, Memorial Day, her grandparents in the same campsite and her eyes, dark with desire. There was no doubt about what we wanted.

I was careful with this knowledge. I told my closest friends, but cautiously, months or years later. It was easy, both the knowing and the not telling. It never occurred to me to tell anyone. Desire was not a public thing. In my family, you were histrionic or you were silent. Desire brought pregnancy or an alcoholic husband. It was swallowed up in the effort it takes to get up at four in the morning to milk and sow and feed and pray and try to keep the house clean, the kids from drinking, the cows warm enough. Life was hard, and my mother's second husband had died barely a year before. I knew the price of a dangerous desire, and knew to keep it anonymous in me. I wasn't victimized or ashamed. I was invisible. My uncles were glad I wasn't pregnant, and my grandmothers expected me to find boys some other day. My parents were glad I was as ambitiously smart as ever. I was glad that I did not need to open myself up, that I had a corner of my life to plant and tend as I wanted.

Again, my life was split: the potent world of an electric desire, lyrical and dark, abutting the prosaic, silencing world of my mother and my improbable upbringing. It was hard, living with the fear of discovery and the knowledge that this would only be remembered as betrayal when my mother finally found out. I didn't eat when I was a teenager. I wasn't hungry, and I never connected this lack of appetite with my low-level anxiety at living these two lives. But this desire saved my life; I believe that. It reminded me that I was not the girl everyone told me I was, not the eternal virgin caught reading about irrelevant body parts in a world that could never feed me. It reminded me of my body, the subcutaneous landscape beneath my careful systems of intellect and disengagement. It saved me from succumbing to my best intentions. It was sloppy, inconvenient, pressing the breath from my lungs and words from my head. It forced me beyond the parameters I'd set to keep from wanting too much, wanting more than was mine. It kept me from a creeping complacency about my soul. I needed to run from myself, from the world of my cousins and my mother, a world I knew could only unsex or devour me. It was an uneasy juxtaposition of imagination and humiliation: days when it was too much for my mother to get out of bed, when I went to honors classes, stole kisses in the girls' bathroom and spent holidays with my grandfather, who wouldn't let my mother's black boyfriend into his home.

This relationship was too long, too secret, too dependent. We wanted to be everything to each other, an orchard, an island, the world created and destroyed for each other. Ultimately, I hid from her as much as I hid from my mother. But she knew me, and recognized parts of me I'd never aired. She faced down my dependency and shame, and she understood my need to name things. She showed me that I could communicate as well as observe. It is hard to believe these things alone. Without them I do not know if I would have found my way to fuse myself together as well as I have.

What happened was I got away. I taught myself new words, I didn't turn into my cousins, I didn't stay with this world-in-a-lover. I write this today as if I knew to choose it at the time. But it was difficult and soul-trying, leaving her and leaving this world. I was smart, but I was luckier. I got away because my parents changed their lives and fed me different dreams than my cousins had. Circumstance intervened again, and the world I could inhabit expanded.

I escaped to my Seven Sisters school, where I found a whole world that would recognize me, ardently smart, publicly queer. I found a place where whom I kissed stopped defining who I was, where having words mattered, where I started eating again, cut my hair, unloaded a decade of fear and tried to never go home. These women, queer, generous and articulate, gave me so much: a history, a shared sense of displacement and hope, a place to laugh in public, a chance to think out loud, permission to touch my friends. I found a place where my public and private selves communicated, if they still knew better than to merge. My desire was no longer dangerous, no longer secret. I could want and dream and work like hell, and I could get what I wanted and dreamed of. These women taught me entitlement, and I held it to me, precious and overdue.

Half a decade after the fact, I came out to my parents, my brother and none of my extended family. My brother had moved to Chicago, far from either parent, and was living the life of an overworked computer programmer: smart, kind as hell and fastidiously financially secure. He was flattered that I trusted him and he hasn't stopped hounding me since. My father took it philosophically, my mother took it personally and I rarely bring it up. I sometimes wonder about telling my grandparents or my cousins: whether they'd keep me from their children or see that I am still the girl who named all the barn cats, all scabby knees and serious eyes. It is possible that they would surprise me. I have not given them the chance.

Today I am defined by longing of a different sort. The queer community has bred as much complacency as comfort, much like the farmland of my youth. I hold separate the stories of my childhood. They are a foreign currency in this landscape I am shaping for my future. The world I have entered denies the world I am from. It's class, it's culture, it's the assumption that the queer community is complete and can sustain me. I can transcribe my past into a convenient mythology—third grade, the dancer, poems on the bus; fifth grade, my graceful teacher, baffled by my disappointment at her marriage; Sara, soap and salvation—I tell these stories and I am recognized. I belong. But there are stories I am too ashamed to tell: my stepfather's crazy dreams, how I broke my wrist at fourteen falling off a horse neither he nor my mother could really afford but owned anyway and that I wouldn't have been riding if he hadn't been drinking. The day he chose exhaust over oxygen, leaving my grandmother to find him in his garage and call my mother, a hundred miles away. How I was next to her when she took that call, held her when she collapsed into my arms, where she has been clinging ever since. There's my mother's sister, on and off of drugs, clinging to her factory job. Her daughter, a mother before twenty. And more than that, our lack of surprise. My mother's condemned house, her specific and impossible plans, the fact that I have abandoned her in a life I let her build. The anxiety in this world is exhausting. It nearly claimed me in my teens. Balancing wants, needs and available resources, emotional more than financial, it isn't easy to maintain your humor along with your sanity and some spare energy for yourself. How do you tell someone that you think your joy is a betrayal of your past? I love these people fiercely, but I do not let anyone know them.

There is no place for this ambivalence in this world I've found. Being queer means being empowered. It is speaking the truth; it is acknowledging desire. It is dating the people you want to date, finding every word you are comfortable with and using it loudly, advocating change, speaking truth to power, accepting that your very existence will always be political. It is saturated with desire. There is no guilt in wanting to belong elsewhere, no sorrow in an exile to this wonderland of hope and acceptance. I am supposed to be proud. I am supposed to be sexual and visible, to desire the women I want unabashedly. This will make me wholly myself. These people, too, I love fiercely. I chose my friends here, I chose my lovers. I owe them much of who I am. And still they do not know me. I am not wholly reflected in their discourse, in the narratives I've been given to piece myself together.

I have given up my past. I have traded it for better skills, more joy, a broader definition of myself, more agency in satisfying my needs. But the fact remains that my children will never play with the children of my cousins. I have paid the price for my desire, given up security, the bonds of time and familiarity. I wish it were not so. I wish I were more honest about my judgment of these people, of myself. I wish I would come clean, stop caring or start speaking. But I don't. I just stand, five years and a continent away, look back at what I've left, and smell loss and a dishonest nostalgia.

Desire has taught me many things. It taught me to look within at a time when I didn't think I had emotions worth nurturing. It taught me to honor the anarchic blood in my veins. It taught me that whatever the cost, I cannot force my own wants down. It has led me to a world where I can be more myself, where I am no longer everyone's virgin, oblivious to the world within me. It forces me to face my mourning for a life I thought had nothing to feed me. It is impatient beneath my skin, frustrating and uncompromising, whispering rumors of a new landscape of wholeness and recognition. It is a radical ambivalence, this desire, and it reminds me that there is still more out there. I draw on it as I try to integrate this dual life, as I search for a space in this terrain for all the stories of my life. I struggle to talk about my past to the people that I love, get frustrated and remain ambivalent about the words I use to explain myself to the world: queer, conservative or otherwise. This ambivalence keeps me fighting to remain truthful, working to simultaneously salvage and scrub off my inheritance, searching for a place to rest these nomadic bones on the shifting ground of legacy and volition.

Las Lesbianas Are on the Other Side

 Daisy Hernández

In Spanish, lesbians are mujeres del otro lado, women of the other side. We are never told where the other side is exactly. It may be at the feet of Mexico's Guadalupe or it may be leading la revolución in Cuba. The other side may be nestled in llama-skin rugs in Peru, slithering through Colombia's jungles, bathing on a beach in Costa Rica or just sitting on the front stoop of an apartment building in Jersey.

In Spanish, we do not talk about what is on the other side. There could be garden snakes, lizards, tadpoles, ice cream cones or a woman's lips. The other side is veiled in more secrecy than the Holy Spirit. When I made my confirmation, I sat in St. John the Baptist Church, dressed from head to toe in white, and I waited for the Holy Spirit to touch me. She didn't. Maybe she was too busy on the other side.

My mother and father speak only Spanish. I, on the other hand, was immersed in classroom English at the age of five and quickly began to use language as a way of dividing my world into sides I could understand. Where I went to sleep was Spanish. Aunts, Catholic saints and actresses from las telenovelas were Spanish. School was English. Boys in class, Bugs Bunny cartoons and office jobs were English. My writing was English.

But nothing splits only in two. The Spanish was either my father's Cuban or my mother's Colombian. Bus trips to Miami from Jersey were Cuban. Cigars, mosquitoes and African gods were Cuban. Grocery shopping on Bergenline Avenue was Colombian. Handmade clothes, airmail envelopes and yellow underwear on New Year's Day were Colombian.

I have kept sides of myself so separate according to language that lovers tell me I sound like two different women. I have spent my academic life studying only English. Spanish has remained a spoken language, sounds that stumble like un boracho into English conversations I have with my sister and other Latinas born in the United States. And so as a butch in Harlem once said to me, "Your Spanish is more lousy than mine's!"

I was born in Spanish and grew up in English. The two sides had little to do with each other until I met mujeres del otro lado.

English was my adolescent rebellion. Other girls smoked pot, had one-night stands and drank beer until vomiting; I wrote in English. At fifteen I wrote in my journal about giving my boyfriend a blowjob. I wrote the details of tastes and highway motel rooms and of pillowcases that did not belong to me.

English gave me freedom. At home, I did not have to hide my journals from my mother and aunts. I would have phone sex in English with boyfriends while my mother and aunts watched telenovelas in the next room. My friends would come over and we would discuss the intricacies of using condoms without any concern that my mother would overhear us. English afforded me privacy, a privilege to keep secrets at home.

I bought lesbian erotica books without hesitation. I kept in my bedroom issues of *Blade* and *HX for Her* and my mother commented that the boys on *Out*'s cover were "bonito." I talked on the kitchen phone with friends about cute girls while Mami fried plátanos for dinner. I did not worry. Whether or not my mother suspected anything, language kept us on different sides.

Men were an escape from Spanish, my overprotective parents and our working class poverty. It was a boyfriend who taught me to drive, bought me a used Oldsmobile, and took me to look at colleges. It was a boyfriend who gave me a reason to move out of my family's house for a year. It was a boyfriend who introduced me to flavored condoms, poetry and Manhattan.

I had only one relationship with a man who was bilingual. We spoke English with each other and Spanish with our families and we broke up after four years because we did not speak the same language. Naked in bed, he reached for Spanish words and I for English. Outside of bed, I read Hemingway and listened to Madonna; he listened to Spanish ballads and watched fútbol.

It was with an English-only man that I first considered women. He was a jock type, six feet tall and all muscle and English. He also had long hair and wore silver rings and necklaces. Having him on top of me—his dark hair either covering my face or pulled back in a ponytail—made me come with such an intensity that I found myself playing with his rings and looking at women.

When I finally decided to pursue women, I went to England. I was twenty-one years old and thought an ocean between my family and me and an unfamiliar land was what I needed to be with a woman. I met no one. Actually I didn't even look. I was too scared I might stay in London for a woman and only speak Spanish by phone once a week when I called home. I was too scared of my own desires to even look for the other side. I was too nervous el otro lado might be far from my mother's house.

I then decided on Washington, D.C. Five hours away from my mother and aunts would be enough distance without loss. I could meet a woman, fall in love and move in with her. All within a week. Of course, I met only gay men. I was more hesitant about moving between sides than I could admit.

I grew up translating everything I heard in Spanish to English for myself and other women. Because the women I knew as a child were immigrants, migration became a way of seeing the world. I came to think of sexuality as places women come from and go to. And so at gay bookstores, female-only college parties and lesbian bars, I alternated between feeling like an undocumented immigrant and an unwelcomed tourist.

Often I felt I had no privilege. I would be in a lesbian-only space, but I saw myself as a poor immigrant woman in an English-only country. I was afraid a lesbian would ask to see mis papeles, and I had nothing to show and no words to explain how I had been smuggled to the other side.

But I am the child of immigrants and not an immigrant myself so in lesbian-only spaces I often also felt like a tourist who gets to look at the natives and try the local customs before going back home. For a time, I even kept my hair and fingernails short and stopped wearing makeup. Yet regardless of what I did to my appearance, I would order a drink at a bar and still feel like a white woman with a bad sunburn, wearing flower print shirts and matching shorts on a Caribbean island. I did not belong to a lesbian culture any more than I did to the Spanish language.

In Spanish, orientarse is to make yourself familiar with lo desconocido, the unfamiliar. It is to become comfortable with a new job, apartment or city. With the other side. Or just with the other.

But how do you make yourself familiar with your own sexuality? Sometimes I wish my sexuality were a place where my mother could send me packages of arequipe and guava pastries. Or if only my sexuality were a city and I could buy a guidebook that highlights the major attractions and has a foldout map of the subway system so I would know how to get around. If only my sexuality were a new job, complete with on-site training and a benefits office.

Orientarse, orientation, sexual orientation. The words come to English and Spanish from the search for an Orient, for a side where the sun rises, a side that is unfamiliar if you are European. It is thought that if you know where the sun rises, then you know where you are on land and where to travel. Then you can find that other side no one talks about in Spanish.

Sexuality, like land, is vulnerable to our definitions. Sexuality is the one piece of holy ground everyone claims by a different name and for a different god. It is the land taken and marked with unnatural borders, cut up into "this is my side, that is yours."

When a friend sent me an email asking, "How are things on your side?" I wrote back, "I'll tell you when I find it."

I am a woman from the other side in search of the other side. I am a woman living in one country who suddenly found the land had changed names. I longed for a woman's lips and suddenly the borders marking my body were moved and I belonged to a different people.

I thought lesbians only happened in English. They were the girls at my college with pierced tongues, women with long, blonde hair and guitars, feminists with short haircuts, movie actresses rich enough to be queer, porn stars my best friend and I drooled over while we swore it was the men we were looking at.

And then I discovered Las Buenas Amigas, an organization in New York City for the Latina lesbian diaspora. In English, the name would be like The Good Female Friends or The Best Friends. It is perhaps the most perfect way to talk about lesbians en español. At least that is what my eighteen-year-old sister said as I drove her to her new all-girl life at Smith College. Good friends. Best friends. My sister and I caressed the words in our mouths: "Mi buuuuuuena Amiga, Laz Buenaz Amigaz," convinced that placing emphasis on certain syllables in Spanish was the equivalent of telling our mother, "This woman is my lover."

I went to a meeting of Las Buenas Amigas expecting to find women like me, part of the first U.S.-born generation, whose first language was Spanish but who speak mostly English. Instead, I found women my mother's age and women my age who spoke Spanish first and foremost. It was as if I had walked into my own home and my entire family were gay.

It was an odd kind of comfort and familiarity that I felt with the women from LBA, as if I were out to my mother and my aunts and they were out to me. I listened to these women from LBA laugh and gossip in Spanish just as I did at home with my mother and aunts. Words were said in Spanish that I didn't understand, just like at home. Except these women knew how I felt about women. We were on the same side.

The first woman I kissed on that side I met at an LBA party. She was from South America, had been in New York less than two years and was more fluent in Spanish than I was. We kissed and her tongue in my mouth felt as invasive as her Spanish-only sentences that I could not completely understand.

I was twenty-three years old, living with my parents and my aunt, and for the first time language exposed me. On the phone, I spoke in Spanish with this woman and I wondered if my aunt in the living room could hear me. For the first time I had to watch what I said to a potential lover. Not because I was on the phone speaking to a lesbian, but because the lesbian spoke Spanish.

The morning after our first date I lay in bed and wrote in my journal about her fingertips on my breasts, about struggling through dinner to discuss my job with her in my limited Spanish vocabulary. My mother in the living room interrupted me by yelling for instructions on how to program the VCR. From my bed I tried to explain but I didn't know the Spanish word for "forward." I kept repeating, "el forward Mami. Primero el forward." I continued saying this until suddenly I burst into tears. I could not communicate with my mother any better than I could with the woman I was dating.

English had given me freedom but it had also alienated me from my family. Dating a woman more fluent in Spanish soon made me realize how little I spoke with my family about the sides of me that are in English. I say very little in Spanish about my career, my dreams, my lovers. I cannot tell my mother how to program the VCR any more than I can talk with her about dating women. I cannot give her and my father the poems and essays I write in English. For my parents there will always be sides of me that exist only in translation.

There were a few more dates after the first one and then I decided to stop seeing her. The chemistry wasn't developing, because of lack of desire or lack of language or something else. She returned to me the copy I had lent her of *House on Mango Street*. The pages were marked by my pen noting metaphors and by her pencil underlining English words she didn't know. Words like grins, slant, albeit, firecrackers, crumbling, otherness, baffled. My blue lines and her gray ones intertwined across the pages.

I realized then that what I needed was a bilingual lover. I don't know what other lesbians look for in a first lover but I wanted someone who could understand me in Spanish and English. I found her. She was Latina, perfectly bilingual and already a friend.

On her answering machine, the message was in both Spanish and English and I became infatuated with the sound of her voice, how she enunciated each English syllable. She slid between the two languages with ease and confidence and I was willing to follow her anywhere.

We went to the supermercado for latex gloves.

I had specific, albeit odd, expectations about the other side. I expected that having sex and becoming romantically involved with a woman would feel similar to that moment history textbooks assign to European immigrants—when hundreds of them lean against the railing of an old boat and catch their first glimpse of the Statue of Liberty. It was a recurring description in my childhood history classes, and even back then I had liked the idea of people traveling through a dangerous ocean to reach a woman dressed in a robe. So when I fantasized about my first glimpse of the other side, I expected she would be in silk robes, holding a dildo.

Sometimes I also thought that if my first female lover were Latina, then going to the other side might be like reclaiming my parents' homelands. I imagined smoking Cuban cigars with my lover who would dip her finger in Colombian coffee and brush her wet fingertip over my nipples.

But going to the other side turned out more as if I had sneaked out of Cuba, traveled through perilous waters on a rickety boat and, when I finally arrived on Miami Beach, looked at the sand, the palm trees and the Cubans, and all I could say was, "Coño, but la Florida sure looks a lot like Cuba."

There is something shocking and foreign and ultimately very familiar about having sex with a woman who speaks the language your mother uses to chastise you and the language with which you write about your mother.

The first night though I just lay on top of my lover, ground against her Spanish moans and came—losing my breath as if I had been punched in the belly and had liked it. For a moment, I forgot what side I was on.

Until the next morning when I washed my panties in her bathroom sink with hand soap and she remarked, "Oh, look at you, how cute! Washing los delicados by hand." I had forgotten that she knew Spanish, that her mother like mine insisted panties are items so delicate they can only be washed by hand, never thrown into the washing machine like the gringas do at the laundromat.

After that, I still often forgot she knew Spanish and that I did not have to translate for her. I had to remind myself that I could tell her exactly what my mother or any other mujer in my house had said without turning the Spanish to English. I had to learn that between us the Spanish and inglés were as intertwined as our naked legs.

In private, she called me Mami. In Spanish, the words used for our parents, Papi and Mami, are also used for lovers or for people we find attractive or just for the equivalent of a "hey baby." I have never felt comfortable calling anyone Papi or Mami but my own parents. However, when I lay in bed with my fingers inside my lover and she whispered "Mami," there was something gratifying about it. Suddenly, by having sex with a woman, I could appreciate that what is incestuous in one language is desirable in another. That who I am in English also exists in Spanish, even when I remain unspoken.

As we spent more time together, I began speaking more Spanish. She introduced me to more vocabulary and phrases and slowly I found myself talking with my parents and aunts about my English life, about my job and ideas for graduate school. I didn't come out to them, but being with una mujer del otro lado brought me closer to my family's side.

A friend confided, "Yeah, my girlfriend's like my Spanish dictionary too." But it was more than that. I've always had bilingual friends. This was about how fucking and loving, sex and desire, language and family can sometimes be on one side. It was about recalling a time in my life when words did not separate me into sides, when words were so intimate they did not need definition or translation.

One night, while holding my lover's hand, I began sniffling with the onset of a cold and she turned to me and asked, "¿Estás mocosa?" In English, it would be as if she had asked, "Is your nose full of snot?" Not usually a life-altering question, but for me it was. They were my mother's words from my childhood on the tongue of my lover and at that moment I paused to wonder if I would ever leave this side.

My STD and Me

⊛ Mara Kaplan

In high school, the midpoint of a miserable, protracted, awkward, sexless adolescence that started at twelve and didn't begin to taper off until twenty-three, I used to try to comfort myself by thinking things like, At least I'll never get an STD. Not that I actually thought about STDs that much, but in safety ed (the half-year joke course we had to take in the tenth grade in my suburban California public school—the semester we weren't taking driver's ed), the creepy coach teaching the class showed slides of herpes outbreaks on both male and female genitalia, and it was pretty gross. Well great, I thought sarcastically, I'll never have to worry about *that*. At the time, it didn't seem like it was *really* a risk for anyone in that classroom—even the stoners and the jocks and the sluts—so being a celibate nerd, and therefore 100-per-cent-guaranteed safe, wasn't anything to be psyched about.

In fact, although I never admitted such warped, inexplicable, lame thoughts to anyone, I felt jealous of girls who had to worry about STDs or pregnancy or getting a bad reputation or coming out or anything else that related to being sexually active.

Not because I wanted an STD of course, but because the risk of STDs represented to me a whole set of problems that were foreign to my own life. Teenage problems related to sex were normal—if only my problems could be so simple.

My parents were quite liberal about sex in relation to social issues (pro-choice, pro–gay rights, pro–sex ed in schools, etc.) and, sadly, very rigid when it came to their own lives. By the time I left for college, my parents hadn't had a sexual relationship in years—although I wasn't aware of this at the time, having developed absolutely no sexual consciousness yet myself. (Perhaps this should have been a clue.) I only learned the full extent of their estrangement at twenty-six when finally, after twenty-nine years of marriage, my mother moved out and my father came out as gay.

Of course this is a long story in itself, of which I will share only a coinciden-tal, STD-related detail: When I was in high school, one of my father's liberal activities was volunteering for the National STD Hotline, and he used to regale my mother and me with funny stories about the calls when he got home. All well and good (albeit a little weird for a supposedly straight, married, white-collar, middle-aged man) until, years later, my mother called the STD hotline office, knowing surely (at least on some level) what she would discover—that my father had quit long before, although he still went out to "Hotline" on Thursday nights. Suffice it to say that since that my parents were closeted for so long, and since both of them chose to repress or hide their sexualities in exchange for the rela-tive security of marriage, it should hardly be surprising that sexual self-aware-ness and self-esteem were not cultivated in our home.

Coming from this environment, I did know all about safe sex from the sex ed factoids I'd been bombarded with. (I even had T-shirts and tote bags from the STD Hotline!) I knew that there was nothing to be ashamed of if things went wrong—why should getting an STD from having sex be any different from catch-ing a cold from sharing a glass? Anyway, if it was curable, what was the big deal? (Of course, some of them aren't curable—but what, I thought naively, was the chance of getting one of *those?*) Teenagers were supposed to be dealing with sexuality and having sex, and all those right-wing politicians who wanted to repress and deny teenage sexuality were a bunch of fascist creeps.

What I didn't get was anything about sex itself. What I didn't get was how to be sexual. What I didn't get was physical attraction, or crushes or flirting or going on dates or making out at parties. My own self-hatred, the sheer horror I felt looking at the contours of my body and the sight of my acne-coated face in the mirror was so intense that it held me, transfixed, in a murky, asexual rut for eleven long years. How would anyone ever be attracted to me? And how could I be attracted to anyone else, when picturing myself with them meant imagining myself as a different person? Putting my real-life self in a fantasy was enough to kill it before it even took hold. My own sexuality, whatever shape it might take, remained mysterious, untraceable, impossible. Nothing seemed as elusive or desirable to me then as sexual precocity, and the beauty, the sexiness, the physical ease that always seemed to go with it. If I could have this, I thought—hell, if I could just be normal—I would take an STD any day.

One day, four years ago, I realized that my crotch was itching. And hurting. Itching, itching, itching, itching and hurting. I figured it was just a yeast infection and started an anti-fungal treatment. It was annoying, though—and not just because of the itch. I was only six months into a new relationship, I was head over heels in love and we were still having sex every night and spending entire weekends in bed and canceling all our other social plans in order to fuck. So going a whole week without sex to let the yeast infection clear up was not going to be fun. In practice, though, it didn't actually slow us down much—we had other ways to fool around. I didn't give it a second thought.

But it didn't go away. In fact, it hurt more. The itching was intolerable and I couldn't stop scratching myself. I constantly had to pee. When I finally dug out a hand mirror in the bathroom and squatted over it to check things out, something on my labia looked like a long, dark-red line. Did I scratch myself that badly? I vowed even more strongly not to give in to the itch—obviously I was making it worse. Still, it didn't go away. A couple days later, I pressed lightly on the red line with my forefinger. Without warning, my finger plunged into a mushy open wound that seemed deeper than I thought possible. The pain was nothing compared to the shock of feeling my finger break my skin. I stared at my finger, horrified. And then I thought, This is something else.

I remembered, very vaguely, that my boyfriend had once mentioned having a cold sore in his mouth, and I knew. I tried to tell myself that it could be anything, but I knew. My boyfriend—who absurdly enough was getting a Ph.D. in public health—came over with his textbooks as soon as I called him. He looked up herpes in the Merck manual while I stared at the cunt reflected back to me in the mirror on the bathroom floor. "Listen to this," he said excitedly. "You *don't* have herpes. The first outbreak is usually accompanied by flulike symptoms: fever, sore throat, headache." I had none of those symptoms. I felt fine. Still, this wasn't particularly reassuring, and neither of us could think of any other explanation for a huge blister on my vulva. But how could I have gotten *herpes* from an innocuous little mouth sore? I heard somewhere that nearly 50 percent of people have oral herpes. Surely, I reasoned, more than 50 percent of people have oral sex. So if I got herpes that way, shouldn't 50 percent of people have genital herpes too? *Do* 50 percent of people have genital herpes? Anyway, why would I have gotten it on my cunt but not in my mouth? We kissed every day, sometimes for hours—and my mouth was still clean. I called the twenty-four-hour consulting-nurse service for my health plan and described my symptoms. The nurse seemed fairly convinced that I had herpes, but told me to make a doctor's appointment the next day to get tested. She was so blasé and matter-of-fact about it that I finally started to panic.

That night, lying in bed, I started to cry. All I could think was, I will have this for the rest of my life. I cried myself to sleep, my boyfriend holding me. The next morning, I woke up in tears. I called my doctor's office, and I could barely talk enough to make the appointment. I choked back a sob when the receptionist said brightly, "and what do you need to see the doctor for?" It got worse: My doctor wouldn't be available that day. The only one in the clinic with a free appointment was a man. The thought of waiting any longer was the only thing that seemed worse than getting naked, putting my legs in stirrups and exposing my poor, infected vulva to a man I'd never seen before. I took the appointment. I left a message on the voice mail at my work calling in sick. I was still crying, and all I could manage to say was, "I'm okay, but there's something I'm really worried about and . . . I have to go to the doctor today and . . . maybe I'll come in later." Click. Whoever got the message probably thought I had a life-threatening disease. I went to my regular shrink appointment that morning. At first, all I could say was, "I have herpes. I know I have herpes, but I still have to go to a strange doctor and get a test so they can tell me what I already know." Finally I explained how I got it, and my shrink, who was a psychiatrist, an M.D., said, "I'm so sorry. I didn't realize you could get it that way."

Then I went to my doctor's appointment and sat in the waiting room. I realized that spacing out and dissociating a little could keep me from crying. The situation already felt like a bad dream, so I went with the dream feeling. I pretended to be in another person's body. When I heard myself saying I needed to be tested for herpes, I thought, This can't be you.

I made it through the appointment. The doctor was okay. I would have preferred a woman, but he was okay. He gave me a bottle of big blue coated pills. He told me the first outbreak is the worst. He told me the sooner I start taking the pills, the faster it will go away. Everyone talked to me very carefully and kindly, but I wondered what they were thinking. I knew they knew I'd been crying. I knew they knew I'd caught a disease from sex. Did they believe me when I said my boyfriend wasn't sleeping around? Did they think I was a fool who trusted the wrong guy? Or, did they just think I was loose and careless and brought it on myself? If anything, I got the sense from them that I was overreacting, with all my tears (obviously they'd seen much worse). Still, for the first time I felt like my sexuality completely defined me. Like I was a bad girl who had sex and got in trouble and needed to go to the clinic to be tested and treated and diagnosed. I had thought I was completely immune to the bad-girl stereotype. Not only had I felt asexual for most of my post-pubescent life, I was a fucking feminist for God's sake. But the truth is, no one was rude or condescending or sexist. The shame came from inside me.

I went over to my boyfriend's place after the doctor's appointment. He was resting on the futon couch when I got there, so I lay down next to him. I wished we could stay there together and watch the rest of the world disappear. It was so hard to believe that there was no second chance to get it right.

My boyfriend said, "I think I have it too." I stared at him, and he said, "Well, now I have these blisters . . . I found them yesterday, but I didn't want to tell you." And then we knew that I'd given it to him—or given it back to him—before we knew what it was. Our love had seemed so beautiful and pure to me, yet somehow this disease appeared between us. Instead of coming together and making love or making orgasms or making a baby, we had made a painful, incurable, shameful genital infection.

Before, I'd felt like our love, my first love, had freed me. Freed me to be as sexual and as sexy as I had ever wanted to be, freed me to give my love only because I wanted to give it, freed me to flirt and play and dance. But suddenly, the part of me that felt so free was being punished, was being trapped all over again. There was going to be no freedom in sex anymore, only consequences. No more playing, only precautions. And it occurred to me that, no matter what happened between us, I would be tied to him forever. Not by desire or true love or even by choice, but because we both shared a copy of the same creepy virus.

During the day I felt okay as long as I was kept from thinking about herpes or that I was walking around with an open sore on my cunt. But lying in bed at night I had no distractions. I sobbed every night for four nights, even waking up in the middle of the night crying. My boyfriend would wake up then too and I knew it was torture for him to see me so upset. He seemed to have it all in perspective; he didn't feel the shame. He just said, "I love you. I'm sorry. I promise it's going to be all right."

Getting herpes felt like the end of my life, or if not the end of my life at least the end of my youth—which, considering that I was only twenty-five and only had been happy and having fun and enjoying life for the past two years, was almost as bad. It seemed like incredibly rotten luck to get an STD after having sex with a grand total of three people. And from a guy who had only had sex with one other person, his college girlfriend four years earlier. We were both such babies when it came to sex, slowly teaching each other how to be adult human beings. At the time, I hadn't even had an orgasm—not with myself and certainly not with anyone else. *That's* how far behind I was. Still, *I was working on it*, dammit, subjecting my willing lover to marathon stretches of oral sex—probably how I got the herpes in the first place.

But it wasn't enough, apparently, to be a late bloomer, to get a late start. No, fate had decreed that I would have only a small window of time for casual sex: two years between the ages of twenty-three and twenty-five. And now my time was up. Just when I was finally getting the hang of the mating game. Just when I was starting to get the sexual confidence I would need for more adventures.

I felt cheated out of all the sexual experiences I might have if only I could be free and invincible a little bit longer. The thought of giving herpes to someone else was horrifying. The thought of having to explain that I had herpes and process the whole thing over and over with anyone I wanted to have sex with—and deal with their reaction to it—was utterly demoralizing. I was certain now I would never get all the experience I thought I wanted. At the same time, I felt old. Old before my time. I was used up, dirty, damaged goods. I had baggage now. At twenty-five, nothing in my life had seemed permanent. Not my job, not my relationship, not my apartment, not even my choice of city. I had no commitments, I could reinvent myself at any time, or so I thought. But the herpes would never go away. I couldn't fathom it. I looked at myself in the mirror and stared at the fine lines on my face that recently had begun to appear. I felt ten years older than I had the week before.

More than a week after my diagnosis, the sore finally started clearing up. Immediately, I began to feel better. The sore itself—painful, ugly, contagious—had made it impossible to feel normal. It seemed to last forever. I'd started taking the acyclovir too far into the outbreak, and it hadn't done a damn thing. For days, my boyfriend was holding me every night, taking care of me, trying to help me stop crying, and I still wouldn't let him see the sore. It reminded me of my years of battling acne, never wanting to show my face to other people. Once again my own skin was turning against me, flaring up, breaking out. Seeing a sore there on my special place made me feel like my sexuality was somehow diseased. But it was a purely visual effect. Once the sore was gone it was easier to imagine having a normal life. I realized that I was okay. That of course I wasn't going to be dealing with it all the time, even most of the time. If I had one outbreak a year, the average, would it really affect me that much?

On the day I could tell that the sore was fusing together, turning back into normal skin, I went shopping and bought a new summer dress. I went straight from the counter back into the dressing room, changed into the dress and wore it out of the store. I felt like a weight was lifted off me.

I went to my boyfriend's place, and we started kissing on the futon couch. I felt sexy again. We kept kissing. And touching. We weren't supposed to have sex until our sores were completely gone and we had finished all the acyclovir. More kissing, our fully clothed bodies melded into each other while our hands kept trying to feel skin through or around or under the clothes. His hand pushing up my short skirt, touching my ass, then pulling the straps over my shoulders to get to my breasts. My hands in his shirt feeling his back and chest, then his skinny boy hips through his pants. Sure, we'd done all this before. But always before, after a certain point, the clothes had come off. This time I realized how sexy it was not being able to fuck. There wasn't enough room on the futon couch, and our bodies were moving around and around with nowhere to go. We started rubbing on each other, as if we were two teenagers in the back of a car trying to get as close as possible to sex. His dick not in my vagina, but on the outside, right on my clit, right where it belonged. It felt like the best sex we'd ever had. I didn't want it to end. I heard myself starting to scream, over and over again, more noise than I'd ever made before.

Afterwards, lying still, I heard my boyfriend say, "So . . . what was all that yelling?"

Given this turn of events, I may be the only person who can say that getting herpes cured her from being inorgasmic. Of course, it's possible that it was just a coincidence that I had my first orgasm right after I got herpes. That it was time for it to happen, and if we had just figured out to try frottage a little earlier I could have had an incredible screaming orgasm.

But I think that in some small way getting herpes actually connected me to my body and to sex. After years of being alienated from my body and my sexuality, and hating the way I looked, it was no small thing for me to feel like a truly sexual person. Sure, I had made a lot of progress, I was getting close. But in a completely subjective, irrational way, getting an STD was like objective, scientific proof: I was sexual, and I had a disease to show for it. For the purpose of viral replication, my cunt was as good as anyone else's. And maybe I hadn't realized exactly how far I'd come, how free I had started to feel, until my sexual independence was threatened. Now my sexuality felt not only more real but also more fragile and precious. Now there would always be more at stake in sex, but was that such a bad thing? The stakes were also raised for my own pleasure.

Maybe, then, something clicked in my unconscious, something along the lines of, *What the fuck are you doing not coming?*

Sex wasn't the only thing that became more real. I have been with the same lover now for four years, and getting herpes was our first test, the thing that brought us closer in two weeks than we had been in six months. Of course, it is not the only thing we have been through that has seemed to tie an invisible thread around our hearts. Four years later, it is low on the list. But it was the first thing, the first thing that made me know I could trust this man to love me.

In a way, I've had it easy. I am still with the person who gave me herpes, and I gave it back to him faster than you can say herpes simplex one. Two months after I found the sore on my cunt, another one showed up in my mouth. The damage, as they say, is done. But we may not always be together. Someday, I might want to fuck—or even just kiss—another person, and it will always be a risk. I'm not happy about it, but I can live with it. All it means is that if someone is going to fuck me or kiss me, they really have to want me. Now that I've had real love, I can't take sex so lightly anymore. I don't think this has anything to do with having herpes. I am just old enough now to want something more from sex.

With a new lover, I will never have the luxury of unprotected sex, but that caution could well save my life. The truth is, I never had that luxury—I'm just lucky that all I got was herpes. And yes, I have been tested for HIV: About a year after I got herpes, it dawned on me that there was no reason I couldn't have gotten HIV from one of my three lovers, as "unlikely" as this might be. What do we really mean when we talk about risk? On the day herpes viral particles entered my cells, if you had asked me if I was at risk for any STDs I would have said, "No way." The first man I had sex with was twelve years older that I, and I knew him to be promiscuous. The first month we slept together we used condoms. For the rest of our three-month affair I agreed to stop because he didn't like the way they felt. I remembered him telling me, "I promise I'm safe, I've never had a sexually transmitted disease." And at twenty-three, I believed him. Now all I could think was, Oh God, Mara, how could you do that? Somehow the preview for *Titanic* got embedded in my brain, and, until I finally got my negative results, I had the same nightmare over and over again: a massive ship slowly sinking in an endlessly wide, impossibly deep, pitch black ocean.

As it happens, all I have is herpes. I would be lying if I said it wasn't annoying. But it just doesn't feel that bad. I would never expose another person to herpes without informing them of the risk; but if I do someday give it to someone else, I know that they will live. The only question is, will anyone who doesn't have herpes believe me when I tell them how little it matters?

My Body, and My Mind

 Michelle Tea

Julie had a call for me and she swore that it would be easy. Julie was full of shit. Once upon a time she had set me up with a magical, seven-hour coke call that required me to do little more than chop up great mounds of cocaine and soothe my temporary boyfriend's intense paranoia, all while naked of course. I hung out, ate pickles, smoked and made $700. Ever since, Madame Julie had been luring me to work with promises of the cokehead calling for me again—keeping me by the phone, sending me out on other, less profitable calls that required me to actually work, until all my hope was killed. I knew that the call of my career had already happened, and the rest of my life as a prostitute would be spent yearning for what once was. *I think he's gonna call tonight,* Julie would whisper through the phone lines, her voice full of promise. *You want to sign on?*

She must have done it to me that night, I can't imagine why else I would've signed on in the middle of a blizzard. I don't know how the cab even made it down my street, a dead-end stretch of potholes ignored by the snowplows. I always knew the cab-drivers. Julie had a special deal with four or five of the drivers for Blue Cab, I think I was riding with the Captain that night, a real piece of work. *You know, I was raped by a woman once,* he said, a normal little burst of compulsive self-revelation. Really, Captain? I said absently. *Yeah,* he continued, *she handcuffed me and then she, she sat on it, and I kept telling her to stop and she wouldn't.* I'm Sorry, Captain, That Sounds Awful. The Captain had sailed boats once, hence the name, but now he drove cabs and sold painkillers. He hauled me through the bleak winter landscape of February Boston, dead everything, a desert of snow. No one on the road but suckers like us. *How come you're working tonight?* asked The Captain. *Julie tell you that druggie was gonna call?* I harrumphed from the back seat. *That guy hasn't called for a while,* he observed. He's Probably Dead, I said wistfully.

That night's call was at a hotel in, I don't know, Boston or Cambridge, every-thing looked different and foreign in the intense snow that blew down on the windshield like a biblical curse. The Captain parked the cab and ushered me through the gusting frost. I hobbled in my heels, holding on to the Captain like a bannister. It wasn't good weather for 'ho fashion, and I hated feeling helpless. The hotel was one of those motor lodges, the rooms broken up into individual cabanas so you could knock directly on the trick's door, instead of having to parade yourself through the lobby like a circus animal. My girlfriend Liz had gotten a call at one of those places once, a fake one. The boys at the desk had rung the agency as a joke, they wanted to see what a prostitute looked like. She looked like anyone, a regular long-haired white girl, with blue eyes that gleamed like weapons, little knife-eyes. Mean, mean Elizabeth. I loved when she was mean to the johns, tormenting them with phone calls, ratting their infidelities to blubbering wives, so much righteous cruelty, my Valerie Solanas. But feminist anger was not the actual root of Liz's wrath—the world was just lucky she had found a cause to attach herself to. Liz was simply mean, and it could be turned on me, her hooker girlfriend, partner in crime, girl revolutionary, as easily as on any trick.

The Captain deposited me at the door and said he'd see me in an hour. Julie had prepared me for this call. She said the guy was into witchcraft, was a wizard or something, and if I acted real fascinated I could probably get him to read my tarot cards and kill a half hour. The guy was big, robust, red-cheeked and bald-ing with a little rim of white hair crowning his head. Now, there are many differ-ent types of men who call prostitutes, far too many for me to catalog here, but there is one type I want to discuss and that is the man who, besides sex, wants a captive audience for his deep and worldly knowledge of everything. Depending on my mood, this could be a good thing. If I was feeling particularly vacant and disconnected I could just Oh Really . . . Wow the better part of the hour away. But if I was feeling more present and ornery I would feel I had to top him at his dumb games. *La Petite Morte,* sighed one john after the deed was done, obviously imagining himself transported into the tawdry but romantic frame of a Toulouse-Lautrec painting. He looked at me, expectant, waiting for me to request a translation. The Little Death, I said sarcastically. He looked hurt. He began speaking cryptically about the kundalini. Yeah, Kundalini, The Snake Curled At The Base Of Your Spine, You Raise It Through Meditation. *You know a lot,* he said, surprised. These guys really thought prostitutes were stupid, which was understandable considering that any woman would have to be an idiot to sleep with them, but I was getting paid.

Mr. Wizard had a little tin lamp resting on the hotel television, and he started in right away. *What do you see?* he asked dramatically, holding out the object. Uh . . . It's A Lamp. *How many sides does it have?* Four. *Do you know why it has four sides?* It was just a regular, square fucking lamp, but I knew what he was getting at. The Four Directions, I said, North, South, East, West. The Four Elements: Earth, Air, Fire, Water. The Four Vulnerable Points On A Rapist's Body: Eyes, Knees, Groin, Throat. Mr. Wizard was clearly startled. These guys all think they're Henry Higgins, dreaming of my transformation into a silk purse. You could see reels of *Pretty Woman* twirling in his head. *Do you practice The Craft?* he asked excitedly. *I could tell the minute I saw you, your energy. Do you belong to a coven?* New Age tricks were the worst. They really thought they were doing something spiritual. No, No, I said, I Just Know Some Stuff. Hey, Do You Read Tarot Cards? *Yes, yes,* he rushed over to a chest of drawers and slid one open. But he pulled out a book instead, some men's movement thing about Thor or the Green Man. *Have you read this? Excellent book.* He started telling me about this really special, really sacred place in the woods where he and all his male friends went to hop fire and drum. That's Really Great, I said. I was bored. I didn't see tarot cards anywhere. *What's your sign?* he probed. Aquarius. *Oh yes Aquarius, that's a very special sign.* Yeah, I Know. *Oh . . . the hour's getting away from us,* he said, glancing at his watch.

That was the very worst call. I need to tell you that I had an orgasm. It was awful. I felt it coming on like a sneeze and I couldn't believe it. What needs to be understood is the lousy relationship I had with the enigmatic phenomenon that is Orgasm. I had only just confessed to Liz that I'd been faking all along. Liz, the laziest lover ever. After I got her off she would lie there like a big wet sea creature, some sluggish lump on the ocean floor. She would tug me into position above her mouth and half-heartedly snack at my pussy. I'd brace myself on the wall above our futon, thighs straining, and when it was clear that I was only going to end up cramped and exhausted I'd fake a gasping buck on her chin, as if she were a trick, and sink back down into bed with her. There were a few moments at the start of our relationship when things seemed promising. Once she bound my wrists behind my back with clothesline, but then her roommate came home all frenzied because the garbagemen were out front and no one had brought the trash down, so Liz just left me there in the bed—door open so the roommate could understand how wild she was, a tied-up damsel naked and panting on her futon—while she hefted a week's worth of trash into the street.

It was tempting to blame it all on Liz and her lack of amorous inspiration, but I knew it wasn't her fault, not really. It was something about my body, my body and my mind. The hard little computer in my head that whirred and clanked like industry, not even sex's rosy lushness could pull the plug. My body, a kind of briefcase to lug my mind around in. At night before sleep took me out, alone in my bed with my hand jammed down my panties—no problem. But never with another person. So you could imagine my alarm at this toad between my legs, this situation I had no erotic connection to. Like the malfunctioning machine that it was, my body was responding. Orchestrating a little coup on the fascist brain that had been training it like a cadet or zen monk to just not want so much, the icky inner drone of need. It was like a baby screaming at my tit, my body, it was hungry and I had no idea how to feed it.

My view was the trick's little grey head, pink bits of scalp flanked by my skinny legs, traitor flesh. I had to make a decision. What an awful decision to have to make. I was going to fake it anyway, as part of my regular whore routine, so either way he was going to think he was a little champ, but I would know. I let it come on. Like most orgasms, it felt pretty good. He pulled himself off me. *Oh Tiffany,* he said. *I always have really wonderful energy with Aquarians.* I went into the bathroom and sat down on the cold hotel toilet. I didn't choose for that to happen. But cosmically we choose everything, interrupted my Aquarian brain, don't we? So on some intangible level I chose to have an orgasm with this creep. Why, to learn something? Learn what? That my body was even more Other than I had thought, something separate, something I was hopelessly stuck with, like a siamese twin. It made its own decisions and I shared the consequences. I looked at myself in the big lit-up mirror over the sink. Scrawny white girl, little tits, bony arms, lipstick clinging dryly to the lips. Was I looking at me or my body?

Back in the room, a pair of headlights shone in through the window. *I think your cab's here,* said Mr. Earth Man. He watched me put my clothes on. *You're going to find a coven, Tiffany. I can see you in a Dianic coven. But be careful, there's a lot of lesbians in those groups. They have no balance. You need the goddess and the god.* Out in the cab The Captain was smoking a cigarette. *You got another one?* he asked, *Or am I taking you home?* I'm Going Home, I said.

When I pushed into the little warm room that we lived in I found Liz alone in the bed, heat blasting out from the metal grate on the wall, an old, burnt smell. The lights were out and there was a ring of glass candles around the futon, the bobbing flames scorching the sides a charcoal black. She was sulking and listening to Ani DiFranco, I could tell she wanted to be alone but there was simply no place for me to go. We shared this one small room, and the rest of the house belonged to the long-suffering friend who was resentfully letting us crash with her. Liz's body was on the bed. She was a Virgo. Always I think these things come back to that, astrology. Liz knew what to eat, what to feed her body, what was good for it. She massaged her skin with the guts of a ripped stalk of aloe, or oil scented with jasmine. She sat in the woods and was content just to be there, watching plants growing imperceivably around her. Liz knew how to take her Space, how to set Boundaries and be Alone, and she could turn evil when it wasn't possible, when I broke her little ring of candles and reminded her that I lived in the room too.

Hi, I whispered, trying not to wreck the somber little church-vibe she had going. The Church of Liz. *Hi,* she muttered. When I confessed to Liz that I'd been faking all my orgasms, I'd expected her to yell at me. Her fury was so unpredictable, and nothing brought it out like weakness. I had expected to feel shamed and incompetent and less than lesbian. It was a shock to feel her twine her soft arms around me in the dark, her hand pulling my head to the hard skin of her sternum. *It's alright,* she breathed, *I totally understand.* There have been studies done with rats and electricity that demonstrate the state of panic and confusion you are kept in if you don't know when the next bolt is going to hit you. It was like Liz flipped an internal coin to determine her mood, if she would zap or cuddle. Her unexpected niceness made me feel sickened and tweaky. Maybe it was because she had so recently been a straight girl faking all her own orgasms with her two billion boyfriends. But I suspected that Liz never wanted a girlfriend, she just wanted a girl friend, to bond with about all the injustices and confusions of being a girl, and sitting up all night talking about phony orgasms was like a big bowl of popcorn and a wide-screen TV. *I totally know what that's like,* she assured me. Was I crying?

Liz scared me. It seemed we broke up daily, though nothing was ever said, the situation never talked about, Processed. Just a disgusted glance when she entered the room we shared and saw me on the futon, tarot cards in a cryptic arc around me. A withering stare as I dumped morning granola into a dish, a violent shrug as I came up behind her and pressed my belly to her back. I tried not to ruffle her mood. If we broke up I would have to leave and I had nowhere to go. Do You Want Some Time Alone? I asked her that night, Ani's warbling trill ringing out from the small radio on the floor. *Um, please,* she said sharply, like I was dumb even to have asked. I wanted to tell her about the call, ask her if her body had ever turned on her, but embarrassment lumped in my throat.

I took a shower and stayed in there forever, so Liz could finish up with whatever she was doing in our room, lying around, being with herself. I washed my crotch with the fear and concern of a mother washing the makeup off her twelve-year-old daughter after catching her making out with some guy in the garage. Who Are You To Me And What Dangerous Things Do You Need? The suds fell down my legs and the water turned cold around me, freezing like the awful snow outside, like everything. When I returned to the room Ani was silent, the candles blown out and the air stinking of hot wax and smoke. Liz pretending to be asleep. I crawled in beside her, her body and mine. Sleep crept in like a power outage, putting out the lights.

FROM HERE TO ETERNITY

(★) Annie Koh

Fifth grade sex ed didn't include a film strip on seduction, nor was there a Q and A on how to be a good lover. But long before my first kiss I'd filled in a vast reservoir of rules, assumptions, misinformation, fantasies, myths and clichés about sex. When I was fifteen and listening to my friends recount their first times—in a graveyard, on a blanket in the woods, with someone else's boyfriend on a pool table—I learned that sex wasn't meant for beds and that an uncomfortable place equaled bona fide badass. I understood from watching *Say Anything* that teen sex meant steamy windows and back-seat fumbling. By the time I got my driver's license, still a virgin, I conceived of all sex as breathy but silent, hands and lips blindly reaching out with sudden irrepressible need. It was movie sex: a silent, sweaty tussle, the boy bare-chested, the girl almost always on the bottom, her boobs splayed by gravity.

I learned to expect what men expected. Magazines advised us about What Men Really Want, what a man will think his due after paying for the date and male-focused fantasies like the easy lay, the sexual wildcat, the horny lesbian twins and the "oops!" walk-in that ends up in an unexpected threesome. Gen X flicks informed me that I should wake up in the mornings with a convenient sheet modestly drawn over breasts to flattering effect. I learned that the way Antioch College had proposed sex, to much fanfare—with rules of engagement, careful discussion and consent—was impossible because lovers never talked about what they were going to do. Sex just happened, just coalesced out of desire and surprise. But of course there *were* rules of engagement.

Floating within easy reach on society's sea of clichés and half-remembered myths were all the sexual scripts I had imbibed. They made sex more accessible. In one breath you can invoke apple pie, baseball, and the hooker with the heart of gold and not ruffle decent company. Scripts are familiar. Like platitudes mouthed at a wedding, sexual scripts provide strangers and acquaintances with commercially sanctioned, widely accepted and appropriate ways to be sexy and have sex. In our awkwardness, we rely on the Hallmark cards of sexuality to express our desire.

Cards can express deeply felt emotions; a mass-marketed cartoon concept doesn't negate congratulations or sorrow. Similarly, sexual scripts can work in tandem with lust. When wielded with thought and leavened with a little wryness, even a tired stripping motif like the Catholic schoolgirl can be a genuine turn-on. The centrality of sex in culture leaves us with a muddle of scripts to draw on, many still actively circulating as fantasies as we stare at ceilings or screens or a lover's torso. Scripts can instigate experimentation and serve as models for adventures. But results may vary. A script can translate easily into boring, corny, uninspired sex. And sometimes, a script can drive an entire encounter, making the situation seem more powerful than you are, making sex an obligation.

My first year in college I reinvented myself as a self-proclaimed bad girl, and in the process I consciously picked a master script, a kind of one-stop library/do-it-yourself guide to sexual experience. On the Web, I found the purity test (list of tests can be found at www.armory.com/tests/purity.html). While this now seems too much like a checklist of sexual clichés cribbed straight from the most uninventive pornos, it provided a plan for sexual exploration. There were dozens of incarnations, all purporting to measure how pure or impure you were through a series of yes or no questions about experiences with sex and substances; most made no assumptions about sexual orientation or even sexual know-how. You got a point subtracted for holding hands, and a point subtracted for having sex with your Doberman. The 500- and the 1000-question tests pretended exhaustiveness: that beyond them there was nothing left to do. My messy and half-abandoned forays into sex had left me anxious for a systematic way to approach my sexuality. I didn't want it to be through the pubescent manual *Love and Sex in Plain Language* that my mother had given me when I was eleven. The purity test's pseudo-objective weightiness, coupled with its aura of "anything goes," served as a rich sexual road map pointing out positions of interest, experiences to stop and savor.

At night, after the sounds of roommates and classmates coming home from the dining hall stopped echoing across the quad, my boyfriend E. and I ventured out. In the humanities building, I stood pressed against a men's bathroom stall, alcohol running red underneath my cheeks; in lecture hall, where two years later I would watch my History of India professor pace, E. and I lay across a table with our pants at our ankles. My campus tour would include the TV room, the philosophy lounge, the auditorium and even the old standby, the bed (kinked up of course).

It ended up not mattering so much that most of these moments were "unconsummated." They carried symbolic weight, the affirmation of a newly embraced sexuality. Fucking while talking to my roommate in a bed kitty-corner to mine, underneath a flannel comforter the same plaid as uniforms at an all-girls' private school in Greenwich, Connecticut—this image and these memories became stories to whisper to each other over the phone months later, ways to turn each other on again and again. The litany of places served as our commemorative plaque. Yes, it was trophy sex, of the same genre practiced by the acquaintance who organized her lovers by ethnicity or the girl who slept with at least one person in every entryway on the freshman quad. But even as I retabulated my score every month, the purity test wasn't the end, but rather served as the means, the excuse to keep on pushing the edges of our blooming late-adolescent horniness. New versions would be passed around, and in the diffuse blue glow of a monitor we'd grin, "Now *that's* a good idea." The whole point was trying new things, playing with old stories but making them our own.

By the time summer rolled around I had dropped ten purity percentage points. We had a car to use and a car equaled freedom in the screen adaptation of the American dream. (Or was it hot-rod sex?) We spent the summer driving from scenario to scenario—in some ways the cheesier the script, the bigger the turn-on. In the middle of a barbeque, the yard and patio dotted with beer drinkers we hadn't met, E. and I snuck out. We offered limp excuses to the two people we did know: either "We need air" or "We're going to get more beer." We drove in search of a lovers' lane, a makeout point, a promontory or secluded cul-de-sac where we could indulge in a reenactment of some '60s teen couple's first time. Fitted into the front passenger seat of his mom's car, we fumbled through the few pieces of summer clothing we had on, a little buzzed and completely horny. We were channeling *Say Anything* and my mind was a receiver for teen sexpots of years past.

Between pushing our shorts off and failing to find the condom I thought I had stashed, a white car approached us from the opposite end of the street. Its headlights glided over the steamed-up car windows as it passed by. And then, like a police cruiser circa 1974, it turned around and stationed itself directly in front of our car, its lights on high beam, shining in. We held our breath, clutching each other. It stayed there, bright and obnoxious, for five minutes, until the driver tired of whatever game he or she was playing and rolled off. We exhaled, naked and relieved. All the elements of this classic American tale had been triggered, and we pushed on to the happy end. It didn't matter that it wasn't a Buick, or that what fell to the ground wasn't a varsity letter sweater. Anything that occurred in a car on a summer night was simultaneously transgressive and pure.

I was so young, but I felt old-ish even then, even at eighteen. Old enough to revisit a teen-sex cliché I actually never experienced the first time around. Old enough to find the camp in it. We tweaked it by cramming into the front seat, the seat back cranked all the way down. (The back seat was something he had actually done in high school, and I had smooched across the stick shift.) We were dumb enough to have sex without a condom—due perhaps in part to its absence from our decades-old scene? It was possibly the best sex we had that summer, barring one other sudden in-car rendezvous. We joked, "Keep your eyes on the road," but the simple act of getting into the car accessed half a century of sexual folklore.

I am a place junkie, and images from perfume ads and classic B movies I've only read about impel me to public sex. I am a location scout for my own private porno; every dark corner, this dim bench in a deserted museum, that clearing in the woods become possible on-site shoots for this reel of memories I add to the 18mm loop of older scripts of encounters. When I found myself on a fog-shrouded and nearly deserted beach, many lovers later, I pulled out my mental list to check if I had done *From Here to Eternity* yet. No, not yet, and I lured my wary lover under a copse of gnarled trees. As we began to unbutton our pants, he stopped and rose up from the bed my coat had made across the sand, protesting, "I didn't come here to have sex," the unspoken accusation "Did you?" shimmying between us. How many of these scripts come unbidden, ready to be activated out of storage by circumstance or desire? How many are conscious choices I have drawn about myself, a mantle, to justify my image as a sexual explorer? Or did it matter that I was using the situation to fulfill a lifelong sexual scavenger hunt if we both came hard and throaty under branches dripping with fog?

Induction to the mile-high club is ideally supposed to be a surprise assignation with the stranger seated next to you, or a badly lit tryst with the slinky flight attendant when she comes by with water and juice during the movie. But the last time I leaned suggestively over the carpeted aisle to flirt with another passenger,

I found I had broken into hives midway over the Pacific. His gasp of horror sent me padding into the toilet to poke disgustedly at my face and give up. Flying with my boyfriend of two years was close enough. I decided to earn my mile-high club membership in this way, and prematurely sewed the patch onto my sexual bragging sash.

E. was having none of it. Early on I whispered my intentions, but the combination of no sleep and transatlantic turbulence outweighed for him the allure of fulfilling a middle-class fantasy. I waggled my naked feet and waited, impatiently. It was a long flight; time enough, I considered. Sure enough, seven hours was long enough for him to move from sullen disinterest to mild interest to action. After the foil-wrapped meal with its abandoned steamed carrots had been taken away and a round of Bailey's Irish Cream distributed, he turned to me and smiled.

When we shimmied into the toilet midway through the movie, though, the brightness of the overhead light busted a little of the glamour. I considered leaving the light off by keeping the door unlocked, but I didn't want an anxious businessman to interrupt us. The facts set in—sex under a fluorescent light beside a trash bin beginning to overflow with paper towels—and I giggled. There's a moment of self-consciousness where the resident color commentators of your brain chorus in disbelief, "Hey, you're really doing this! You're standing in an airplane toilet 35,000 feet above the Atlantic about to have sex!" E. sat down on the closed toilet lid, and I was straddling him, kissing him. And then . . . Should I be able to say I followed the instructions to the letter, losing the color commentators, then getting so "caught up" in the moment that my cries of passion echoed down the plane? Or does the story line leave us caught *in flagrante delicto* by a flight attendant who had been peeping the whole time? Or was the situation itself what made for sexy sex, the maneuvering in a phone-booth-size toilet of love hurtling in the stratosphere being enough to send two twenty-year-olds into a dull roar of desire? I had been conditioned more effectively in scripts than he had, but it was both of us casting ourselves with comfortable familiarity in this mythology that heightened the excitement by making it ours.

After we crept out of the cramped bathroom, startling the brown-haired aunt type coming up the aisle, there was an audible "check" in my head. I suspected that three years down the sexual road I wouldn't be able to recall the sex itself, that it would fade unmemorably. Sure enough, sitting here post-handcuffs, post-blindfold, post–digital porno pictures and other purity test activities, I can't remember if we had enough room to go down on each other.

So far, so good. Although the purity test sometimes resulted in sex unmemorable beyond the question to which it answered a resounding Yes, each assignation was still a light-hearted consensual ramble. But the trouble with uncritically embracing such an external guideline was that I also left myself susceptible to other cues and clichés—ones considerably less in sync with my own desires. For a full two years I'd abdicated the navigation to a 500-question test that luckily matched my new-to-sex urge to try anything. This map had served me relatively well, but I'd never consciously determined what I wanted from my sexual encounters. Sex turned into a series of Mad Lib forms where I plugged-in "place," "proper noun," and "time" to churn out a short sex scenario. Fun, sort of flexible, but still a script, one that did not train me to write my own lines or craft the outcome. What did I want? Where and when? I immediately responded to cue cards, visual signs, other people's desires. But the tidal troughs and crests of my own sexual desire were obscured. I knew that a flawed society held onto flawed ideas, but still thought I could discard outdated clichés: the ones that reek of backward sexism, false definitions like the ones you marry and the ones you don't, false obligations, as when dining and wining translate into sex.

But there are other stories in my sexual canon, chapters and verses that I don't produce as anecdotal trophies at spring picnics. I prefer to hold silent in an upset stomach the dissonance between a chosen identity as a carefree sexual explorer and injunctions and behavior that seem to burble up from a primordial goop of old world patriarchy. Comparing the memories of my purity-test adventures with those less comfortable, more forced encounters, I feel as if I am two different people. Context alone seemed to determine whether I felt playful and adventurous or as if sex was something over which I had no control.

There were mornings when I woke up with my hangover in my mouth and my hand draped over an unfamiliar stomach. There were mornings where instead of a fearless sexual Amundsen I thought of myself as some sort of unwitting slut at worst and at best a nice girl who couldn't say no. At 2 a.m. I heard echoey directives like "He's putting you up for the night, you should sleep with him." Who implanted these devilish lies that led me through sex like a somnambulist until I stood up with a headache of vague regret at another bout of unwanted sex? I began to acknowledge the power of situations, but without fully understanding that my responsibility was not to this sheaf of social scripts but to internal dictates of comfort and desire.

How to have sex in fewer than ten steps. 1) You meet at a party, 2) he mixes you a drink, 3) you move on to a bar, conveniently losing your respective friends at the door, 4) he buys you drinks, 5) you dance, 6) he asks you back to his place, 7) fuck, 8) repeat until shiny.

I follow directions well, even directions imprinted on the underside of my conscious mind. On a muggy summer night, I encountered an acquaintance at a party, mixing gin and tonics on a kitchen counter. While we automatically chatted and flattered, our torsos began the slow trapezoidal tilt of mutual interest. We moved on to a bar, leaving my friends at the door with an overzealous bouncer. He bought me shots. Or was it cocktails? I danced, confusedly. I lost my favorite orange plaid summer shirt on the dance floor, foreshadowing events to come. He asked, "Do you want to go?" (or was it a declarative, "Come back to my place"?) and I went. My house was on the way to his house, sort of, but I didn't bring this up. I just skipped drunkenly to his house and then stumbled through a dim and dirty apartment to a bed. Right after he brought me a glass of lukewarm water I passed out. I woke up the next morning unmolested and realized I had to meet my aunt for breakfast. And before I left, we fucked, because I couldn't think of any other ending to the night before. I fucked because I couldn't imagine saying no. What kind of girl doesn't sleep with a guy she went home with?

If I could take a cross section of that night or any other night, stain it with some emotional ink that highlights the exact moment where sex turned from being an unlikely possibility to a probability, maybe I could pinpoint where the script shoulders its way in to the proceedings, insinuating itself where it is not expected. Here, I could point, here at 10:22 when he puts his right hand on my left hip. Or maybe it's at 11:58 when I grimace after the shot of tequila. Or—to flip to a later date specimen—maybe it's here, atop a neglected vista point, when he pulls me into his chest and moans, "Oh god I want you so bad." And I mentally sprint through the available responses I have and can only come up with the mandated, "Me too."

I tried. I tried to trick the script by improvising. I paid for the cab back. Or we came back to my place. Or I paid for dinner. But once the script had been invoked and the evening sexualized, I was obligated to the foregone conclusion. Both he and I understood the rules, and that shared knowledge bound me. He would know if I broke them, and I felt guilty for even considering it. His expectations and my hyperawareness of his waiting for the preordained fuck played a referee role. He was just as bound as I was, though, so it was only fair—so I believed. But because so many scripts invoked a male pursuer and a female pursued, the process was his to initate, mine to follow. In the board game Life it doesn't matter if you inherit your aunt's skunk farm or become a doctor, there is only one ending for you and your plastic station wagon. Once I rolled the die and began the game I could only end up in bed.

Friends told me to stick up for my desires. I had figured out what was expected, what was normal, but I hadn't listened enough to myself to remember what I wanted. In the meantime, I expected myself to be impressed with fuck-ins until dawn. It didn't matter that I wasn't a morning sex girl or that I wasn't a sex marathoner; lovers couldn't entice me with tales of their stamina. What I had relied on was incoherent: snippets of scripts, single scenes, barely sketched scenarios, a synopsis here and there, all patched together with a glossy pornographic veneer. It was part old-country fear of uncontrolled instinctual passion between an unchaperoned woman and man and part post-'60s compulsion toward free love—only a prude wouldn't revel in making love. I imagined myself helplessly rooted to the street, or the couch, or the bed, or wherever I was, while SEX rolled inexorable and impassive towards me. I didn't know how to stop a juggernaut. The smartest thing I could do was jump out of its way.

Two months after I sat in a restaurant watching my friend's horror as I told her how I let sex happen to me and then promised her and myself never to let it happen again, I successfully jumped. In a March snowstorm, I insisted on a ride from my male friend's apartment to the non-sexual haven of a girlfriend's place across the river. Yeah, he gave me a ride. And yeah, I'm sure he knew it meant, "No I don't want to have sex with you." But I didn't have to say it. I didn't have to name it. The men are not the villains here; this is no rape story. Just the befuddled acquiescence of a girl lulled by twenty-odd years of social conditioning and the happy orgasm of a boy willing to play along. I was proud of myself for jumping out of the juggernaut's way. I thought that was enough.

Three months later I had moved to a new city. The day after I opened my suitcases, I ran into an old acquaintance for the first time in four years. One afternoon I called for a ride across a bridge; he obliged. A week later at 2:00 a.m. he called, bored and a little bit slurred after a hundred dollars of liquor. The next day he bought me lunch. At midnight we went cruising for soda and hamburgers. Half of me knew that P. was a nice guy, the other half wondered why I was spending time with someone who couldn't believe that a girl didn't like Tiffany's. We were both lonely in a summer of absent relationships, mine three thousand miles away, his two thousand miles farther. Was that it? Or was it two twentysomethings playing at the age-old game of the mutually beneficial relationship? In financial insolvency, I've flipped to the back of the free weeklies, looking (idly, I told myself) at personal ads: "Generous Professional, WM 45, ISO SF 18–25." I never called, but marveled at the number of men and women willing and looking. There was too much nostalgic history mixed in for this to be a cold cash transaction: I knew P. from school. But I was living on a part-time nonprofit salary, and he offered to buy me groceries. I accepted once, but left them in his fridge, too embarrassed to retrieve them.

Where was the point of no return? When we ran into each other half a block down from my apartment, I didn't experience a frisson of destiny that told me we were fated to have sex. The sense of obligation snuck up slowly. Watching DVDs of bad teen flicks together, I could not have predicted that two weeks later I would watch myself in a mirrored closet while he moved on top and inside of me. I called my boyfriend to let him know that I had been steamrolled by the juggernaut again, and he hung up on me to let me know that he couldn't wait for my next revelation.

Three months later I quick-froze the borrowed scraps of my sexual MO and put them aside. I knew I was prone to letting external situations dictate desire— or the shoddy simulacrum of desire. Which was fine if all it meant was every time I rode the bus or train for an entire year my spine pulsed down to my crotch. But it was not fine if the trappings of a date were enough to convince me to topple into sheets with someone I didn't want to sleep with. I still hadn't learned to play sex with my own rules, and so I decided not to play sex at all. In my journal I underlined sample monologues of refusal: "I'm not looking for a sexual relationship right now." I rehearsed saying, "I'm practicing celibacy." A friend tells me she abandoned sex for two years until she learned to rewrite her own operating system. In a sex-saturated culture, saying no can be a bold statement and an exercise in strength of character; I was pleased to announce my moratorium on sex to my friends. In the calm of no sex, I would be able to decipher the difference between invasive scripts and friendly aids to sexual exploration.

But I am not asexual. My desire is resilient, stubborn in the face of scribbled vows of celibacy. It follows me on my commute to work and insinuates itself while I'm standing in line at the library. It chides me for conceding defeat to outdated scripts, even while I argue that it is only a strategic retreat. Is choosing not to have sex the only method of control I have? Have I needlessly shunted aside a healthy, enjoyable sex life? I flip-flop. I am not consistent in my celibacy and take hiatuses from my hiatus. I deliberately didn't bring birth control on a cross-country visit, but found desire anyway, between one hand laid atop another and in the fact that he hadn't bought condoms either for fear of appearing presumptuous. I still use clichés on occasion, playing with the rumpshaking singlemindedness of a stripper or trying on a dominatrix demeanor. I wish all that I had gathered from the pornos, dredged up from the Internet and mined from the novels was a proclivity for sex in strange places. But mixed in with planes, trains and automobiles was a cue-card mentality that prompted me to clap at the Applause sign even if I had nothing I wanted to applaud. Now I run from celibacy to status quo and peer at everything in between. Which may be as it should: No sexual code of Hammurabi could account for the idiosyncrasies of desire or predict the conjunctions and disjunctions between sentiment and lust. There is no simple navigation from here.

POSSESSION

 Askhari

Preview
The first time i made myself come, i was lying under a ceiling fan. Swirling. Around. Around. Around. i came so hard, so much: i gave myself a headache. Without closing my eyes, i felt my breath multiply. i could feel. The urgency of being abandoned and rediscovered all in the same century. i tore my own shirt. Somewhere between South Carolina and Silver Spring, there was a bare body the breadth of the Black Sea.

The first time i pushed myself beyond my boundaries was because i got to thinking about how soft and aching with color i am. i pulled my satiny smooth shirt through my legs. Repeatedly. Repeatedly. Repeatedly rubbed my own thighs. Together for some satisfaction. Nobody had touched me in months. Nobody. Not because i wasn't pretty or sweet smelling, but because i did not allow any ole dick or finger or tongue up in there.

This here is personal. Peaceful. Powerful. Precious. HIV-free. Healthy. Secure. Worth every after-midnight telephone call. When you touch this here, you got to know what you are doing. Because this here has known uncensored joy. Has known unconstrained abandon. Uncontained passion.

Nobody had touched me in months including me. i busied myself trying too hard to be too revolutionary and liberating to and for everyone else. My mind. Continuously crowded with thoughts of love and revolution: i forgot to leave room for lust. And good new fashioned feeling good. Some say: i work too hard, too much. Some say: i think too hard, too much. Others say: i think and talk and write about sex too much for my own good. Tell me: what they know about good? Huh? Tell me, what harm i be doing by discussing sex; writing about sex; putting a finger in it, a candle in it, a slender warm well oiled flashlight in it?

i just wanted to be near me.

i offered my body to myself that night. Under the ceiling fan. Spinning. Around. Around. Around. i fingered this here. Like this here was the revolution. Uninterrupted, i touched quiet flesh between my own stretch marks and scars. After, i talked softly. Perfected my poetry. Whispered to myself. Smiled. i rubbed and licked and loved the parts of my self i could reach. i was rubbing and licking and loving. Ah . . . i was loving. i pleasured my own self. i mean, after all: this is mine. i say: this here is mine.

Feature Presentation
Whose pussy is this?

Dig. i love Black men. Do you hear me? Love them. But, my alone actions do not always involve men. Often have nothing to do with them. i do not have to rely on Black men for pleasure.

i do not have to be careful. i can take my time. i do not get jealous. i can be quiet or loud. i don't need lace panties. i love to sing.

Me touching myself should not be threatening. My masturbation should not be menacing. My private joy does not jeopardize the existence of Black men in my life. And if on occasion they want to watch—sometimes, that is all right with me. Sometimes, it is not all right with me. What i do during my peace of mind times is about me. About choice. i do not choose to rely solely on Black men for my personal pleasure.

This. This is me claiming my own body. And space. And place. This is me gathering my selves together in my own name. This is me knowing what i want. And need. This. This is me beneath my own equator. Hot, wet and unbothered. This here belongs to me.

And now: whose pussy is this? This is mine.

And so now: i am fingering off-pink folds between key strokes. Feels good.

You know you are smiling. You want me to describe my strokes. Tell the steamy story to you in *Technicolor*. You want to hear the seductive sounds i make in my softened solitude. You want to know how loud. How long. How hard. How far. How fast. How deep.

You want to know if it was good. And now i got you thinking about me doing this shit while you are reading, and your thoughts make you a participant in my pleasure. Dig? You know you like this. You know you want this because you are still reading and you are still smiling. And check this out—even if you *are* still fully clothed, you are my partner in the possibility and meaning of masturbation, otherwise known as my epiphany dance: *Swing low sweet chariot and let me ride*.

Credits

And now, with my own fingers and other assorted objects, i am saying deeply, loudly, boastfully: i do not distract myself from desire. i am unapologetic. No. i will not say i am sorry. Not for any of this. No. No. No, i will defend my private moments publicly with poetry and prose. i proudly put on display my sometimes insistently intimate need for contentment and its relationship or lack thereof to the outside world.

Come by here, my lawd: stretch *this* across a thunderstruck sky because i am saying this out loud and not for the last time in a warm, womanly and honestly rebellious voice. Whoever is listening or reading should know that: i came/come with my own set of dynamite.

BECOMING GENTLEMAN

⭐ Sara Johnston

The gendering of sex entered my life at the same time you did. The first time I pulled the harness over muscular thighs, positioned my only, virgin dick over my aching cunt and asked you to lead the way, you placed one small hand on my back, your fingers burning your scent into me, and your other hand held my dick as you made space for me to thrive.

I thought I was going to die.

I thought I was going to come that instant.

I thought I was going to cry.

I did cry and so did you, your nails digging into my back, marking my muscles as if you would own them. I did not know that would soon be true. My hips rocked slowly, unsure, nervous, scared to hurt you in the ways you've been hurt so many times before. I thought that I would be horrible at it. Nothing like a "real boy." Instead, I fucked you so slowhardfastsoft. Butch to your femme. Boy to your girl. I wanted to heal you with tenderness and validate your power with my strength.

I remember being so scared that I would be like all the others. Letting you lead and then taking over as the words "no" "that hurts" "please stop" drowned in your own throat. I wanted to fuck like a boy, but not like the ones who have torn you into tiny pieces in order to feel big and powerful. I wanted to fuck like a girl, but not like the ones I imagined barely touching you, not noticing the blank stare, the to-do list in your head and the sudden silence of memory. I wanted to reach inside you, touch your ribs, taste your blood, heal broken bones. Sex with you is like nothing I have ever known. Our bodies together create firestorms under skin, burning flesh as sweet as lavender. With every movement you take me further into your heart, you murmur, "he-she-girl-boy-prince—I love you."

I remember the night you asked me to keep my boxers on while we made love. Fear, passion and gratitude came flooding down my back, into my hips and through my dick. I was scared that you wanted me to be a bio-boy, thick in the shoulders, hard chest, my dick skin and blood and muscle rather than silicone, psychologically attached. I felt choked with insecurities as I fucked you as best as I knew how, the way I thought you wanted it, as if I were one of your old boyfriends, hard, slick and male. Later, under sweat-drenched sheets, our bodies sticking to one another, my dick still standing straight up as if I hadn't been fucking for over an hour, a clear reminder of my cunt hidden underneath, I confessed to you my fears of not being boy enough for you. You cried in my arms, hanging on to my heart, and said that I was exactly what you wanted. Mixed up fruit cocktail of gender that makes you hot every time you look in my eyes. You said I fucked you so tender, so well that night, but not because I gave what I thought you wanted. It was the complexities of my body and genders that drew you to choose me and want me.

I bought my first dick almost one year before I actually got the courage to use it with someone else. The first couple weeks after my purchase, I kept it stored in my drawer, still in its wrapper, hidden nicely out of sight. I remember the afternoon I slipped on the cheap harness, pulled the dick through the ring and awkwardly tucked it into my cotton Everlast boxer-briefs. I slipped into my jeans and almost came with the combined pleasure of pressure on my clit and the not-so-realistic bulge in my pants. I remember parading around my room, an ace bandage wrapped tightly around my breasts, baseball cap pulled low and a package settling in my pants, all of it screaming fag-butch-boy-jock-queen. After five minutes of this I looked a little too long in the mirror, saw my "D" cups escaping their binding, the bulge a little too high and my eyes a bit too soft, and I urgently tore off my clothes, unwrapped my chest and stepped out of my harness with fear, desperation and unrecognizable desire.

My recent exploration of masculinity has progressively closed off parts of my body to you. I have internalized some of the images I've been handed of male and female, masculinity and femininity. Fucking with a strap-on is a gendered act for me: my body feels different, it feels male, I feel right. To have your fingers inside my cunt reminds me of what hides behind my dick; it is an abrupt and confusing shift of identity that throws my realness into a whirlwind of contradictions. At this point in my search, I don't like to be fucked as much, I like your fingers soft and curved. Penetration feels vulnerable to me, your mouth on my breasts is barely felt. Through these feelings I still like to be fucked every once in a while, mostly in the ass, where it does not feel so vulnerable, where my female body, girlhood, is not being coaxed to the surface. Sometimes my masculinity feels invalidated through being fucked. I struggle with this because I know it to be a myth. Your fingers touching the inside of my thighs, your lips coaxing sounds like silk from my mouth remind me of how much I crave your mouth on my clit. Lying there, my dick resting on its side next to me, I feel unreal, my head trying to catch up with the touches my body aches for.

I know that masculinity does not own fucking, nor do I want it to, and that is why I am slowly working to reconceptualize masculinity and femininity within a context that feels right to us. I see the tears in your eyes when I shake my head slowly as you reach to touch me. I know my genders are what draw you to me, and I work hard for the day it all makes sense. I often think back to the night you wore the harness, sporting my hard dick, positioning yourself to do the fucking. We were both scared. I encouraged you, and held your back the way you hold mine, leading you in, and as you began to move tears slipped past the walls I have constructed, clouding my vision of my sweet girl fucking me. It was too early, we should have waited, I was not ready to spread my legs that wide and open myself so much to allow you in. I wanted to give it to you, I wanted you to know how it felt to have someone open up and give so much. But I couldn't. We didn't really talk about it again. My fear of being fucked by a girl and your fear of fucking a boy. We know that we will be able to do it some day, but in a different framework. I could not become your femme and you could not be my butch.

The first time we had sex, I saw your soft hands, round hips, hair spread out on the pillow. I felt your nails digging into my back, and I stopped cold. This was forbidden territory for a dyke like me. You were all girl, yet nothing like I had ever known. How could a girl like me fuck a girl like you as if I were a boy with a silicone dick and not have a gender freakout? My breasts rested on your own, my hands were caught up in your hair, my hips rocked hard like I should've been born with a dick, like I should've been doing it a long time before. I wanted to be the gentleman I'd never been allowed to be.

As many times as I have slipped my dick on and have received what you offer, I always have known that sex is not just about dick. I am not butch because I look sexy with swirly-colored silicone resting above my clit. I am not butch because I can fuck you tenderly while at the same time bite, pinch and let my muscles show. I do these things because I am butch. I am also butch when you lay me on my back, your long curly hair creating pools of mystery around my thighs, your fingers deep inside, filling my ass, my cunt with sensations I have never known. Your whole body brings me to climax. Sometimes this exact feeling creates the contradictions, as I confuse penetration with masculinity and make assumptions about your femininity that are wrapped up in internalized images of gender. Sometimes I wonder if it disappoints you; your transboybutch spreading his legs wide begging to be fucked. I worry that you think I am too much of a girl, not butch enough, not a boy, not masculine.

When we have sex it is only you and me in this world. I can only see you, I want you to drink me, swallow me whole or nibble me up bite by bite. I want to live inside you and suck you dry. I want to be yours. I like it when you call me your boyfriend, he, him . . . but I am also afraid to lose she and her. When I opened that present this Christmas and peered into the box, a black satin bra and underwear shattered the assumptions in my eyes. You had said I would never expect this gift, that it was something I could never guess. I had laughed and joked, "What is it? Girl underwear?" Turns out I *could* guess it. Then again, I also had no idea. The note tucked in the corner read, "Because I also love you when you are my girl." I could barely make out the soft pattern through my tears, and your words sounded muted by all the noise in my head. But I could hear you faintly when you told me I never had to wear them, you just wanted me to know. At that moment, everything clicked, an earthquake shifted everything right into place. I understood all you had ever said to me about gender and about what you want. My fears about being both boy and girl had nothing to do with you and everything to do with my own internalizations of gender and masculinity. I was finally able to let my breath out, and I curled up in your arms and cried. That night when we had sex you touched me everywhere, and I was so scared, yet so relieved. Your fingers melted my insecurities, and the words on the small scrap of paper echoed through my body with the vibrations of truth. I finally understood that it was me you loved, not some imitation of male that I thought you wanted.

Your femininity has encouraged my own masculinity, fed, bathed and clothed it, fingers caressing old wounds of confusion and self-hatred. Sex has become our dance of genders. Sometimes urgent ways of validating what was not always visible: your queer femininity and my queer masculinity. We explore parts too hidden to verbalize, queering our own queerness. Sex has opened old scabs, healed fresh scars. Your femininity gave my masculinity energy to shine. I notice it mostly when you touch me, when you grab my arms and lead me to your body, when we walk in step down the sidewalk. Trans became familiar to the way I was touched, the way I fucked, the way I use my body to turn you on and the way I have begun to use my clothes on and off my body. I have started to respond more intensely to the femininity you have worked into your body, the femme identity that spills from your pores, opening skin to make a home for me. I have always experienced myself as masculine, yet I did not understand what that meant until your hands grasped my back, pushing and pulling, enveloping, swallowing the movements of my hips, my own small hands in your hair encouraging words to rise from your skin like mist.

It's your hands that I remember at night, resting like ghosts on my back, your fingers tattooing rhythms into my skin, touching bone. When I fuck you long and hard, the marks on my back penetrate my skin. When you fuck me, legs wrapped around my waist, leading and guiding, it is my hand on your neck that touches the inside of your throat. I coax words, silky and stiff, from unrelenting lips. I am tongue-tied and heavy without your eyes reflecting my image back onto my body, yet your hands have given me the encouragement I need to be strong and intentional in my differing identities. Sometimes seeing is all we need to feel powerful in our own skin. I dreamed of your body last night, curves as soft as moonlight over the ocean, inviting, creating space for me to inhabit, to pull your skin around me safe and powerful and home.

FEMME DYKE SLUT

 Tara Hardy

I was born in a town on a dirty river and I am the slut my mother always said I would become. I am a femme dyke slut. I create openings in my body to inspire the lust of other female-bodied persons. In that town on a dirty river, I was born to work, and I've had to work at this. But simply having an opening is not the challenge. The challenge lies in the active and taken-for-granted art of receiving—like what the throat does. The sexual counterpart to the squeeze of swallowing.

The opening is not the work, because long ago in that small town the farmer, my father, ripped my barn door from its hinges. Everything warm-blooded fled. Not even the shadow of desire, or the horsy steam from her nostrils, dared approach my gaping frame again. He left me fixed open, dilated, a pupil in constant light. For years, my cunt had the vacant stare of the insane.

It has been work to coax her into yearning again, let alone receiving. I have done that work with the help of my butch lovers. It has been butches who have gotten my catatonic

175

second mouth to speak. They understand damage. They understand stone. They know what it is to wait for desire. They too have been thrown to the bottom of that dirty river, lying there like a drowned eye waiting for a reason to feel.

Who has thrown me there might surprise you. Sharon, my mother threw me. There were years when my name could as easily have been "Slut" as "Tara." She was trying to teach me to pass (as she had always hoped to do) as middle class. And middle-class girls did not wear red heels with their skintight jeans. Middle-class girls didn't suck off boys in the back seats of cars for drugs or beer, at least not without some attempt at a coverup.

I'll never forget the day the snow thawed enough to see the dirt again at the end of our pocked driveway. There, among the rivulets of water, a condom shone like a slagging moon against the brown Michigan earth. It must have been discarded from a car window during one of the months when I lacked faith that the snow would ever melt again. I didn't have the guts to remove it in front of the kids at the bus stop, so I just stepped on it with the toe of my thinly soled boot, not moving until everyone else had boarded.

My father discovered it later that afternoon, and found reason to mention it at supper. He knew that my mother's fury at my overt sexuality would strengthen the seal of silence about his own forced liberties with his daughter. Consistently, in this way, he used her to ensure his access to me. Because as long as my sexuality had a pulse of its own, she believed (we all did) the seed of evil lived in me.

And because my sexuality was clearly feminine, it was femininity she tried to beat out of me. When I was as young as four, she beat me up for changing my shirt. My hair had been freshly cut, and I wanted to check my look in my white blouse with the broken-shell buttons. In order not to not muss my 'do, I pulled the sensible turtleneck in which she'd dressed me over my hips and made the switch. When she found me, her fists were accompanied with phrases like "boy crazy" and "raise you to be smart not pretty" and "don't you want to make it to college?"

She beat me not because she didn't love me, but because she was trying to protect me. The kind of feminine sexuality I stood to inherit in that factory town was anything but understated. It was not spawned from the nondescript pools of "natural" looking cosmetics I later encountered as a Merry Maid in the bathrooms of rich women. It was bold, direct and unmistakably hungry. It was fuckable. Which in my world today means ferocious, but in her world then meant vulnerable to being used and discarded like trash.

More desperate, however, was her need to protect me from rape, which she, along with everyone else in the late '60s, believed was caused by the blatant flagging of female sexuality. While feminists conceded that short skirts were not an invitation to rape, they certainly weren't wearing them. In fact, lesbian feminists had concluded that de-gendering meant a certain safety and strength. Women who posed nude for magazines were condemned as worse than the men who peddled them; if only women would stop participating in this exchange, stop being sexual agents, stop acting like objects, we could all get out of sexist jail. But that "jail" was defined by white and middle-class women.

Which brings me to naming who else has thrown me to the bottom of the river—lesbian feminists. Because I think we agree with my mother. And I say "we" here because while I criticize certain interpretations of feminism, I refuse to be thrown out of the club. My stilettos are firmly planted, and I'm not going anywhere.

This wasn't always the case. I wore a red scarf around my neck to my first dyke bar, which, let me tell you, was an unwelcome accessory. I was stuffing it behind the heater after the first twenty minutes, along with the rest of my girly flair. For years I stopped being a slut. I lay around in bed with women, not above or below them, talking politics and trying to love my leg hair. (I remember shamefully trying to dye the hair so it would be less apparent but still enough to pass the dyke test upon inspection.) The women I dated wore corduroy jumpers and drank herbal tea. To them, I tearfully confessed my years of slutting about and begged for feminist redemption. Which was sometimes, reluctantly, bestowed upon me. Years later, I woke to find I had, in fact, become my mother's ideal, her sexually muted daughter.

In the university community where I finally came out, muted, shorn and nondescript earned one membership and authenticity as a lesbian. I remember the cheers from those who had previously ignored me when I arrived at the Pride Parade with my newly requisitioned gone-to-seed-dandelion hair. More than one woman actually clapped me on the back, telling me, "Now you look like a real lesbian." I coughed and grinned.

This is the only moment when I can remember receiving any kind of lesbian recognition that was not connected to the "ticket" of a butch or androgynous lover who was more visibly queer. And I can hardly explain the confusion it created as I was praised and finally accepted as queer only when I was the farthest from myself that I had ever been.

Those claps on the back were congratulations for rejecting a femininity assumed to have been imposed on me, as well as to be an invitation for abuse. But the fact that femininity has historically been used as an excuse for violence against women does not mean it is that invitation. We do not make ourselves safe by eliminating the excuse. Erasing flagrant gender identification has only resulted in polite and, in my case, dead sexuality.

In the mirror after the Pride Parade, the gaze of my unrecognizable reflection haunted me. I felt separate from her, as if she might snub her nose, turn away, leave me. I wanted to reach in and touch her, ask her how to be her. As I worried, she tried to look smug, tough. Instead, she looked defeated.

Dimly, I hoped my new cut would at least win me some dates. But I wasn't sure it would. My sexuality hadn't been revealed, it had been clipped—for the cause. I was stiff and awkward in my sensible shoes and button-downs. In many ways the changes made me more obvious as an imposter.

It took me twelve more years to understand, let alone convince anyone else, that it wasn't dyke I was faking, it was gender (and class). I had blunted and imprisoned the girl in me. All those years later it was only by uncovering my undeniably brazen girliness that dates started pouring in. Living authentically in my body, I, remarkably, started getting laid.

Reclaiming my slut identity, and therefore my sexual, gender and class identities, has meant moving from female to feminist to femme. And today, if I were a cocktail, I'd contain shots of all three.

Being a slut, a femme dyke slut, means living in the exhaust pipe of the feminist "she-volution." It means pulling myself out of its recycled cud, bringing out my shavers, raising my hems and painting my nails into gleaming lethal queens. It means declaring "my femininity does not cause your rape." Having had enough of dolphin sex and kiss-your-tit-in-the-garden music, being a slut means fucking wide, fast, often and for my own pleasure. If being penetrated for my own pleasure and not solely the pleasure of another is not revolutionary, I don't know what is. Being a slut means using the dick no matter who's wearing it.

I don't want to give the impression that femmes are always or only penetrated. I am still femme, in fact I am intensely femme, when I am strapping it on and penetrating another. Femmes have dicks. We use them. Well. And my dick is a girl. I conceptualize my dick as female, whether she's in my mind, my drawer or hanging off my studded leather harness. Giving pleasure through penetration belongs as much to me as any other, and I don't have to manufacture a maleness that is not part of my gender spirit in order to own it.

Only a couple of years ago I came to understand why doubting (or even hating) myself as a femme has everything to do with misogyny. I was lying in bed with a butch girlfriend, telling her how I'd been called a gender conformist that day. Without fully being able to articulate why it wasn't true, I was angry. I asked her whether she'd rather have me be more butch. Being overly familiar with this line of questioning from me, she shook her head and started telling me about her day at work. I interrupted her to say, "You don't have to cover up your wanting me to be more butch by dismissing me. You could at least tell me the truth even if you think I don't want to hear it."

She smiled at me, brushed the hair out of my face, and said, "Just listen."

At the time she was driving a school bus for a living. She told me how a girl had gotten on the bus that morning and approached her presenting the hem of her dress in her little hand. My girlfriend was nervous, afraid she wasn't going to "get it," whatever the specialness was. She said she immediately wished I was there, to help her understand. With much relief, she saw that the girl's hem was lined with velvet. She nodded and said, "Oooh, velvet. Very soft." The girl beamed and took her seat.

At that point in the story I started to cry. I felt so seen and was so unfamiliar with that sensation that I felt exposed.

"I'm a girl! I'm a girl!" I cried through my tears.

My girlfriend looked me in the eye and said, "I know."

"I've been trying to cover it up. Trying not to let it show so much," I said. "But I'm a girl, I can't help it." I paused. "You love me anyway?"

"I love you because you're a girl," she answered.

In that moment I felt deeply how hard I'd been trying to cover up my "girlness," perhaps since I'd been born. Because contrary to popular belief, not all of us got encouraged to be feminine from our mothers—an assertion I've heard from a number of femmes.

When my mother was beating me at four for being too much of a girl, screaming I'd never make it to college, I didn't even know what college was. But I was pretty sure that no one there ever dressed up like I did, then lay behind the couch and masturbated to fantasies of Elvis. Her message was clear—sex made you stupid. But that didn't stop me. Defiantly, I continued to sweat with early lust for that swivel-hipped rock star, my first King of Drag. Even on our black-and-white twelve-inch, "Jailhouse Rock" kept me behind that couch for hours.

I'm still a sucker for a butch woman with a sneer. A sucker for a masculinity so sure of itself that no amount of biology or socialization can convince the body that it shouldn't live there. Today, because I desire masculinity when it occupies female bodies, I thank God there are dykes who do Elvis. Because it has been butches who have helped me heal. It was a butch who led me to my own dirty, sweet, forbidden river and said "swim."

In its flow I've found nothing short of salvation. Recently, I took my butch/trans/boy-dyke/she-Elvis lover inside me. This particular time, I reached an incredibly deep logjam of grief and I felt it loosen. With a tight and insistent hold on my G-spot he encouraged me to go to it, to turn it over to him. I've had other lovers who were afraid of my sexuality, of its power, of the ravenous girl inside me who has the means to swallow them whole. Because I am risking trusting that my lover can handle my lust, my greed, I started to give it to him. But pressure on your G-spot can make you feel like you have to pee. With work, and his encouragement, I stopped caring if that actually happened. I stopped caring what foul or delicious thing sailed from me as I grasped, desperately, at pleasure.

That's when I felt the grief literally begin to leave my body. I stopped breathing and started pushing—out! I saw old wounds come into view and then fly out of me. Glimpses of garden tools, bug-stained hands, onions in my father's fist—they appeared and exploded. I was emptying of pain and filling up with myself. And power. I stopped caring about the source of the pleasure, and started following it, no matter where I found it. I told myself to go after it, to feel as much pleasure as I could.

At one point, my eyes tightly shut, I started having a feeling of things getting tiny then huge, tiny then huge. I remembered having that feeling as a child when I was being touched, and knew suddenly that as a child I'd had orgasms. That this tiny, huge feeling came with pleasure. Again, I didn't care about the source. I wanted it. Lust. Pleasure. Thunderously, terrifyingly, I wanted it.

I realized that I need my little three-year-old orgasming self integrated into me in my adult life. It never was my femininity that caused my father to violate me. My femme did not invite him. But my femme is rescuing my tiny, potent, primitive self. I love her pleasure, no mind the source. And I need her.

It concerns me that femmes are at best regarded as the dinosaurs of the dyke community and at worst parasites who trade on "traditional femininity" in order to pass. To begin with, femininity has never been part of my family tradition. The women in my working-class family have been workers—women with bulges due to starchy diets, feet misshapen from cheap shoes and smoker's skin even if they haven't smoked. As workers they were supposed to be asexual and not obviously gendered.

Perhaps in response to this, many in my community, including myself, choose a sexual expression that is direct, loud and unmistakable. Sadly, this choice has often been misinterpreted. Because in a world whose watermark for being liberated is the position as far as possible from female, a loud femininity has been assumed to be extra oppressed. I believe the exact opposite is true. I think working-class women resist by stepping outside of "proper" to make a sexuality that is anything but lacking agency. In contrast to the understated, deflective femininity of the privileged, ours is a wide-mouthed, unapologetic ability to devour.

Another means of resistance in my femininity is that it rebukes the tradition of making marginalized women—women of color, working-class and poor women—labor so the women in the middle could be fancy, uncalloused and pale. I resist constructing my femininity at the expense of another. Practically, this means I buy my clothes secondhand and not from corporations that operate sweatshops in or outside this country. I don't hire people to do shit jobs for me— one of my strongly held beliefs that has come from cleaning other people's houses is that everyone should have to scrub their own tub. I do my own laundry. I've never had a facial. I don't wear fur. I resist diets.

But I do construct my femininity, consciously. It is not by default or assigned. I choose it and sustain it. On purpose. In the dyke community there's a belief that being femme is some kind of natural expression of being female; the contradictory belief also exists that many trappings of femininity are in fact unnatural. But that crazymaking notion is not my point. My point is that I get up every day and decide how to present myself to the world, just as I witness butch, trans and FTM people laboring over how to present themselves—not because we're vain, but because how we're read is connected to safety, credibility and recognition.

Once, an FTM friend commented that femmes have it easy when it comes to fashion. Easy? Each morning I face the task of dressing myself in a way that expresses my femme gender identity, but that also makes me recognizable as a dyke. I balance dressing as a dyke with not wanting to be mistaken as anything but femme, since I want to be seen. Added to the mix is the need to not draw male attention, because if that's the only attention I get all day, I'll feel like the traitor I'm accused of being. Easy? Some days it's a wonder I make it out of my apartment.

I want to liberate femininity from its history—in my mind, in my body and in my communities. I want to liberate it from the hands of the privileged who withhold access to it, and use it as an excuse to oppress others. I want to demolish its reputation as cause for violation. And I want to take it from under the pestle of the dyke community and celebrate it as a radical expression of queerness.

I want to use my femininity, as Minnie Bruce Pratt describes, as a site of resistance. It is resistance when I use it on the street to deflect hostility from cops, bashers and other bigots directed towards my butch, trans and FTM lovers and friends. It is resistance when I use it to inspire desire in persons very different from the heterosexual white men who were meant to use me in maintaining their supremacy.

It is resistance when I rescue my femme sexuality from a mother who hated it, a father who used and tried to kill it, a culture that says it's worthless and a queer community that devalues it and keeps it invisible. When standing waist high in that old river, I bend to retrieve the stone from its cast-away place. Slipping it into my pocket, I feel its heat spreading beneath the worn seams of my thrift store jeans—no matter who is smirking or spitting in my direction. Wearing other people's garbage I dare to name the mirror powerful. Passionate. Beautiful.

Dreaming of a Color-Blind Affair

 E. René Parker

When I was nineteen, I was just beginning to have sex with some consistency. I had only had sex for the first time the previous year, and I was still uncertain about whether I was doing it "right." (It would be some time before I figured out to use my own satisfaction as the only gauge of good sex.) The white guy I was with, whom I had been seeing for about six weeks, was from Atlanta and had moved to the East Coast to do an internship on Capitol Hill. After our first late-night romp, he jumped out of bed screaming, "Wow! Wow! Wow!" Fishing for a compliment about my sexual performance, I asked, "Wow what?" He came back toward the bed with lust in his eyes and said, "Wow!" kissed me on the forehead, "black women's pussies really are hotter inside than white women's!"

That night, we cuddled in bed and he quickly went to sleep while I cried into my pillow, unable to say or do anything that would communicate how hurt and used and disgusted I felt. He truly believed that in sharing his personal discovery about my genitalia he was paying me a compliment, and the value of my own feelings shriveled in the face of this certainty. Disabusing him felt like a hopeless cause. What being with men meant to me then was the affirmation of my womanhood—being a woman meant *being desired* by men. So I tried to captivate this man, to seduce him, to make him want me—but I couldn't find a way to reject the twisted response I had somehow elicited.

It's not hard to figure out what was going through this boy's mind. After a few bad experiences with non-black men, I became more critical of what I eventually came to term the "erotic exotic": the images, stereotypes and myths of black women and interracial sex that always have surrounded me, creating a degrading fantasy about my black, female sexuality. Learning to name and denounce this experience has become something of a personal mission. As a southern black woman, I am one of the United States' homegrown, erotic-exotic female creatures. I am the object of centuries of thoughts about race and sex that are as old as Europe's first contact with Africa. Many of my early lovers saw in me a black woman innately endowed with savage, mystical sexual powers. To them, I was the "trophy black girl," the one they banged and then bragged about to their friends.

Being exotic to white men—and sometimes white women—means being different: different from the women in their family, different from the other women they have dated, different from their "norm." Most women of color will know what I'm talking about. Racially and ethnically "different" women are perceived as sexually *badder than bad.* Women from other places or cultures are flavors to be sampled. A man stands to learn a sexual secret by breaking a social taboo.

As a black woman in the South, I learned about erotic-exotic fantasies through the southern archetype of the Negress or Voodoo Queen. I absorbed this archetype in childhood and have been forced to navigate around it since—both in my own mind and the minds of others. American society with its history of slavery, civil war, and Reconstruction, imagined the black woman as the woolly-headed Negress: uncouth, unkempt, and without class. While the well-endowed black buck wanted nothing more than to rape virtuous white women, the Negress wanted to be fucked by any- and everyone, preferably from behind or anally.

I cannot recall one porno movie I have been subjected to where the solitary black chick in the film did not get fucked doggie-style with gratuitous camera close-ups of her ass, fetishizing the mystery of "black tail." Anyone who thinks such stereotypes no longer exist doesn't understand that racism is as much an unconscious psychological disease as it is an issue of civil rights and social myths.

However, the boy from Atlanta was not the only one who understood our sex that night in terms of myths and fantasies. What made me vulnerable to him was my own fantasy—a post–sexual revolution, post–civil rights version of traditional romantic love. This was my fairy tale: when I found a boy who wanted me (no matter what race), we would have sex; sex would inspire love; and this love would transcend race, magically wiping away the entire history of racial oppression. Thus, any lasting, committed relationship I had with a non-black man would be a shining example of the power of love.

This might seem like an unlikely dream for a black girl to have. My own culture and history certainly taught me that I should stay away from white boys. White men hurt black women—so went the lessons learned in childhood. Slavery, the Civil War, the movie *Imitation of Life* and the television miniseries *Roots* all pointed to the evils perpetuated by white men on the bodies of black women. And yet, as much as I was told, taught and shown such evils, I couldn't believe that they had anything to do with the white friends I'd known growing up. Before personal experience taught me otherwise, I wanted to believe that since I had managed to overlook so many negative stereotypes about whites, they would recognize that those about blacks were just as foolish.

I grew up in a white working-class suburb where the color line was entrenched socially and geographically. The city of my birth also had been racially segregated. Because the black neighborhoods held economic and social problems that my mother did not want to be part of her children's lives, she moved my sister and me into a suburban neighborhood during the early 1980s. Living in a predominantly white suburb and attending predominantly white schools, I never had the privilege of "automatically" choosing partners who shared my racial background. Even though I didn't actually have a boyfriend in high school, the taboo against interracial relationships in a mostly white environment still felt unjust—a social barrier to dating whoever might catch my interest. Racial differences never repelled me in an aesthetic sense. My crushes were all on punk-rock boys who listened to Suicidal Tendencies or the Dead Kennedys and performed in the local late-night screening of *Rocky Horror*. So I decided early on, before I had any sexual experience whatsoever—and before I became conscious of all the other social codes that determined my sexual choices—that I could date any boy I wanted, of any race, and no one was going to tell me who to "do."

I was a bookish preadolescent, and my mother, then in her late twenties, would not have wanted it otherwise. Because she got pregnant so young, she taught me a mantra that would both plague and help me for years: "Boys and books don't mix! Boys and books don't mix!" Thus books, and the myriad sexual fantasies they inspired—not the one-track minds and fumbling hands of the adolescent boys at school—nourished my developing sexuality.

My romantic adolescent fantasies never were limited to black men. My books were by white authors, with white protagonists. Jacqueline Susann's *The Love Machine* and the sexual addiction (not then coined as a term) of the enigmatic Robin Stone whetted my early sexual appetite. Through Robin Stone's sexploits, I learned about the sexual freedom that men possessed and women did not. Jackie Collins's character Lucky Santangelo in *Chances* and Ayn Rand's character Kira in *We the Living* became my female role models of lust and love respectively. *I* wanted to be the hero in love. My novels promised me both the all-consuming love of Romeo and Juliet and the passion of Prince's *Do Me, Baby*, feeding me the classic ideal of romantic love combined with sex for its own sake in a contradictory yet intoxicating mix. The female characters were independent, extremely sexual and adventurous, and yet they still inspired deeply romantic love relationships. Reading their stories made me long for sex and at the same time made sex seem inseparable from earth-shattering love.

Knowing that these were fantasies didn't mean I understood love or sex in reality. I did know that should I cross the color line in selecting a boyfriend, my fate could be the same as Juliet's—social death. By eleven, I had seen Juliet die many times in my local summer Shakespeare festival. I thought she killed herself not just because she thought Romeo was dead but also because all of Italy and the entire Capulet clan disapproved of their relationship.

I knew about young "redneck" and "whigger" girlfriends who did cross the color line. These girls were also called "nigger lovers" and "dirty butts" by white boys and girls in my school halls and on my neighborhood streets. Their butts and breasts were groped, grabbed and fondled by black boys who may have thought they were "more man" than the other black boy the white girl kissed, "made out with" or let "go all the way." Even these black kids persecuted white girls who had sexual contact with black boys, which only goes to show how deeply these warped stereotypes were ingrained. When I got my first kiss by one of the neighborhood white boys and he thought we should keep our tryst secret, I didn't take it personally. I knew then that my reputation had to be protected if I didn't want to go through what my friends had.

I stopped talking about my romantic and sexual fantasies with my mother at age eleven, when she slapped me for saying that I wanted to live on the island of Knossos with my Greek husband. "No *way*, no *how* will I be the grandmother of any half-breed grandchildren!" Her words still ring in my ears. In my teens, I decided she needed to get past her prejudice, and I refused to tell her my prom date's color. Without waving it as a flag or badge and not perceiving myself as liberal, enlightened or cool, I decided to become a transgressor of the sexual rules dictated by my family and my culture.

Sexual attention was something that I craved when I got to college, after being the asexual and unapproachable "smart girl" in high school. I didn't want to have sex with someone of a particular race, I wanted to have sex, period. After applying to schools all across the country, I went to a Catholic all-women's college in D.C. because it gave me the best financial aid and would allow me to live, with expenses paid, in a fast-paced northern city far away from the prying eyes of my small town. (More than anything else, I wanted to have sex outside of the purview of my mother and everyone I knew.) I shake my head now thinking that I ended up at a small, all-women, essentially all-white Catholic school when sex was my main goal. But at the time, and with limited resources, it was certainly my best option. By the time I got to D.C., my whole body was wound tight with the need to have sex. I lost my virginity six weeks after my arrival, with a guy I met in an art supply store.

In spite of my desire for sexual independence and my determination to cross the color line whenever I damn well pleased, I was still the teenage girl in thrall to the heady version of love I discovered in my paperbacks, unaware of just how distant those romantic plots were from real-life relationships. I could have tried to choose my lovers based on my own sexual desires or whims, but I didn't actually know yet what these were. What I truly wanted and waited for was for men to choose me, to sweep me up, to make love to me and prove my worth as a woman. In practical, how-to terms, I translated this to mean that I should make men desire me, and from that point, have sex with them. After sex, the rest would follow magically.

When the art supply boy and I went our separate ways, my first sexual explorations as a "woman" consisted of going to nightclubs with my girlfriends from my dorm. All of us felt the same need for male affirmation of our sexuality and attractiveness—this wasn't something we could give to each other. And because it was an all-women's school, finding men meant heading off campus and going to the kind of bars and clubs that I now think of as meat markets.

At school, I was once again surrounded by whites. There was only a handful of black women, and most of these were international students. (As a black woman from the South, I was something of a domestic international student myself; as the admissions coordinator told me my first year, I was the first student from that region in close to twenty-five years.) When we went out to bars, I learned that being the erotic-exotic black girl in a predominantly white dance club meant that everyone noticed me, at least initially, and granted me the attention I craved. I loved to go out dancing, and my girlfriends always complimented me on the way I danced at our late-night slumber parties in the dorm. Yet, according to the men in the club, *my* dancing style was viewed as better, sexier than my friends'. Men would come up to me and tell me how sexy and free I looked on the dance floor, usually as part of a pick-up line.

I often got offended when these men crudely attempted to mimic the cadence and intonation of black speech, assuming that I would respond positively. "*Girrrl,* you have some *serious* moves. Then again, I never met a black person who did not know how to dance," they would say, or, "You prove that there is at least a little bit of truth to the rhythm thing." The stupid things that came out of their mouths, along with the mimicry, always turned me off. Many of the white men I met in the dance clubs plainly stated that they didn't *usually* find black women attractive—but there was something *hot* about me. I was erotic, sexy, desirable, allegedly more worthy of fucking than other black women. In lonely moments of wanting to feel like a desirable woman and not the "smart girl," I ignored the things that offended me and accepted their words as compliments. I wanted to have fun and have sex and be a woman finally, and, for the first time, I was getting real sexual attention.

When I hooked up with a man at a club, I had my standards: he had to be cute, he had to turn me on and he had to have his own place—no way was I going to bring a man back to my dorm room. This level of screening may have been appropriate for a one-night stand—which most of these encounters indeed turned out to be. I wanted to have sex with the men I met and never felt shame doing it. But considering I still assumed love and affirmation would instantly follow sex, my "standards" were, shall we say, inadequate. I never thought I deserved the poor treatment I sometimes got from men, but I also invariably repressed my own anger and attributed their racist and sexist views to upbringing. True love still held the promise of transcending race altogether.

My critical awakening finally happened. As a D.C. college student during the late 1980s, I could legally drink beer and wine. Georgetown nightlife included a range of bars and discos with men in the armed forces and from universities like Georgetown, American and George Washington. When I dance in a club now, I close my eyes. This is why: I vividly remember a circle of men hooting and cheering at me, giving me long, lecherous stares, and swarming me with offers to buy me drinks when I stopped dancing. I was frightened because I couldn't figure out what I had done to gain so much attention, and yet I was elated because their hoots and cheers meant that I was sexy. Leaving the dance floor, I played down the intensity of the moment. I humbled myself and tried to appear appalled (as I thought any good southern woman should), while secretly pleased that I had commanded so much attention.

In this small club, off a side street, I remember hearing a military man with a jarhead haircut say to his friend that he would *definitely* get laid by me. I was a "sure thing." In a casual aside, he added something to the effect that the way I was dancing, I was doing everything but verbally propositioning men for sex. And so I learned that an acceptable dance move in my mother's house since childhood could be likened to a sexual proposition in a dance club up North.

To the men, I was a seductress. I was the cause of their arousal, responsible for their hard-ons; ergo, I *clearly* wanted sex. Penetration is the next step— isn't that girl-lesson number one? This was even part of my own thinking about sex at the time, wrapped up in my romantic notions of what women *did* to men. I'd known quite a few teenage boys who guilted their girlfriends (my friends) into having sex with them by declaring that they would get blue balls if they didn't have some kind of release. "Some kind of release" either meant a hand job, a blowjob (which you only told your best friend about because you risked being called a cocksucker otherwise) or intercourse. One friend told me that she gave her virginity to a boy because she "couldn't stand to see the man she loved doubled over in pain" from blue balls. The whole idea that women caused men to lose sexual control sickened me at the same time that I half believed it to be true.

If being a woman was about being desired, I couldn't deny that I wanted men to be attracted to me. Yet my wish to be a woman whom men wanted became a trap when men began to harass me for sex—the presumption that women were always responsible for men's sexual response intensified all the more by their perception of me as an oversexed, erotic-exotic black woman.

Later that night, I had to fight off an unwanted sexual advance from a young Marine. He claimed that because I had made eye contact with him while I was on the dance floor and later accepted a drink from him, I had agreed to have sex. Our fight was in immediate view of the bouncer sitting at the front on a stool. He ignored the whole thing until my girlfriends, all white, saw me struggling and pleaded with him. They said I was innocent and convinced him of my naivete because I was "from the South." Finally, the bouncer intervened, and the Marine relented, spewing out, "Black whore! Dirty black slut! Fuck you bitch!" down the street at me.

I remember thinking in the cab back to my room that the bouncer must have agreed with the jarhead. Why else did he let the guy hassle me so long? My friends also must have felt I had caused some of this, offering up my being from the South as an explanation for what had happened.

Though my mind was racing in the cab, I was scared, numb and angry. He had gotten physically aggressive. He had pawed my hips and ass and grabbed me by the forearm. I had to twist, turn, and side-step beer-laden kisses to keep from being trapped. A half-remembered image from *Roots* had flashed in my mind, and it occurred to me in horror that I had just relived a scene between Kizzy and Master Tom.

I didn't let myself dwell too long that night on the possibility of being raped. But I was furious knowing that I wouldn't have had to fight him off without the doorman's help, if I had been white. During slavery, raping a black woman was not a crime, and it carried no legal penalty—it was a given. And more than a hundred years later, we are all still living with this. In the cab that night, I was hit with the reality that I will be *presumed* to be without virtue and therefore will be open to attack. Paradoxically, being easily identifiable on the dance floor as the only black girl meant that I was *invisible* and on my own in a conflict. I would have to be my own protector.

What I learned, finally, was that I was a sexual object for reasons that had no connection to my own body or personality. When the Marine assaulted me, he made me over into his own twisted, racist fantasy of what a black woman should be. Until that point, there were times when I felt conflicted in my interactions with men, felt confused about what I, as a woman, was "asking for" or felt responsible for men's responses, because I still believed—on some level—that their reactions had something to do with me personally. Indeed, my entire fantasy of romantic passion hinged on the assumption that how men responded to me would confirm my desirability, my womanhood and the power of my love. It took a violent assault, which I knew I had done nothing to incite, to reveal that I was living out fantasies—of race, sex, desire and romantic love.

In the years since, I still have not limited my sexual relationships to black men. What have changed are my own expectations, and my personal and social consciousness. Twenty-five was a crucial age, because I had a repeat version of the incident I'd experienced at nineteen. When my white companion responded after sex with, "Hey! I never made it with a black chick before!" I bolted out of bed. I got dressed, told him that he would never make it with this black chick ever again, left and slammed the door behind me.

What is hardest for me now is coming up against the subtle eroticization of racial difference. An old boyfriend once said to me, "I just love the contrast between my white arm and your black arm." But the beauty of this visible contrast was all in his mind. White skin holds no secret thrill for me—I thought the contrast was minimized because we were dating each other in the face of social opposition. In moments like this, I am forced to wonder whether there is something else my partner carries into bed with us, if some old image, dream, or whiff of "black sex" makes our sex something more (perhaps I should say, less) than what is between us. I have a very low tolerance for this kind of speculation. Though I've dated interracially, I'm not seeking contrast. I'm seeking mutuality.

In unapologetically dating white, Arab and Southeast Asian men (in addition to black men), I've sometimes endured the threat of social punishment as well as the kind of racial exoticization I have already described. I brought no one home to meet my mother until I had been living on my own for six years and was enough of an adult that I knew she would have to accept my partner and me—whether or not she approved. But I never hid from her the fact that at any time I could be involved with a non-black man. With all but one of my white lovers, I was never invited home to meet their families either. But I learned to see it as a kind of threshold for whether we could ever have a viable relationship, because too often I was made into a strange, threatening secret. "When my grandparents kick, I stand to inherit close to a hundred grand. I don't want to do *anything* to jeopardize that," one lover told me, explaining why I would never be able to meet his family like his previous girlfriend. I knew then where I stood.

For many people the thought of interracial sex is still viscerally shocking. Some of the queries I've heard from friends and acquaintances make it seem as if they have a vision of my partner and me having sex right there in front of them. I've heard everything from an off-key rendition of the *Jungle Fever* theme song to "I hear white boys eat pussy funny since they don't have big lips like brothers," to "Don't you feel like he's the slave master?" to "I bet you go to a brother when you want the real thing, don't you?" Instead of individuals we both become flat, cut-out icons, perceived solely in sexual and racial terms. It's hard to tell if these reactions stem from the idea that we are both traitors to our race, from the fear of miscegenation or simply from the force of the taboo. I also have been told that my "sexual curiosity" was "misguided." My sexual curiosity may be abundant (and occasionally misguided), but I soulfully believe it was never beholden to race. Still, people consistently confess their curiosity to me about what interracial sex is "like."

In spite of these obstacles, the taboo against crossing the color line still strikes me as yet another double standard, whose only function seems to be my sexual disempowerment. Crossing it *always* has been the prerogative of white men, and I feel that this freedom to choose sex partners of any race should be mine. The hurt I've experienced with interracial sex never has made me regret my choices. Anyone as naive as I was in the beginning is going to feel pain, and I've been hurt by black men too.

A recent article in a black women's magazine, "Dating White," proposed that black women are now dating white men "simply because we can." Maybe some black women can play around with white men, and for them sex with whites is just another form of trophy sex. But if I learned anything from my experiences with white men, it's that I *can't* play games. I don't have sex with anyone now unless I'm serious. But because of my openness to being with men of other races, I was able to have two important, fulfilling and sexually empowering relationships, first with an Arab man and later with a white man. I entered these relationships wiser and more seasoned: finally sure enough of myself to know what to look for in someone else; finally mature enough to choose who to sleep with rather than waiting, passively, for love to happen to me; and finally shrewd enough to sniff out the ones whose sexual curiosity is truly misguided (although sometimes I still make mistakes). Yet these relationships, too, eventually had to end. I'll never know for sure whether race contributed to the experiences, beliefs and sensibilities that made us incompatible.

I believe that when you are a black woman in this country, you can never fit a Eurocentric standard of beauty and desirability. Your dark skin, woolly hair, black features and body shape are marks not of your individual beauty, but of your savagery. Your experience of exoticization is literally carried in your own flesh. You can expect certain white men to view you as their sexual proving ground. It is easy for me now to dismiss and criticize these staple elements of our culture, but as a nineteen-year-old black girl still learning what to expect from sex, it was much harder to distance myself from them. I could criticize stereotypes, but was still too young to fill in the gaps they left behind, too vulnerable to every cliché that came out of a man's mouth. Becoming critical of them was the precondition for discovering my sexual self, and being able to choose the right partners to share my sex.

My racial identity, my femininity and my southern heritage are all part of a convoluted web that has produced my sexual spirit. Part of my own sexual consciousness has been flavored by that place called "the South," and I too have often considered it the "exotic" region of the United States. The air is hot, moist and fragrant. The scent of magnolia and catalpa linger in the warm breezes. Georgia peaches and pecan pies are sweet, juicy and sticky. Crawdads, gumbo, jambalaya and red beans and rice are flavorful, spicy dishes that, once tasted, are not soon forgotten (for better or for worse). These symbolic aspects of the southern landscape and its history and people intermingle with my sense of sensuality and sexuality.

My southern heritage and culture helped build a paradise of sensory memories. I am a product of this exotic region through birth and socialization, and by choice and imagination. Yet this same culture has created a purgatory inside me. A purgatory built upon the desire for freedom to express unapologetically the breadth of my sexual spirit. In dating and sleeping with white men, I never wanted the rape story between white men and black women to be mine. Instead, I wanted a new story—a fairy tale.

When I think about my past relationships, I am reminded of the Black Uhuru song "Colourblind Affair," and the slow yet upbeat dancehall grooves echo my own feelings of loneliness, loss and hope. Creating yet another story, one without a fairy-tale ending, has proven more challenging than deconstructing old myths. But I'm still a romantic at heart, searching for that perfect mate, of any race, who could play the Sid to my Nancy, the Sartre to my Beauvoir or better yet, the Prince to my Vanity. Someone who will move with me between my southern hometown, his family's living room and my dream house by the Mediterranean Sea.

THE ALLURE OF THE ONE-NIGHT STAND

⊛ Meg Daly

Names have been changed to protect people's anonymity.

I remember being seven, sneaking into my mother's bedroom and rifling through her dresser drawers. They were filled to brimming with wool sweaters, cotton blouses, silky stockings, velvet scarves, denim jeans, satin chemises. The drawers exuded subtle scents of old oak mixed with faded perfume and a hint of skin and human warmth. I furtively tried things on, right over my clothes: a slip that fit me like a gown, a clunky amber necklace, too-big fancy shoes. This was a private ritual. It was a way to glimpse the future, see what it might feel like to be a woman. Getting caught would have ruined the magic of my glamorous, invented self. If someone were to walk in on me, I would have been exposed as just a kid in ratty corduroys, playing dress up with her fantasies.

I carried this feeling of illicit exploration to my initial teenage sexual encounters. My first time having intercourse was a one-night stand, and from that moment on the one-night stand became a sort of enigmatic lover in itself, a lover I would court for years to come. Because it is based largely on fantasy,

194

or at least on the suspension of the mundane narrative of one's life, the one-night stand provided me a keyhole through which I could view an alternative story of myself. It was the fascination of raiding my mother's closet drawn out to its more extreme conclusion: from being a little girl donning lipstick and heirloom jewelry to being twenty-nine and casting myself in a role of my own making. One-night stands have been a way for me to fully explore the range of my sexual self—though not without my fair share of risk and emotional drama.

What there is to learn about sex or oneself during a night with a stranger is different from the self-knowledge gained in a romantic relationship. The essential nature of the one-nighter is that you know the person very little, not at all or not in a sexual way. Plus, there is a shared, unspoken agreement that the thrill of your evening together is bound up with never engaging in such an act together again. Because of these boundaries, one-nighters allow me to explore fantasies and feel adventurous in a way I may not in relationships. Relationships, on the other hand, challenge me to forge a bond beyond sex, to form friendship and commitment. What attracts us to our romantic partners is often very different from what attracts us to people we sleep with only once.

I didn't realize my first time having intercourse was going to be a one-nighter, though the clues were obvious enough. My friend had to drag me, drunk and terrified, into a room wherein waited a boy I had a crush on. Earlier at the party, I had suggested to my friend Kathy that perhaps I could "do it" with this boy, in an eager attempt to catch up with her. Kathy had had sex for the first time a few months prior, and described to me the luscious feeling of sweaty bodies pressed together. After I said I wanted to do it, we spent some time getting good and sauced, and then Kathy urged me on. I balked, and that's where the dragging routine came in, with me laughing and screaming and her tugging me down the hall to her brother's empty bedroom. Once there, the boy in question jammed his latexed cock in me and worked away till he came, my head banging against the headboard all the while. When he was done, I kissed him, unaware that sex should be any other way. Losing my virginity was not non-consensual. It was not, on the other hand, exactly what I would have liked or consented to had I known I had a choice or a voice in the matter.

Oh, to have been raised like some boys who are given the message they can derive pleasure or power from such unappealing, adolescent fumblings. But no, my idealistic feminine heart longed for "connection," and any sexual feelings that surfaced during my teens quickly got sublimated into my quest to be *wanted*. I engaged in several more one-night trysts, half the time thinking if I slept with the guy it would lead to a Relationship, and the other half just acting from a blind and urgent need to be touched. Most of these encounters during high school and college ended with me in tears, and the guy nodding off into sleep. The worst one ended in me being forced to have anal sex by a man with whom I'd otherwise been consensually fooling around all night.

It wasn't until my senior year in college that I realized I could actually enjoy sex. No one had ever discussed sex with me as a teenager, and like most kids I knew, I learned what to do from porn. Which is to say, to lie back and open my legs. Fortunately, I attended a liberal arts college in Oregon where I was inducted into the vast and enlightening world of feminism. My friends and I challenged ourselves to reconstruct our lives as females. We set about growing our leg hair, freeing our voices, raging against rape and economic disparity and (in our more private moments) finding our clitorises. One sunny day during my junior year my friend Sara handed me *For Yourself: The Fulfillment of Female Sexuality* by Lonnie Garfield Barbach and told me I had to try it out. Try it I did, and for the first time in my life I had an orgasm. Ever since then, I've divided my sex life along the lines of B.O. (Before Orgasm) and A.O. (After Orgasm). In the B.O. days, I was essentially numb to my own pleasure. A.O. kicked off a minor feminist revolution inside me, marked by sexual assertiveness and heightened appreciation for my own and other women's bodies. Once I felt the power of a female orgasm, I wanted more. I wanted more of my own, and that desire led to wanting another woman.

Learning how to orgasm was, in a sense, a physicalization of all the feminist theory and sisterhood-is-powerful feeling I'd been immersed in for four years. Orgasm felt like the ultimate celebration of being female, and I wanted to run right out and share the party with my fellow sisters. It wasn't a rational progression so much as a progression of desire. As I learned to plumb my own depths, I became curious about doing so with someone else with similar body parts. Given the ways in which our society restricts and vilifies women based on anatomy, it made sense to me that some degree of freedom could be found by sharing sexual love with another woman. Two women together creating a hoopla of female sexual energy could, I presumed, get themselves "back to the garden"—a Sapphic, feminist garden, that is.

My insular, idyllic feminist community at college would have been the perfect realm in which to explore lesbian passion. However, I was either too scared or too unlucky to act on the fantasies that had begun surfacing. I'd spent enough time reading Adrienne Rich and Audre Lorde to open up a longing for a deep, unbounded female connection. This longing was not reflected in my sex life. I still bounced from one-nighter to one-nighter with men, with a few short-lived heterosexual relationships in between. I maintained a few flirtatious or otherwise ambiguous relationships with women, but none were consummated physically.

After I graduated college, I moved to New York City, a metropolis my mother, when visiting from Wyoming, dubbed "a den of iniquity." The risks and dangers of sex multiplied now that I was away from my small college campus. It took me several months (during which I fell into bed with a few male acquaintances, and developed mad crushes on female friends) to realize that the rules had changed. Sex with strangers took on a new edge when someone could disappear the next day without a trace. My approach to sexuality became influenced by the tough, skin-baring attitude I saw on the streets. I worked at an edgy performance-art space, as well as for a queer publisher. I began reading transgressive sexual literature. As quickly as '70s Sapphic ideals had popped up on my lavender horizon, they were subsumed by a more visceral, less vanilla form of lesbian desire that was emerging in lesbian circles in the early '90s. All those flowerlike images of vulvae I had dancing in my head sort of fluttered away when I opened the pages of magazines like *Pucker Up* and *On Our Backs* and saw women in states of very real and very raunchy desire. I saw that lesbian sex wasn't necessarily just going to be about gently stroking each other's clits. Lesbians, I quickly learned, might like power play, butch/femme roles and dildos, not to mention S/M, topless dancers and porn.

Enter Leila. Leila was my first one-night-stand partner with whom the sex was great, no strings were attached, and a baseline of respect was maintained. She was also my first lesbian lover. Up until this point, one-night stands largely had been about passivity on my part. But the influence of feminist literature, my discovery of my ability to orgasm, and the feeling of freedom that came from graduating college and recognizing I was now the author of my life finally allowed me to act on my own desire. My encounter with Leila was orchestrated by a mutual friend. When, after several beers and a plate of fries, Leila suggested we go home together, I happily agreed. Leila was beautiful, more femme than the butchy girls to whom I later found myself attracted. She rocked my world, and more specifically my body, in a whole new way. She introduced me to the pleasures of biting, whole-hand fucking and deep, guttural coming. I was attracted to her because she was so different from me at the time: flamboyant and earthy, a smoker and drinker, classy without artifice and savvy as hell.

The morning after what proved to be a wild ride in bed, Leila and I ate breakfast and lounged in Central Park. We remained acquaintances, and even slept together another time a year later. But no other bond was forged. No great friendship, no emotional torment. In retrospect, Leila represents a turning point in my understanding of my sexuality. My introduction to lesbian sex was not the one of soft caresses and gentle tongues I had imagined it would be. Leila exemplified a woman uninhibited by the nature of her sexual hungers. And by choosing to sleep with me, she unwittingly invited me to follow in her footsteps. That our sex was rougher and yet more mutual than what I had experienced with male one-nighter partners revealed to me that I felt safer with a woman. Whether the trust was warranted or not does not diminish the importance of that feeling. If I'd been with a man who had bitten my nipples the way Leila did I might have feared I was being treated as a plaything. Instead, I felt physically thrilled in a way I'd never imagined. Leila opened up a new realm of fantasy and desire for me. When I started having sex with women, I began to desire a range of sexual play.

That said, anyone who thinks one-night stands with women are less complicated than with men is peering through a very narrow lens. My experience with Leila turned out to be a bit of an anomaly. With women, I soon realized, I doubled my chances for discovering hidden agendas and expectations. At least with one-night stands and men, I had pretty much figured out that there was little chance of a relationship developing. I still felt hurt by this sometimes, but only because I hadn't yet learned to own my desire with men. I hadn't yet learned I could fuck and run, just like the next guy.

Generally, when I went to bars to meet women, the courtship began with personal conversations. We told each other about our past lovers. We mentioned hometowns, familes, goals in life. Sure, we were drinking and flirting and touching legs; but we were already halfway into building a relationship when a casual one-night thing was all that was supposed to be happening. And the real zinger is that even after all the emoting and talking, chances were at least one of us was still only in it for one thing! I learned the hard way that I had a randy teenage boy living inside me who didn't give one whit about relationships or love. One-night stands with women brought out the part of me that was turned on not so much by being wanted—my old heterosexual paradigm—but by the act of want*ing*.

For instance, there was Maria, a Brazilian butch with an easy smile and— dare I say—dark bedroom eyes. We met at the infamous Friday night Clit Club in Manhattan. I had gone to the club alone, with the vague plan of getting laid, or at least distilling my physical existence down to a sweaty, sexually charged body on a dance floor. Maria was introduced to me through a mutual acquaintance. Her playful, direct eyes caught mine, and a silent pact was formed. She had a soft-butch appeal and her advances were self-assured without being smarmy. I let her be my suitor for the night, and let myself play out my fantasy of being wooed by a butch woman. She took me out to breakfast at four-thirty in the morning and then to her small Chelsea apartment. Her studded tongue danced in me through the dental dam. It was hot, safe sex and I left the next morning pleased with this contained experience that seemed both mature and respectful, if utterly fixed in time.

Unexpectedly, Maria called a few days later—I'd given her my number as a matter of formality, not invitation. She insinuated that she expected our relationship to continue. I was baffled. I acquiesced to letting her come over, but I was waiting outside my apartment building when she showed up. Maria sat down on my doorstep and wept when I told her I didn't want to continue seeing her. I stroked her back and lamely told her I thought she was a really nice person. (Now where had I heard that before!) I couldn't stomach this new phenomenon: I was the one who was supposed to do the falling in love and the getting rejected. I didn't know how to handle my new role as the rejecter. Creepy thoughts snuck in: Had I used her? How could I call myself a feminist, much less a lesbian feminist, and be dallying with women only for sex? What made me different from those male Casanovas I had deplored in college for doing the very same thing to me?

In fact, one-nighters are not usually about knowing or even caring about each other—they are predominantly about getting off. If both people knowingly agree to this, then there's no problem. It was by way of one-nighters with women— who seemed safer and more familiar to me than men—that I realized my expectations during one-nighters with men had always been a joke. When the trappings of heterosexual roles and stereotypes were removed, I discovered more of the totality of my human capabilities and traits. I discovered the ability to desire openly, and the confidence to accept someone else's desire for me. I began to see that I could be an agent, an active participant in my own sexual life. Why this lesson came to me through trysts with women has to do, in part, with my own sexist brainwashing. In previous heterosexual encounters, I had little training for how to be sexually autonomous. If you put me in a bedroom with a man, I became passive. With women, heterosexual rules were no longer in operation. The field was wide open, and we could play.

On the flip side, I presumed all women were trustworthy and would not threaten or do bad things to me. My wake-up call arrived in the form of a tough, androgynous woman from Brooklyn whom I met during another foray to the Clit Club. Michael was everything exotic to me. Her name was sexually ambiguous, as was her appearance. She wore a men's white tank top, no bra and baggy jeans. I caught her checking me out while we jam-packed on the dance floor, each dancing with someone else. Quickly we gravitated towards one another and there was nowhere else to go but body to body. Hers was wiry and taut. She had dark brown skin, offset by her dyed blonde hair and two gold rings in her nose. We were quite the odd pair, me with my pale skin looking like I had just jumped out of a Dove soap commercial, and her looking like Me'Shell Ndegéocello in street clothes. We were pure fantasy to one another. We didn't even learn each other's names until we were out on the street headed to my house.

The truth is I was attracted to her in part because she was black. Plus, she exuded a sort of machismo and sexual knowing that contrasted with the aloofness that some butch women wear like so many rainbow rings. Since it was only a one-nighter and only about sex, there was not much else to like but each other's physical appearance. But the sexual chemistry fizzled once I took her home; we were all elbows and knees jabbing, teeth clashing inadvertently. We were totally out of sync, and our connection lacked even a shred of sensuality. My fantasy bubble popped with the harsh realization that sometimes desire for a stranger is better left on the dance floor.

In the morning I made her breakfast—her request, to which I eagerly complied, anxious to bridge the uncomfortable disdain growing between us. Little did I know that Michael was casing my apartment for something to steal. She settled upon my eyeglasses, which I'd left in the bathroom. I fed her and ushered her out the door. No numbers were exchanged. After she left, I searched for my glasses, to no avail. Sleep-deprived and fuzzy-eyed, I sat down on the living room floor and sobbed. I was terrified. It had not occurred to me that I could befriend, much less have sex with, a woman who might act maliciously toward me. What if she had stolen something more valuable? What if she had been violent? I chastised myself for not ending the evening back when the sex turned sour. What was this need of mine to be nice to someone who was not particularly nice to me? Did I think I owed her breakfast in the name of sisterhood? All sense of the thrill I'd felt left me. I was reduced to a gullible robbery victim and she to a thief.

After Michael, I swore off one-nighters for a while. But the enticement was too strong. Besides, the problem with Michael was that she wasn't trustworthy. When I was honest with myself I had to admit I'd had a bad feeling about her way back at the club, before we ever left. Trust plays a funny role in one-night stands, because trust is both antithetical to and essential to a successful one-night affair. I *have* to trust that the person is not going to harm me, while at the same time I know that I *can't* trust them with my feelings or with any hope of future intimacy. The very excitement of a one-night stand is based on the fact that I don't have a long-standing relationship with the partner in question, and thus, I really have no reason to trust her (or him).

It was my discomfort with this paradox that led me one night into the arms of my friend Sam. I thought I could skirt around the trust issue by having sex with someone I knew, and someone I trusted I wouldn't fall in love with. Sam was a work friend with whom I'd flirted shamelessly, under the guise of all talk, no action. But when he finally propositioned me one weekend when his wife was out of town, I said yes, much to my own amusement and confusion. Because Sam was a man, and married, and because I identified as lesbian, I assumed it would be easy to keep things purely physical. I approached sleeping with Sam like a fetish. Sleeping with a man seemed like a kind of goofy, risqué act. I certainly didn't think it would make me question my sexual orientation. I thought fucking Sam would be akin to letting a girlfriend tie me up—something I'd try once but not make a habit of. It had been a while since I'd seen a naked male body, and I wasn't so sure his would turn me on. In fact, it didn't, but not because it was male. We tried fooling around, but neither of us derived much pleasure from it. Once I was there in his bed, I felt too nervous about the fact that I was participating in a betrayal—of his wife, and of my lesbianism. He seemed nervous too, and couldn't keep his erection. We were both drunk and skittish and so instead of the wild fucking I'd envisioned, we fell asleep in each other's arms.

When I woke up, one of my contacts had fallen out and had crusted to the pillow. I took it as yet another metaphor for my skewed vision. I had thought Sam and I could treat each other like strangers, bring our flirtation to fruition and then walk away. Instead, I was plagued with guilt over his wife. More painful, though, was the tenderness that had leaked into our brief affair. I hadn't expected to come away caring about him. I berated myself for wanting more, and for wanting a man. I was angry with myself for not knowing better than to sleep with a friend.

As it happened, my vision was more deeply distorted than I thought, because I hadn't realized what Sam symbolized to me. First, Sam awakened me to the re-emergence of my bisexual desires, with implications I couldn't face at the time. Concurrently, I desired him precisely because he was married—not because he was unattainable but because he was *marriageable*. Sam had the kind of marriage I might want, where both partners kept their names, their individual careers, and a sense of originality and non-traditional aesthetics. He and his wife were literate, avant-garde, urban, creative people. I wanted both to *be* Sam and be with someone *like* him. Maybe, ultimately, I felt anguish over Sam cheating on his wife with me because it ruined my fantasy of him as the perfect spouse.

You know what they say about hindsight! At the time, I couldn't make sense of what the experience with Sam had meant to me, so I chose to cut off all contact. Not only that, but I stopped having one-night stands. I had lived in New York for more than three years, and in that time I'd had several short-lived relationships with women, and ten one-night stands (with men and women). At age twenty-six, I'd had nearly thirty sexual partners. After Sam, I started to take stock of my sexual and romantic life. I'd been acting rather blindly but could no longer deny that I was drawn to being sexual with new people. I was not doing what many of my friends were doing: building long-term, monogamous relationships. I was out exploring the multitudes of desires I could feel and experience, yet I was also behaving like an undercover agent. There was the good Meg who kept trying to get a girlfriend, and the misbehaving Meg who kept trying to get laid. Something in the one-night stand adventure—with equal parts risk and thrill—kept bringing me back for more. I often felt excited and empowered, or at least enlightened, after each new affair or relationship. Yet an ugly sense of shame inevitably came rushing in when the high wore off. What I really needed was a Susie Bright–like fairy godmother to help me put an end to the self-loathing I sometimes felt. I wish I could report that I engaged in all these trysts with the same sort of humor and self-assurance that someone like Bright possesses in her stories. But most of my one-nighters felt rather furtive and desperate. Again, I liken myself to a teenage boy: part blind desire; part gangly, awkward limbs; and part kid-like innocence—lacking much grace or wisdom.

No *grande dame* of seductresses stepped in to wave a magic wand for me. But the sexual freedom and agency I tapped into when I slept with Leila blossomed into a life of sexual curiosity and adventure. As I've gotten older, I've become more comfortable with my "loose" tendencies, as well as with the risks involved in promiscuity. I consider myself lucky not to have contracted any STDs, not to have been assaulted, not to have been robbed more substantially, not to have been raped more than once. Brief sexual affairs contain an edge of danger, both physical and emotional. That's part of the appeal. One-night stands clarify the distinction between sex and love. Love is hard-won and timeworn, hopefully enhanced by lots of great sex. One-time sex is by nature not conducive to love, but searing in its raw human urgency.

Speaking of raw and human and urgent, my last one-night stand to date holds up as quintessential. It had been four years since Sam, and in that time I'd happily come out as bi. I'd also transported myself to the West Coast and summarily pursued a solid relationship with a man that lasted a good year. We were not soulmates, however, and when it ended, I headed out into the singles world yet again.

This time, the guy I found wasn't married or marriageable. John's appeal was rooted in that illustrious mystique surrounding rock 'n' roll musicians, and I finally got to act out a composite of all those teenage fantasies I'd had about David Lee Roth, Bryan Adams and Prince.

To be fair, John looked like none of the above, though he prided himself on his resemblance to a famous movie actor. I met John after a show he did with his band at a club in Portland. We flirted ever so briefly. The band had a few more shows before going on to Seattle, so I reappeared at the next gig a few days later. I stayed until the show was over, joined the band for a beer and the next thing I knew I was driving John back to his motel in a far-off suburb of Portland that I would have no reason to visit otherwise. He ever-so-tactfully asked me up to his room. I accepted. John, of course, traveled with a stack of CDs and a killer portable sound system. He put on some slick tune or other; I don't know what it was because I was too busy trying to decide if I wanted to fuck him. He was really sexy, but I felt strangely dispassionate. I needed him to fan the fires of sparkly illusion. (Step One in my recipe for a perfect one-nighter: the right attitude. I could take it or leave it, putting me in a position of simultaneous desirability and potential agency.)

As if on cue, he pulled out a copy of an Annie Dillard book. (Step Two: a literary wooing.) He must have known just how to make a writerly type like me swoon, though I'm not sure Dillard would appreciate being so employed. Then he kissed me. John had the unfortunate and perhaps guy-like style of kissing that consisted of sticking his tongue straight out, like, well, a cock. At this point I told him I'd made a vow to myself not to do this one-night stand thing anymore. He said, "Vows are made to be broken." (Step Three: unoriginal and movie-like lines add to the ambiance of living out a fantasy.) Perhaps it was this cheese-ball comeback that actually set things in motion. I nearly warbled out Sheryl Crow lyrics: "Lie to me. I promise, I'll believe." I knew it was artifice and desire, each of us constructing our little illusion about who the other person was for those few hours. He was my high school fantasy come true: a rocker boy with a brain. If only he had rehearsed his lines better. (Step Four: the imperfection. It wouldn't be perfect without a flaw.) After a few insincerities from John, I relented and undressed, holding on to Step One's cool ambivalence.

But wait! He had no condoms. John threw on his clothes and braved the torrential Pacific Northwest rains. He returned, sopping but grinning, with a slim box of Trojans in hand. It was perfect! (Step Five: Safe sex with a guy so unprepared for a one-nighter he doesn't have any condoms on hand adds to the illusion that one-night stands aren't common practice for either of us.) Finally, I climbed on top of him, stroked his long hair and made him moan. Then he climbed on top, took me for a wild ride, and we came like crazy. Twenty minutes later we did it again, girlish boy and boyish girl tangling up the sheets. I even caught a glimmer of affection in his eye.

We slept for a few hours, I got up, showered, dressed and left. "Keep in touch," he said as I meandered down the orange motel hallway, out into the brilliant sunlight, still feeling kind of drunk, legs like rubber bands, lips slightly swollen, not an ounce of love in my heart.

That's where the fairy tale ends. I was so taken with this ridiculously imperfect perfect night that I tried to coax John back to town for a replay. Major no-no. My overzealous attempts to woo him (Flowers sent to a hotel room! What was I thinking?) effectively scared him off. We traded a few emails, which devolved into mutual insults and a miniature-sized ugly breakup. Luckily that ended abruptly, and I haven't spoken to or heard from him since.

That is as it should be. I'm glad not to be in touch with most of my coparticipants in one-evening trysts. I look back at my one-night stands to date with a mix of remembered lust, giddy pride and stinging embarrassment. I'd hate to be corralled with the likes of the Spur Posse, that group of Southern California boys who kept a running competition of how many girls they had sex with. Yet, I revel in the swaggering pleasure that comes from saying "I did it this many times, in this many ways, with this many people." Why shouldn't I? Let's face it—those same tongues that caressed my ears, my neck and my breasts have certainly told the tales of their travels. Having turned my own tongue loose on the page, I am reminded of Anaïs Nin's provocative maxim: "We write to taste life twice, in the moment and in retrospect." With all these one-nighters now safely behind a scrim (dare I admit I'm monogamously involved?), I can savor (or spurn) my private strips of celluloid, my dress-up satin chemises, my beguiling, blistering, ever-revealing one-night stands.

The Virgin and the Fuckdoll

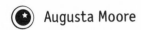 Augusta Moore

You know you've done it, I mean after you've done it, or maybe while you were doing it. You said it, or you whispered it or slobbered it somewhere between that and that, but you *said* it, I know you did, and it wasn't that you didn't mean it, because maybe you would have if there'd been a third date, or just maybe as you hold hands with your sweetheart on your eighth anniversary you can say with smug hindsight that you just knew. Uh-huh. More likely you did mean it—for exactly twenty-three seconds—but you did, and it was gold until the next morning. Or until you got your breath back.

Maybe it shocked you when it came out—like a swear word in your grandmother's house—and just like then you would do anything to take it back, you blushed, you thought you'd die, you hoped no one else had heard, and then you ate a cookie. But I heard you. I did. You said, *"I love you."*

And then again, maybe it didn't shock you a bit. Maybe you got addicted to saying it because it was natural and pure and *love* goddammit, and it oozed like melted chocolate out of your mouth, not just after sex but during coffee and while you brushed your teeth and even when he annoyed you but you didn't get angry—no, you were charmed. Maybe it played that way for weeks, or years. *I love you.* And then maybe you didn't say it so much, except in bed, when slow wake-up lovemaking or a feverish make-up fuck brought it all back again. Or did it make you forget?

Who's to judge? If you're one of the lucky ones, the first time another human being touched you places only candles (Jesus, Mary *and* Joseph!) or vegetables (lots of betacarotene) had ever touched you before, you felt many things and among them was a rush of something so unlike I-like-my-teddybear/car/the red-white-and-blue that you had to call it something and it was probably love. It's not so many years later (but many more than you admit to your mother), and now with the serenity of a love monk you can say that it was childish fumbling, it was a crush (all those things that your mother did say then), but it wasn't really love, was it? It wasn't about shared goals, it wasn't about the crinkles around his eyes, the way he made *linguine alla vongole,* or even the fact that he made you wet to your knees when he looked at you. He did, oh I understand. But it didn't have to be him. He was there in the moment, and, in the terrible midst of those precious baby love steps, that moment seemed like (dare I say it Judy?) *forever.* And it was good—after all, you didn't know any better—and it was love.

But as you ambled your way through life and left your footprints on a number of lovers, there came a time when you *should* have known better. But if experience didn't allow you to enjoy bedding down, at least rationalization did. The sex got better, and as it did so too did your reasons for allowing relationships that everyone (including your mother) knew were wrong—for one reason or another—to continue. Because every time you finished, you suffered that sweet sexual amnesia that convinces you something that feels like this has *got* to be good for you—it's got to be love. It's just *gotta.*

It wasn't my finest moment when the realization set in that when I claimed it was love, it wasn't, or didn't turn out to be, but it kept going—the sex, at least. And it was going *well.* I am a compulsive monogamist, a girl who falls in love in the time it takes to kick off a shoe and sticks with the relationship until the dazzle fades, some two or four years later. At that point, rationalizing the need to flee comes slick and easy. After all, a girl who hasn't broken thirty lives dog years in the span of a four-year relationship. I could switch false idols, careers and a whole shoe wardrobe in less than six months. Generally speaking, after about two years with the same boy, I get bored; I win a game that he didn't even realize we were playing, in which I push and push waiting to see if he will push back—any sign of backbone, not to mention hellfire, would keep me there. But I push and he acquiesces; I wait an appropriate mourning period (usually too long), yawn and split.

But then came a time, a painfully amoral and glorious time, in which that boredom came fast—as in two weeks instead of two years. The flag was planted and the battle over barely after the pants came off, with no time to intellectualize my changing needs. Why bother? My needs hadn't changed, and neither had my boys. *That* was the problem. So I dropped the expectations and traded work for leisure: like a sneak blizzard during which I drank the snow on my tongue, ripped my shirt off and let the flakes prick my chest, made snow angels like there was no tomorrow and invited the neighborhood boys over for all sorts of wicked, cleandirty play.

I deserved it. I was coming straight from five years of sin livin', time that counts like marriage to many of us. I did the breaking up, rather ambivalently and with a lot of whiskey and second thoughts. But, after the deed, the fact remained that the house was empty, and the bed, more important. Let me admit to being a wretch who needed someone to sleep with, someone to yell at, to hang out with on Friday nights to feel a little bit normal.

So it began, in a rage of smartboy attraction whipped into a frenzy by a skinny, elegant body and cheekbones and deep, soulful eyes and long, wavy hair I'd have died for. Because we were in grad school, his mind wooed me first. I was aching to be impressed. I dared him not to bore me. (Besides, he was pretty.) I did believe, in the beginning, that having conversations during which we said things like, "Don't you agree the political is personal, the personal is political, and that inclusion of the personal is not a masturbatory and impolitic foray into the private?" was sexy.

As the weeks droned on, I plucked out the "personal—masturbatory—foray—private" and tuned out the rest, trading monologues on Hegel for amazing afternoon monkey sex. Thankfully, my soul-eyed Beauty's long-windedness was matched by graceful stamina in the bedroom, allowing for endless exploration and possibilities. I mean, he was *always* hard. It was like having a warm dildo with handles that kissed too—the fictitious ever-ready pool boy lover in Judith Krantz novels. But the script was tweaked, and maybe a little more Krantzian than I realized. My Beauty was beautifully passive and feminized, while I jack-booted all over that delicate soul, allowing myself to believe every time we fucked that I felt some glimmer of fondness, some ray of affection for him. And I did, for *parts* of him.

By night I bedded my Beauty and by day whined to my friend Julian. "I can't stand the way he *shaves*. He never listens. He's so self-absorbed. He's such a child. He's always flipping his stupid hair. He cribs Metallica songs on his guitar, for Christ's sake. I'm fucking a Wittgensteinian buttrocker."

"Then why don't you break up with him?"

Why indeed? I got away with the anti-feminist I-don't-wanna-be-alone ploy for a couple of weeks, until it became evident that I was spending more time alone, or with Julian, than I was with my Beauty.

"Just admit it."

"Admit what?"

"He's your fuckdoll. Just say it and get it over with. You'll feel better. *Fuck-doll.*"

Ouch. This might sound pedestrian to some of you, but I *didn't* have sex casually. I was a serial monogamist! And it wasn't as though I was plumbing the local malt shop or anything; he was legal and single and I did (for a minute) believe there might be something there. Having a fuckdoll sounded so cold, so masculine, so self-serving. It was, dear reader, oh it was. And it was delicious. I realized, in that moment and with that compound noun, how freeing sex without love can be—even sex edged with dislike; because nothing was at stake emotionally, everything was a possibility. I didn't worry about the long-range trajectory of our sex life—did we do it enough, was there enough variation, did he find me as attractive as he used to, I didn't like my body so he must not, why do we spend weekends cleaning the catbox instead of fucking—gone, every one. In their place, out came the toys, the ropes and the ice. This relationship wasn't work (hell, there *was* no relationship), so the sex wasn't work—it wasn't tragic or drenched with meaning, tearful or soulful. It was wild, experimental and all about me me me.

Instead of thinking silently about the nanny/employer fantasy to make myself come, he played the part and I exploded. Protesting in vain that his wife might hear, what if the kids wake up, sometimes I asked him to creep into the bedroom while I was feigning sleep. Sometimes I made myself *sixteen.* Between student meetings I would sneak into his office, hike up my skirt and squirm in his lap, laughing when I left him with a hard-on and a fresh-faced sophomore with sentence fragment issues outside his door. We fucked in every room of my house, and never once did I worry about the spread of my thighs on the bathroom counter or if my stomach pooched down when I was on my knees. The smell of apple blossoms and the sound of trains still rim my memories of the backyard, and if the neighbor was watching from his window so much the better. I was in control, and that was sexy. I was sexy.

I'd like to think my Beauty got something out of the deal, but I have to admit that other than sex the feelings were not balanced. I had evolved from a very penitent serial monogamist to the sexual equivalent of Eric the Viking in the sack, with nary a thought to the fair maiden I ravished nightly. He loved me, and I used him, and though I was honest, when his selective hearing kicked in I didn't really try to make him hear me. I've never been the kind of girl who could play at real one-night stands—my first (and only) resulted in a chocolate croissant binge and days of Catholic whore guilt. My play with him was the perfect equivalent. A boy I reinvented daily so that I could overlook the faults and take seconds of the good stuff. Because I didn't love him, in retrospect maybe didn't even respect him, I was attached to nothing that I risked losing in the rebirth. Instead, I found the deliciousness of sexual power after years of accommodation, patience and virgins. I think my time was due to discover what (some) boys discovered a long time ago: selfish, hedonistic, flesh-bent fuckdoll relationships teach you a lot about what gets you off.

My grad school romp was not the first time I set about dividing love and sex in an attempt to distill the latter down to its naughty, thrilling essence. But karmically (at least) my initial attempt was doomed from the get go.

I was in a rut at the time, but my LTR wasn't over yet. I was waiting for someone else to feel for a pulse and pronounce it dead. In the meantime, I needed to feel alive, so I settled on a fling, otherwise known—within the confines of a comatose yet still breathing LTR—as an affair. Immoral and bad and all about sex. The kind of relationship that's all about dosing a girl with a Percocet/therapy/ Girl Scout Cookie injection of endorphins and *I feel pretty* . . . This kind of fling is about feeling wanted—I wanted to be wanted. The fact that the affair is forbidden and will make you go to hell is exactly what makes every touch, every glance electric ecstasy: tastier, tactile, terrific. Oh, how I needed terrific. I may end up in hell yet; but even now someone up there is laughing at me.

I tried desperately to fall into a torrid affair with a moody cynic who basked in my it's-all-about-me glow. We did secretive sneaking and planning and he looked at me with one cocked eye and breathed brooding, bad-boy things. I was so up for terrific that I overlooked the sloppy goldfish kisses, called them fervent passion or too much scotch. I patiently moved his hands not *away* from sweet spots but *to* them, like a piano teacher. Then came the moment that left me as cold as that aforementioned fish. The boy was no Brando. He was a virgin.

Let's be clear that I never set out to deflower anybody. I was in my mid-twenties for Christ's sake—where were all the sacrificial teenage girls? While I enjoy the *Graduate,* I also know Mrs. Robinson could have gotten a better lay than good old Ben. It annoyed me to diagram out where to put knees and how to support weight on one's forearms and to have to suggest forcefully, well, you might be done honey but you're not going anywhere quite yet. Worse yet, unlike those sacrificial teen girls, I'd had plenty of boys who *knew* things, so I was quite aware of what I was missing. I wanted a good fuck without having to hold class.

He came, I bolted and I never touched the boy again. He wrote me long, sad letters and blamed his alcoholic depression on me. He wanted desperately to have another chance (many more chances actually) to become a proper lover and go off into the sunset with me. I'd gone fishing for a great fuck without love, or without what eventually comes with love to spoil it all. Which is to say that I didn't want to have to think at all—I just wanted my mind blown. I got a coital catastrophe attached to a little boy with single-minded devotion.

It wasn't until I made that little boy a man, and that magic moment when sex and love and lust fuse together and you can't tell where one ends and the other begins never happened, that I began to realize what I'd done. The sex was terrible, and while he was whispering *I love you* my eyes were wide open. I had no desire to say it—being denied both the throes of lust and the sweet comfort of a known body. Without good sex, there was just no pretending it was love.

Looking back, I realize that when I told myself I was looking for a quick fuck I was still looking for much more. I wanted the drama of love. I wanted to say "I love you" partly because I felt like a goddess, and partly because I was spent and limp and partly because I meant it too. Maybe I chose a virgin sacrifice because I actually wanted all the devotion and affirmation his inexperience would inspire. Maybe I even set myself up to be disappointed in bed—knowing deep down that a fling was no way to end a relationship. (What reason did I really think the fling would give me for pulling the plug? *Love?*) If I had just owned up to the dying LTR and ended it, if I'd been a real man (as it were), I could have given both my partner and myself a real chance to find a better alternative.

In my later playdates with my Beauty, however, I wasn't trying to fill a void. I was doing the opposite, using my lack of emotional attachment to leverage myself into greater sexual heights, so that when the next LTR came around it had a chance of being phenomenal (and it is, dear reader, it is).

In the end, I can't claim either of the experiences as ones I'd care to repeat—though I'm glad to have them under my belt. I now know that stable, decent and caring aren't enough for me in a relationship no matter what Mom might say. I need theatrics; I need a lot of fantastic sex. But the sex can't stand alone. Behind the scenes, theater is empty and garish. If I'm aware that it's solely theater, I can't enjoy the show. I need to *believe,* at least in the moment, and it takes at least some component of verisimilitude to make that happen. Better still if it's the real thing.

In the end, the virgin and the fuckdoll taught me the most by letting me, or making me, be the initiator, the deflowerer and the user. In the process, I explored some of my stereotypically feminine hang-ups about sex and love, including not asking for what I wanted and not allowing myself sexual pleasures without some pretense of a committed relationship. I'd been sold the love story, wherein the heroine waits passively for her forever-after hookup. I'd been hypnotized by the idea that only Catwoman was sexy and badass enough to purr and growl and lay out the latex while making her desires seem as normal as pudding. Playing the he-man to these passive boys, I said when, I said where and I said how often—whether the latex was out or not. It led me to a place where I both owned my lust *and* yearned to share it with someone I wanted to talk to when I woke up.

It came to me that there are precisely 1,076 different ways to have sex, not involving contortionists (but maybe the bearded lady). Optimally these are fueled by a maximum endorphin–giving mixture rich on passion (at 60 percent), with love, affection and tolerance weighing in at an even 40. (I now believe in this balance the way middle-aged men with expensive cars believe in octane ratings.) Yes, I give passion that much credit, and it flies in the face of the glorious story, the one in which sex lands a leading role but no mention in the title. But I'll take the sex story over the love story anytime: A really good sex story has a love story built right in.

I admit, sometimes my carburetor gets a little out of whack; my libido overheats and my tolerance plummets. Love makes you hot—and unbearably fragile. In the throes of love it takes one rebuffed advance to annihilate ten years of good therapy. When passion runs too high, sometimes your partner gets flattened like roadkill and you might not notice until you're a mile down the road.

I found what keeps me purring, but wouldn't dare prescribe it to anyone else. Hell, you can run a car on corn or the sun or by plugging it in, as long as it makes your little engine go go go.

FAKE DATE

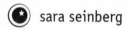 sara seinberg

How long have i known bender? five years? something like that. maybe six. she's been my friend for a long time, let's just say. my right-hand man. my sibling. my pseudo-husband. she's my stand-in, the perfect date for when there is no actual date. we finish each other's sentences all the time. sometimes i just trail off in the middle of thoughts because when i look up into her wide indulgent eyes, it's clear i don't need to finish. she's always right there with me. even our arguments are half spoken, half gesture. she's like an appendage, an organ found after history had nudged it from my body, a prehistoric fold of tissue they took from me before i popped red and screaming from the scar in my mother's belly. but i found her. or she found me. i can't remember. but that's how i always felt with her. found.

let me tell you this about her . . . she's a genius. a photographer, a writer, graffiti artist, renegade and romantic. one of those people who can stop certain moments, color them with a tiny word and a ridiculous image and bring your rigid heart to its knees. and if you never knew your heart had knees, bender could break you off a little chunk of muscle, sprinkle it with pepper and feed it to you in the face of a hunger you never knew you had. sexy. she's sexy in a quiet way. always the one in the corner at a slow rolling boil drinking ginger ale. and handsome. goddamn near perfect looking. spikes of dark hair saluting san francisco's fog. dark eyes, soft and sad, framed in eyelashes reaching out in forty-six pieces brushing butterflies into unsuspecting stomachs. two tiny tufts of curly hair on her chin, a beard. people say a bearded lady, but she's no lady. i watch people at nordstrom stare when she helps me pick out lipstick, but she just smoothes the ace bandage down over her flattened tits and picks up the next color. says, *baby, this'll look real purty on you.* even here in san francisco, folks can never make the call. boy or girl? i always thought, who cares? she looks good, right? and that mouth. a mouth they oughta make laws about. soft soft lips, full, and two spikes of metal shoved around the bottom one. they turn slightly up at the very corners all the time like she's got a secret. a smirk to charm the panties off a nun. i can tell you about that too. that secret. we got one. i suppose after the last year, we got a couple. not to brag.

the thing is, all this came to pass without one conversation about it. there were no plans, no discussions. the phenomenon built itself bawdy and sick in front of everybody, and no one saw a thing. it felt like shoplifting things you never need with a pocket full of money. It felt like lobster for breakfast with two pitchers of homemade sangria on cape cod, a beach across the way and no job to go to on monday. it felt like drag racing, like drugs you hid from your parents in high school. anything that fun had to be kept quiet. we knew that without ever saying it. we knew it like you know the sun is always gonna chase daybreak back to the sky. we knew it like taxes, like death, the inevitable things. things that must happen. and our thing was silence.

it started when i forgot to pay my cable bill or i couldn't or i didn't care or something and it was playoff time. the niners had somehow gotten their shit together and made it out of the wildcard game and into the division games. it was a shitty year for them. i didn't care. i wasn't a niners fan as much as just a fan of the game. now i mutherfuckin' love football. as much as shoes or the mac counter or any other femme vice. all those guys on the vast green field, goal posts holding court in the sky, cheerleaders falling out of their sparkly uniforms on the sidelines. grown men, lined up in those tight pants, the quarterback slipping nimble hands between the legs of a burly center, hut one, hut two, hut hike and just beating the hell out of each other for piles of money and glory. it's so absolutely hedonistic, so entirely gratuitous, and quite frankly, so homo. the patting of hundreds of tight asses every season, visions of locker room showers, a bastion of fag porn. all of this occurs to me somewhere while i watch it, although in the moment, i'm as much on top of the game as any guy in the bar, doing shots and screaming my head off and making sounds like a wild boar of a girl wishing for a dick.

so by the third quarter, i'm pretty tanked. the game is tight. i have an awful feeling atlanta is gonna pull it off. it's terrible here when the niners lose in the playoffs. the fans are really crazy. that's why they call them fans. short for fanatics. i never knew that, but i saw it once in this performance piece. you really do learn something new every day. but anyhow, the people go nuts. maybe it's worse when they win. traffic in the mission stops and men with painted faces and no shirts pour onto the pavement, placing their fragile bodies made of only bone and water and tissue in front of two-ton machines. cars careen to halts, honking commences and beer bottles shower the streets with glass. when they lose, the energy isn't as high, but it's meaner, especially if it's close. there may be no widespread party mayhem, but there's fights. brawls. god forbid you have an atlanta jersey draped across the only rib cage you call home. drunk angry niners fans get in your face like somehow you are the one that gave steve young another concussion. like you are the one that knocked jerry rice on that fine ass and stripped the ball from his blessed thousand-point arms. they are angry like you fucked their wife. but something about all that testosterone really does it for me. the smell creeps quietly into my nose and always finds its way to other venues, venues south in the body, venues that respond like a fire drill. i just prefer the testosterone in a crowded bar rather than isolated in my bed, you know what i'm sayin'? i like a guy who really just might not be a guy in the rest of the world. but here, in playoff season, the rain pelting the january streets outside for the sixteenth day in a row, bender was the guy who was always there. i just never looked for her.

when young took yet another pummeling, i reached down and grabbed bender's leg. it was a tense moment in the game. nothing more. i wasn't aiming for anything, although i don't think i ever could have missed this. i forgot to check for the swagger, the one that girls get when they pack. part pride, part discomfort. part man, part dyke. it's nothing i ever checked for on bender unless i saw her out on a date with someone, or we went out together prowling, but sometimes she just wore it for herself, a nice day for a hard-on. who could blame her? this i was sure of: she had not put it on for me. we weren't like that. it was clear. in fact, after one particularly brutal breakup, i had tried to manufacture this crush on her because i really had to focus my mangled heart someplace else. after a few weeks, she was like, *sara, what is going on? why are you acting so weird? you are really freaking me out.* and that pretty much cured me. a good slap in the face. you know, sometimes that's all a girl needs. but there was this huge bulge in my palm all of a sudden and i looked at her and just said, *whoa. sorry, sailor* . . . but something kept my hand there. a mute fascination with the spontaneity of finding your hand on the cock of your best friend in a straight bar during the playoffs, a speechless moment of time zipping through my blood in a pang. she looked at me and slid those lips across her teeth into a sneer and said, *you don't look so sorry, little lady.*

i didn't even have time to freak out. in that one instant we both became entirely different characters. she'd never looked at me that way or said anything remotely indecent to me at all. maybe we just knew each other so well, we already saw the game. we knew the rules, the outcome and the uniform, and there were so many people in the bar, it seemed as private as an hourly hotel room. no one was looking at us. no one was looking at anything but the tv. and so then my hand started moving and she tossed her head back and smiled and moved her baseball cap over her eyes. she looked good. toothpick poking out over a lip ring, breathing real even like she had it coming. like she knew the whole time. people would break out into cheering and moaning over the game every so often and bender would open her eyes and laugh. she never once looked at me. just chewed on that toothpick and came sitting real still in the bar like a goddamn praying mantis. i only knew she got off cuz she finally put her hand on top of mine, grabbed it so hard i thought all those tiny bones would shatter, and she leaned in real close and said, *who knew you were such a filthy little bitch?* i said, *you knew. you know everything about me, sailor. so fuck you. buy me a drink.* and she stood up, walked that huge-dick walk over to the bar and came back with a smile and a cocktail. the niners lost and the only thing we talked about on the way home was the game.

now you might think that changed things. you might think we started fucking all the time because here we were, two people who loved each other already. spent the night in the same bed all the time and never a fresh moment. here was an open door. what could be better than fucking your best friend? i mean, really, what could be friendlier? you might think we tried to keep it up and eventually we ended up in a relationship like your pals jonna and lou who were friends forever and one night just took the plunge. they've been together ever since, arm in arm, shacked up in hayes valley with a kid on the way. or you might think we ended up like the majority of friends who have sex, awkward and estranged. where both people are on different pages and trust falls through cracks in the hardwood floors. you might be thinking about that guy frankie in college and how you were so close, but as soon as you spread your legs, something happened to the ebb and flow of the conversation. hesitation crept in, jealousy, regret. these things placed wedges into minute places and you hammered chasms into a bond you thought was made of some material sent down from olympus. some atlas-tough grade of steel nothing could shatter. but then you were wrong and here you are, eleven years later, reading this story and wondering whatever happened to that guy. your friend who used to stay up till four o'clock in the morning listening to metallica and helping you with your physics homework.

but i swear to fuckin god, nothing changed. we were still the exact same pals we had always been, dorking out all the time and talking about our respective toils of the heart. we went on photo adventures, shot warehouses and street scenes. we tagged the neighborhood with stickers, we ate lunch, we went to see bands. she was always my date. she'd scope out perspective fellas at the bar for me and i'd raise eyebrows across the jukebox at ladies while we poured quarters in and played patti smith over and over. i think another four or five months went by before we turned to look at each other like that again, like possibilities, like things with skin, like creatures with matching chemicals.

it's different to get away with it at a dyke bar than it is surrounded by hollering meat. the perils are different. the concerns. in one place, you fear for your physical safety while indulging your physical pleasure. in the other, you are avoiding a torrent of gossip. you are avoiding the risk of public knowledge affecting your private fun, outside forces pressuring a label or an answer. things change in dyke culture when people know who's fucking who. but there we were, within the red walls of the tiny dyke bar on a dark intersection of mission streets, sitting on our stools drinking ginger ale by the pint. just hangin' out. the two of us were on our way to get matching tattoos the next week up in north beach. tattoo city. chris conn. that guy can do more with detail than anyone i've ever seen. if i peer down at my arm right now, i can make out the bolts in the fire hydrant, a battalion of ink stains on my arm with bender's name across the banner. but at the time, we didn't know what the banners were gonna say. a bunch of us were there that night, kicking up our heels and laughing. a drama-free evening. and in a town where you've got a trillion dykes and everyone knows about everyone else's business, their cheating, their breakups, their hep c, their ex-girlfriend's new girlfriend, their penchant for pain, a drama-free evening is gold.

so sydney comes up to us and bender buys her a beer. she listens in for a minute and then asks us if we're going to some fancy art opening. we nod. she asks who my date is gonna be and i huck my head towards my man to the left. she says, *oh, your fake date. bender, you're everyone's favorite fake date. maybe you should get that tattooed in the banner . . . fake date.* and i say, *yeah, buddy, you get fake date and i'll get mercy fuck.* we all laugh at that, knowing i haven't had sex in six months and mercy seems like the only thing that can get me laid at this point. and this probably reminds bender it's been quite some time for her too. sydney wanders off to say hello to the lovely ursula. i look back at bender who isn't laughing at all anymore and i say,

what's up, mister?
i just thought maybe i was feelin' a little merciful is all.
oh really? you don't say . . .
that's a nice dress there, sugar. and i don't see one pantyline.
that makes sense. there are none.

she just stands up and strolls towards the bathroom. i watch her walk. she's got the swagger. i smile, but i don't follow her. i just sit there waiting and playing it cool. i actually marvel at how hot the whole thing is, the notion of its silence. the notion of the game we are playing. we both get to win. who doesn't wanna play a game like that? i feel the thunk of the spit i swallow through a tight throat and look towards bender leaning on the jukebox. she twitches her goatee towards me and i smile. but i still don't move. i just turn and talk to sunny tending the bar. i watch her pour guinness stout into pint glasses, the foam taking so long to sepa-rate, cream-colored swirls of bubbles running away from the mahogony that settles to the bottom. i watch like a witness. like a scientist. i can feel bender's eyes from across the bar, and knowing a guy is looking at you that way and chewing his toothpick into splinters makes your head feel different. like the guinness on tap. all the foam rises to the surface and anything solid waits at its furthest point. your head is split in half, the foamy part spinning and light enough to blow away, with all real concerns tucked away at the bottom. the phone bill, the staff meet-ing, the possibility that having sex with your best friend might get tricky . . . these things are so far away. you can't see them from where you are. then bender calls sunny over and hands her something. she comes back and gives me a napkin from bender without thinking twice. *hey girl, bender needs you over there.*

the napkin says this:
get your ass over here now. i only ask nice once.

can i tell you how weird it is for your best friend to get you so worked up you can really barely see? i have walked from that bar stool to that bathroom 962 times and never lost my way. but that night, it took forever. i stopped to chat with everyone i could find. and at every stop i'd look over at bender, acting like i had all the time in the world. knowing she was just there waiting for me to show up at the jukebox. every stop along the way built up the column of tightness in my neck and made my head spin a little more. it was a way to make what we were doing obvious to anyone who cared to see it. but people only see what they expect or what they want to understand. there was all of that, and there was the fun of making somebody wait. and if you can't torture your friends, who can you torture? there she was, just as cool handed as paul newman, just shaking her head at me and laughing. she looked like a guy who missed dinner. a hungry steel worker with the whitest teeth and a dry throat. she looked like a dream. it must have taken me twenty minutes to get to her, and when i did, she reached out real slow and wrapped her fingers around my wrist. i had forgotten what her hand felt like last time. a grip of strong fingers is more to a dyke than a hand-shake. it's an invitation. it's a gift. it's dessert. she dug her fingertips into my vein and pulled my ear up to her mouth.

are you tryin' to make me mad? you think i got all the time in the world to wait for you? you think the world only waits for your dance card? what kind of shit is that, makin' your date stand around with his dick in his hand while you chat up the entire bar . . . leave him with only a jukebox.

surprisingly, all i could say was *sorry.* but i didn't even say it. the word was lodged at the back of my tongue and all i did was move my mouth. she put on this voice like an old comfortable pair of levi's, the thick grime of oil under a mechanic's nails, the sweat in the rim of a cowboy's hat, the broken teeth of hockey players. talking sweet and mean all at the same time. i got to be the girl she kept looking for, the girl who followed orders with just the right amount of shit-talk and just the right amount of fear.

i don't think i heard you, ma'am. i just saw your lips do a jig around your teeth. you know, i been watchin' your mouth all night and seems like now all of a sud-den you don't got so much to say. but i think i can keep you occupied.

then she shoved me towards the open door of the bathroom so hard i forgot she was bender. she was this other guy. she was not the same person who ran hot baths for me with green salts and rosemary lemon oil and brushed my hair out

FAKE DATE

when i got sad. she was not the one who took me to the doctor's and waited with me while they shuffled my blood away to some terrible gray lab. she wasn't the one who showed up at my reading with orange and yellow flowers for her best friend. i heard the door shut behind me and before i could turn around, she had me up against the wall with a fistful of my hair wound around her fingers. i think i may have yelped. i don't remember. she grabbed my arm and yanked it high up my back and plowed her knee up between my legs. i could feel the toothpick in her mouth doing a small and quiet samba behind my ear. her breath was hot and thick like new orleans in august. and before i knew what was happening, i actually couldn't move.

you think it's cute, makin' me wait? you think that's fuckin' funny? you know the score. i don't need to tell you nothin', do i? i know you've done this before. just like you said . . . i know everything about you. i know what you want. i know what you eat in the morning. i know how you like to get fucked and i have the fuckin' keys to your house.

her voice was entirely calm. she just talked like she was reading me a laundry list. she never said anything loud and she never sounded angry, but every part of her skin that touched me was hot and every muscle in her arms was flexed and i just stood with my legs shoulder width apart and my face pressed into the graffiti dripping off the walls. *don't move. stand exactly like that and don't move.* she gave the order like it was some sort of punishment and i listened as the metal of a belt buckle unhitched. click. click. buttons opening with a small heave of denim. and then she sighed. all i wanted to do was watch. but i didn't move. i felt her behind me, a singular motion towards my back.

i'm sorry, sugar, but we gotta make this quick. lot of pretty ladies out there waiting for the bathroom, you know. and we can't think our business in here is any more important than theirs. now you need to be quiet and you need to relax. that's all you gotta do here.

and holy hell, what else would a girl in that position do? it wasn't as fast as bender planned. we started liking it too much and then the pounding on the door started, so she just threw me on the floor and fucked my head off until we both got dizzy. then she got up and held out her hand to help me do the same. she licked her lips while she put it away and as i passed her on my way to the door, she grabbed me by the neck and pushed me up into the wall until i could barely breathe. then she spit the toothpick out and kissed my forehead, like she does every time she says goodbye. we opened the door and there was sunny. first she looked mad, then confused. she said,

oh, it's you guys. i thought someone was fucking or shooting up in there.
then bender started laughing and said,
no sunny, it was just us.

after the first time, we hadn't actually done it. a hand job in a sports bar four and a half minutes into the fourth quarter is not the same as sex. at least, it offers you the comfort and blindness of really believing that. but getting banged on your back with your dress hiked up and your favorite bartender throwing her fist into the door while you come brings a whole different focus. it really is your best friend on top of you, handsome and kind, acting like a lonesome cowboy in a brothel in a forgotten texas town, a little bit mean and perfect, fucking you like you always told your best friend you wanted it. that's what best friends are for. you tell them everything. you tell them what you're not getting everywhere else, you tell them how you wish guys would talk, you tell them about the cadence of your heart. you tell them the things you cannot tell your one-night stands because that is all they are, and you don't care enough about them to tell them anything other than you don't eat breakfast in the morning, even though you do and you go meet bender at the cafe and tell her all about it. you tell your best friend the things you don't tell your lovers because you can't find a way to say what you want without them hearing the word *inadequate* in the back of their heads. but you tell bender, and she stares at you and nods her head and laughs and understands and has nothing to lose because she is bender and she will always be there next to you. and when she shows up for coffee, her neck still covered with bruises from the date she had, you smile at her and pound your fist into her arm and you call her a stud and you can never quite picture her having sex because she is your best friend, and best friends don't do that.

but now you know. you have told her every last thing you long for in a guy. you know exactly the way to talk to her because she's sat sprawled on your bed four hundred times telling you the seventy-two different ways girls drive her nuts. you have trained each other perfectly, although you never meant to. and once she actually has been the guy with the perfect voice, the perfect pressure across your throat, the perfect sneer across the perfect mouth, the perfect kiss on a sweaty forehead, your thighs still trembling in the yellow bathroom on 19th street, something shifts. you begin to wonder, what if? you begin to watch her in a way that catches you off guard. you begin to think twice about staying in her bed when it gets late, not because you don't feel safe, but because you do. you begin to stop looking at other guys at clubs because there is one next to you, one who knows everything there is to say, one who has seen the ugliest side of you and still plods through every awkward pebble in the road until you find the smooth black pavement again. you begin to think, am i missing something? are we missing something here?

and still you say nothing.
she says nothing.

even the next day when you have lunch and your neck is purple on the left side where she dug her fingertips into the muscle, and your spine is sore from the concrete floor and her lip is swollen from biting down on the piercing to keep herself quiet, you stare at the road map of your sex on each other's faces and you pour the sugar into her coffee and she hands you the cream and you have no stories to tell each other because you were both there. you have nothing to talk about because there has been a silent agreement about the silence you are keeping silent about. so you get jacked up on caffeine and go see a movie to shove the sex from your minds and replace it with something solid to talk about. you watch brad pitt and edward norton beat each other senseless over and over and all you can do is picture them fucking, but you are not alone in this. you are in san francisco. at least 89 percent of the audience is picturing the same thing. it's not a bad place to take your mind on a walk. but bender keeps interrupting your faggot stroll of escape, appearing in your daydream, placing her palm on your right cheek and putting her other hand over your chest and telling you to breathe.

you give it a week. you wait for it to disappear like it did the last time, easy and smooth like crayons, but it doesn't go anywhere. it gets worse, and it starts to feel like every time you see her you are lying. you are either waiting for another nod of her chin towards an alleyway or a pool table or you are waiting for her to say it's over or you are waiting for some subliminal message from the world to tell you what to do. it's only been a week, but losing the angel on your shoulder changes the sky in a pretty short period of time. and finally one night as you lay on her bed, you say,

bender, we can't do that again. or we can, but then we'd have to get married.
she laughs. *i know.*
you do?
yeah.

is it okay?
yeah.

and she turns her head and you look at each other and your entire body swells and subsides with relief and she moves her face towards yours as slow as you can imagine and you close your eyes and your mouth goes slack and you feel the metal around the pink skin before you feel her lips and she softly kisses you goodbye in a way just like you told her about the slowest kiss in the world you always dreamed of. and finally, you both close your eyes and sleep like normal people for the first time in a week. in the morning she brings you coffee as you rub your eyes and you say,

morning, sailor.
that's captain to you, little lady.

and you laugh and you pull your tired legs from under the covers and slip them one leg at a time into bender's jeans.

Flat

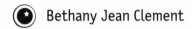 Bethany Jean Clement

W e'd go to the local bar to drink that summer, and he was usually there. I'd pretend I didn't see him for a while, and then not talk to him for a while more after finally vaguely acknowledging his presence. If he wasn't there I'd watch the door while elaborately appearing not to do so, and if he didn't show I was disappointed, but you'd never have known it.

Sometimes he and his friends would get us high out back; the bar was hot, sweaty and smoky and wretchedly drunk, cheap-beer drunk, Rainier-Ale drunk, walleyed-no-longer-capable-of-seeing-the-balls-on-the-pool-table drunk. That place felt then like a swirling suicidal hell, as if these people had already slain themselves and were doomed to party eternally in this sweatbox, never a breath of cool air, just to be borne about on the hot acrid winds kicked up by the fans, no dancing, for no one danced at that place, no matter how much they wanted to. No relief, only more beer.

Then we would sometimes take each other home and fuck. In fact, I called him the Fuck; only some remaining shred of civility kept me from calling him that to his face. One time the Fuck took me home and put something I didn't recognize but that I liked on his stereo as loud as it would go—and that was loud, it was a hell of a stereo, I could tell that even though I was stupendously drunk and we only had a record player at my place—and I saw him in triplicate as he descended on me. What is the comfort of seeing double, or more, a thing well seen and more than enough seen once?

That spring I had worked at the House of Foam. Foam is, I found, an under-appreciated substance; foam is in couch cushions, car seats, cases in which people store guns or gems or oboes. I had an eighty thousand dollar bachelor of arts degree and I was spending my days learning the arcane system of foam, the numbers to describe density per square foot of various types, the virtues of closed-cell versus open-cell. I memorized standard bed sizes in inches (foam makes a very comfortable and durable mattress) and sewed upholstery fabric into strange shapes to fit around strangely shaped pieces of foam that would then fit into strangely shaped places on people's boats.

The industrial sewing machine sped out of control with the slightest depression of the pedal; my fingers were jeopardized by the weird electric saw I used to custom cut foam for those oboes to nestle in. I had to drive a long way out of the city to the suburban strip mall where the House of Foam was located, and there was nowhere good to eat lunch, and someone stole my leather jacket from the back room at work. My boss was a woman short of stature and temper, and I wasn't making much money. I was thus surprised to find that somehow I had been imbued with a real American work ethic: I did my best in the intensely boring, muffled world of foam.

Foam is seasonal, I was also surprised to learn. My boss laid me off at the onset of summer; the boat cushions for the year were done, the rich were yachting, blissfully unaware of my labor supporting their asses as they sipped cocktails. I was demoralized; and concurrently, coincidentally, my love, Leo, left me. I suppose "left me" is the wrong phrase, since we were not frequently together. We were having a "long distance relationship." He telephoned to say he wanted to have fun with his friends over the summer. It seemed love was seasonal as well.

I commenced grieving. At times I entertained a macabre debate: would it be better if he had died? An angel, frozen in time, versus that soul for whom my love was too much, out there somewhere walking, eating, having fun with his friends, forsaking me still with every unshared breath. In my sorrowing, a peculiar self-aggrandizement arose: I could love deeper, more fiercely, and I did pity he who might attempt to be my equal but could not.

I never fantasized about my own death, but being unemployed left me plenty of time to sit on the porch, morbid, smoking cigarettes. My roommate, Annabel, wasn't working either, the economy was bad, and she spent the days lying on the carpet in the living room listening to an ancient, scratched copy of *Let It Be* by the Beatles. She lay close enough to the old turntable that she could blindly but expertly lift the needle back to the beginning. She wept calmly over the loss of her own true love, her high school boyfriend. We fed each other's fits of angst, long stretches of denial. What did we know of love? It was what had gone before; it was the absent reason for all that we did and failed to do.

I deduced a fatalistic formula: it takes as long to get over them as you were with them. You have to symbolically transform every moment of that time with one moment of your pain-tinged own before you can win your heart back, most of it anyway; the whole thing is only magically restored in the fleeting instant before you give it away again. By my calculations I had many months' and Annabel about six years' penance to do.

We lived in a shitty neighborhood, and our house was small and hot; but we had a nice yard, and our neighbor had a big gun. He liked us and told us he'd make sure we were safe. His assurances gave me a sense of impending but eluded doom. I did feel safe: yet unease stalked me, warm breath on my neck nightly. I frequently dreamt that I was still awake, tossing and turning, ghostly apparitions of unthreatening but bothersome acquaintances, partygoers milling in and out of my darkened room, perching on the edge of my bed to chat, and I, the tired host, too polite to ask them to leave.

I filled the moments on that hot still porch with loathing, blowing them full of smoke and watching them drift away. I waited, sickening with boredom and self-pity. Nightfall was a relief; my thighs would not stick to the painted boards of the porch, I was free to get up, move into the twilit yard, experience an empty desire, nonspecific; to be filled with beer, smoking, the Fuck.

So we spent our days: I smoked, Annabel wept. At night we drank. The first time I saw him, Annabel had said, "You don't want to get involved with him. He's bad news." He was a beauty—tanned, muscular, malevolent looking. He had long thick dark hair that I realized was appallingly longer and thicker and darker than my own. He did not leer; his smile was wide and sinister, implicating you in that knowing devilishness, knowing what he wanted he would make you want, what he wanted he would get and give.

I invited him to our house one day; the daytime seemed safe. I decided I didn't care enough to wash my face or brush my hair for this rendezvous. We went to the video store and got a movie and got high and watched it and drank beer with the front door open, the afternoon sun a shifting trapezoid on the dust of the air, the floor; we were elaborately casual, two young, shiftless people on this still day. My boredom was unadulterated. Then, the hallway, dimness, he, his hands. "I don't think I want to do this," I breathed, between one kiss and another. He laughed, "You don't think?" He already had his hand up my dress and the wetness he found there belied my words; ah, I thought, even my own body betrays me now, as he laughed again, "You don't think?" The foolishness of life, of protestations, of virtue, of any thought at all; there was only the giving in, the giving up.

Sometimes we would go night swimming after the bar closed, Annabel, me, he and his friends. Air, finally; the canal, made to join two lakes, buzzed with pleasure-boaters during the day. At night it was dark, shiny and deep. We leapt off a high platform. I would float on my back and marvel at the firmament, still holding. I would be wanting to kiss him there in the water where I felt, momentarily, all right, but the sides were steep, no footing, just me, wishing hopelessly.

Once there I asked him to come home with me and he said no. So we parted: the lurch of disappointment, barely felt. Later in the fall, a girl named Tina, small, honey blonde, desperate-eyed, would stagger up to me at the bar; I rarely went there anymore, and I would regard her soberly as she decried the Fuck, told me how he had pitted us against each other all that summer, how he would leave her, callously, telling her he was going to meet me, and wasn't he an asshole? This with the intonation of desperation; and I would agree, because I felt sorry for her, because she had known, and cared. I hadn't known, and had I known, I wouldn't have cared; but I wouldn't want her to know that, the depths of my apathy, merely out of respect for the tears threatening to spill out of her drunken blue eyes.

That night after he had turned me down, Annabel and I got in my car and I put in a tape of Hendrix playing "Like a Rolling Stone"—at the beginning he says it's for everybody here with hearts, any kind of hearts, and ears. I drove on one of my favorite roads, a winding one with traffic islands in the middle, and I could feel my mind sliding in and out of lucidity, abstractly, distantly. At the end of the song I rewound it to the beginning, turned it up and drove faster, my foot, disembodied, heavier and heavier on the accelerator. Annabel had a gleeful and vacant grin. Under that slow hazy sea of unreality, the tiny voice that usually guided me was distant, echoing, slurred. This, one moment; the next skimming gently to the edge of a curb and the steering wheel pulling recalcitrantly. We bumped to a halt: me, Annabel, the car. I switched off the radio.

"Annabel," I said, "I fear I have flattened a tire."

"Really," she said. We got out and I burrowed blindly, blurrily, in the trunk and somehow turned up the packet of pieces, which I placed on the ground near the sadly deflated tire. Annabel and I stood and regarded it.

"I know how to do it," she said, "I know how to do it." She kept repeating this as we stood. I lit a cigarette and softly cursed the night. "Fuck," I said under my smoky breath, and then louder: "Fuck. Fuckety fuckety fuck." The dark was thorough, so late it was almost early again. The bushes at the side of the road mocked me; distantly, houses slept. I sat down in the black grass, and for no apparent reason I thought of that day, the dim stillness, his hand sliding up my skin and knowing that in the other room the motes of dust were still floating endlessly in the slanted beams of the late afternoon, my half-hearted protest, his disbelieving laugh, the shedding of clothes simply because there isn't anything else to do.

Then careening around the corner came a VW bus. I leapt up, to the best of my ability, and waved. The bus swerved over and the lawnmower engine cut; the door flew open and a fellow stepped out to (strangely, romantically) the sound of Frank Sinatra at high volume.

And so we were saved: he greeted our incompetence nonjudgmentally, worked steadily in a nimbus of activity. I watched in slow motion, with an oddly detached, expectant gratitude. We thanked him profusely, completing each other's sentences like a doddering married couple. He refused our offers to make him dinner, buy him a beer sometime, would not take our phone number. He just wheeled off into the night.

I piloted the car home slowly, in silence.

To what do I owe my survival of that season? Shiftlessness is one thing, but to be bereft of a sense of possibilities, to be young and to spend your time drinking beer, and cheap beer at that, and fucking someone just to do it, perhaps as some feeble lowing cry of hope: it was all I had the heart for, and it was something in its very meaninglessness. It said, this I can do.

Why do we chain ourselves to the past this way, even in youth, perhaps even more in youth? Why do we allow the past to extract more than we have already given? Why would you spend your moments, your very life, in some hopeless, fruitless penance, when you know not what you have done? It is perhaps a luxury of being young, to think that you have time to spare, that you can make any one moment other than what it is: your life, the present, hung in dark space like a star on an invisible chain.

Fate is a tiger you've got by the tail: for some reason, then, it turned on me and only yawned.

BONE TO BONE

 Chelsea Cain

S tretch the moment. The river rocks worn smooth and gray by the current. Rotting pine cones. Nothing before or after right now. Not needing anyone but him. Not wanting to be with anyone but him. Unable to imagine longing for anyone but him. The sensation of pressing my face against his soft cheek, pressing our flesh together until we are bone to bone. Knowing this.

Standing together on the banks of the Metolius River. The clear, see-right-through-to-the-bottom-of-things water that came from a glacier that came from snow that came from a glacier. Walking with him, both our hands in my pocket and feeling that every pine needle every blade of grass of that place is precious. Wanting to memorize all of it, every sensation: The cold burn of the air on my cheeks, the smell of Ponderosa pines and cedar and wood fires burning in the nearby cabins, the feel of his warm hand, the lap and purr of the current. The feeling of not wanting the feeling to end.

Sex to me is like this moment by the river. This place is me. I live here with my mother's ashes, fully formed beneath the water, a sort of lady of the lake. I brought him here to peel back my skin and show him the river that runs through my flesh. My body is long and pale and soft, but this place glows with a thousand particles from a thousand places running underneath the surface.

I want to tell you that it is sweet and strange and befuddling and profound and wicked and pleasurable and holy. It is a river of sensation. It rushes, rumbles, laps. It is a way of melding, wonderfully, a brief Niagara. Every cell finally sure that it is engaged in exactly the right activity.

The moment, entering me, is thoroughly surprising every time. This is the inside of me. This is my most electric alive part. This is my vulva, my vagina, my clitoris. This is my most naked self. Inside each other's skins. Exchanging cells. I can feel all those little bits of him on my bare belly pressed against my bare belly this is the center of me this is my inside this is all of me.

We like to be touching, always. He runs his hands along the curve of my waist. He will do this for hours, quietly, perfectly entertained. After sex, we lie on each other for as long as we can, pelvis to pelvis, still connected, the sweat a puddle getting cold between us. Hearts racing. Blood dispersing. When we finally break apart it is with regret and promise and remorse. Miss me.

It is better when you are completely honest.

My mother, before she died, said that life was like floating down a river on your back. You're always worried about what's up ahead, craning your neck around to see what's up ahead, stretching to catch sight of white water, rocks, logs. When you're dying, she said, it's like being handed a map of the river, suddenly you know what's coming, and for the first time you can just float.

Stretch the moment. I try to remember to float. When we spread her ashes in the Metolius I made that my mantra. I made sentences in my head as I let handfuls of her drop through my fingers into the river, gray ash and chunks of charcoal and bone. Float float float float.

Plank widths, he says, are the smallest thing measurable, the width of the threads of the universe. I like your plank widths, I say. What's that about my plank's width? he says. You should be a physicist, I say.

Electron. Proton. Nucleus. Atom. Quark.

When he is inside me that is all there is. That is the most important thing, and all the rocks and white water and logs just disappear. We fit. My nose in his ear. His nose in my eye socket. Toe to toe. Penis to vagina. Chin to clavicle. We line up. When he is inside me I can feel him in my marrow. There is nothing more that I want than to have sex with him. Together, we are blood and bone and semen, like the Metolius.

I want to walk more with you by the river he says after the first time because he understands what the world is. The too-huge world that seems less so when we are together walking. I want to walk more with you by the river he says, and I think yes yes yes, because he understands. He likes this place he likes me he likes the river. He understands what we are to each other. You are my one true love he says, and we laugh at how silly it sounds.

I don't tell him he is like the river. He is my Metolius.

We go back to the cabin where my mother and I came a few weeks before she died. Her insides were swollen then from the cancer, her cells already poisoned. She wanted to drive down to the river but she was too weak to walk so we sat by the water with the car windows rolled down and listened to the sounds of it. Summer then. Clear and warm and green. The river a rush of glacier water a current of clean clear water over red and gray stone. She closed her eyes and memorized the sound of it.

When she died it was with that same expression on her face, as if she could still hear the sound of that river running.

I can hear it too. And when I let myself I can go to that place, not to the banks, but actually under the water, submerged. It is a cold pure feeling, another world.

He lays with me. We rest against each other and even the touch of him against the back of my knee, my bare skin, glows a ripe pink. He comes inside me and I crumple under the weight of my own skin. If I could hold my breath longer I would live under water.

At the cabin we sit and lie down and talk like ordinary people. As if we are not made of water. We play board games in front of the fireplace and make pasta and watch movies and then try to will the snow to fall. We spend a lot of time looking at each other, which is a lot like sex I think only smaller and less so. Sex is that sort of looking times a thousand times a hundred thousand. Look at me. In my head I am thinking I love you more than anything more than anyone else in the world. I don't say it aloud, but it ripples through my body, a strong undertow. That is what I think when we are having sex. I love you more than anything more than anyone else in the world. I love you more than anything more than anyone else in the world. In those moments when we are inside each other these are the only words I know.

There is a place on the Metolius where you can see up the river and around the bend, where there is an island of grass and a big old log that stretches into the water. There's a cabin on the opposite bank, one of those square summer structures from the thirties. No one around. I think that if you went in from that spot you could float a long time without obstacle. If you could somehow survive the cold and the current. You could cross your arms over your chest and push your feet out straight and point your toes and just run with the water; you could float for miles. Underwater sometimes, if you could hold your breath. If you listened. All that water, pressing into you, that feeling of being completely surrounded, supported, a second skin. I feel him. He holds me up, his particles pressing into me all over, holding me together while my tissue sheds and scales into the water. Ineffable now.

I close my eyes and let the thick water carry me. The human body is 85 percent water. This is me. This is my belly, breast, nipple. Epidermis, dermis, subdermis. Connective tissue. Spleen. Bile duct. Kidney. Large intestine. Small intestine. Veins. Heart. Frontal lobe. Hippocampus. Cerebral cortex. Brain stem. Muscle. Lungs. Ovaries. Bronchial tube. Tongue. This is the Metolius. I yawn my body wide, until our flesh surrenders and our bodies become shadows dancing on the glossy surface of the water. I think: Float. I think: I love him more than anything more than anyone in the world. I think: I am the lady of the lake. I think: I am the clitoris. I am the Metolius. I am the glacier water. I am the pine needles. I am the smooth cold rocks. I am my mother's ashes. I am the fish. I am him. I am my mind's own words disappearing. I am my mind's own words floating away from my body. I am my mind's own words getting smaller and smaller and farther away. I am all river.

ETERNAL NOVICE

⊛ Karen Bullock-Jordan

S ex is my life. I know that sounds melodramatic, but really, if I could be sure I would never have any kind of sex again, I would take a quick header off the nearest tall building.

Now it's not like I don't *have* a life, 'cuz I do. It's not that I don't have other interests, 'cuz I do—reading, shopping, playing/listening to music, movies, card games, politics, etc. It's just that my prime motivator in life is sex: S/M sex, "vanilla" sex, the potential for sex, planning for sex, spontaneous sex, savoring the afterglow (and of course, telling all the details to my gal pals).

I know that some people out there think of sex for its own sake—meaning, not specifically as an expression of love or intimacy—as "just sex." My experience of sexuality, if not my whole definition of sexuality, is something fundamentally different. Eroticism and sexual energy are the filters through which I experience the world, and my own sexual spirit infuses everything I do. Sex is like a religion for me—a way to connect with the universe, with its energy. The "Letter from the

Editor" in *Essence* magazine used to have a profile drawing of Susan L. Taylor that showed her long braids trailing out behind her head, mixing with the night sky, the cosmos. Maybe it's not what the *Essence* folks had in mind, but that's exactly how I feel during good sex—like I am exchanging energy with the universe. Sex is a way of playing with another person, bonding with them both physically and emotionally, each initiating the other into new experiences. Most of all, sex is fun. And like other games that engage body, mind and spirit, sex can be a mirror for everything else in life.

It would not be an exaggeration to say that I have become something of a sex guru over the years. All this time, I've been talking and writing about sex. Been beating people over the head with my outspokenness. I've answered questions, dispensed advice, spoken on the interconnectedness of politics and sex, encouraged strangers to talk about their fantasies, and organized groups so women can find, talk to, teach, learn from and fuck each other. Sometimes I even get paid to do these things. But I've also found that no matter how much I think I know, every sexual episode can be a learning experience, if I am open to it. My sex-guru status notwithstanding, I am always learning from my brand-new experiences, and am realizing all over again how much there is to learn.

Many of my best learning experiences have been S/M-related, something that has always made me quick to promote S/M. But the fact is, you don't need to push external boundaries to push internal boundaries—plenty of vanilla sex has shaken me up and left me a little different than before. In fact, these days I seem to be having something of a vanilla renaissance. (Which just goes to show that no matter how much you've done already, as long as you are growing and changing, sex is going to change too—yet another reason to view sex as a voyage of discovery.)

It's not that I don't want to do S/M anymore, but in the last few years, I haven't met many bottoms that I'm attracted to. And after a painful breakup with my "boy"— an S/M play partner whom I loved and with whom I had an intense relationship—I've found it harder to "get it up" emotionally and put myself in a topping headspace. Also, in the aftermath of my "divorce" from my partner of eight years, I'm itching to sow my wild oats. When we were together I was free to have all kinds of S/M experiences, but our agreement called for no vanilla sex outside our relationship, and I had only been with two other women before I met her. So in relation to vanilla sex I have suddenly found myself on the "less experienced" side (if experience is measured in number of partners)—rather a novel experience for me. The realization that behind my sex-guru exterior lurks a true vanilla novice has given me a whole new appreciation for sex as a learning process, and inspires me to share a few of my discoveries.

Place is often an integral part of transformative sexual experiences (S/M-leather conferences, play parties and public sex all come to mind). I have been going to the Michigan Womyn's Music Festival regularly since '91, right after I came out into S/M, and was told by the other S/M girls in my town that Michigan was an experience not to be missed. And now, having gone so often, I have to say that even with all the negatives—tofu cooked for thousands, the anti-S/M sentiment, the anti-trans sentiment, the increasingly expensive costs, the increase of alcohol abuse by campers in the Twilight Zone, the incessant white-girl-non-rhythmic drumming, and forgive me, but the music—I'd rather have my hair pulled out strand by strand then miss Michigan. What better place is there to learn something about the power of cunt?

There is something magical about being in a women's space on such a grand scale for an entire week. The energy is almost palpable. I like the feeling of being in the wilderness with the security of knowing I'm surrounded by thousands of women. There is also a feeling of camaraderie among the S/M dykes, a feeling of being at a tribal gathering, that makes my time there memorable. I can't speak for the other seasoned players who attend, but I feel like I can let loose at Michigan in a way that I can't anywhere else. I can't say that every year I've played a lot or had a lot of sex, but some years, I'm in constant motion: One year I had at least one scene a day, sometimes two, and by the last day, because of a scheduling conflict, my partner at the time and I had two scenes going on at once. Even the years that I played very little, I had so much fun that I needed days to reacclimate to "regular" life after I returned.

After a few years, I felt part of a core group of girls, and the experience was becoming like a family reunion: you know, like you only see this whole group of people at this one event, and you may or may not have contact with some of them in between, but when you all get together again, it's like you never left. I had played with a number of the girls, and had a fair number of non-S/M sexual experiences under my belt. At the time, my one regret was that I had never fisted a woman. I had only been fisted by my partner, who was much smaller than I and had very small hands. I, on the other hand, had very large hands, and had not been able to get one into her cunt (though not for lack of trying).

My hair had become something of a joke these years at Michigan. I never knew what to do with it, so lately I had just been letting it go its own way— which meant that after my shower my hair would lie flat against my shoulders, and as the day wore on it would slowly poof out, till by nightfall I had a look even Chaka Khan would envy. One day I was sitting by the campfire and asked my lover to get me a bandanna from the tent. She brought back a red one and I started tying my hair up. In the S/M handkerchief code, red means fisting (worn in the left pocket it means you're a fister, in the right, that you're a fistee.) As I knotted the handkerchief, E yelled across the firepit, "I see you're wearing a red hanky—which side do you wear it on?"

I was flustered but desperate not to appear so. E was part of my little "family," but up to that moment, I had not spent much time playing with her. I was a little intimidated by her, and had categorized her in the group of "heavy players" that I would be too gun-shy to play with. Then I decided, What the hell? I told E that I had been fisted many times, but had never successfully fisted a woman. She replied that she'd love to help me "bust my cherry," and we made a tentative date for late the next day, as I was presenting a workshop and needed to use the morning to prepare for it. The next morning, I'm going over my notes, frantically editing and scribbling, when she shows up. She's talking to me, but I'm only half listening, since I'm focused entirely on trying to quell the nausea that I normally feel before speaking publicly. She leans over and says that she knows that I'm busy, but she's been thinking about my fist all night and she really needs it right now, it won't take long. So, with a willing and ready woman eager to help me have a new experience, what was I to do? You guessed it: I dropped my notes like a hot potato and prepared to get busy.

The year before, my partner and I had further opened up our relationship and become polyamorous. She had brought her new lover with us to Michigan, an S/M novice who, coincidentally, happened to be best friends with my other lover (how's that for incestuous lesbian relationships?). While this woman was somewhat overwhelmed at the various things going on, she was content to watch and eager to learn. She held us both in some esteem as these wild sex radicals (which we were, and are), and I wanted to keep my reputation intact.

The spot E and I picked to do my first fisting happened to be right near where my partner's lover was sitting watching a scene (I think it was the first one she had ever witnessed). E got on her back and I gloved and lubed up, and then I started fucking her. I had read many pieces on fisting, and had seen a couple of demos (one of which featured my lover) and of course had been fisted many times myself. So I had these tapes playing in my head as I was fucking her, going over the "proper" technique. Go slow, work one finger in at a time, apply more lube. E was not a fisting virgin by any means, and was becoming increasingly frustrated by my slow build-up. She kept urging me to go ahead and "do it," but I refrained, 'cuz I wanted to be sure to do it right.

Finally she says, "We're running out of time!" and reaches down and grabs my hand and pushes it into her cunt. My jaw dropped, but wanting to retain my aura of cool, I closed my mouth. To feel her swallow me so simply, to feel her walls hugging my hand, was simply mind-blowing. Even through the glove I could feel her heat and wetness. I also had the odd visual of appearing to wear a metal bracelet, as her numerous labia piercings lay neatly against my wrist. At one point, while I was still trying to appear nonplussed, E did a 180 till she was facing away from me. Then she began hurling herself up and down on my fist, and my cool was lost forever. I felt simultaneously like I had never had sex before, and like I was starring in a porno movie. I flashed back on a scene from one of the earliest real lezbo porn films by Fatale Video, where a butch/femme couple is having sex, the butch fisting the femme, and the femme does a 180 on the butch's fist. Every time we watched that movie, my friends and I would rewind that part and watch in slo-mo, demanding, "Can anyone really do that?" And boom, here I was, and it was happening right at the end of my very own wrist!

There is no comparison to the humbling feeling of awe at the power of a woman's cunt. I had always believed intellectually that cunts were powerful and women's sexuality was powerful, but until that moment I hadn't truly realized how screwed—uh, I mean, *skewed* the paradigm of power in relation to penetration is. In the patriarchal view of sex, which seems to permeate most of the world's thinking about vaginal penetrative sex, the power rests with the male. The variations on the vanilla missionary position—woman on top, or female dominant—get most of their kick from their opposition to standard male power and control. Even in lesbian sex, in my world of butch/femme sexuality, the power still implicitly lies with the penetrator—witness the discomfort, jokes and evasions when the subject of butches getting fucked by femmes comes up. In recent generations this is changing, but as my ex-partner (who is only six years older than I) constantly reminded me, when she was coming out, the term "butch bottom" did not exist.

With my fist deep inside this woman, my fingers so captured by her inner muscles that at times I wondered if I'd ever get them back, I felt privileged and given to and humbled. It reminded me of something my first girlfriend had said to me when we were talking about this same subject. She'd said, when you walk into a house, which is more powerful, you or the house? Sure, you can damage the walls, but the house can collapse and kill you. At the time, I just shrugged it off. But fisting E, I realized she was right, and finally understood the incredible power of receptivity.

While I don't know everything about sex in general or my sexuality in particular, I do have a certain wealth of knowledge about my body and had been feeling confident in the last few years that I knew what I liked and didn't like, what I was capable of and not capable of. For example, I was pretty sure that I did not like anal sex, was not capable of a G-spot orgasm, and with the exception of swinging from the chandeliers, had been in most of the sexual positions possible for two people who were not contortionists. I believed that I could map my vagina and knew the pleasure spots and the various methods and implements that could be used to stimulate them. I thought I would never be able to come from penetration without the use of a vibrator. I believed I knew exactly what I wanted to explore—namely, certain kinds of S/M experiences. As far as vanilla sex went, I was pretty sure that while things would get better, they would not get different. However in the last eight months or so, most of these beliefs have been exploded as the myths that they were.

I've always been a "trisexual," meaning I'll try almost anything at least once. I wouldn't call myself a trend follower, but if I hear of new or different things, I'm definitely going to give them a whirl. Sometimes the initial experimentation is so powerful that I know that this is something to incorporate into my life. Sometimes, the whole process of experimentation makes me wonder what the hype is all about. A case in point is all the hoopla about the G-spot orgasm. I have had lots of friends who ejaculate: one who eventually had to invest in rubber pads for her mattress, one who even did a demo at a play party my partner and I hosted, and my ex-partner. I went to panels and demos, read about it, and of course tried it myself, but I was not a convert. I didn't like the feeling of having to pee (and I have no inhibitions about urination or anything like that, it was just uncomfortable and distracting from my other feelings of arousal and excitement).

I was also not-so-vaguely bothered by the public sentiment in dykeville about it. It quickly became *the* orgasm to have . . . what separated the wheat from the chaff, so to speak. I had women tell me it was the closest thing to God, that it beat clitoral orgasm hands down. I heard women ejaculators actually express pity for non-ejaculators, as if having only clitoral orgasms meant that you were hopelessly inhibited and doomed to a non-evolving sex life. In my mind, this simply became another way for women to judge themselves sexually inadequate. Experts were quick to clamor that this proved that male and female orgasms were more similar than different, which pissed me off the most. It seemed to be a quest for validation of women's orgasms, by showing how they were in fact like men's orgasms.

Once I met a woman who was determined to make me ejaculate. Although she was sexy, and most of our sex was hot, her tunnel vision got on my nerves—especially when, in the post-coital glow, she kept up some New Age rigmarole about the spiritual aspects of ejaculation. Part of the problem with sexual trends is that once you start to hear all this hype and pressure, especially from your own partners, it gets harder and harder to know how you would actually feel about it. After this experience, I just ruled it out completely.

There is a spot inside my cunt, very near my G-spot but not on exactly my G-spot that I like to have stimulated during sex. One day, my present lover was fucking me and hitting that spot quite rigorously and well. I was close to orgasm, and suddenly I felt like I had to pee, but different. I wanted to see what would happen, so I warned her that I felt like I was about to spurt. She said okay, and started fucking me harder and then *whoosh!* It just went on and on and I completely soaked the sheets. We were both giddy afterwards and her new nickname for me became "Puddles." I have to admit that I did feel some new and different sense of my own sexual power with this forceful gushing going on in my crotch area. I felt sort of like Queen of the Jungle by soaking the sheets (the towel, the mattress, etc.). The spontaneity added to the overall experience, and the ability to be with this woman and let go in a way I hadn't been able to before was special to me. However, I am still not one of those enthusiasts who thinks it's the ultimate in orgasm. If it happens, it happens, but I don't *work* at it. Rather than converting me to the gospel of G-spot orgasms, the whole thing really showed me to trust in myself and not let myself be too influenced (one way or the other) by sexual trends.

Learning experiences can come from the least likely places. I recently started a sexual relationship with a straight man, the first time I've had a penis inside me in almost twelve years (I'd had sex with my ex-boyfriend a little over a year ago, but it didn't involve vaginal intercourse). I had identified as bisexual a year or so after I first came out, but finally rejected that identity for a number of reasons. One, I had mainly called myself bi because I thought that "real" lesbians wouldn't allow me to call myself a lesbian if I was still attracted to men, even though I had no intention of having sex with them. Two, while I thought that I might have sex with a man again sometime in my life, I thought it would be with a gay man. And I couldn't imagine actually having a relationship with any man. And finally, as I saw it, there was group A (women) and group B (men)—this was before my own trans awareness came about—and if I had a 98 percent chance of finding someone compatible in group A and only a 2 percent chance of finding someone compatible in group B, and the percentage goes to 100 percent/0 percent if we were talking about love, then it made no sense to my lazy ass to waste time with group B, or to imply through my identity label that I would.

Lately, though I had been contemplating sex with non-queer men because before I got involved with my current lover, I was experiencing a period of intense sexual draught interspersed with fucked-up relationships (from minor to major) with women, and I wanted some sex without the drama. I felt that although sex with boys would come with its own drama, it would be less heavy 'cuz I wouldn't be invested in it. I also had to confess that as someone with rather awesome control of my cunt muscles, I felt like some of my best tricks were being lost to the universe.

My favorite saying had become "a penis is just a dildo substitute"—you know, when you just can't get the right dildo. I mean, yes, penises have some drawbacks over dildos. They don't stay hard forever. They only come in one basic shape, so expressing a sense of humor (dinosaur dildos), fashion sense (dildos colored to match your favorite G-string and bra ensemble), religion (goddess-shaped dildo) or appetite (dildos shaped like food) is difficult. You generally cannot get them sized to fit, and from what I remember, it's hard to switch to a different size once the sex act has gotten underway. Also, if you're not very careful you can get (gasp) pregnant. However they do have some bonuses—penises are free, don't break if the cat gets hold of them, their colors don't fade with use and they don't have to be boiled for seven minutes in your spaghetti pot.

I had met a man whom I found attractive, and the feeling was mutual. I told him on our first date that I was a dyke and that I had a girlfriend, and he seemed okay with it. I was very curious and was aroused by the idea of sex with him, because it felt so "naughty"—which was refreshing for a jaded ole dyke like me. Going all the way back to straight boys almost seemed like the final frontier. And when I found out that he was an amazing kisser, I decided, *Adventure time!* and went for it. I expected that the sex wouldn't be that great and that I would have to teach him about foreplay and where my clit was and how and when to use his fingers, 'cuz hey, that was what I remembered sex with straight boys being like.

Suffice it to say that none of this was true. I was astounded. The first night, I even learned a few things, which really hooked me. There were new positions that I hadn't ever tried, there were variations on familiar positions. He stretched the flesh on my inner thighs, which caused my vaginal wall to collapse down into closer contact with his cock. I was amazed by our foreplay, having had a hazy memory that men didn't know what to do with their fingers in a cunt. Once again, he surprised me, doing it for a longer time than I had expected and even doing some new things. I kept asking, "What is that?" and finally he said he was snapping his fingers inside me.

I am a self-identified size queen, and while I have a few smaller size dildos, most of my regularly used ones . . . let's just say they aren't to be found on any human male. His penis was smaller than any of my dildos and yet nothing felt lacking. In fact, some of the positions and angles we tried would have been impossible with a larger penis. My fave cousin said (as I described this to her) that it was a well-known fact that men with small penises were better lovers, 'cuz they worked harder and had by necessity become more inventive. I'm not sure how accurate this statement is, first because I don't have any other recent experiences with men as a basis for comparison, and second, I'm still not sure if his cock is smaller than the average bear, or simply smaller than any items (with the exception of a few fingers) I've had in my cunt since at least the early '90s.

I remember a bunch of ridiculous thoughts flitted across my brain during the afterglow. The first was, Oh my god, what are they teaching them these days!? The second was that I should have told every straight man I'd had sex with that I was a dyke. (Earlier he had confessed that he was really nervous and had felt some pressure to perform, because as he put it, "Women know how to please women.")

The dildo I wear that makes me feel like I actually have a cock is very large (nicknamed "Big Daddy"). It's uncomfortable to pack 'cuz it's so inflexible, but the girls like it when I wear it. Driving to work from his house the next day, I wanted to go throw out all my huge dildos, buy some smaller ones and then pick up chicks and show them what I could do—probably not his intention. But the fact is, great new sexual experiences just make you want to go out and have more sex to road-test them in all kinds of new terrain. As for sex with boys, well, I yam what I yam. I had been having these mini–identity crises as I contemplated having sex with him, but while I thoroughly enjoyed the act, and goddess willing, will continue to do it with him, I'm certainly not about to start trolling for dick. The magical energy that I feel when I have sex with women (even casual sex) was missing.

I think I'm at a point in my life right now when it's important for me to be surprised, to learn that I don't know everything. Even a year ago I could not have guessed that I would be thoroughly enjoying vanilla, missionary-position heterosex right now. At the same time, I'm entering my sexual prime. My erotic and sexual energy, which have always been considerable (some might say overwhelming, or awe-inspiring), have increased ten-fold. It may sound simplistic and sappy, but sex, great sex, and lots of it, keeps me happy. And sex of whatever sort offers inexhaustible chances for self-discovery.

Which is lucky—'cuz it gives me a reason to go on living.

My Way or the Bi Way

 Beth Lisick

Clearly, I was bisexual. I mean, sure, at nineteen I hadn't actually had dictionary-definition intercourse with anyone yet, but I just sort of figured that, intellectually, bisexuality made good sense. What self-respecting California-born-and-raised UC Santa Cruz student wouldn't be open to the imminent joys and adventure of loving all? What kind of person would discriminate so haphazardly against one sex? Oh, wait, not even haphazardly, but so ridiculously in adherence with The Herd. Yeah, that was it. You know, the sheep. The church. The government. The fuckin' man, for chrissakes. If you actually thought about it, and I'm talking *thought* about it here, in the sense that only a suburban Catholic refugee could. Reevaluating everything from the NFL to strawberry harvesting to the spelling of the word "history," I was more than ready to go to battle with my presumed sexual orientation. It all made perfect sense in the hazy redwood forest of my mind.

Now don't let my seemingly late bloomage fool you. (Okay, if you must know: Freshman year in the dorm room with nice Mendocino County–mountain-biker boyfriend, while listening to Bob Marley. It was very nice. Really.) I had actually been a sexual pioneer since the fourth grade. I wasn't into any of those spin the bottle/three minutes in the closet baby games. I was wearing my tight Sassoon jeans tucked into my brown pleather boots, and I was ready for some hot behind-the-bushes action. I always made the first move, whether I was comandeering the handball court on the playground or seeking out the haunted house at the amusement park. Skateboarders, BMXers, AYSO soccer players: I loved the tough guys. At least until I was thirteen or so and converted to what is still my fave: the smart and mischievous dork musician. I digress. What I'm saying is that it was always and forever boys. I loved fooling around with my boyfriends, didn't care if people called me a slut and would do everything with them except the proverbial "it." Why? I still don't know, probably the Catholic thing, but I was very relieved I had made that choice when scanning the crowd at my high school reunion a few summers ago. Those boys didn't have shit on me.

So, let's talk about the ladies. Though I have never been one to go nuts with lust over strangers on the street, it is only a woman that will make me stop, do the double take and think, "Yow!" At age thirty-one, I cannot ever recollect seeing some random dude—buying a record or driving a cool '62 Valiant or something—and thinking, "I really want to fuck him." But the way I felt seeing a hulking chick with tattoos on a motorcycle or a twee mod girl with a cool dye job or Martina Navratilova (with questionable haircut or not) had me thinking I was ready to hit the open road and do a little exploring. Have I set the stage here? In sum: Open-minded girl, not uptight about sex, always dated guys, goes to college, embraces idea of bisexuality. Um, have you heard this one before?

Oh, but I was different. I wasn't doing drugs, going to orgies, reading Anaïs Nin, having threesomes with my boyfriend, having threesomes with my girlfriend's boyfriend or making out with other former straight girls at the kegger. And this wasn't some Hollywood fantasy with a guest appearance by Kelly Lynch in a body stocking either! It was a philosophy. While I may have joined the women's rugby team and been flattered when they attempted to lure me to hot tub parties during the full moon on a deck overlooking the Pacific, I didn't have anything to prove. I just knew in my heart that I was bisexual, and why did I have to go sleeping with girls to show anyone? Those rugby players were just like the senior football players at my high school, a tight-knit club of swaggering jocks I wasn't going to let prey on me. I checked my trademark "Sure, why not?" attitude at the sidelines for them. As a matter of fact, I made it all the way through college without kissing a girl, assuming the whole time that I just hadn't found the right one yet.

After graduation, I moved to a small railroad flat in the Mission District of San Francisco. I was living with my boyfriend, whom I never saw because of my absurd schedule working as a baker. I'd wake up at 3:30 a.m., head down to the Embarcadero in total darkness and crank out bread and desserts until noon. I'd clock out, totally exhausted, go home for some lunch, a little wine and a nap. Except I always drank a lot of wine and would stay sleeping well past my self-imposed two-hour limit. I was miserable. For the first and last time, my job was my life. What was there at work to get remotely excited about? The head chef seemed potentially alluring in his checked pants and white coat, until he came in on his day off wearing a tie-dye and open-toed shoes on his way to a Phish concert.

But wait—what about Bernice? She always was vaguely flirting with me, trying to figure out if I was into girls or not. Because she was a bit of an old-school lesbian, the fact that I was acquainted with the music of Joan Armatrading and had the bleach-blonde crewcut got a lot more mileage than it might have with someone my own age. She apparently received the signal to move ahead, and I didn't get in the way. Bernice was totally cool. Ex-military police with brown feathered hair and a rail-straight boy body. We'd reload the flour bins together, and I'd ask her about being in the army. I'd never met anyone who got paid to boss people around on Guam. Through her tough veneer, I could see that she was almost as confused about it as I was. It was weird and I definitely developed a little crush.

One day she straight up asked me out. Just like, "Let's go out on a date after work sometime." As was my custom for many years, I replied with the resounding Sure, Why Not? I used to do this all the time, winding up at baseball games or in Reno. I was attracted to things that had an equal chance of being futile or sublime. So, we had a few beers at The Cafe on Market Street, and I, emboldened by Anchor Steam on an empty stomach, thought we should go get something pierced downstairs at the Gauntlet. Well, the wild descent into a debauched marathon of drinking and piercing ended when I got a small ring in the cartilage of my upper left ear and she did her earlobes for the first time. The afternoon date was over. Bernice pulled up next to my truck, and I decided to be bold. I leaned over the stick shift of her Jeep, completely prepared to launch into a full-on makeout session. Her tongue was hot and beery, her face a lot softer than I'd imagined. I grabbed her perm by the back. There was no way I was doing any half-assed kissing my first time with a girl. I knew how to kiss and I was going to demonstrate that. After a minute or two, I retreated. I felt nothing—except a little sore around the ear as pus started to seep out. Damn! I reasoned she just must not be the girl for me.

I marched onward, deciding one afternoon to satisfy my urge for lady sex with some erotic videos from Good Vibrations. Even though this whole "sex positive" business had been drilled into me for years, when it came down to it I was a little embarrassed to stroll into the neighborhood sex shop at 2:00 p.m. in my baking uniform and rent porn. I realized that the employees, with their open, friendly faces and early '90s sexual sophistication didn't give a shit what I was doing, but I still tried to select something that didn't look too explicit. As fate would have it, I wound up with some indescribably hilarious video of lesbians stripping for each other in cramped apartments and poorly lit rec rooms to a muffled soundtrack of women's music. I passed out with my chef's coat on and my undies on the floor, unfulfilled.

Perhaps what I needed was a gal pal. All this making eyes with the telephone repairwoman and embarrassing innuendo with the FedEx dyke was getting me nowhere. Could I just be the Madonna to some fabulous Sandra Bernhard character? You know, wowing the crowds at the AIDS danceathon in our cutoff shorts and spangly halter tops? And then if that worked out, could I become Sandra? Did San Francisco have its own Ingrid Casares?

I can only guess it was through the power of positive thinking that I finally got some action. The kickoff took place while I was fast asleep on the couch at a friend's house (which I suppose it is sort of like being molested, if you want to get technical). I woke up to find this gorgeous Scottish girl, a mix of male, female and otherworldliness whom I had nicknamed the Androgynaut earlier at the bar, leaning over me, kissing my neck, whispering in my ear, her giant's hands on my lower back and in my hair. This might be somebody I could get into, I thought— for about a minute, until I remembered that she was the new girlfriend of a friend of mine. A friend who also happened to be asleep in the next room.

Maybe a year later, I was in Seattle to perform at Lollapalooza. A bunch of spoken-word people were invited up to read, and even though we were relegated to the third-stage tent and it was costing me money to travel I decided to go. (The Sure, Why Not thing.) Life with the boyfriend was definitely on the rocks, and it occurred to me that this might be a good time to give it a whirl. Go out with girls for a change. Fly my gayrod flag high. Reach for the rainbow. And Seattle was teeming with saucy punk vixens. I crashed over at some other poets' apartment, some pals of the 7 Year Bitch girls we'd been hanging out with earlier. I could start living my rock and roll fantasy now.

When the last two people awake at the party were this lanky red-haired girl and I, and she just so happened to be moving to Paris the next day, it was a done deal. We got into bed, and instead of playing it nice and naive I decided I should take charge of the situation. I basically appointed myself the top, even though I'd never been naked in bed with a girl before.

Overall, it was pretty okay, even though I do wish I had gotten her name. There's no doubt I enjoyed myself, but it was similar to the way I enjoyed waterskiing for the first time. Or eating snails. I jumped in with a positive attitude, realizing it was an activity beloved by millions, but it didn't exactly work for me. I couldn't surrender to the situation on a sexual level, not to her tiny moans when my fingers were inside her, or to her teeth on my neck, 'cause I was too wrapped up in taking mental notes. Oooh, it's weird how it sort of feels like I'm touching me. Am I enjoying this? I mean, besides the "new frontiers" angle, am I into this? Are we currently experiencing hot girl-on-girl action? I felt like I was doing research and the results were coming back negative. It frustrated me to no end that this could be happening. There was a sexy twenty-year-old girl writhing underneath me with her legs hooked over my shoulders, and I was not turned on. What was I? Some kind of sexual mutant?

After this experience, when I was in my mid-twenties I stopped putting pressure on myself to go out with girls, even though I *still* assumed I was bi. I kept holding on to this notion that evolved individuals could enjoy sex with a person regardless of gender, if they would just free their minds and let their asses follow. I thought my feeling open to being with other women automatically made me bisexual. Then a funny thing happened. Through the spoken word scene, I wound up getting to know more and more of the incredible women writers and performers in San Francisco. And nearly all of the ones I was crazy about were dykes. I stopped thinking I needed to fuck them and started realizing I just wanted to hang out with them. I couldn't believe there were girls who knew a lot about hair products whom I actually wanted to be around. For the first time, I met people who could deeply appreciate the aesthetic of a perfectly formed beer belly, or cultivate a scuzzy redneck look and bring it to new heights. Having spent my childhood as a tomboy, I totally dug the genderfuck aspect. Straight women hardly ever do drag, and, if they do, they'll dress as a man. It was a revelation to understand that a biological female could dress in fishnets and stilettos and still be in drag. As a person who has never been comfortable in groups or identified with a community, I almost felt I had found the chosen people.

Unable to face the facts about my heterosexuality, I gave it another try when I traveled across the country with Sister Spit, an all-girl spoken word group. In the summer of 1998, I was one of twelve performers on its monster summer tour, and the only one who was pretty much straight. A couple of the others had been involved in relationships with both men and women in recent years, but Sister Spit is really a dyke thing at heart. So it was six weeks with many gay bars and gay crowds and a lot of people assuming I was gay. Whatever. I'd be lying if I said I didn't notice, but it just wasn't a big deal. There were a few awkward situations, maybe a girl at the show would have a crush on me or something, but there were always eleven other babes from whom she could choose. The only confrontation I had the whole time was in Tucson when my boyfriend's mother's girlfriend (got that?) somehow felt I had betrayed the lesbionic sisterhood by infiltrating the group.

There we were on tour, we've made it all the way to Provincetown, where we are guests of all the cool dykes in town. We pull in late, we head straight for the bar and everyone is there to greet us. Immediately, I hone in on this tough girl in a cowboy hat whom everybody seems to know. My latent bisexuality awakens from its slumber. I start fantasizing that she's been waiting all summer for the new crop of Sister Spit girls to arrive. (She later confirms this as fact.) Then I take inventory of who on the tour is currently available, i.e., not doing it with someone else on the tour or planning to meet someone in P-town already. Hey, my odds are looking good! Oh shit, I forgot, I'm not into girls, right? But that can't possibly be, when my only plan for the evening is to make this one realize I will be her San Francisco tour girl for Summer '98. I check myself. Is it because I haven't had sex in three weeks? Is it because if I hook up with her there will be a comfortable bed and a nice shower in the morning? Is it because everyone else is planning to take drugs and swim in the ocean and I just want to sleep? We're talking, sort of flirting, and she tells me she has two jobs: construction work and part-time sales at the local sex shop. A nice combination. And then it turns out she has one of those great Dyke Names for the New Millennium. Rocky. Trouble. Buzz. Pistol. Bob. Sold! I go home with the Cowboy.

A full moon, the warm summer air, holding hands with a hot local dude in the streets of gay mecca ground zero. If this is not a litmus test for my bisexuality, I don't know what would be. We will solve the riddle by sunrise tomorrow! As we walk through the streets, I am really pleased. I don't know where we're going, but the town is so small I figure it'll be easy enough to sort out in the morning. All I want is for this girl to take me home and fuck me all night long. The problem isn't so much that I am inexperienced, as I have long believed that enthusiasm and willingness to learn go a long way. The problem is that I'm sure she assumes, as most people I meet on tour do, that I am gay. I decide to come clean right away. It would be really bad to wake up after a night of screwing and tell her I am straight, right? She might even want to have nothing to do with me. Would I be pissed off if I took some guy home who was on tour with the Straight Male Traveling Circus and he turned out to be gay? Even if we had fun in the sack?

Now we're hot and heavy, making out back at her house, and I decide I'd better say something quick. We're kissing, and the whole time I'm trying to figure out how to word it. "Um, you know, I'm basically straight." No, that's lame. What about, "Just so you know, I have a boyfriend. I hope that doesn't bother you, but I totally understand if it does." Too pathetic. I settle on that old cliché "I've never really done this before," which is sort of a lie. But if we are headed where I think we're headed, it might turn out to be the truth after all. I am not looking back.

Trooper has the situation dialed. Asking me what I want without being too chatty and letting me select the dick from her extensive employee-discounted arsenal. Whoa, did I just say that? Letting me select the dick! I am going to do it with a chick wearing a strap-on. That's what I'm thinking while she's doing various sexual things to me. I'm thinking, when is the part going to come that's unlike anything I've ever experienced? Something is going to happen very soon that's really going to do it for me. So, now I'm doing it with a chick wearing a strap-on, and apparently I'm just not into it. I mean, she is totally attractive to me and we are naked and the sea air is drifting through the window and I am on top of her with my legs straddling her and she is doing something I love, perhaps slapping my ass or talking nasty in my ear, and I am not exactly balancing my checkbook in my head, but I am not excited. For the record, I am also decidedly not bored. It's extremely interesting to me that I cannot have an orgasm right now. It is like a physics problem I must solve immediately. I am astounded by my inability to get turned on at this very moment. I am an embarrassment to womankind.

Less evolved. I am obviously less evolved than my bi friends. It's upsetting. It's a snore to be straight in the year 2000. I find it anti-futuristic. I think Sharon Stone was just quoted saying she was actually a lesbian, except she has sex with men. (While I applaud Sharon's sassy boldness, I think she may have just needed a juicy soundbite to publicize "If These Walls Could Talk" with Ellen and Anne.) But I've come close to thinking that way, especially when being "straight" makes me feel predictable, conservative even: "Oh, I only like this one kind. I'll just take the kind with the penis, thank you." But even though it's been a struggle to accept this about myself, I've finally come to terms with the fact that a certain percentage of people are just born that way.

Ain't Had None. Can't Get None. Don't Want None.

(★) Diana Courvant

I could hardly think, though I'd been trying all day to catch myself in a writing mood or even a creative moment. Part of it might have been a blood sugar thing, since I'd been skipping meals lately. Eating hadn't come easily because my pain pills hit hard on my stomach. I would have skipped a dose, but even at full strength my pills never got rid of the pain entirely. It was always there, in my knuckles, ankles, elbows, knees. It was in other places too, though I couldn't complain. Three years ago the doctors didn't even realize how my thyroid was making my joints worse. At the time, I couldn't type at all. Every time I touched the keyboard it felt as if I were pressing on the sharp end of a tack until the point was deep in the bone. Since they started regulating my thyroid hormones I have been able to type again. The tacks disappear for days at a time. Of course, now I need about eleven hours of sleep a night and sometimes a nap in the afternoon. Feeling tired never goes away anymore. It's not just a blood sugar thing. So of course I understood, after a moment, what the survey was asking with the words, *"How do you deal with sex play with a partner?"*

It was a survey written by some authors without disabilities to find out about how people with disabilities have sex. They were trying to write a how-to sex book for people with disabilities that would finally tell the story of what is best for the person with disabilities and not that person's partner. As a first step, they wanted to get some feedback from people who had disabilities. I knew what they wanted to hear: Having sex isn't easy. Once in three years I found myself in a comfortable position cuddling with my lover. The only times I have enough energy for sex my lover is at work, or school. When I finally feel creative, I have to decide whether to use my creativity to have sex or to write.

Yes, they also wanted to hear about how those problems are solved. How do I use pillows to support my joints so I can have sex ten or twenty minutes longer? Do I rearrange my sleep schedule to be awake for my lover? How much of my creative energy do I spend on writing, how much on sex, and how much do they overlap? It is important stuff to talk about, and that's what they wanted to hear. That's what they wanted to learn. But that's not what they asked.

"How do you deal with sex play with a partner?" the survey asked. *"How do you deal with sex?"*

The wording of the question wasn't an accident, even if the people writing the survey never realized how I would see the question in the first moment. I only knew what they meant to ask after I looked at it from their point of view.

I guess if you're able-bodied right now, it's easy to see sex as a problem for people with disabilities. It's not only easy: it's traditional. I don't go to bars much. As a queer woman, I don't have many to choose from. As a wimp, I don't like the smoke. When I do go to bars, though, it's easy to see that women with mobility devices don't get asked to dance. I use crutches to walk, but I most often use office chairs to dance to better protect my joints, and to swivel in ways a wheelchair just won't. Dancing on my crutches works too, but I need a lot of room if I don't want people to kick them out from under me. Crowded clubs don't usually have the space. Still, office chairs ain't hard to find. I've never been to a club that couldn't find one when I asked. So why don't I get asked to dance? Why don't my friends who use wheelchairs or scooters get asked?

It's not just that other queer women don't know *how* to dance with women using crutches or canes, scooters or chairs. Several of my friends put on a workshop on how to dance—how to lead, how to follow—for women using chairs (of *all* kinds) and the people who want to dance with them. Nobody without a disability showed up. Yup. Nobody. Best any of us could tell, nobody wanted to dance with us, no matter how fast I could get that office chair to spin.

In Colorado, I was at an anti-violence conference. I didn't know anyone there, but some of the women that I'd met were going to a queer club downtown. I tagged along, and so I could use my crutches and wouldn't have to feel weird explaining why I wanted an office chair, I sucked down a couple of Long Island Iced Teas. Properly tipsy, I didn't hurt so much dancing on my crutches—or at least I didn't notice the pain as much. It was my first night dancing on my crutches when I really let go. I had a great time, spinning, shuffling, swinging back and forth. But nobody asked me to dance. The next night at the same club I ran into some women who were really inspired seeing me dance the night before. One of them asked if I would marry her. Two more said, "Me too!" They borrowed my crutches to try swinging and spinning on them. But none of them ever asked me to dance.

Dancing is a topic of its own of course, but also a metaphor. When people say, "it takes two to tango," they are just as likely to be talking about getting together in the bedroom as in the ballroom. I taught a workshop this summer, called Disability, Sexuality, Community, Activism. One participant, Mary Bennets, gave the best nutshell description of society's assumptions about the sexual experiences of people with disabilities: "Ain't had none. Can't get none. Don't want none." These assumptions are so pervasive and powerful that when *Mouth,* a magazine for politically active people with disabilities, finally put out a sex issue, a librarian wrote in that she was canceling the library's subscription. She couldn't tolerate the idea of lending any more copies of *Mouth* to people with disabilities. Though it was easy to figure out why she would cancel the subscription just then, she didn't have any trouble putting it in her own words: "It is unseemly to bring sex to the attention of the disabled."

In academic books, previous sex how-to's and a myriad of autobiographies, you could read the same story: sex isn't for people with disabilities. *The Disability Studies Reader* tells about a girl with spina bifida who wanted to know if she would be able to have satisfying sex when she grew up. Her doctor only told her that her vagina would be tight enough to satisfy any man. The author that tells this story is as appalled as I am at the doctor's oppressive, uncaring response and presents the story as an example of problems with society. Yet nowhere does *The Disability Studies Reader* talk about how to create a sexual culture where people with disabilities are considered desirable partners.

The how-to sex books already published (and there aren't many) are just as sexist and heterosexist, and care just as little as the anecdotal doctor about the people with disabilities that are asking questions. The books that focus on women with disabilities are just long drawn-out versions of the same thing we see in

Cosmo every month: How to satisfy your man sexually so he won't leave you in the lurch. They'll give you advice like: if intercourse is painful, try exciting him with fellatio first, so you'll be able to continue long enough for him to orgasm. Don't look for advice helping a disabled woman to orgasm!

Autobiographies of women with disabilities offer different versions of the same story: Heterosexual women end up divorced if they gain a disability and can no longer satisfy their husbands. Over and over you hear about the partners of women with disabilities, especially men. You hear about the partners' sexual needs. But you don't hear much about the needs or desires of the women living with disabilities.

Hell, even this book is guilty. When the original call for essays was posted, out of all the topics suggested to contributors not one touched on dis/ability. Even our best efforts, from *The Disability Studies Reader* to *Sex and Single Girls*, keep falling short. And America's dominant society is pretty damn clear: sex isn't for people with disabilities.

Even after I begin a relationship with a lover, it's not like I'm done struggling with those assumptions. For the last ten years I haven't had a lover who didn't tell me at one time or another that she was worried about hurting me during sex. Then there's the assumption that if I am hurting, I'll want to stop right away. Occasionally I like having my wrists tied to the bed. I also enjoy the times when my lover takes the phrase "wheelchair bound" literally. (It certainly doesn't deserve to be used the way it is normally!) Besides that, I'm as vanilla as they come. But for years now I've hurt every minute of every day. It's not going to magically stop just because I want to spend some sextime with my lover. Even without practicing S/M, pain and sex are inextricably linked.

My lover and I care about each other. We support each other. We feed each other. So it's hard to ask her to do things that I know will hurt. It's even harder for her to feel loving, happy and hot if she knows that she's hurting me. For more than a year, we couldn't spend five minutes in bed without processing about how to do what so my joints wouldn't hurt. Sometimes it felt like we spent more time processing about sex than doing it.

We started talking about sex because of the violence and sexual abuse I'd survived, and my still intense fears growing out of those experiences. We bought some washable kids' felt pens and drew lines, designs, words on my body. "Touch here," my body read. "Not here," was written in other places. "Kiss," "nibble" and "bite," were written in still other places. Carefully, slowly, we shared more touch, more skin, more pressure. With it all came more pain. The joy of wrapping my legs around and between hers came only by bending knees, hips, ankles.

As we kissed, those joints would cramp, would lock themselves, my pain binding me to my joy. The painful disentangling of ourselves, straightening and stretching of my long legs caused my lover shock and sadness. It was hard to communicate how I'd learned to love the feeling. My pain had become my body's way of speaking the longing for my lover that only increased the more we touched and kissed.

Later, as trust replaced fear, we became more spontaneous and energetic in our sex. We tried fucking after carefully placing pillows under my body. Being fucked was wonderful, but the rocking of my joints and the pressure on them caused more pain even than wrapping my legs around hers. Pushing myself onto her fingers or dildo passed a wave of pain through my body. Often I would hold my breath in, trying to still every motion I had the power to control—every motion but the fucking, the reaching for, the kissing on my lover. I didn't want to stop any of those. I only wanted the energy to keep on, to grow this fertile feeling of joy. I wanted the orgasms that crept closer and closer, washing through me at first rarely, intermittently, unpredictably. Often I would have to stop, though, the pain becoming too intense, crowding out the joy. I would cry at how close my body was to the explosive relaxation of all my cramped joints. My lover would hold me as I tried to tell her that I didn't regret the pain, as I searched for the words to describe how the inescapable pain gifted me with an unignorable sense of the preciousness of my joy.

After two years, I thought we'd both learned a ton. I'd learned which pillows were softest, which angles were best. We both got to know my body so well I'd started having orgasms almost any time my lover wanted to give me one. Then one day I mentioned hurting all through sex. She'd forgotten. I mean she hadn't forgotten that I hurt sometimes. She hadn't forgotten that if I moved the wrong way I could strain myself. She'd just forgotten that every time my body rocks, I feel another wave of pain. She'd forgotten that if I remain perfectly still, I'm still a shallow pool of pain. It felt like she had forgotten that I have a disability.

I know that it's normal to get turned off when you cause your lover pain she doesn't want. I can understand why she didn't want to think about it, why she wouldn't want to dwell on it. But I wanted her to remember it. Why else had we talked so long and processed so much? It sure as hell wasn't just to live up to lesbian stereotypes. We'd talked about more than disability. Rape issues, transsexual issues, monogamy issues: we'd talked about it all and come through to a place where we were happy with each other, in love with each other. Over years we'd come to a place where for the first time in my life I felt like sex was happening to a real, whole me. New-Agey or not, feeling truly loved for my whole self was giving me the best orgasms of my life.

If my lover was forgetting who I was when we made love, had sex, fucked, my whole new state of orgasmic grace was at risk. Finally feeling like I'd gotten sex right, I didn't want to lose it. Sex was too precious. We talked again, processed again, dealing with our physical and emotional feelings. We did it because dealing with our emotions, with my disability and with my pain is worth the sex we share.

That's why the survey question was so offensive. Sex play was what we both wanted, what we both had worked for. Sex play was funny, joyous, loving, ecstatic, precious. Surrounded by a culture that seems intent on stopping our sex, we had acted on our own desire, played in/with/during sex and found happiness. We'd talked for months and dealt with any number of issues to find our joy in each other. Our sex itself wasn't an issue to "deal with"; others' ableist assumptions were.

How do I deal with sex play with a partner?

They really thought sex was the problem? My mind was spinning just thinking about it, though maybe that was my blood sugar again. Offensive or not, I tried to come up with an answer to their question. Even typing lightly, my fingers were hurting. Of course, it was worth it anyway. It would have been worth even more if I could have watched their faces as they read my answer:

Well, first I try to schedule lots and lots of time with my therapist so that whenever my partner wants to have sex I'm never more than thirty-six hours from safe, effective professional help. I also keep the Portland Women's Crisis Line number programmed in the speed-dialer of the cordless phone (on our second phone line with an unlisted phone number) so I always have access to a reassuring friend. I keep the volunteer schedule taped to the side of the bed and highlight the names of the ones who are friendliest. I also try to read my affirmation books as much as possible.

Then, when my partner wants her sexual needs met, we both have a drink to help me relax. She takes me to the bedroom and undresses me while I count Fibonacci numbers—you know, the 1,1,2,3,5,8 series where each number is the sum of the previous 2. When I get to 4,052,739,537,881 I start to lose track, so I start over. I mostly don't notice as she's getting undressed, but I know she does because eventually I feel her skin against the inside of my legs. Then I hear her turn on the Hitachi and feel her press it directly against my underwear. I open my eyes a little to check and see if she's looking at me. If she is I usually just freeze. I get all paralyzed until she's not staring at me anymore. As soon as she's not looking at me, I bite my lip as hard as I can. The pain usually distracts me from her kisses on the inside of my thighs, but sometimes I feel them and flinch or react. I usually moan when that happens and try to pretend I moved because I'm really excited. Usually she won't stop vibrating me till it just becomes too much. I try not to, but my body just doesn't want it any more so my hips buck trying to push the vibrator away from me. I wish I could just ask her to stop but she thinks our sex should be mutual and doesn't believe me if I say that I'm done without having an orgasm. All my orgasms are really quiet when they happen anyway, but she wouldn't know. She thinks the only way to have an orgasm is to spasm out of control, but at least that means she stops after I buck for a little while.

Then she kneels over my mouth and she uses the vibrator on her clit. I'm still not sure if she realizes how little I lick her, I'm just so glad she loves her bunny pearl. Sometimes this part is okay, but if she uses the Hitachi on me too much then I can still feel my crotch vibrating long after she stops pushing it against me. Sometimes I get scared that my labia might never feel normal again. If I cry, though, after she comes, I can wipe my tears at the same time as I wipe my lips and chin dry. It's not that she doesn't know that I cry—she's really sensitive—but that's also part of the problem. We both know that because I'm disabled I'm not ever going to want sex. But if she never gets her sexual needs met, we won't be able to have a long-term relationship! And then, because she's sensitive, we have to take into account that she'll feel too guilty to initiate sex if she always has to deal with my crying. So she always leaves the room right after we have sex and then I can call the crisis line if I want to, but I don't always. That way she never has to deal with me being all emotional around sex and doesn't have to feel guilty for meeting her sexual needs once in a while.

Then if I still feel like I need an emotional release, like if it's not one of my favorite volunteers on the crisis line, I pick up my journal and make up sarcastic answers to stupid questions like, "How do you deal with sex?"

On the Altar

 Cecilia Tan

Imagine me blindfolded, or maybe my eyes are just squeezed shut, or maybe the room is total darkness. Imagine the hands of many people caressing my skin. Imagine the feeling of being lifted up, gravity replaced by tactile overload, as the group sticks better to itself than to mother earth. It's a nice erotic fantasy, one I had as a teenager. But I never could have a fantasy that was just some anonymous sex. I had to know who the people were, why they were together, how they met. In my suburban teen world, I couldn't imagine a scenario in which people I knew could, or would, participate in such an activity. What could bring a whole bunch of people together for the purpose of sex and erotic fulfillment? I had enough trouble figuring out getting just two people together. Clearly, my vision could never be enacted in modern America, so I turned to science fiction to create narratives for my fantasies.

I was an avid science fiction reader as a kid—a geek—and always was dreaming up my own far-flung planetary societies where group marriages and erotic rituals were regular occurrences. I created groups of people who worshipped their deities through public sex rituals or who were like sexual sports teams, working together. Nonmonogamy was an important element as well: I wrote soap operas in which my characters found ways to overcome jealousy, have "sexual friendships" and otherwise connect sexually with each other outside of traditional marriages or courtships. Was it a coincidence that even then I tended to fantasize about communities and frienships rather than about anonymous orgies?

Maybe those early fantasies shaped my later tastes, or maybe, though young and inexperienced in "real sex," I had an inkling about what would fulfill me later in life. Either way, my sexuality was never one-track.

It started with a party. It started at a science fiction convention, appropriately enough, where my first girlfriend and I threw a bondage play party so we finally could meet, face to face, all the many people we'd bonded with (no pun intended) over the Internet on alt.sex.bondage. We wanted to see if we could get along as well in real life as we did online. We participated in daily discussions over Usenet about safety and politics and leather community "tradition," and we figured, hey, it was about time we got some of these self-proclaimed perverts together in a room. So, with the help of a few other folks we knew through the newsgroup, we booked a pair of rooms at the hotel for a gay- and lesbian-themed science fiction convention and posted an invitation.

My girlfriend was also my first S/M play partner. She taught me the poly jargon, words like "primary" and "boundaries." She and I were supposed to be primaries, principal partners, while everyone else was supposed to be a "secondary," a sex buddy, if you will. She taught me many things, including how different a woman's finger feels between my labia, how different a woman's nipple feels in my mouth. She was the top, the one in charge of our relationship. Or so I thought at the time.

The night of the party arrived, and people of both genders we had flirted with over email appeared in the flesh. I thought I finally had found my far-out world. Here were all these people, brimming with sexual energy and mutually interested in having public sex, group play, connecting with one another. My girlfriend wrestled me onto the bed at one point, and several other people we had been flirting with (or, at least, I had) joined in, holding me down, while they blindfolded me, put clips on my nipples, teased me with a Swiss Army knife (love that fish scaler attachment!) and dripped cognac into my mouth. Here was my fantasy, the many hands coming together on my body for the common purpose. I was both the priestess and the sacrifice on the altar—I felt like all the energy in the room was funneled through me. Blindfolded, I couldn't see anyone, but it didn't matter to me who was who—individuality was second to the goal of the group. You know, I don't remember if I came or not. In a way, it doesn't matter. To have the focus of the group like that was one of the most arousing and fulfilling experiences of my life.

Apparently, it wasn't so for my girlfriend, who later admitted that her boundaries had been crossed. She hadn't felt justified in saying so, because she hadn't actually stated those boundaries yet. So what I had thought was a magical, friction-free convergence actually wasn't. The submergence of the individual into the group was a blow to her self-esteem, I think. She didn't admit this to me until months later, when we were processing the fallout from my two other ongoing relationships, both with bisexual men.

In my mind, at that time, everything was clear. She was my girlfriend and primary, Clash (not his real name) was my punk soulmate and fuck buddy (his term), and Fred was my lover. I desired each differently; each brought up different needs in me and fulfilled them in distinct ways. I was twenty three, living in the big city and craving erotic adventures. I'd discovered a world of sexual outlaws, bisexual community activists and leatherfolk, and the concept of multiple partners was not as new to them as it was to me. It was the age of Queer Nation and ACT UP, and we all carried condoms and latex gloves in our leather jackets. A typical weekend went something like this. I'd go out dancing with Clash Friday night, stay over at his house experimenting with our bodies, fuck again in the morning, then go home, shower, get a nap. My girlfriend would come to pick me up on her motorcycle in the afternoon, and we'd have a nice dinner somewhere before she'd take me home, tie me to the bed with a scarf and finger-fuck me until I was screaming. Trying to be a butch top or something, she would then leave without coming herself. At midnight Fred would call wondering what I was doing, and I'd meet him for a late night snack in Chinatown, and then we'd wrestle on the floor of his apartment until dawn.

All three relationships had different flavors, different purposes, but sometimes they also fell short of them. My girlfriend was trying hard to fit the image of the leatherdyke top, mentoring me, giving me thrills, and I was willing to do whatever she wanted, try whatever she suggested, learn whatever she had to say. But she wasn't very demanding about her own needs, and we both came to feel that our sex was one-sided. She would tie me up and torment me, then satisfy me, which was great fun, but I was hungry to know all about how to make love to a woman, to find out what she liked and what women tasted like. Once, just once, I remember her pushing my face down to her crotch and letting me lick her off. I had been wanting to do that to someone, anyone, for years. As far as I know, she liked it. But she never asked me, or ordered me, to do it again. Since I was the supposed submissive and student, I figured she would tell me what to do differently if it wasn't working for her. But that never came to pass, as if the power dynamic I was expecting never actually came into play.

Meanwhile, Clash wanted to be the model sexual outlaw: we protested together with ACT UP at the statehouse, went dancing at gay bars, stickered Boston with "Bisexual Pride" stickers. He was the first queer "fuck buddy" I'd had, and the dynamic was completely different from a het relationship, even if the plumbing was basically the same. The two of us could lie in bed and talk about his boyfriend's dick size and cruising rituals. It was egalitarian in a way that none of my other relationships had been. Clash was trying hard to do it all, break all the boundaries, so I knew getting together with him on any given day was bound to yield another erotic adventure. We both craved novelty, and he was endlessly inventive. He learned how to make an ice dildo at home with directions he saw on the Internet and had a wonderful time fucking me with it. He finger-fucked me in public at an all-ages punk show. He decided one day to see if he could make me come without touching my clit, an experiment that exhausted us both. He was so willing to try anything, actually, that at one point he asked me if I'd do an S/M scene with him: I said yes, only to find out that he considered anything that actually caused pain to be abuse. (He eventually would change that tune, after meeting a top Daddy of his own and reclaiming his rebellious bottom nature, but it took a while.)

Then there was Fred. He was the true sexual outlaw, who hustled his ass on the streets for cash, but who really, really knew how to show a woman a good time. Fred was the first one to bite me during sex, the first one to whip me, the first one to really blow my mind with S/M role playing. It was so innocuous, at first, when I went home with him. We were talking, sitting on the floor in his almost empty apartment and drinking beer out of cans, and then we were necking and kissing one another.

And then he was on top of me, and not letting me up, all the while licking my neck, which happens to be one of my most intense erogenous zones. Interesting, I thought. He was my size and weight, yet I couldn't flip him over. I was sure that if I wanted to, I just could have told him to get up. But it was fun to struggle. He never gave in. I think we wrestled, while he licked my neck until I almost came, for forty-five minutes or more. In the end, it was I who gave up, and I suddenly realized that he'd literally dominated me. I was thrilled. All kinds of feelings had raced through me, from rebellion to surrender. I felt overcome in a way that my "willing" submissive role play with my butch mentor girlfriend did not inspire. Sometime after that, he showed up at my office one day, we went out to lunch, and he pulled me into an alley and slapped a leather cuff around one wrist. Fred was a pro, I was pretty sure by then—he knew the moves so well that it was easy to play along. I showed up at his apartment that night, and we did a scene so similar to my girlfriend's and yet so different. Yes, I got tied up and so on, but he let his hunger drive the scene, and satisfying his pleasure was integral to the power dynamic. I felt wanted and desired in a way I didn't when it was all about me.

Fred also orchestrated the first genuine orgy I ever participated in: not an S/M play party, but a group sex experience. He insisted that two things were necessary for it to work. One, you had to have an odd number of people participating, and two, you had to have at least half bisexuals. "Otherwise you just get a bunch of pairs of people fucking," he explained. "And we could just go home to do that."

An orgy is a funny thing. The focus shifts from one person to another at different times, as people team up and then split apart, as various desires shift and ebb. Multi-orgasmic women like me ensure that it goes on for a while, while the guys try to hold off as long as possible. We went through a lot of latex that night. Under the admonition not to pair off, I didn't have intercourse with either of my two lovers, instead experimenting with the people I didn't know, such as Fred's ex. She was another outlaw, stripping in a peep show as if it were an empowering thing and not just a job. I don't remember who did what to whom and in what order—you'd need a scorecard to keep track. I mostly remember moments. At one point she parted my legs and sucked my clit, and other people were around us—drawn in closer to us the closer I came to coming. Then after I came someone else worked on her, and we lay about in a fleshy mass of stroking and groping until she came close to coming, and then all eyes and hands were on her, bringing her up. And then on to someone else. And someone else.

So for a while I juggled three relationships and three sets of erotic needs. In the end, though, my girlfriend was coming to realize that she wasn't getting her needs met through the role she had prescribed for herself. So we were no longer primaries, and, although we remained friends, we just didn't have much time or impetus to see each other socially. My other two sexual friendships fell apart around the same time. Fred's ex-girlfriend got back together with him and then declared him off-limits to other women (and men). It was hard to see each other casually, because the erotic attraction was still very strong and, I confess, we couldn't help ourselves when we got together. I was against being dishonest about anything, as was he, which meant that when we told her we'd broken the rules, much trouble and strife resulted. So I stayed away. It was a difficult way to lose a friend, but I stood by what my girlfriend had taught me about how primaries got to make the rules.

And remember how Clash kept insisting we were just fuck buddies and how great that was? He kept up that story right up until the day he torpedoed our friendship by admitting that he'd been in love with me all along and that my obliviousness was driving him to suicide. He'd been craving a love relationship all along and had hoped somehow that when I broke up with the others I'd change my feelings for him. He never understood that my feelings for him, and the others, were entirely independent. They were three separate relationships that grew from three different parts of myself. I never played them off each other, nor did I ever try to weave the three of them together into one big family.

In many ways, it was as if I had dated them one after the other, rather than simulatenously—except that by having three lovers at once, I quickly jumped up the learning curve of my sexuality. After all, it would have taken years to gain that much experience and self-knowledge if I'd dated them serially, and, in the end, it was the alchemy of multiple inputs that helped me clarify many things about myself. For one, I now knew a wide range of common S/M activities and psychological states. I disliked some; I liked, craved and wanted more of others—I wanted to see if I could go deeper into submission, I wanted to know more about women, I wanted to retain the queer flavor of my life and identity even if my next lover were a het man. I also learned to negotiate shifting boundaries and learned that my own boundaries are pretty loose and far-flung. And I baffled all three lovers with my complete lack of jealousy. You never really know if you're the jealous type, I think, until you've got competition for someone's affections.

Anyway, it so happened that all three relationships unraveled at once. Maybe it was fate. I was single again and wondering if I would ever find partners who were not jealous, insecure, or confused or unclear about their needs and who could meet my appetites in bed. Having done the heterosexual monogamy thing earlier in my life, I knew I wanted someone non-monogamous, someone bisexual or with a queer sensibility, someone unafraid to experiment or have erotic adventures, someone with self-confidence and self-knowledge equal to mine.

Sometimes fate delivers. One month later, I met corwin, the partner I have been with for nine years. It was basically love at first sight, so if he wasn't the type to be comfortable with non-monogamy, I was in trouble. But fortunately he and I agree on just about everything when it comes to sex, love, relationships and boundaries. Our initial attraction took place (where else?) at an S/M play party of the group that had grown out of that alt.sex.bondage gathering. Our community. We were in a private home, and corwin had come with a date who wasn't his steady girlfriend, which I took as a good sign. Then there's our extremely striking physical resemblance to each other. Back then, when he was younger and more lithe, corwin was mistaken daily for a woman, and not just because of his long, dark hair. I, meanwhile, often was mistaken for a man, especially in my Boston neighborhood, where many long-haired, bespectacled

Berklee College of Music students lived. Put us together, and you could cover plenty of polymorphously perverse ground with only the two of us participating. My hunger for diversity might be assuaged, I realized, with such a person.

And it is true; each with fairly wide-ranging erotic tastes, we have much to enjoy together. Not to seem flip, but we can try just about anything. Sometimes we cross-dress, and I play dashing young prince to his helpless princess. I can take on a more femme dominatrix aspect as well. I can be rough with him or spoil and indulge him. I can order him to pleasure me, or I can seduce him. We can go to sex parties together or with our other lovers. Because we both present androgynously, I suppose you could call us heterosexual but homogenderal. I call us polymorphous.

But even when corwin cross-dresses he can't substitute for a woman. I'm still bisexual, and I still want to dive into female softness sometimes. Being "poly," I have that freedom, as does he. We have all kinds of dynamics with me as his Top, even one where I order him to tie me up and whip me. This doesn't work quite as well for me as when someone else does it, since corwin can't actually overcome me, but we can play purely for fun. After nine years together, we have very few surprises left for each other, but I find that going out and having experiences with other lovers recharges my libido and gives me new ideas.

My current secondary lover is the first macho heterosexual man I've dated since high school. He's a womanizer (if I can use that term in a positive way), which is exactly the quality I need: I don't have to be butch around him. He can take up all the butchness. We both work at a Renaissance Faire, so there's a mix of hyper-masculine and hyper-feminine roles at work, i.e., princes and wenches and the like. He's a knight, by the way, and cultivates a dashing cad persona that isn't too different from what he's "really" like. He sweeps women off their feet and ravishes them. This means I don't have to work very hard much of the time; the expectations of both our roles are well understood. (Not that the relationship is free of processing.) One of the first questions he asked me—in between kissing my neck and undoing my bodice—was, "Do you think it's possible for friends to love each other?" My answer? Absolutely. So I seem to have found another sexual friend and adventurer. Our well-defined boundaries set us free with each other and with others. Since corwin is sexually submissive to me, it's nice to have someone else do the driving. (corwin has other relationships where he is the dominant partner, so he gets both sets of needs met.)

And once in a while, I take part in a threesome. When most people in the mundane world think "polyamory" they think "ménage à trois." But really it doesn't happen to us that often. The major difficulty corwin and I have is that the men and women I am attracted to invariably are not his type, and vice versa.

Though there have been one or two exceptions, like that sweet boy who rode his motorcycle here from Atlanta, whom we did get into bed, and the knockout stunning dom from San Francisco, whom we didn't—yet, anyway . . .

My best threesome experience was when I was the third. They were younger than I was and craving erotic adventure but leading fairly conservative lives (well, they were in theater, but, compared to my march on the statehouse/street hustler lovers, they were conservative). I'd had a crush on her for years, and he'd had a fantasy all his life about doing two women. She orchestrated it: brought him up to visit me in Boston, called on the phone, then came up for a second visit. To this day, one of the most erotic memories I have is of her lying between my legs, both of us on our backs and facing him, my hands cupped around her breasts, while he fucked her. It felt right, to have her there in my arms while her lover was inside her. Like something for which I had waited a long time.

The dynamic of the ménage was complex. The couple functioned as a unit in some ways. When she was the focus, it was because she was the beloved of both of us—as she lay there between my legs, we both poured our desire into her. When he was the focus, it was because he was the man, the phallic element, which affects both the logistics and the development of the experience. When I was the focus, it was because I was the "spice," the two of them adding me to their bed (even though technically we were in my bed), and to the way they interacted with each other. I was different and new, and it was wonderfully empowering to give myself to them like a gift. I suppose some people might have felt slighted or lonely that night when they left, but not me. I was their tour guide through an erotic place outside their experience.

Not every polyamorous person or couple operates the way I do, but I think most of the poly folks I know subvert the basic assumption of couplehood, i.e., that Mr. or Ms. Right should do and be absolutely everything you could want, that he or she can satisfy every need, every desire. It's such a pervasive myth, akin to "love will solve all our problems," and results in secret infidelities and serial monogamy that can be hard on the family. Some poly folks I know just don't feel comfortable with only one person. They want to weave a big central family together in order to fill emotional needs that just one person can't fill. I am not quite like that—I don't want a triad marriage or a multi-parent household. But I do want a larger erotic community, and the freedom to connect with and express the many divergent parts of myself with secondary partners.

I suppose you could say my adolescent fantasies have come true, but I didn't have to go to another planet to experience them. Alternative communities exist; people of radical sexuality find each other and band together. I have valued being free to seek fulfillment of diverse erotic needs outside of a single relationship, but that is just one aspect. The freedom to operate outside the mainstream is also critical—I'm not comfortable conforming. But I keep coming back to my dreams of the hands, my dreams of the group brought together for a common purpose, of the boundaries of individuality giving way to a group community eroticism.

So I keep trying to find ways to re-create that reality. About a year ago, I gathered a group of more than a dozen friends in San Francisco to heal my broken heart. Yes, it's true, not every relationship, poly or otherwise, ends happily. One of my secondaries had burned me very badly several years before, and on the fifth anniversary of the meltdown my friends, my tribe, my chosen erotic family came together to heal me.

We created a ritual, and they agreed on the common goal. But I did not know exactly what they would do to me. The first thing they did was blindfold me and lay their hands on me. I again was the sacrifice on the altar, the vessel into which the group would pour its love, desire, need. This time, they did it not just to me, but for me, to bring me back into my body, to center me there, to re-awaken my desires that had retreated. They took me through the cathartic, cleansing fire of their sadism, their desires and their love. In the circle surrounding me were gay men, bisexual women, committed couples and single adventurers. In some ways, I felt I had been every one of them at some point in my travels, and each of them gave me back a piece of myself. I hold all these facets of my sexuality inside me, in tiny drawers in a big jewelry box of my identity, drawers that I can open and explore at any time.

I Am One Lousy Lay

 Susan Jane Gilman

I am one lousy lay. I am the queen of erotic mediocrity. I am Nyquil with breasts.

What's more, I don't care.

Let me be the first to admit that, during sex, I just sort of lie there. I have no discernable sense of rhythm, and I rarely make any noise—except when clearing my throat. Which I do a lot. Don't ask me why, sex makes me phlegmy. Also, I have an ant farm on the shelf near my bed, and sometimes I get so busy watching the ants march around that I forget I'm in the middle of having sex and the guy has to say, "Um, excuse me. Yoohoo. Over here."

Oh yeah, and I hum. Whenever guys go down on me, I just start humming—show tunes, mostly, or those little jingles from *Schoolhouse Rock*—"Lolly's Lolly's Lolly's get your adverbs here," and that one about the Nineteenth Amendment. Guys say it freaks them out, but hey, you know how it is. Once you get those songs stuck in your head, you just can't get 'em out. I mean, I once sang the preamble to the Constitution for, like, three weeks in a row.

I own one slinky, sex-kitten teddy that's been lying around on the bottom of my underwear drawer since 1989. Whenever I dig it up and put it on, the thong rides up my butt and gives me a rash. So I just end up wearing stretch pants and bunny slippers—which I usually insist on wearing to bed, too. Men complain, but look, I tell them, my feet are cold. "You like to keep on your socks," I point out. "It's not like your Mr. Rogers look is erotic haute couture either."

My other sexual shortcomings?

Besides the ant farm, the humming, and the bunny slippers, let's just say that I've been ordering the exact same lunch meal at McDonald's for seventeen years now, and I'm inconsolable whenever the milkshake machine breaks down. In other words, I don't exactly subscribe to the variety-is-the-spice-of-life school of thought—and you can imagine how that translates onto the mattress.

My calf muscles cramp easily. I get lockjaw in no time. I giggle at inopportune moments. I find erectile dysfunction screamingly funny. I yawn audibly. Sometimes, in the middle of foreplay, I point out how the cracks on my ceiling look a lot like the profile of former Russian Prime Minister Boris Yeltsin. And if I happen to finish before the guy does, well, then I tend to lose interest altogether. "Hey, wanna do something else now?" I say, "Why don't we watch a little MTV or play Cranium?"

Don't get me wrong. I really like sex. Yay sex. Orgasms are great. Yay orgasms. Yay intimacy, too, for that matter.

It's just that, sexually, I happen to be a Type B personality with a really short attention span. So sue me.

Look, it's not like I don't *try* to get with the program. Every morning, I get my big bohunkis out of bed—a major accomplishment right there, considering I'm a night owl. In order to look my sexiest, I shower and exfoliate. I floss and moisturize. I blow-dry, curl, spritz, and primp. I stuff my legs into pantyhose, prop up my boobs in a Wonderbra, grease my underarms with a Lady Speedstick that smells suspiciously like floor cleaner, and do the whole white-girl-putting-on-makeup-in-the-bathroom-listening-to-Motown routine.

I poke contact lenses into my eyes. I dress, accessorize, and manage to elbow my way through the orgy of the rush-hour subway while doing only minimal damage to my 'do. Major points for that alone, no?

But then, I work all day. In my pseudo-glamorous job as an associate editor for a corporate publisher, I spend hours reading manuscripts, talking with agents, interviewing authors. I write cover memos, synopses, marketing plans. I proofread and edit. And oh, am I ever on the phone—you might as well glue it to my ear.

I also gossip with Cheryl in the next cubicle, drink overpriced latte and waste time reading my horoscope on the Internet finding out how compatible I was supposed to be with all of my ex-boyfriends. I do this in a room with 100 percent florescent lighting and 0 percent fresh air for roughly twelve hours a day.

Sometimes after work I hit the gym. I pay eight hundred dollars a year so that twice a week I can climb, pedal and ski to nowhere for twenty minutes. Of course, when I'm finished with my workout, I have to shower and exfoliate and blow dry and primp all over again. It's exhausting! By the time I get home, microwave dinner and have my boyfriend come over, frankly, I'm just too tired to be a sex goddess.

Geez. Is that so horrible?

Nowadays, it seems, there's so much pressure put on us gals to sexually perform—as either madonnas or Madonna, virgins or whores. On one hand—the far-right one, of course—we've got these zealots railing against female sexuality and telling us to keep our legs crossed. In this Paleolithic world, women are again encouraged to see sex as sinful and shameful, and ourselves as both precious vessels and vassals to men.

If we slip up (or, I guess, down), we're urged to become "born-again" virgins—roughly the sexual equivalent of what we used to call in the playground "a do-over." Yeah, right. Like who's kidding who here?

On the other hand, we've got the rest of the culture just egging us on. "Give Him the Best Sex Ever!" read headlines in women's magazines, along with "100 Surefire Sexual Techniques." Advertisements imply that we can drive men to their knees in a sexual frenzy by eating Doritos in a library. We've got stars like Madonna and Courtney Love constantly pushing the envelope, seeing just how far they can go, how supersexual they can be. On television, on the Internet, on the airwaves, there are women boasting, gloating, gyrating, flexing, showing off their new breasts, writing about their "sexcapades," confessing, bragging, revealing, flaunting, begging, singing "give it to me one more time, baby."

In the face of all this, it's easy to end up feeling hopelessly inadequate—like we're never hot enough or fuckable enough—that something is fundamentally wrong with us if walk around our boyfriend's house in sweatpants and don't have sex on a motorcycle every day. Hell, it's even easy to feel inadequate if we don't have an empowering relationship with a Hitachi Magic Wand.

"I feel like sex is now a competition," a friend told me recently. "It's like we have to prove we're the best and the baddest and getting it all the time."

Yeah, well, not me. Frankly, I'm proud of the fact that I inspire narcolepsy in men. I see it as a badge of honor that I'm so dull in bed, *guys* say to *me*, "Wait, that was it?" I'm proud of my, ahem, shortcomings, of my wandering mind and a libido that runs more hot and cold than a New York City radiator. I'm proud of the fact that I am generally one lackluster, perplexing, ho-hum piece of pootie.

Because, if you ask me, *real* sexual liberation means having the freedom and the self-esteem to be one truly horrendous lay. It means the freedom to be indifferent, or lazy, or even to—gasp—actually be interested in something other than giving a fabulous blowjob. In a culture torn between tits and tightasses, between hype and hypocrisy, only accepting our limitations and imperfections will really set us free in the end.

That said, I'm putting on my bunny slippers, picking up my ant farm and climbing back into bed. I've got a whole lot of not-so-hot lovin' left to do.

DOING IT RIGHT

 Julian Bell

I wish you could come into me," she said.

So did I, at times.

This time though, she meant she wanted me to pretend that I had a dick. We had nothing really dicklike around, no dildos, nothing. So I put my hands to where a dick would be and she moved my legs with hers under me, so that we were in a position that resembled boy-girl missionary position fucking. It made me wet, but also it made me tremble. It made me feel very inadequate. I could push inside, but I couldn't wiggle my fingers against her cervix. I couldn't dally around in the vulva with a couple of extra shorter fingers and/or thumb. I couldn't explore those strange crevices or angles or vast open spaces as she clenched at my knuckles.

I could push too hard and it could hurt. She whispered to me, "I love you with a dick," and I did my best, but I wasn't very good. Her back stayed flat, her hands lost their movement, and maybe she was concentrating on something I didn't understand, some sort of place I didn't yet know about, but we lost our rhythm. What started as intense pleasure driven by the anticipation and excitement and newness of the experiment leveled out rather quickly. And I found myself in a sexual role that had become completely detached from my own desire.

Performing an act without desire made me feel ashamed. Like acting straight and attracted to boys when I was younger, I wasn't being true to myself. Up to this point, I had experienced direct and indirect homophobia and had dealt with the fear of coming out to family and friends, but I had never felt ashamed of myself, my body, my sexuality. Until, in the least expected of places, I felt ashamed in bed with my girlfriend.

This was the same sort of anxiety that I had begun to feel, on a more general public level, since I moved into the lesbian community. Here was a whole group of people who, by rejecting heterosexual norms, challenged mainstream ideals with their love and their bodies. Who all moved their bodies and directed their desires in different ways than they were supposed to. I saw queer culture as a resistance not only to traditional gender roles but also to all the rigid structures that went with them, all the scripts that regulated how bodies could behave and how sex itself should be performed. I naively entered the queer world thinking that queer folks had unanimously voted out these scripts, and the idea of normative behavior, period, from queer culture. When I moved into an urban dyke community, I was completely unprepared for the conformity I found. This community had its own norms and standards, and a great sense of what was cool—including a code of sorts for bedroom activity.

In a way I fit that cliché story of the young dyke who expects the dyke world to be some kind of utopia and gets disappointed. I admit that I thought there was more possibility for freedom in a dyke community than I ever could have. Forgive me, but I wanted it to be the Land of Canaan. I wanted to walk into a bar with my dyke chums' lips glistening with honey. But more often than not I walked into queer spaces where a discussion was going on and discovered that only certain sex stories would be told, only certain dyke images would be affirmed.

I heard about women with new tattoos and piercings, women who slept with several women, the glamorization of butch and femme characteristics and jokes and innuendoes involving anything in sight that could be construed as a phallic sex toy. The women participating in these discussions didn't necessarily wear much leather, own many sex toys, practice polyamory or multiple-partnered sex, or identify as butch or femme. But still they talked about these subjects all the time. Somehow these images, these specific dyke personas, were brought up in conversation again and again, and discussed with a sense of awe, as if the world of butch/femme, sex toys and body art were more "cool," something that we somehow should achieve as queer women. This was the stylish, even trendy, world of lesbian sex.

When I came to queer culture, I was out, really out, for the first time in a new city. And I was in love. I had driven 3,000 miles to be there, from a place where there isn't a rainbow bumper sticker to be found. I had just graduated from college and swore that never again would I hide my affections, or confine my sexuality to a midnight rendezvous in a residence room. Being a lesbian would mean more than a Woman's Resource Center video showing of *The Incredibly True Adventures of Two Girls In Love*, or the token Adrienne Rich poetry on English exams. No. I arrived in October, and two blocks away from the apartment I shared with my girlfriend the street was lined with rainbow flags still left over from Pride. We hung a Fire poster in the living room and old postcards we had sent each other of Vita Sackville-West and Georgia O'Keefe prints. Not only were there delicious-looking dykes everywhere, there were very obvious dyke couples to be seen shopping for cereal at Safeway and kissing goodbye at coffee shops. I felt solid, legitimized knowing that these people around me knew something about my experience, knew about the nature of my love, my desire and, yes, my sex life, and that these things were counted as real, as normal and real as they would be if my partner were a man. The same female hands that opened someone's vulva the night before poured sugar into a cup of coffee beside me at a cafe the morning after, unapologetically. Seeing such sights that had never been part of my everyday experience had me thinking that anything was possible.

I had resisted a lot to get to this city. I had resisted an urge to stay safe at home. I had resisted very strong (albeit platonic) feelings for, and proposals from, a very good boy from my mom's hometown. I had resisted grad school, and two opportunities for salaried jobs in my field. This was in the name of love of course, in the name of finding myself, but also in the name of believing in alternative possibilities. My first boyfriend kissed me on my parents' bed with what felt like the biggest tongue in the world. I looked at his eyelids, the ceiling, the wall, until one day I just got up from under his kiss. I walked out of the room and told him that if he wanted a girl to touch him there he could go out with someone else, and I never opened my mouth to him again.

It wasn't just my own anxieties about being queer that kept me so chaste. What made me keep my pants on all those years was that I was terrified of my body being manipulated into something it wasn't by someone else. When I was growing up, sex as I knew it seemed to be all about seducing me enough to warp my body into acting out a specific part. This was the ever-desired role of the soft-spoken, manicured, skinny girl. This ideal was enforced by sex scenes in movies, beer commercials and makeup companies' recognition of a pre-teen market—their ads and the kids at school who fell for them. This hyper-heterosexualized girl seemed to revolve entirely around the dick, of which I was also terrified. I was terrified that by accepting it, my body would succumb to a singular thrust, would pivot around a pitifully banal pillar only to be washed out in the end. To acknowledge any sense of the sexual within myself—it seemed—I had to consider the dick, my relationship to it, my desire for it. I had to think of myself in terms of the dick, or I was not sexual. And so I wasn't.

Or I wasn't in the way that counted. I did have a taste for thin cotton night-shirts. They made my skin tense and I liked how they swayed against my waist. I imagined hands swirling around my waist like that soft material until my nipples got hard enough to lift it away from my skin. I kept a close watch over the curve of my maturing arm muscles, enjoying the smooth long lines that flexed when I moved my fingers. I imagined the muscles at work in perfecting how my fingers moved. My relationship with my body then was friendlier than it ever would be again. I was happy with it, happy moving in it. I knew there was an importance to my dexterity, to disciplining my motor skills to be all at once forceful, gentle and precise. There would be subtleties involved, and the angle or pressure used to touch my clit could make or break a situation.

I read a lot, too, when I was in high school and later. Poetry, I found out in college, was full of lesbian sexuality, and it was going through a trendy phase in academia. I read letters from Vita Sackville-West writing to Virginia Woolf about their naughty behavior on the sofa. There was Adrienne Rich "stirring our body hair and moving together like underwater plants," there was Audre Lorde "making love in doorways, never meant to survive." This literature—startling, vivid, intimate—impressed upon me the idea of possibilities, new ways to love and touch, sexual expression that went beyond what the girls said about their boyfriends. I wanted (though granted at some distant future date) to make love to a woman, I wanted to dive into her, I wanted to touch all over her skin with my fingers and then I wanted to put my fingers inside her. I wanted to feel all of my body against all of her body. I wanted to invent a careful rhythm. I wanted to hear her gasp and sigh and be careful with me sometimes, and sometimes forgive me if I trembled.

Before I came out, these daydreams, this literature and the attention I paid to my own body were my moments of satisfaction, of satiation. Though not the same as having sex, these moments did contain a certain intimacy, a communication with my body that is unique to the sexual experience. Can I say that these are really my first sex stories? If I did offer them up to my lesbian community, would they be accepted or dismissed? This was the first time I kissed a woman: I had a terrible crush, and I told her so, and when it was her birthday I fed her a lot of rye whisky from a bottle I had bought duty-free. And there was a snowstorm and we had gone out dancing where we touched a few times too often. When everyone else went to sleep, she sat beside me. We talked beside each other, and then we talked with her hand on my thigh, and we giggled, with my hand testing the joints and knuckles on her hand, and maybe I touched her cheek then, I don't remember. Then we were kissing and everything that was wrong with me and the world was going to be okay from then on. We kissed all night, kissed, bit, touched everything. I thought it was both wonderful and terrifying to have breasts in front of me where there shouldn't be anything but hard chest. We never got drunk enough again together to go for another try. That night we just played, experimented, enjoyed ourselves. I'm not sure what degree of sex this is. Sex for most of my friends then meant when the penis goes in. The rest was just "fooling around." I guess I'm always just fooling around, but it doesn't feel so much like fooling to me. It feels like sex.

Eventually I met some very beautiful and generous women who indulged me and honored me with their honesty and their skin. In those few rooms where we shut out the assaults of sexual regulation, we reintroduced ourselves to each other. We did make something out of our contact. The first woman who undressed me had quick, attentive, intelligent hands. The second had a fearless tongue. I began to learn how we are capable of speaking to, and into, ourselves through our bodies. This is where language and sex arrive at their most intimate. This is where they are inseparable, in that confusion of limbs, hair, liquids, mouths . . .

There are few people who really know what it means to come out as queer. Unless people have done it themselves, there is a guarantee they won't understand just what it is like for you to verbalize your desires for human beings of the same sex. After coming out as a lesbian, it took me nearly three years to come out of the bedroom. What I mean is that I ever so slowly began to wear the physical acts and sensations of my own sexual life in the way I moved in my everyday world. It was more than coming out as queer, it was coming out as a sexual being. It took those three whole years in private to nurture my sexual identity (what I identified sex to be for me) before I was ready for the public opinion onslaught attempting to transform into boring, dead normalcy whatever adventures I'd concocted behind closed doors. Not surprisingly, much of this public opinion was that of mainstream culture, the prudent, white, middle-class culture of my upbringing. In this world, I was targeted by marketing schemes, by men, by other competitive and judgmental women, not to mention by anxious family members wanting to see a nice young fellow over for dinner. These were the heterosexual scripts: whom I would sit beside at dinner, how I would dress, how I would speak/walk/cross my legs, how I would have sex and how much, and especially with whom, and what might come out of me nine months later.

I had two younger brothers who played soccer in a league at our local park, so many summer evenings I sat out on the green grass watching them run. And I couldn't help also watching the other families, the moms and dads, the accountants and lawyers and computer programmers and fiscal agents who expressed their sexualities in business suits and salt and pepper hair.

In the winter the boys play hockey. The first time I tried to put all the pieces of the uniform and my brother together before game time I had to ask someone's mother how to do the garter belts. I laughed at myself, deciding I was probably the only lesbian in the locker room. I had never worn garters and never would, but I did secretly imagine how, were we living in another time, this lesson would have been useful in taking someone else's off. I hid my smile though, aware of how distinct my daydreams were from those of the moms. But when the boys went out to play and we went to the concession stand for coffee and then set ourselves down in the stands, I stopped feeling so different. These women had made many of the choices in their mates that I had to make as well. They were all mothers, and therefore had experienced areas of their body and sexuality that I had not, and, like me, they constantly had to negotiate their way through society's regulation of their bodies. They were living through the same stereotyping of femininity that I did, and had resolved for themselves the conflicts between self, society and image in different ways, ways I could learn from. Some of the moms were more butch in appearance and attitude than the butchest lesbians I've ever met. Some put on their makeup and sprayed their hair even before the 6:00 a.m. games. Some were going through divorces, having affairs, trying herbal remedies. Some were getting plastic surgery, some were being treated for breast cancer. They had a lot of respect for each other and me, and the time I spent with these women taught me lessons in diversity that I wouldn't have learned on my own, from books or from my supposedly sexually subversive peers.

Still, they were all moms, and most had husbands. They were definitely survivors, but as straight women, their survival seemed more easily attainable. They had me questioning myself, my own survival potential. I knew the media was bullshit, advertising was bullshit and its heterosexism was so obvious it wasn't penetrating. But the happiness, the community, the family—all looked so good on the soccer field and over hot chocolates in the arena. I didn't feel threatened as a lesbian, I never felt ashamed. I just had to confront that repeat image of the mom and dad couple, the success of it. I learned some things about self-image from these women, but I would always keep myself to myself. My desires were always private.

When I finally came out as a lesbian my desires became public. That meant that when I went out in the lesbian community, I was subject to public scrutiny, and the scrutiny was always directed at my sexual potential. It was in lesbian spaces that I learned that style was necessary, and, for the first time since junior high school, I worried about whether or not I was cool. But it wasn't just cool vs. uncool, stylish vs. frumpy; rather, there were certain scripts laid out for me. In some ways it seemed worse than the hockey stands. I could choose butch or femme, which were back in fashion. I could choose the skinny-framed adolescent boy look. I could be a jock, or a nature girl. I could be punk. That was about it. Suddenly it mattered, too, because supposedly I wanted these women and wanted them to want me. Who, exactly, would want me would depend on the style I chose. For the women who happened to fit into these roles—for whom they were not roles at all, but expressions of who they were—they were probably fun, liberating, sexy. But for me, the idea of adapting my image to a pre-existing style didn't make me feel like a survivor; rather, it felt like a cop-out. The uniformity I encountered shocked me. The queer couples I knew generally matched. For a while my girlfriend and I were termed "the Birkenstock lesbians."

When we would come home, and my girlfriend would say, "So and so said you're cute," that meant I was okay, accepted. Few people said I was an interesting or fun or intelligent person. It was "cute" or nothing. I had gone from opting out of sexuality in the straight world, to having my sexuality precede all else.

Soon after I moved to the city, I got a job at a bookstore. One Friday night, my co-worker was sitting cross-legged on a stool behind the cash register, absent-mindedly flipping through *On Our Backs*, the lesbian porn magazine, as if looking through a recipe book.

"Oh, look at this!"

She rolled her stool over to me, and I hoped I wouldn't blush too much. I found myself simultaneously turned on and bored by *On Our Backs*. Maybe it was because on Friday nights I sold too many copies of the magazine to very straight-looking men. Maybe it was because the looks on the participants' faces were too staged. Rather than inspiring thoughts of sex—the intricacies, the arrangements, the impulse and innovation—the spreads seemed like a forever-stationary theatrical tableau.

All my co-worker wanted to show me was an ad for a dildo. In the top left corner of the page was a picture of someone wearing a new dick. A bold headline stated something about "new" and "buy now." A small article described the chemically simulated skin. "This dick," she said in awe, "is made with this new stuff that makes it feel like it's really skin. I've actually touched one of these. It's amazing." To me, the only amazing thing was her automatic assumption that I would be interested in this special, even more dicklike dildo. Yet this was not the first casual conversation I'd had that was all about the dyke dick, where an interest in dicklike penetration was presumed from the get-go.

"Wow," I said. "Great. This will just revolutionize lesbian sex forever." For the rest of that night at the bookstore, I imagined all of the dykes who had come into the store over the course of the week—the older longstanding couples, the tough women, the cluster of university prof dykes, the excruciatingly sexy young dykes—all going to bed with each other and their new just-like-a-live-dick strap-on. I was afraid to add anything to my sarcastic comment for fear of being called repressed, or a prude. I was afraid she'd ask me what tools my girlfriend and I used (none) or when I'd used a dildo (never). I was afraid that she'd ask me anything about my sex life, period. She talked about hers all the time. She had put up magazine pictures in the bathroom of women she thought were hot. They were sinewy and tattooed, wore dark leathers and greased their hair. She spoke of picking women up in bars in San Francisco, about the phone sex she had with one now that she'd come home. I was afraid that she'd ask me to share my stories and that the truth would be inadequate.

The truth was that I did want to experiment with penetration, and even though my girlfriend and I didn't own any tools you might find in a sex-store catalog, we sometimes were what you could call "kinky" and introduced other objects into our sex life. And when we moved into the dyke community, we began trying a lot of new things: We read a how-to article on fisting. We visited a sex store together for the first time. I read Joan Nestle's stories about sex with her butch lovers, about reaching over in bed at night just to rest her hand on her lover's torso, only to find a leather strap and the beginning of evening adventures. I fantasized about how it would make me feel to have a cock in my pants. I fantasized about what it would be like to have a cock in me. Believe me, these encounters were all stunning and worthwhile.

But, over time, all this new sex information started to run together, and worse, become predictable. If there's a number one turn-off in sex, it's predictability. The porn was full of women's frowning attempts at looking lusty or handsome or whatever bored, uncaring expression someone had decided was supposed to make me wet. The scene was always gray, clothes dark, lighting gothic. And when these scenes did proliferate and become predictable, I realized that I couldn't find other options. There seemed to be only the dark, gray, pouty world of lesbian sex. There was still a "right" sex to have, to desire and to perform. These images were supposed to be "alternative," but in my urban queer world this uniform "alternative" was all there was.

"She said you liked to be creative," a friend of mine told me my girlfriend had said about my approach to sex. "Creative" came out like a foreign word, like I was doing an art project. Or trying to be special. As when my girlfriend said to me, "You think too much." I wasn't trying to be anything, except someone who could please both of us sexually. Someone who tried to look for new erogenous areas and possibilities for peak sensations, even if many times it didn't really work. There was status and guaranteed pleasure, apparently, in adhering to certain accepted practices. Coming up with other ones was discouraged.

I had only been sexually active for three years, all with women. I wasn't interested in tying my sexuality to a particular model. Wasn't that the whole problem with straight culture? I wanted to hold on to the excitement and promise of endless possibilities. What do lesbians do in bed after all? We can't learn from many movies, from popular culture. From childhood we're surrounded with images and stories of heterosexual sex; for lesbian sex, the silence is deafening. But with no common denominator, anything is possible. It could involve a dick, sure, or it could involve two dicks, or it could involve something else of a similar shape. It could involve candles, food, pictures, leather, cotton, music. Lesbian sex to me was sheer improvisation, it worked only according to the pleasures of you and your partner, independent of some socially implemented ideal.

The truth is, as our community has grown and gained visibility, the discourse of lesbian sex has grown as well. We do now have resources, images, stories, models for lesbian sex. Even if they aren't part of North American pop culture, you don't have to look too hard to find them. But in the process of creating a discourse, we also create new norms and expectations. Stories can expand our sexual possibilities, or they can limit them.

Somehow improvisation and playfulness got lost in the stories I heard of queer women's sex. Just like in high school, I felt like my sex was not "real sex" because it didn't match the stories around me. Once again, I was just "fooling around," because the things I was into were not considered sexy. "Sexy" was only what was pre-scripted as cool queer sex. But "cool" degrades what dyke sex is; it delegitimizes the practice of women having sex with other women. And those who write sex with dildos into the script as "good sex" can do as much damage to the practice of penetration as they do to the sex that is left out.

Penetration and butch/femme, after all, were once marginalized in the dominant lesbian feminist culture, and are now being re-claimed. For many dykes, penetration with dildos or strap-ons is sexually empowering, a liberating way of playing with sex and gender. But when the dyke community imposes ideas of "cool sex" and "popular sex" upon itself, even something like penetrative sex gets regulated into certain preferred modes. Instead of breaking the boundaries of accepted sex and working to build something new, conversations about new sex toys or accessories always seem to reduce the discussion to the same old story.

For me, in the bedroom, dicklike penetration never felt comfortable—always I felt as if I were trying to copy something else, be it boy-girl/penis-vagina intercourse or a dyke sex ideal. Where was the potential for invention, improvisation—I was failing miserably with my makeshift digital dick. I knew some dykes could queer sex and gender in endless ways with their dicks, but I couldn't get over the feeling that I was back to the banal, patriarchal dick I had struggled so long to resist. My girlfriend became frustrated.

One night she turned me over.

"Do you wish, sometimes, that I had a dick?"

I had wished that sometimes. Or rather I'd thought about it, wondered about it after conversations like the one I'd had at work, but hadn't expressed it out loud even to myself.

She knew much better. She went inside me with something that could no longer be called fingers because they felt so different. No longer animated, playful, ticklish, teasing, this was one smooth, bendless, singular and serious tool. After a moment I felt I wanted it very much, this dick. I asked her for it night after night and asked for it to continue even when it hurt. But in the moment that it went into me, I was terrified. Her fingers lost their personality and reminded me of the dildos made of glass at our local sex store, cold and smooth. I had never been penetrated like that before. I guess some would say I'd never been penetrated at all before. This was the sex that she wanted more and more, and that I learned to think I wanted, finally, after resisting for so long.

Gradually, in my own bed, I made love as a caricature of my dyke self to a caricature of my dyke girlfriend. Even alone, we became the sexual selves that we thought we should be. The very skin that gave us everything that was our sex changed, or we changed it, or we let it be changed. It wasn't a sudden or total shift. The shift was far more subtle, and far more powerful. Some other story had worked its way into what we told each other. There was a script for my hands to follow, and they had to work in relation to the script, either with it or against it, but always taking that script into consideration.

One night, a bunch of us from a dyke political action group were at a bar where we were holding a fundraiser. The subject of conversation was, of course, sex. And why not? We were a bunch of young, hot women on a night out. And, after all, what makes us the dykes we are is that we have sex with other women. This is the part that those who hate us hate most. This is the very area where we are silenced. So even this kind of talk in a bar is resistance. Talk, any talk, about lesbian sex is essential to our survival. It is another instance where sex and language are mutually dependent, in the vocabulary we create for our own sexuality and desires. And I love talking about it. I love talking about lesbian sex second only to having lesbian sex. But on this night, as is so often the case, the talk went sour.

"Hey you, we were just talking about having a threesome, you want to join us, we could make it four?"

"Ha, ha. Where's the waitress."

"Oh, my god, she's so fucking hot."

"The ass, it's the ass in that skirt."

"She's super cute."

"Yep, and check out these. Nice tits." (Gestures here with hands at chest).

"She's super fucking cute."

I'm serious about the words in the above conversation. Granted, there is some sort of empowerment in re-claiming words like "tits" and "ass" for our own usage. But please, this isn't reinventing language as much as appropriating a dull and offensive way to objectify and sexualize a woman who is an open target just because she is working in a service job.

There was a raffle that night, and a friend of mine, one of the few who didn't share the details of her sex life with the rest of us, won the gift certificate to a sex store. As she went up to the stage to collect her prize (and it was the most coveted prize), the rest of our supposedly aware, politically conscious group joked about it. She won it? When would she use it? Does she ever have sex? This joking laughter frightened me. What constituted "sex" for them that made my friend unworthy of the prize? Who says that a trip to the sex store requires a partner? Who says she doesn't have a partner or more than one partner? I found comfort in my friend who won the prize. I did not know anything more than the others about her sexual portfolio, and I admired her privacy on the subject. It became clear to me that in this withholding, she protected her sex stories, her philosophy of sex and her sexual activities from scrutinization by the dyke authority. Looking back, it seems ironic that she had to protect her most intimate stories from a community that prides itself on telling its stories. Her silence produced a stereotype of its own, one of prudish celibacy, but I could see how it was less harmful than the alternative. I also realized I saw far more potential in having sex with my friend than with anyone else at the bar that night, with or without the gift certificate. I've lived in two other lesbian communities since then, and in both I've seen the same stereotyping, the same regulation, the same separation between how sex is commonly practiced and experienced and how it is talked about. We watch the same movies, read the same magazines, are part of the same North American dyke pop culture. The idea that the dyke world might automatically resist social regulation by dismissing heterosexual, traditionally gendered ways of life needs to be complicated further. Dyke or no dyke, social norms operate within us and seek to govern our behavior, how we move our bodies and our concept of who we are.

If queer women cannot feel comfortable talking to each other about the very things that make us queer women—our attraction to other women, our desire for other women and our sexual experiences with other women—where can we go to be ourselves? How can we demand rights and respect from a society steeped in heterosexism when we cannot expect respect from those in our own community? The distance, the prejudice, the fear we overcome to find ourselves naked with each other is immense. To resist those pressures, I need to be more or less free from pressures to conform when I'm with other dykes. And in my experience, we are not there yet. Because we too often succumb to a kind of normativity—a dyke normativity, but one that, like heteronormativity, tends to discourage our choices of lovers, and our ways of loving.

I wish I could say that maybe I am still that baby dyke who wants the storybook utopia, that soon I'll see the light and not feel so critical of the dyke community. The norms embraced by heterosexual culture still make me feel controlled, even panicked, certainly not very sexy. Is it so strange, then, that norms are created, upheld, relied upon in the queer community, when we are so often attacked and put down? Does establishing a certain code of behavior make us feel accepted when we are not accepted in so many communities? Does the dyke community still have issues (and how could it not?) with bodies, and how bodies are expected to connect and disconnect? As the queer community becomes more accepted in the urban mainstream are we drawn to "radical sex" even as our own norms begin to function in the same way as those we left behind? So often these are the questions on my tongue when I open my mouth to lesbian women.

A Celibate Sexpot Ties the Knot

 Lisa Miya-Jervis

For most of my post-pubescent life, I've been—oh, how to say this nicely?—sexually focused. I was, in rapid and overlapping succession: 1) a sex-starved budding girl who thought about it all the time but never had the opportunity to actually do anything, 2) a teenage sexpert (once I finally gathered enough experience—paltry though it was—to take a stab at advice-giving), 3) a sex-positive feminist extraordinaire, 4) an overall sexual überbabe. But now that I've found myself by turns crankily celibate, happily celibate and happily married, I often wonder how the sexual überbabe, the crabby would-be slut, the asexual queen of productivity and autonomy and the married girl can all be me.

I do understand how I got from there to here. The short version: As an adolescent, I suffered from must-have-boyfriend syndrome, mistaking my abundant, purely physical sexual desire for deeper feelings for another person. Like so many American middle- and high-school girls who have been bombarded with our culture's gendered double standard of sexual/emotional attachment, I didn't think it was okay for me to just want to mess around, so my fevered brain automatically translated my lust into crushes on specific boys I thought I must be in love with. (Luckily, however, by senior year I met someone I actually was in love with—and who was in love with me— paving the way for an actual sex life to replace those painful and mostly unrequited crushes.) In college I saw my way past the boyfriend requirement and discovered the Good Vibrations catalog, *Pleasure and Danger* and other essential texts of sex-positive feminism. I finally understood what it was I wanted, and was perfectly happy with no-strings sexual companionship as often as I could find it. Then I was single for a long while—quite testily at first, but soon contentedly focused on work to the exclusion of the sexual part of my social life. I had sex maybe three times in two years. Then I met someone who made it worthwhile to tear myself away from my desk, and promptly married him. Cue happily-ever-after music.

No, it's not the progression that gets me—it's the combinations. When I was celibate, was I still sex-positive? Was I no longer an uberbabe? (I certainly didn't feel like one.) Now that I'm married, do I have to renounce the little slut inside?

See, I've never been one of those oh-sex-is-okay-but-what's-all-the-fuss-about kind of girls. More like the sex-sex-where-can-I-get-more-sex kind. In college, when men talked about their hormone-addled teen years spent popping boners at the very thought of anything from Phoebe Cates to the smell of their favorite jerk-off towel fresh from the wash, or when they spoke about their desire for easy, anonymous, no-strings-attached sex, I always thought, "And men are different from women because . . . ?" Once I got over fearing the stigma often attached to sexually forthright females, I wasn't shy about seeking out sexual partners, or about articulating just what I was expecting out of an arrangement.

At the beginning of my celibate years—a.k.a. my horrific dry spell, the winter of my discontent—my lack of sex life was circumstantially enforced and most certainly not by choice. I was frustrated as hell, constantly scoping men out at parties and finding myself unable to connect. I wanted sex, and I couldn't find anyone willing to have it with me. Sure, I could take care of myself just fine (and had been doing so for years), but who wouldn't crave the foreignness, unpredictability and pure tactile sensation of another body instead of a vibrator every once in a while?

After a year or so, however, I grew curiously accustomed to my sexless state. I actually grew to like not having sex. Sexual frustration gave way to a feeling of peacefulness. "My horrific dry spell" became "the time of great productivity the likes of which I will never see again," and the most contented period my tortured psyche had ever seen. Finding someone to play around with seemed not only complicated (You mean I'd have to start a conversation with a boy? Flirt with him? Touch his arm and suggest that I buy him a drink?) but also messy and unappealing (You mean I might eventually have to tolerate his tongue in my mouth?). I observed my friends in serious relationships and thanked my lucky stars that I didn't have to consult anyone else about what to have for dinner or smell anyone else's morning breath. I no longer went about my day with my erogenous zones humming, killing time on public transportation with quick fantasies about fellow passengers. I was flat: no waves of heat rushing between my legs at the sight of a set of pouty lips at the post office, no hardened nipples caused by a whiff of an aftershave worn by a particularly skilled ex-fuckbuddy. Just flat. George Clooney could have knocked on my bedroom door in nothing but silk boxers and I would have thought, Hmm, those look like they would be quite comfy for lounging around in bed reading. Where can I get a pair?

I blossomed professionally—all the energy that used to be spent finding partners and spending time with them was now going to writing and editing, with voluminous and gratifying results. My social life became focused on what I truly wanted to do with my evenings rather than what I thought might give me an opportunity to get laid—more dinners and drinks with friends, fewer parties where I knew only one other person and stood near the food scoping in vain and pretty much having a terrible time. For the first time in my life I had ample time to myself, many delicious hours all alone with no one but myself to answer to, and it made me realize how much I love being alone. I did a lot of reading, devouring some classics I'd never had the time for, and developed quite the taste for mysteries featuring ass-kicking female private investigators, reporters and lawyers. I watched a lot of movies. Mainly, I recharged from the constant mental churning of work—which I never would have been able to do if I'd had company.

After a while, my libido waned even further. I hadn't thought it was possible, but I even lost interest in sex with myself. Sure, I had the occasional insomnia-inspired wank, but it was usually more to reduce stress and induce sleep than to experience pleasure. I would often hold my vibrator in my hand at bedtime, intending to turn it on and give myself a thrill. Most nights I fell asleep before turning the dial, and I'd wake in the morning with the hard plastic poking my leg. Oh, I'd remember sadly, yeah, I was going to masturbate. I didn't know what to make of myself. I mean, it's one thing to not want to deal with sex partners in all their complicated glory. But to yawn at the prospect of a no muss, no fuss, battery-powered orgasm?

This was serious. I had built a whole personal philosophy on the notion that a woman could be as sexually voracious as any man—when freed from social restrictions like disapproval, double standards, and all those stupid studies about arousal that refuse to admit that perhaps women's answers to certain questions are influenced by cultural assumptions about what gets women hot—with myself as my own prime example. Now that I was feeling more and more asexual every day, where did that leave all my strong, sex-positive, I-am-woman-hear-me-scream rhetoric? What if I was wrong—what if women really did have puny little sex drives, and I had burnt mine out in a few short years of screwing around? What if this sexual flatness was my true nature, and I had just been struggling against it— overcompensating for years—and now it was finally winning? What if the old me never came back? Despite my otherwise calm, contented life, I was terrified.

These overanalytical ravings lurked beneath my calm exterior for a while, and eventually they ran their course. I accepted the fact that, for the time being, I was a woman who chose, night after night, not only to curl up with a book instead of another person, but to store *Middlemarch* instead of *My Secret Garden* on her nightstand. Indeed, I reveled in it. While there was always some part of me that looked forward to the time when my desire would rev up again, I came to see myself in a way that was beyond sexual. It was truly refreshing. I had been expending quite a lot of energy in being my own sexual role model, and no matter how much fun that was, it was also a relief to stop for a while.

You see, as much as I still believe in the potential strength of women's sexualities, the relentless sex-positive view can be wearing. Clearly, for me it was creating pressure to be a highly sexual person all the time, and thus muddying the waters of my own desires. It took a little too long to occur to me that I should stop worrying that I was betraying my beliefs, already, because how could I be if I was doing exactly what I wanted? Isn't that what sex-positive feminism is supposed to be all about? Of course, it would be so much easier to deal with these libidinal valleys (which are, of course, perfectly natural) if not for the fear of embodying the stereotype of "feminine" (read: passive, emotionally motivated) sexuality. Unfortunately, with the Mars and Venus franchise still going strong, it doesn't look like we're going to be rid of that onerous cultural concept anytime soon.

So, about two and a half years after my circumstantially enforced celibacy had set in, and about a year and a half after my sex drive took its major nosedive, I felt myself heating up again. My distaste for sex with a partner turned to curiosity; my craving to feel another body against mine returned. My frustration at not having any playmates returned as well, along with my willingness to seek them out. And so, like a tentative groundhog poking her snout up out of her hole at the end of a long, cold winter, I accepted a date. A nice young man named Christopher asked me to accompany him to a co-worker's wedding. Never being one to turn down an opportunity to get dressed up, drink excessive amounts of wine and watch two people at a very happy moment in their lives, I said yes.

My celibacy came to an abrupt end two months later. After our first kiss (brief, gentle yet frankly sexual), and our second (on fire), on the occasion of what would have been our third I allowed Christopher to lead me straight to bed. It was definitely weird: I was nervous, I was letting someone else take the lead, I was demure, for fuck's sake—but, most important, I was interested. Very, very interested. In short, I was not acting like myself. This was not a familiar version of me—not the aggressive sexpot (I didn't kiss him until our third date—or, more accurately and even more uncharacteristically, I didn't let him kiss me until the third date) and certainly not the go-away-I'm-busy perpetually single girl. In fact, I had been assiduously holding Christopher at arm's length, getting used to the fact that I had more fun and more in common with him than with anyone else I'd met in I didn't even know how long, and that I thought about him all too often when he wasn't around. I was pretty uncomfortable, which in turn made me confused—I wanted to get closer, but I was afraid; I wanted to go back to my business-as-usual routine, but I knew I had finally met someone too special to dismiss summarily. I was worried about having sex (what if I wasn't good at it anymore?), about not having sex (what if my cherished libido was gone forever?), about pretty much everything else (what if I hurt him? what if he hurt me? what if the world ended and cut short our time to find out?).

As soon as we started sleeping together, the old me was back in a flash. We couldn't keep our hands off each other, and rushed home to bed from dinner parties before our hosts could even brew coffee. I was mighty keen on preserving my routine, undisturbed life, so I set strict limits—two nights a week, max—and forced him out of bed early each morning after so that I could work undistracted. I flirted with other men and stuffed my pockets with their phone numbers. I was in heaven—not just from the hormone high that comes from all the sex we were having (although I'm sure that had something to do with it), but also because I'd been reunited with a part of myself that I had worried was gone forever. Yup, I was back, and loving every minute of it. My self-image was in harmony with reality once again.

And then, once again, it wasn't. I was chafing under the limits that I'd placed on my relationship with Christopher, slowly realizing that not only did I want to see him three, even four nights a week (horrors!), but that hashing over my day with him was becoming natural. I got that warm-all-over feeling whenever I thought about him, and sometimes the thought of going home to my empty apartment made me wistful instead of relieved and happy. I had those numbers sitting on my nightstand, numbers belonging to men whose pants I thought I was dying to get into, and I didn't even want to dial them. Once I allowed myself to see through all my fears—that the disruption of my cozy little single-life routine would mean the end of the world as I knew it, my career discipline and my intense female friendships—I realized what was happening. I had fallen madly in love, and it was (gasp!) a good thing. Six weeks later I asked Christopher to marry me; another six and we were living together. Five months after that, we were honeymooning.

The most common reactions to my engagement were, in order of frequency, "Why?" "You're kidding" and "Are you pregnant?" (The only person who uttered none of these was my mother, who was, most notably, absolutely speechless.) And why shouldn't my friends and family have been surprised? Hell, I was surprised. We certainly had no "reason" to get married (if "reasons" can still be said to exist in these days of extralegal long-term partnership), not even a conservative grandparent who would have been scandalized by cohabitation, or a need for health insurance. And pregnancy? Please. The notion that you have to be married to have kids is about as outdated as the manual typewriter. Besides—and all my friends should have known this about me—had I been pregnant my first stop would have been the nice Planned Parenthood doctor, not the justice of the peace. No one could understand our decision, but it made perfect emotional sense to me. I had fallen head over heels in love with a person who was, both in a day-to-day sense and in the grand scheme of things, perfect for me. We like to do all the same simple, sedate things (read, cook, eat, talk, flop around on the couch doing not much of anything); he respects my work and my drive concerning it without being ambitious himself. He is utterly Southern California calm to my wound-up New York neurosis. He has the most beautiful singing voice. He can make a turkey; I know all the sides.

Although marriage per se had never been on my agenda—I knew there was a good chance I would never marry or even pair off in a long-term way, and that had always been fine with me—now that I had had the staggeringly good luck to find someone whom I not only loved passionately but who I knew would be a good partner with me, I wanted not just to make it permanent but to make a big public statement about it. Thus my entrance into the ranks of the married.

Sometimes, and I hope it doesn't sound disloyal of me to say this, I miss those celibate single days. I gained a lot from them—not just time and energy but also a profound and undiluted sense of myself and my real desires (and I don't mean sexual ones). I took no shit. I did exactly what I wanted to all the time. I was selfish in the best sense of the word, making every last decision, from the monumental to the trivial—Should I take this job? What do I feel like snacking on?—based only on my own considered opinions, whims and cravings. Having no one to consult on these matters can bring a startling clarity that I think is impossible to underestimate. And it was in no small part this clarity that made me so sure marrying Christopher was the right decision. I knew very well how to be alone, and I liked it, thank you very much—ensuring that I was coupling up out of genuine, person-specific love, as opposed to an adult version of must-have-boyfriend syndrome.

Of course, now that I'm married, I'm stuck with a new set of contradictions to resolve. With all my carefully tended feminist ideals—including my commitment to bulldozing outdated ideas about what women want sexually and emotionally (especially when these are linked in marriage), and my frustration at the persistence of such myths—it's no surprise that my own role as a married woman presents a little cognitive dissonance. Now that our first anniversary has come and gone, "my husband" trips off my tongue as easily as "my Good Vibrations video rental account," but I still find myself identifying with single women more than married ones when the conversation turns to commitment, independence and the pleasures of being alone. "I'm not one of them, those smugly coupled women who think that true happiness comes only to those who pair up like Noah's animals," I want to protest. "I know your single life is just as fulfilling as my married one because I lived it. Just because true love clonked me on the head out of nowhere doesn't mean I don't relate to your tales of late-night shagging with the luscious bartender, or the exquisite luxury of an evening spent absolutely alone on the couch in sweatpants with some kind of quirky snack that everyone around you has always found repulsive."

Plus, there's the question of my credibility: How trustworthy can I be now in insisting that there are plenty of women out there who couldn't care less about using their genitalia as some primitive honey-trap to ensnare a mate, à la *The Rules?*

Couple all this with all those wifely stereotypes ("Not tonight, honey") that, although they have been in their death throes for years, still carry an alarming amount of subconscious cultural currency—and it's a lot of pressure. I'm having trouble applying some of what I learned when I was celibate—that the ebb and flow of desire is a natural phenomenon that doesn't necessarily have any implications at all for anyone's sociopolitics. The old impulse to make myself into the perfect embodiment of the strong, sexual überbabe still surfaces sometimes. Then I start to feel like Christopher and I need to have just as much sex as we did when we first started dating (and where can I find the time for that, now that I'm no longer on the hormone high that allowed me to function on four hours of sleep a night?).

And not only do we have to keep up our premarital pace, but I, like any self-respecting überbabe, have to match my husband's every seduction with one of my own (not for me to sit demurely on the couch and wait to be led off to the bedroom, of course). I have to learn all over again that sometimes life—a bad back, a busy schedule, incompatible bedtimes (my man's a night owl; my idea of sleeping in is getting up at 8:30)—gets in the way of sex, and that's not always an entirely bad thing. I have to learn to stop taking my libido's temperature every hour on the hour like an overanxious babysitter.

Even though I'm a far cry from blasé about my less-than-raging hormones—I admit to feeling relieved when our sex life steps up on vacation ("phew, it's not me, it's my schedule . . . "), and I'm disappointed in myself when I'd rather watch *The Practice* than practice a new oral sex technique—I'm slowly coming to know emotionally what I've always known rationally: that all this ebbing and flowing is perfectly natural. Christopher and I have, if we're lucky, a sex life that stretches ahead of us for half a century. Does it really matter how many times we have sex next week? Even more important, when I measure my sex life in encounters per week, I'm using someone else's yardstick. Counting is the way so-called analyses of men's and women's desires are set up (you know the ones purporting that men think about sex six times per hour and women only six times per day). I guess that's why I feel compelled to do it—if I can rack up a good enough count, then I'm somehow doing my part to knock down the sexual double-standards that wreak havoc in so many women's lives. I can't believe it's taken me this long to realize just how ridiculous that notion is. That's not the way it works at all. The true promise of sex-positive feminism is not to make way for the triumph of the überbabe—that would just create new and different hoops for women to jump through. Hoops that are more fun to master than those needed for the John Gray/Condé Nast Tour of Gendered Sexual Roles—but hoops nonetheless. No, the goal of sex-positive feminism is to enable all of us to express our sexuality to its fullest, live our sex lives as we want to, without guilt or stigma or external imperatives. Now that I've gone through all these stages and realized that I'm still myself, and still have my politics and my analytical capabilities, I've finally learned that lesson.

WHAT KEEPS ME HERE

 Carla Richmond

Someone once asked me: "What's it like to sleep with the same person for eight years? Is it like eating the same ham sandwich for lunch every day?"

At the time I couldn't think of an appropriately witty response. I was distracted by a rush of anxiety and doubt that burned in my chest and sought desperate exit through my palms. I felt challenged and vaguely offended by the question. I mistrusted the questioner's apparent awe and admiration, feeling only the sting of accusation. It was as if she were peeling the face off an inviting piece of fruit because she doubted the promise of its vibrantly colored skin. As if she hoped the blade of her knife would reveal worms and rot and make the fruit more interesting. Certainly by maintaining an outwardly stable and undramatic union my girlfriend and I were conforming to some dishonest heterosexist model. By sleeping with the same person again and again and again we were missing the point of being lesbians. Having bad sex (or no sex) seemed as serious and shameful an offense as sleeping with men. I myself lived in fear of lesbian bed death and felt certain my friend was posing this question because she had somehow read these fears.

I replied with a bland, "No," wishing for a humorous response to lighten the moment. I don't remember what we talked about afterwards. We must have moved on to something else.

Dearest Sarika, you are the shadowy presence, the heroic figure that walked out of my sixteen-year-old sci-fi fantasies where lovers share thoughts, crawl beneath each other's skin and wind their souls into one another. I wanted to write this honestly, to fashion an essay like a love letter without clichés, that could contain our love for one another like a velvet-lined box that holds lost teeth, broken jewelry and cherished awards. I wanted to create a receptacle for all our imperfections and eight years of lessons learned from one another: devotion and joy, intended cruelties, unintended slights and loving sacrifices.

Literature is filled with stories of people falling in love and losing love. Apparently, staying in love does not lend itself to art or journal writing. It does not lend itself to poetry. The art of daily living is chronicled on the backs of used envelopes and on Post-its curling off mirrors. It turns up in the pocket of the pants fresh from the laundry, transformed into a weightless ball of pulp. It accumulates like dust or habit. Becomes as worn as comfort. Time in a relationship stretches like bodies in frumpy clothes laid out on a sofa. My head in your lap listening to the echo of your voice through your chest as you recount your day, distracted by your digestive movements, the thumps of your heart, the whistle of air through your lungs. It is measured in drool on pillows, bills, birthdays and armpit smells. It is a series of days fitted into one another like bodies comfortably spooning on a single bed that have learned to accommodate each other even in sleep.

Our relationship is a slow diffusion, the bleeding of one liquid into another. So much so that when I look around the apartment and perversely imagine our breakup, I get exhausted trying to distinguish "mine" from "yours." (I decided that we would be better off having a stoop sale and splitting the profits.) If I had thought to save our phone messages, I could string them together into an epic poem and at that plodding pace tell our story sweetly, not through passionate eruptions but through a series of: "Meet me here," "I'll be home then," "This or that needs doing," "I miss you," "I miss you," "I miss you."

3/21/92—The First Night: Everything amazes me: the fit of our bodies on the dormitory-issue cot, the fit of my mouth on your cunt, the feel of your tongue on my breast. I am amazed by the odors that rise between us. We have created an incredible smell.

Our heavy, sweaty limbs are thrown over each other. We stare at the moon that is just visible through the jailhouse-sized window in your bedroom and realize with a start that it is the first day of spring.

Later, I tell my friend, "We can't stop touching each other. Even when we're sleeping she gives me little kisses on my back. It's the most amazing thing."

12/28/92: You are beside me, in our bed above The Bread Shop. Your breast rests on my arm, brushing the hairs there with each breath. My index finger is hooked into the circle of your navel ring. With my chest pressed into your back, I focus on matching the deep rhythms of your dream sleep, shifting to complement the restless movements of your body. You twitch violently like an unfortunate rag doll caught in a dog's mouth. This pattern of tension and release—your only manner of letting go of the day—settles you heavily into the mattress and brings you eventually to rest. I grip you tightly with each muscle spasm and imagine that the circle of my arms soothes you, fends off bad dreams and smooths your passage into sleep.

10/8/98: My tongue drags clumsily across your body, scrawling question marks across your abdomen, around your breasts. Is this a good night? The right time? Do you want me to touch you at all? I'm terrified that, after years of learning your body, I have forgotten how to touch you. As if knowing your body so well has dulled my senses. Over the last few months, sex has become something that we have in spite of each other, battling towards orgasm, too often falling short of it. We exhaust ourselves striving to make our bodies meet when our eyes have avoided each other for weeks. At times likes these, sex is a surrogate, a make-shift bridge across the distances we cannot name or explain. It is a desperate attempt to manufacture closeness when we have not yet understood what made this distance necessary.

We kneel before each other and put all our prayers into sex. I pretend not to see the exhaustion in your face, the tension humming in the air just off your skin. I pretend that at this moment we are not struggling to define ourselves apart from one another, that your decisions about your future do not terrify me. Our tongues spar perfunctorily, our lips rigid and unresisting. I suckle your neck fiercely as if I could rouse passion to its surface by sheer force. All I arouse are angry red blotches. I pause awkwardly between caresses, anxious and confused. Your breasts seem unrelated, your limbs an impossible distance. In a panic, I catalogue erogenous zones, struggle to remember how I have pleased you in the past. I work your breasts and clit with blind persistance—the fatigue in my neck and my jaw adding to my frustration—until arousal becomes irritation and you shrug me off.

We slump down, worn with the effort, wanting nothing but rest and the comfort of arms. Our bodies meet at last, resigning themselves to sleep. We mumble "I love you" to reassure one another. I plant kisses on your back, not wanting to see the defeat and fear reflected in your face. As your body sinks into sleep, I gingerly trace its lines but your skin feels like waxed fruit. My fingers slip, I cannot hold you in my grasp. My arms are insufficient, too small to contain us both with all this space in between.

4/21/99: I am alone. The part of you that I have grown accustomed to accessing seems faded and indistinct. The boundaries between us are clearly marked: as lines in the dirt, as trenches splitting the earth, as cobbled walls with holes to peer through. In our first years together, the feeling of being absorbed by you was erotic, welcome, exhilarating. I'm not sure when that changed, when the soft wool blanket that had warmed and comforted me was suddenly pulled over my head, making me sweat and gasp for air. At what point having people confuse our names or our voices on the phone stopped being cute. Once it happened, I found myself wanting to go back, to find the line between your life and mine, before they merged, to drag my friends across to my side and draw up visitation rights. Maybe the person who made those friends doesn't exist anymore, has been so fundamentally changed by you she is gone forever. Maybe it's like trying to turn a frog back into a tadpole, to breathe underwater when you've lost your gills to evolution.

This pulling back and pulling in—is this the rhythm of relationship?

I used to take walks in the city on Fridays. Walking alone encountering people as myself. Relishing that you existed to no one I spoke to, or more correctly, that you were not necessary in order for me to exist. I read somewhere an aphorism: You can only truly love someone you don't need. Or something like that. It was something about the separation between loving someone and needing someone. I used to call your magnetic pull, that desperate need to reconnect with you—love. I had begun to think that my relationship with you was what I gave to the world. No wonder I was so pissed at you, felt your decisions spinning me out of control. I was terrified that I could not survive apart from you. In my habit of indulging in overdramatic fantasies, I used to imagine taking off to a foreign place somewhere alone, forging a life of Friday walks where everyone would see me—as if you had never existed.

7/5/99: You have been in South Dakota a month now, and I've learned something incredible—I can live without you. For weeks now I have been making plans with friends, hanging out, having long telephone conversations, taking walks alone. I found the space I needed without ever leaving. Without noticing when I took off or where I landed. This process of breaking off has brought my self into high relief, like an image strongly backlit by a penetrating spotlight. Now I feel whole, surer of myself than I have in a very long time. Now I can miss you.

Can you feel me touching you?

What do you prefer? Morning sex. Evening sex. Make-up sex. Is this what you want? Do you want it muffled? Raucous? Do you want me to beg? Tied to the bed? Kneeling in the shower drawing you into the bowl of my mouth? Ass up? Flat on your back? Pressing you from behind? Do you want to be warned? Do you want to have any idea? In earshot of my parents or yours? Is this a good time? Not yet? Now? There? There. Lights on. Lights off. Candles. Incense. Chocolate body paint. Blackberry-flavored self-heating body oil. In line for the bathroom. Pressed against the stones of a dried river bed. Does this hurt? Do you want it to hurt? Can you feel me inside you? My hand. Deeper? More? Too much? Not like that?

Can you feel me fucking you?

Can I use my teeth?

Do you want me to stop?

I arise wet from the shower and pad to our bedroom, feeling warm and loose in my skin. I smooth lotion into my breasts, over my abdomen and ass, intent for the moment on my nightly ritual. Your knees are hunched around the book you are reading, the covers bunched around your ankles. Your hair across the pillows is already drying in tight curls. I am distracted by the slackness of your thighs parted in careless invitation, remembering how your labia cling slightly to my lips, the feel of the differently textured whorls gathered on my tongue.

How will I know when you are open to me?

By the angle of your thighs? The answering clench in mine? The varying texture of your breath?

I pounce on the bed and burrow my face in your lap, make strange noises, sniff elaborately. I kiss you full on both wings and look up. You are laughing at me over your book, not tightening your thighs or pulling away. My tongue parts you with a single broad stroke, following the wave of your body upwards. Your hands that held the book now stroke your breasts, setting a fevered rhythm for me to follow that beats in the walls of your cunt, that beats against the palm of my hand, under my tongue.

Your skin under my hand is damp, slack as your limbs in sleep. It is smoother than I remember, marked in places with acne scars, and inviting blackheads. My strokes across your skin are measured to lull you, in time with your deepening sighs. I follow the channel of your spinal column, trace the generous curve of your hips, slide over the cheek of your ass, firmly hefting its weight in my palm. I trace the bold tattoo at the base of your spine, an image repeated on my body. I follow the curve of your side, sledding into the parabola of your hips, slipping forward into the basket of your pelvis, testing first the bone, then the still damp flesh, raising soft sounds from you.

I love this body. I love this skin. Every part of it.

Our relationship is a work in progress. Sometimes we glimpse the finished work we are creating, in those moments when we find each other whole. We stand before each other clearly illuminated and distinct, absorbed in our own light that seals us together away from distractions outside ourselves. It is the space where we do not assume and where we remember to ask, where what we know and what we just don't understand about each other are vast and arouse our curiousity and wonder.

Most days sex with my partner of eight years is less than great art, better than a ham sandwich, and wholly unpredictable. At times it's non-existent. Other days it's off the scale. There is a freedom, an incredible joy and an urgency in realizing that I don't need her, that I can talk and breathe and flourish without her—but that I'd rather not.

SILENCE AND THE WORD

(◉) Mary Anne Mohanraj

This is a true story.

In the dark, there's a woman in bed. Her lover's hand is between her thighs, and he is rubbing what he thinks is her clit, but in fact he's almost an inch off, and she doesn't know what to do. She wants to tell him, somehow, but it's not an easy thing to communicate. She tries raising her hips a little, hoping that he will figure it out and slide his finger down that crucial inch, but instead he just rubs harder, undoubtedly thinking he is exciting her. She makes little sounds of frustration, but he doesn't understand what they mean. She knows that she should just say something—even if it's only "lower," but the word has gotten caught in her throat; it's buried down somewhere deep. She can only say it in her head, over and over like a mantra: "lower lower lower lower . . . " She doesn't know why she's doing it. It's not as if he can hear her thoughts, but she wishes he could, because, while it might cause problems, it would be easier than this. Finally, he gives up on getting her off this way and slides his finger inside her instead, gliding over her clit, accidentally, in the process. She gasps, but he thinks it's because of the finger inside her, and she doesn't know how to tell him what he's missing.

That's me.

At the San Francisco Barnes & Noble store, a woman is reading an erotic short story called "A Jewel of a Woman." She hasn't read this story out loud before, and it's a little more explicit than she remembered. "I once tried that trick you read about, where you stuff a bunch of pearls deep into your pussy and then pull the strand out slowly, one by one. It felt so good, so fucking good as those pearls came out, grinding against my clit one by one . . . " She thinks about dropping her voice a little when she says "pussy" or "fucking" or "clit," especially since the children's section is just a few steps away. But the managers must have known what they were letting themselves in for when they scheduled an erotica reading, right? And they gave her a mike anyway. So what the hell! Instead of getting quieter, she gets louder, and sexier; she licks her lips and pauses before the forbidden words; she draws them out—she does her damnedest to seduce the people sitting in the metal folding chairs, seduce them with her voice and swaying body, and by the end of the story people are halted in the aisles across the store, listening, people who hustle away, embarrassed, when she stops. She doesn't care because she knows that, for a few minutes, she had them. They were hers.

That's me too.

Forgive the third person—it's easier than saying "I." If I had to say "I couldn't say that" or "I did this," then I'm not sure I'd be able to write this at all. But maybe I could—that's what's so odd. It's a lot easier to write this stuff down than to say it out loud. I've been writing erotica for seven years now, and it still surprises me how easy it is to write, "She wanted to fuck him silly, until his eyes were bugging out . . . " or even "I took his thick cock in my mouth, licking it up and down . . . "

Maybe it's because erotica is fiction. That would be one explanation—that even though there's a little of myself in all my characters (even the gay men), it's never quite me. My characters can often say and do things that would terrify me in real life; I can use them to explore all sorts of possibilities. They can have sex with strangers, or with their best friends. They can be blindfolded and beaten. They can do desperate, crazy things for love, or for a really good fuck. They're just characters.

Even when I'm reading my stories out loud, my audience doesn't know which ones, which parts are really me. Even if I tell them, "This one is autobiographical," they can't really *know* where autobiography ends and fiction begins.

It's different at night, in the dark, in bed.

He is kissing her, her cheeks, her neck, her throat. It feels good, but something is bothering her, something is making her more quiet than usual, not as responsive. He notices. He stops and asks, "What's wrong?" She shakes her head. She wants to answer, to ask for something, a small thing, but she can't. She is afraid of the words, and doesn't know why. She is afraid of his answer to her simple request. She is a little reluctant to say anything at first. Then her silence makes this seem more important than it should be, and it becomes even more difficult to talk, to say the words. She feels paralyzed. He has dealt with this before. Silence, and the stillness of her body that signals distress. They have sometimes played twenty questions—him asking the questions, trying to guess what is bothering her. She can manage to nod or shake her head, but, too often, he can't even come close to asking the right questions. Tonight, though, he has a new idea. He gets up, walks naked to the living room, gets a pencil and paper and brings them back. Turns on the nightstand light, hands her the paper and pencil, turns away while she scribbles a few sentences on the paper. She feels ridiculous, and almost doesn't have the nerve to give him the paper, but she does. She buries her face in his chest while he reads her request. He doesn't laugh. He reaches out, shuts off the light, turns back and tilts up her head and starts to kiss her again. This time, on her lips. He kisses her for a long time. He doesn't say anything, and she is grateful.

See—it's not just that fiction is easier to write than nonfiction. Writing it down is easier than speaking it. The writing lets me distance myself. The hand moving across the page is further away from the heart of me than the air in my throat, struggling to form words. If you read this, and then we meet some day, you will know these things about me, these things that I have written, that I have told you. Probably I'll be embarrassed, but it will be an embarrassment I can live with. It will be so much easier than having said the words out loud.

She feels so silly having him get a pencil and paper that she tries to teach him the sign alphabet. It is all she knows of sign language—the shapes of letters, A, B, C—but it is enough to make small sentences, with patience. In bed, in the moonlight, she can spell out: W I L L Y O U G O D O W N O N M E? She usually doesn't even have to spell out the whole thing; he figures it out around the D and takes her hand in his to still it and then smiles and slides his mouth down her body. What is funniest is that sometimes he forgets what letter a shape means, especially when she hasn't done this for him in a while. Then she ends up sounding out half the letters as she says them, so that she feels like a grownup talking over the head of a little kid, spelling out the letters of words she doesn't want her to hear. It's silly, it's ridiculous—but it's working. It's better than pencil and paper. It's much better than nothing.

My lovers are always startled when they realize how much trouble I have talking in bed. They're mostly quiet themselves—I like the quiet types, and so lovemaking tends not to be too talkative. For most things, body language and muffled sounds do well enough. Sometimes we go weeks before they figure it out. When they do, they almost always say the same thing—"But you *write* this stuff!"

"It's not the same," I explain. After a while, they believe me, especially after they see me trying, and failing, to talk. Sometimes they accept it as yet another of my strange quirks. One or two have really wanted to know why. I've gotten frustrated enough with the whole business that I've tried to figure it out too.

The nearest I can come to figuring it out is that it has to do with being naked. Not just physically naked, though that's part of it (I have no problems talking about sex while sitting on the couch, fully clothed, using sufficiently dry and clinical terms).

When I talk about sex in bed with a lover, I am physically and emotionally naked, open and vulnerable to someone whom I am inviting past the barriers, the boundaries, someone who has seen and touched all my private spaces. It's intense, and scary. To put my real desires, my most intimate thoughts, into words, and to say them out loud in a private space where there is no possibility that I can pretend that I was just joking, reciting, performing—that's just plain terrifying. It's the most naked act I know.

It's a lot easier to run away and hide.

She has been with him for years. She knows how to translate his code words; speech doesn't always come easily to him either. So when he finishes, and asks her, "Are you okay?" she knows that he is really asking if she is satisfied, if that was enough, or if she'd like him to do something else. He is even trying to make it easy for her—all she has to say is, "No," and he will try to satisfy her. Sometimes when she needs to, she manages to say it, but this time, the thought of the conversation they might get into (as he tries to find out exactly what she wants) exhausts her. So she says "I'm fine," and pretends to herself that she's answering another question entirely, because while she's not really satisfied, not sated, she's not really thrumming with tension either—she's okay, she's fine. It's true enough, isn't it?

You see, I was raised to be polite. I'm not someone who swears easily—it takes a real crisis to get "fuck!" or even "dammit!" out of my mouth. When upset, I am more likely to cry or be silent than shout. Being polite means not saying things, a lot of the time. Not saying things that might upset someone else, things that might make someone uncomfortable. I can hide my powerful naked emotions behind a sheltering, softening cloak of politeness; and that's how I was raised—that's how most of us are raised. That's how you get along with people.

If I ask a lover for something, and he doesn't really want to give it to me, we are both in an awkward position. Does he refuse, and deal with my disappointment? Does he agree, and do something he doesn't really want to do? If he thinks my request is ridiculous, or disgusting, won't we both just be embarrassed? It's easier not to ask.

Yet I'm not sure that silence is ever a real solution. It's just easier than speaking. I don't want to just be "polite" with my lover.

She has bought a copy of Exhibitionism for the Shy, *though she has always distrusted self-help books. She is on the first exercise, where you stand alone in a room and say the forbidden words out loud. Just the words at first, disassociated.*

Fuck. Cock. Pussy. Cunt.

Once she has practiced that for a while (it's not so hard), she moves to the next step—owning the words.

My pussy. My cunt.

I like fucking.

This part is difficult. She almost gives up right here. But she is tired of not being able to say what she wants to say. She is tired of resorting to pieces of paper and letters hand-spelled out in dim light. It would be so much better to just be able to say it. She feels silly, stupid, ridiculous all over again, saying these words to an empty room—but she says them. It does get easier with practice.

I want you to lick me.

I want you to fuck my pussy, my cunt.

So why are *those* words so particularly difficult? There are lots of things I could ask for, lots of things that a lover might say no to, that might be upsetting or disappointing—yet they're rarely as difficult to say as "Will you kiss my breasts?" (Try it. Go alone into the bathroom, close the door and try saying the words out loud. I hope you have an easier time of it than I do.)

Is it because we're not supposed to like sex? Is that a specter of my mother, hovering in the background, listening as I say those scary words? Am I hearing the echoes of all those years of "don't look, don't touch, don't do . . . " Whether said or unsaid, the message was clear: just don't. So that if I do, I do it quietly in secret, in the dark, under the covers, soundlessly. Or, if overcome by passion, I might scream, and there's an excuse, isn't there? "I couldn't help myself . . . " So whimpering and moaning might be okay; that's just my body taking over.

But when I put the words to it, when I say, "I want you to fuck me, please . . . " then I can't pretend that I just happened to fall into this bed, oops! or that I was simply overwhelmed by my body's desires, 'cause there's my mind forming those words, sending the message to my mouth to open up and say them out loud.

I have to admit to my lover and even worse, to myself, that I consciously choose to be here, having sex, and that goes against everything I was ever taught.

I know not all of you have my background, and I do wonder how much of my difficulty comes from the way I was raised (of conservative family, in a culture where sex came always after marriage and a woman's needs were often subjugated to a man's). It would be easy to put it all down to that: to being female and Asian and unmarried. That's undoubtedly a lot of it, for me—but it can't be all of it. More than a few of my lovers have had similar difficulties, and while they are also unmarried, they are neither female nor Asian. It seems to me that most cultures teach us to deny our sexuality, deny the strength of our desires.

Strong desires aren't polite, aren't civilized—it's no wonder society wants to control, soften, silence them. But if everyone tries to silence their own desires—then no one gets what they want. We all just end up being polite, and deeply frustrated, together.

She has been with one lover for eight years now—long enough to trust him, a little. She has written him notes, said a few words in the darkest part of night, written messages with her finger on the skin of his back. He doesn't always understand, but he has never laughed at her.

A few months ago she called him up and left a message on the machine.

"I wish you were here.

If you were here I would like to

go down on you."

There are long pauses between the phrases. When he listens to the message, he can tell that she is having trouble breathing, that her throat is tight and that she stopped partway through to bite her lip, to swallow.

"I would like

you

to go down on me."

She wanted to be more explicit, more detailed. She wanted to tell him how she loves the taste of him, how she longs to bury her face between his thighs, and then have him do the same to her, have him lick and suck and dig his fingers into her ass and lift her off the bed, but she couldn't quite manage the words. Still, it's more than she would have said to his face. She asks him later if he liked the message.

He says he did.

She is thinking of leaving another message sometime soon.

I could stop here, say nothing more than I already have, not push any further. The sex is pretty good at this point, after all. I've had a lot of practice, and I don't really need the words.

But the desire is still there. The desire to speak, to be naked, to be known. To be honest about desire, to be able to trust someone that much, with something that scary.

It's the same desire that drives me to write erotic stories, and to keep an online journal and to write this essay to you. I am trapped in my separate, often confused, head. And one of my deepest desires is to first know myself, and then be known for who I am, to be loved *as* I am. An entire being, sexuality included—however naked and embarrassing and ridiculous that may be.

Writing the stories, writing to you, scribbling notes or signing letters: each attempt is scary. Though exciting as well—you should understand that part. Writing down the words makes my throat tight; I was shaking as I typed some of the sections above. My breath came fast, and my fingers are still cold. I write best when I'm scared and sweating—and the satisfaction when I finish is sometimes just as good as being fucked really well. Sometimes better. And that satisfaction comes whether or not I ever show the piece to anyone else; I am admitting something to myself in the writing of it. But sharing it takes the writing a step further.

When I first started writing erotica, when I put those words on the screen and then sent them out over the Net, to hundreds or thousands of readers, it was a huge relief, an opening that let me start exploring desires that I had no other access to, desires that had been deeply buried and unspoken. I could say so much more with my fingers than I could with my throat; it gave me a freedom that I had never known—a freedom that at the same time only went as far as I could handle, that I could take in small steps and stages, so it wasn't quite so frightening.

When I write about sex, I can control how much I expose myself, my desires (just as I could in all of those intermediate stages above; I could always erase that machine message). I can hide, a little, behind the name of "fiction," or limit how much truth I spill in nonfiction. (That's not really me who wants to be tied down to a bed and spanked—that's just an example, just a character. Right?)

I can hide behind the relative anonymity of the pages—and that protection lets me push myself further. My characters can be as exhibitionistic as they desire . . . and when they are, a part of my own truth steps out into the light. Every time I manage to communicate my desires to a lover, a reader, a friend—it gets harder to hide. I've spoken a scary truth, and it's out there now, inescapable.

And when that trust is rewarded—every time a lover, reader, friend responds by accepting who I am (and sometimes sharing some of their own scary desires)—it's the most intoxicating feeling I know. Like riding a rollercoaster up and up, nerves taut, the heartstopping pause at the top, and then screaming all the way down. Every time it works (doesn't fling me off, doesn't crash and burn) makes me want to try again—and push a little harder, go a little faster and farther this time.

So that maybe, eventually, I can be completely naked and unafraid.

Every once in a while, if I speak very quickly and don't think about it at all, I can just say what I want. That sounds so simple, doesn't it? It should be easy.

I want to tell you what I want.

(Un)Safe Sex

● J. Keiko Lane

D o you want me to fly up there to be with you during the trial?"
She was waiting for my response. I wanted to tell her yes,
come be with me, hold me through this. *Hold me through this.*
I looked out the window of my Victorian duplex at the flame
and ochre leaves that looked like wide, open hands.

"No, I'll be fine," I said to her silence, "I'll call you after
it's over." I hung up the phone before she could argue with
me, before I could change my mind. This was not the first
time we had argued about whether I would let her fly from Los
Angeles to Portland to support me through this rape trial. This
was not the first time we had argued about whether I would let
her hold me.

Four months earlier I had walked down a dark, uneven country road into deepening forest with a woman I'd just met. Both
of us writers, we walked down that road for several nights,
telling stories, holding hands. She had been abused as a child
and was still remembering in pieces. I told her I had been

raped a year and a half earlier, in my college dorm room, by a man I knew. Both of us caught between memory and desire, a photo and its negative—how our bodies reach for our lovers with quickened breath, with all the desire to know and a deep fear of being known. How when we reached for our lovers we never knew if we were reaching for the woman in front of us, or the piece of our own story we saw reflected in her body. We talked about the fear of remembering, how she was trying to remember, how I was trying to forget.

One night we lay down in the middle of that country road, looking up into the dizzying darkness of those woods, the air pulsing with bats and owls, with stories we could not complete.

Late that night I watched her undress, then climb softly into the single bed. I turned the light out before peeling off my own clothes. "Shy girl," she whispered as I slid into bed beside her. "Are you quiet?" she asked, nodding toward the thin wall separating my room from our sleeping friend. "I'm quiet." We kissed until our shyness fell away. I stopped her when she reached between my legs. "I don't have gloves," I told her. And we didn't. I did not tell her that in the light of the moon through the window I was watching her hands, her mouth on my breasts, and feeling nothing of my own body except my hands as they touched her. I closed my eyes, saw him over me again, always him, my arms pinned, flesh tearing, room red and spinning, the gasp from my unstartled throat the only sound as I watched from somewhere outside my body, not wanting to wake my friend just behind the thin wall. So silent you wouldn't know I was there. She slipped her hands between her own legs, whispering "Is this okay?" and I smiled. She bit down on my fingers, her legs wrapped around mine, rocking on her hands between her thighs. I lay there feeling all that heat surrounding my body, wishing it would thaw the chill that rattled my shaking breath, watching her body rock and spasm. Then she kissed me again and curled tighter around me. I held on as though my life depended on that heat.

A few weeks later I sat with a friend in the waiting room at the Gay and Lesbian Community Services Center in West Hollywood, flipping through old issues of the *Advocate, OUT/LOOK* and a local queer newsprint with my face on the cover, posed with friends from Queer Nation and ACT UP, smiling and jubilant after an action for healthcare for women living with HIV. One of the men in the photo had died within weeks of that action. When the test counselor called me in, I sat at the scarred desk facing a tired looking man not much older than my own twenty years. I stopped him quickly when he started talking about care services and asked me if I had a support network I could turn to while waiting for results. When I told him most of my friends were positive, he seemed to think that meant implicit support, that they knew I was there. Then he asked why I had decided to get tested, if I had any reason to believe I might be positive. "I haven't always been as careful as I should have been. And I know woman-to-woman transmission occurs."

Later, driving home, my friend asked if I was planning on telling any of the women in ACT UP the real reason that I was waiting for results. "No," I told her, "they expect me to be stronger than that."

"You still haven't told them you were raped?"

"No."

"Why? They love you, they'd be there for you."

I didn't know how to tell her about the involuntary flinch that happens when a woman hears another woman's story of rape, how the body either remembers its own story, or imagines it to be possible. How it is easier to sleep with women who don't know and pretend desire is untouched by fear. How there was already so much grief in the community that I couldn't bear adding another layer of story. "Whatever happens," I told her, "I would rather they believe it came from pleasure, not pain."

A few days after getting tested, an old friend asked me out. We had spent many nights of Queer Nation meetings and defense actions together, days of worry when friends were in the hospital. Parties and relief when they came home. Memorials and vigils when they didn't. Our first date was a going-away party for another Queer Nation compañera. She picked me up at my parents' house where I was spending the summer, charmed both of my parents and led me off to the party. Standing out on the balcony high above the train tracks and the pink glow of dusty hills in the late night summer sunset, she smiled as she bent down to kiss me, my back against the railing, her hands laced in mine. "Flowers," she said to me, "you kiss like flowers." We both laughed at the silliness of it, the joyous silliness of that night. Most of our friends were still alive that summer, and dropped in on the party. We danced to disco and salsa, her thigh between my legs, my arms around her neck. Late that night, cooling off on the balcony, she asked me to go home with her. I wanted to. I really did. She was fierce and playful and sexy. And I was not sure that I could be.

Sitting in her car outside my parents' house, I told her I was waiting for test results. She told me that the past few years while I had been in Portland she had been doing safe-sex education at women's bars, passing out condoms and gloves and dental dams. "We can be safe," she whispered as her teeth grazed my ear. When I shook my head no, she asked if impending test results were the real reason I was sending her home alone. "No, I'll tell you another time," I said, between kisses, guaranteeing myself another day with her. Neither of us was likely to let the challenge slide. We had known each other too long for that. Hers was not a question and mine not a promise of the truth, only a promise of whatever story I was telling myself at the time. I had no idea what version I would tell her.

Over the next few weeks, I told her the whole truth, or at least the truth as I understood it that summer. Maybe it was because of the way the short dark hair at her neck bristled when a man I didn't recognize approached me on the street and reminded me that he was an old family friend. As I remembered him and chatted, she stood with her palm wide and flat against the small of my back, her other hand on her hip, cautious and protective. Maybe it was the day after I got my negative results back and didn't feel any more at ease, when I finally told her about the man on campus, and she told me about the one who had haunted her. I must have looked stunned. She smiled at me. "Girl," she said, "none of us are as strong as you think you should be."

And that evening she kissed me long and deep and no longer gentle, murmuring in my ear that she knew exactly what I needed, exactly how to give me my body back. I don't know if she saw the tears in my eyes, saw me flinch at her tenderness, at my grief mirrored in her eyes, inseparable from the desire. "Then what is there left, legally? Any campus recourse? You know we'll be there. We've fought for harder, and you are worth everything else we have ever done. You believe that, girl. You believe me."

None of us are as strong as you think you should be . . . You believe that, girl . . . All these years later, that's what I remember most. But how long it takes those words to echo until we reach out and grab at them with all we're worth, because our lives do depend on them. Whether anyone is watching or not. The disappearing act is not just the response of our bodies in fear, that attempt at molting flesh into air, into memory. It is the trained expectation that there are only two choices, invincible or destroyed. It is the shame that tells us to press our hands against our own mouths, biting down on our own lives to keep from making any sound, to keep from telling any story.

One hot night a friend of ours threw a big party. It was one of those still August nights in Los Angeles where at 10:00 p.m. it was still ninety degrees outside and ninety-five inside, even with all the fans blowing. We packed into that apartment, dancing and drinking tequila. A friend who we had thought would be dead by then toasted to his new boyfriend. I wrapped my arms around her neck, dancing, her hands on my ass, her teeth against my bare shoulder. Maybe, I thought, I would go home with her. I pulled her closer to me, liking the sticky heat between our bodies. She bit down harder. *Yes, leave a mark. I want you to leave a mark. I want to wake up with this desire as evident on my body as your hands are now.*

I went outside to talk with a friend. A few hours later the rest of the party came out onto the lawn, turning on sprinklers and hoses, trying to cool down. She came over to me, leaned in and kissed me, and I turned away, dizzy, smelling the tequila. Remembering that the man had smelled like smoke and alcohol. I said goodnight. I drove myself home. Shaking.

The last night we were alone together was a few nights after that party. She went out to a local queer club where she met up with the rest of our outlaw friends. I stayed at my parents' house, sitting on the side deck watching the stars push their way through the smoggy air, listening to the salsa music that floated up the hill late at night. We had a system. She would drive by after leaving the club. If I was still awake and wanted company, the light on the deck would be on. It was visible from the street. I always left it on. That night there was a meteor shower that was rumored to be spectacular seen from the desert a few hours away. She got to the house at midnight and sat down on the bench next to me, quiet for a moment, breathing in the scent of rosemary, lavender and gardenias that grew in big pots along the edge of the deck, looking out at the forest of eucalyptus and tangled bougainvillea vines that sheltered the house. She filled me in on the gossip of our friends she had seen at the club that night. We laughed and she leaned over to kiss me. I shifted, straddled her lap, her tongue rimming the ticklish roof of my mouth, then coming up for air, her fingers pinching my nipples, my hands kneading her hips, our bodies rocking in time with the salsa floating up from the bottom of the hill, her hand reaching down my jeans, my mouth against the taut muscles of her neck, teeth grazing her skin, biting down to keep from making any sound. "There's no one here but us. Let me hear you," she whispered into my ear, "let me hear you." I sat up, looked into her eyes, quiet.

"I'm going to drive out to the desert, watch the meteor showers. Come with me?" she implored, her hands running through my hair. She was silent, looking into my eyes, her smile sweet, gentle. Then, quieter, she said, "You're not coming with me, are you?"

Yes, I wanted to tell her. Yes. I'll go anywhere with you. Yes. I leaned my face into her neck again, breathing in the smell of the club, tasting it with the tip of my tongue, breathing in all that salt slick uncertainty of our lives.

"No. I can't," I whispered into her neck. I couldn't look her in the eye.

Back in Portland, I told myself that I said no to her to prove to myself that I could. I could say no. My choice would be respected. Years later, I still regret that no. Not because I thought she could have been the love of my life, but because I did trust her, her touch, her history and our friendship, trusted her to give my body back to me. I just wasn't ready to want that body back. But learning to say no as a knee-jerk response isn't worth anything if we can't also learn to say yes. To say yes to each other in the dark or in the light of day, when we are all reaching hands and mouths, searching out screams and tears and stories. *Yes.*

Right after I got back to Portland for the fall semester, a student I had met a few times the year before started flirting with me. She was young and butch, all brooding eyes and narrow smile. Heavily ringed wide hands, tight jeans covering muscular thighs and an ever present leather jacket even though it was still the tail end of a hot, sticky summer. I finally took her to my bed, a few short weeks after she began following me around campus, a few short weeks into the planning of the rape trial. We went to a movie, then drank red wine with my housemate on the porch of our old Victorian duplex. I was not what she had counted on. I pulled hard on her nipple rings. I snapped the gloves over my knuckles loudly, kept pulling her hands away from my still clothed body with my left hand, my right hand working deep inside of her, my knees spreading her legs wider, until she stopped trying to touch me and grabbed at my arms, trying to pull me deeper into her. I worked at her until she stopped saying my name, until she made noises I know made my housemate blush in the next room. I bent my head down, teeth scraping her thin skin. I left marks.

  She never got any closer to me, though we had sex several times before the trial. Maybe I took advantage of her inexperience, knowing she looked and talked a wilder life than she had lived. I knew she would not have the language to cajole me into telling, into the deep sorrow over our broken and recovering lives that I wanted to cry out into the arms of some woman I had yet to name. Into some woman I had yet to become. I cannot say that I took her to my bed wanting anything more from her than to watch, to remember what was still possible, even if I would not be the one to cry out my desire into the rooms of that old house. She never knew my story. I never knew hers. Maybe I was exactly what she was counting on.

  Two weeks before the rape trial, that young butch girl and I were in L.A. I was visiting my parents and checking in with my ACT UP and Queer Nation family. She had flown down with me and was supposed to be visiting a friend. But she had spent most of the week at my parents' house with me, meeting my women, my beloved women, a few of whom I had finally told about the impending trial. A few of whom had not raged loudly but had looked me dead in the eye and said, "Tell me his full name." One day, having coffee at a little women's coffee house with her and the woman I had dated that summer, I realized that I had gone back to Portland and picked a young version of the woman who had tempted my heart and body until I was too afraid to move. I had found her younger self, the one who didn't yet know what to do with a story like me. The one who had no idea how to see me, what to look for. Later that afternoon, back at my parents' house, the younger woman inside making a phone call, I walked my friend out to her car. "Is she really going to be there for you during the trial?"

"No."

"Will you let me? I can fly up, be there when you need me."

I looked into her dark eyes, a worried smile crinkling their edges, her hands firm against my back. I pushed her back up against her car, leaned the full length of my body against her, answering her concern with my tongue, sure and confident in her mouth, my hands reaching up for hers, pulling them away from my body, placing them, gently, back on her car. I leaned away from her and we both smiled, hearing a stirring at the doorway of the house.

"Was that for her benefit or for mine?" she whispered into my ear.

"Mine," I whispered back at her, grinning. "This time, it's all for me."

I tested negative that summer. And every time I have tested since. The man who broke into my dorm room and raped me, kneeled over me, pinning me down with his knees, had rolled on a condom, drunkenly slurring, "We have to be safe, now. We have to." I had smelled the latex of the condom and remembered weeks earlier in Los Angeles, my gloved hands helping a friend dress an open sore, my friend smiling with me. I felt my body tear and the warmth of blood between my legs and closed my eyes, trying to hear back to my other life, the life where that friend laughed as he said, "Don't pity me. I don't regret a moment of my life. Remember that. Don't regret a moment you choose. Announce your choices."

My last lover and I were not safe together. It took me years really to feel the body and spirit of a woman pressed up against me, to feel her desire and my power to satisfy, to search out her cries until she cannot be quiet. I cannot put another barrier between us. It has taken me years longer to begin to want her to feel my desire for her, to feel my own body open to her mouth and her hands on me, to learn not to be afraid, not to be quiet.

It has been years since I lost that rape trial and I am only now starting to see the trial itself, the telling, the human breath of it, as a sort of beginning. Not a victory, but a hint of possibility. Years later I still see the man who raped me around town. Not the ghost of him when I visit our old campus for poetry readings and plays, but his actual, human face and body and hands, walking down the street, at the grocery store, at a movie theater. One night, driving home on an empty street in the dark Portland rain, I glanced in my rearview mirror to see that he was the cyclist riding next to me. He caught up to my car at a stop sign but never looked into the windows of my car, never knew it was me. As we both turned right around the tight corner, his wheels slipping just a bit on the slick street, my car hugging the curve, I thought about how easy it would be to let my fingers ease just a fraction on the steering wheel.

My old friends from ACT UP and I rarely talk about emotional and physical risk anymore. Perhaps the new cocktail has depressed the urgency of our fury and action, or it is that so many from our old community are dead that those of us still alive don't have the energy or the desire to talk about what we won't do. We are too busy imagining what might be left. So, I continue to get tested. The women I sleep with, few and far between these days, are also tested. I know all about making latex sexy, about making it a game, about how it can mean respect and caring. I have passed out condoms and gloves and dental dams at parties and warehouses, winking and tossing my head back and laughing conspiratorially. But I don't want this to be a game anymore. I want to taste and smell the difference between desire and fear. I want to feel the invisible fracture where laughter covers an eternity of tears, and the moment when that eternity ends. I want to always remember that differences begin with locating the overlap and then tracing a path of stories. I will not put anything impermeable between us.

No, that isn't a promise I can keep. It may not even be a promise I want to keep. I know sometimes latex isn't a game, it is the necessary way we honor our commitments, or the concession we make to keep us all still satisfied and hungry in the middle of the plague. Sometimes it is the most loving common denominator. In my outlaw clan, men and women pull on gloves and condoms and dams when it is the only way to love and honor everyone involved. But sometimes it is another excuse, a safe policy that lets us stand a little farther away from our desire.

I will not put anything impermeable between us out of fear or memory. There is too little left. And too many stories lost. For some of us sex was never safe. It has always been that balance of sorrow, the ghosts of the girls we were and of the women we might have become. But look who we are now, I hear all of my women chorus. Some of the voices frightened, some rageful, some proud. I have learned to look into the eye of the determined survival of the women I know. The laughter and teasing, unflinching desire that dares each of us to tell a story whether we want to believe it or not. Say it, we dare each other. These are not contradictions. These are the coexistent truths that will whisper and scream out until we finally hear them. *Tell me the truth. Tell me your story. Tell me who you are.*

A Blackgirl Taking Control
of Her Sexuality

 Siobhan Brooks

This essay is dedicated to my mother, Aldean Brooks

I*t's a late-night shift at the Lusty Lady theater, and there are no customers. I am working with Cinnamon and Octopussy, and we decide to sit on the carpeted floor until a window opens up. We're glad that the windows are down for now because it's three in the morning and we've been dancing since midnight. I sit in silence and listen to the Nine Inch Nails CD that's playing. I've been at the Lusty almost a year, and I still feel shy around the other dancers, especially Cinnamon. She's beautiful: dark and tall, with a round body.*

I look at our reflections in the mirror under the neon light. Funny how little I know about some of the dancers. The only conversations I've had with Cinnamon are to comment about how rare it is that management is allowing two Black dancers to work the same shift. We are all bored, staring at our bodies in the mirror. Cinnamon is looking at me, then at Octopussy, looking between our legs. I find this amusing—she is like a little girl discovering sexual body parts for the first time. She looks at me and says, "Let me see your pussy?" I slightly open my legs for her, and we all three sit and examine each other, admiring our bodies. Cinnamon has a clitoral hood piercing. "You have a nice pussy," she says, and motions for Octopussy to see it. I smile at her and say, "Thanks." We're about to become friends.

I am a Black bisexual woman, and a former exotic dancer with a college degree. I am also the product of the Sunnydale housing projects in San Francisco—a.k.a. "The Swamp." When I started dancing at the Lusty Lady, it was like I'd found another world: for the first time I no longer had to be afraid of my sexuality, or to hide it.

My mother loved me the way most Black mothers love their daughters in the projects, with survival as the main goal. But because she had few resources, my survival was not guaranteed—one false move could jeopardize it. As a child my life was endangered whenever I wandered a few feet away from my mother and the one bedroom unit we lived in. I knew not to go into John McLaren Park because of the rapes and murders of young Black girls that occurred there. I knew not to walk down the corner of Hahn and Sunnydale—day or night—because of the agendaless, rowdy, justifiably angry Black boys who guarded that corner. It was their turf and they determined who would pass and who would not; I knew to take a detour if I didn't want to be sexually harassed. And, of course, at any time I could expect catcalls from the guys in the neighborhood driving hooapies and sporting gold chains—I'd get called a stuck-up bitch for not responding to them.

My sexuality was completely wrapped up both with the dangers I faced growing up, and with the various ways I tried—or was taught—to cope with them. Long before puberty, I knew not to *ever* have sex and become pregnant, because my life would be ruined by a permanent incarceration in low-income housing projects, and I would never finish school. My mother, who had been a teenage mother herself, instilled this belief in me—and there seemed to be some truth to it, because in my community the young Black teenage girls with kids were repeating the cycle of poverty. Even though the Black community values children, I could feel the disapproval in the air when young mothers boarded the bus struggling with babies and strollers. I saw the hard stares of older Black adults. My mother had become pregnant with my sister at age sixteen in San Francisco and was removed from school and sent back home down South to her grandmother to have her baby. She only completed tenth grade, so she could only get service work as a maid in hotels, a job she had until I was born.

It makes me sad now, realizing that sexual repression, rather than sexual empowerment, was supposed to protect me from pregnancy, STDs and rape.

Like many parents who don't want their teenage daughters to become pregnant, my mother chose not to tell me anything about my body or sex. She probably was repeating a tradition her grandmother passed down, of not talking about it. When I started my period at thirteen, she got upset and kept asking me in a worried tone if I was *sure* that's what it was. For years, I never saw my vaginal opening (I masturbated by rubbing my clit against a hard surface, so I never penetrated myself). When I turned fifteen, I got a yeast infection from taking antibiotics for acne. The medication for the yeast infection was a vaginal suppository that had to be inserted like a tampon, but I didn't know how to do it and I was scared I would hurt myself. My mother was of no help: She got the same look of distress she'd had about my period. It took me three hours to find my hole, but afterwards I felt so excited and proud. I started to look at my vagina with a mirror every chance I got, but it still took me years to get over the feeling that there was something bad about my body.

Femininity—in both appearance and behavior—was one of my mother's defenses against all the threats of our world. I now feel like my femininity is innate, that I am femme, and I doubt this is only because of how I was raised. Nevertheless, femininity was beaten into me. My mother dressed me up in little fake-fur coats, lacy dresses and Buster Brown shoes, partly to compensate for the fact that we lived in poverty. Every Christmas she would buy me around twenty gifts, half of which were clothes. My mother was very femme, smoked More cigarettes, wore heels in spite of the fact that they disfigured her feet over the years, and put on a wig and a suit every time she went out. When she dressed me up, I felt loved by her and I also liked the comments I received from other grownups. I did feel more feminine in those clothes, simply because I couldn't run around and get dirty. Being careful with my clothes was an extension of being careful with my sexuality: I was supposed to be "special," just like my clothing was "special." But I became afraid to express my sexuality because my mother ingrained this "specialness" into me: If I became outwardly sexual I could get pregnant, and then I would be dismissed from the pedestal.

Now, I think of my femininity as a natural extension of my sexuality, but as a light-skinned black girl, I found that people always associated my femininity and attractiveness with my skin color. In my community, light girls were always told they were pretty, and the image of the pretty, feminine light-skinned girl was a stereotype to which I was expected to conform. Older Blacks made a conscious effort to try to protect me from danger—including the Black girls who told me I spoke like a white girl and beat me up. Meanwhile, I watched the darker-skinned girls being consistently ridiculed and harassed for being dark, and for not having "good" hair. By privileging lightness, the beauty standard of the Black community I lived in reaffirmed the inferiority of Blackness. Even though I was valued for being light, I could never be white, and inside I suffered from self-hatred in regards to my hair texture and physical features, like most Black people in this country.

Even my own mother had internalized the notion that Blackness was demonic and ugly. No matter how "pretty" she or other people told me I was, I had to struggle to unlearn this negative view of Blackness before I could think of myself as attractive and feel confident in my sexuality. My mother, who was dark-skinned, tried to make sure that I felt loved and important, even while that encouragement was based on her own self-hatred. She loved to take pictures of me while cutting herself out of them. When I was a child, out with my mother, people would always comment that I was a really pretty girl, or that I had "good hair," *and* that I did not look like my mother. The implication made me angry. My mother always hid her natural hair under a cheap black wig. I believe that my mother felt unattractive her whole life up until her death at sixty-five of emphysema; she died four days before my twenty-sixth birthday. On her deathbed was the only time I saw her real hair: two short gray braids on the sides of her head. At least she died in her natural state—no wig, makeup or sunglasses to hide her Blackness.

The comment "you're not Black like the others" (from both Blacks and non-Blacks) haunts me in various ways wherever I go. Whenever a boy expressed interest in me, it was always followed with comments like, "You're really pretty. Are you mixed?" Or, "You're really sweet and quiet, not a loud hoochie like the other Black girls." I never felt like I could live up to the toughness I associated with Black women—I thought we were all supposed to be quick-tongued, neck-rolling bitches. So after consistently being told that I was not "really" Black, I took on qualities associated with white women: polite, submissive, pretty.

My mother always wanted to reinforce this kind of femininity as a shield against the dangers of sexuality—my own or anyone else's—but this model only made it harder for me to control my sexuality and set boundaries. Because I wasn't supposed to be sexual (or assertive and contradictory) at all, I didn't develop the tools to communicate what I wanted or did not want sexually. I felt caught between sexual stereotypes of Black women (loose) and white women (pure), but it was the image of the light-skinned Jezebel, or whore, that always seemed to strike closest to home: desired over darker-skinned women for her "light" skin and submissive personality, she is still Black, more sexual, and sexually available to men of all races. It made me even more vulnerable to the sexual harassment that seemed to hover like a constant threat.

As a teenager, I felt like I had no boundaries: I allowed strange men to invade my personal space just because I felt like I couldn't say no. I never liked being harassed, but I found myself giggling, smiling and acting girlish in response. I didn't want to be seen as an "angry" Black woman and risk losing attention—even unwanted attention. Once, when I was on the bus with a white friend, an old, drunk Latino man started flirting with us. When we ignored him he began dropping grapes down my blouse. I was so embarrassed, I just froze and sat there hoping he would stop. When he got off the bus my friend and I laughed—nervously. Another time I was getting off the bus and a Black man was trying to get my attention. He was leering and his pants were sagging, so I ignored him. When I got off the bus he shoved his hand up my skirt, and I felt the imprint of his fingers for minutes after he left. A police car happened to pass by at that moment—but that's all it did, it didn't stop. A crowd of people saw what happened and came to see if I was all right. I was glad they were around, but all the attention made me feel embarrassed and I just cried. I was also reluctant to tell some of my friends because I could imagine them saying I should have fought back—Black girls don't let niggas do that to them without whipping someone's ass.

Since I never felt comfortable expressing or even acknowledging my sexuality publicly, I ended up finding sexual outlets that were somehow secret or removed from my everyday life. I used to dance to new wave music, naked and with full makeup, alone in my room. Unlike rap or other Black music, the music I danced to (the Cure, Depeche Mode, the Pet Shop Boys, late David Bowie) created a space for me to imagine myself and my desires outside the realm of Black stereotypes, as well as creating a gender-bending, glam aesthetic that—even then— clicked with my inner femme. But I always had to shut down the desire to show off my body and my sexuality as soon as I left the room.

In my late teens, I started accepting rides from men in cars. When I walked to the bus stop, at any time of day, men would stop and ask me if I needed a ride. If they looked dangerous, especially if there was a group of them, I wouldn't get in (at least I had some sense back then). But if the guy looked nice, I would get in and in each case (I did this around ten times) he took me to my destination. Once a man asked me for a massage, which I did not give. Looking back, I can't believe how lucky I was that nothing really bad happened to me. I never felt like I was really in control of the situation or even my own actions. It was like most teenage rebellion: I know it's dangerous, but I want to see if I can live to tell about this.

After school and on weekends, I dated a select group of guys whom I would make out with without the rest of the school knowing. These were never boyfriends—they were make-out buddies. I didn't want people at school to know what I was doing and with whom, so I found ways to experiment with my sexuality secretly. Everything had to be hidden.

I was one of those girls who did everything but sex. I had so little control but I always felt like that was the only thing I did have control over: not letting a man penetrate me. I was frightened of intercourse after growing up with all my mother's warnings about pregnancy and after being a teenager in the epoch of HIV and AIDS. But even though my reasons all stemmed from fear, I still felt that my ability to refuse sexual intercourse until I was truly ready for it was empowering. I had sex with a man for the first time, using a condom, after a couple of years of counseling in college. I knew it was the right time and so I was able to be open to it and to make it happen. At twenty-one, finally living on my own, it was the first step I took toward gaining control over my own sexual expression and enjoyment.

Still, my sexual agency didn't develop overnight. About a year later, I had sex with a young guy I met at a bus stop. I didn't want to have sex with him, but I felt like I had to because I came up to his apartment. He had white crust on the side of his mouth, but that wasn't enough to make me feel like I could say no. I thought he was wearing a condom, and when I found out he wasn't I pushed him off me and left. I ended up contracting chlamydia—fortunately, the only STD I've ever had. I didn't want to have sexual intercourse with just anyone, but in certain situations I still had a hard time saying no.

I started dancing at the Lusty Lady Theater while a women's studies major at San Francisco State University. My financial aid was delayed that semester, and I discovered that many of the women in my department (most of whom were white) stripped as a way to pay for school. A few worked at the Lusty Lady, which was managed by women and was known as a feminist alternative to male-managed strip clubs. I started out doing it for the money (when I auditioned I kept thinking, "I can't believe I'm doing this"). But after my financial aid came through, I stayed in the job because it was enjoyable and gave me a way to begin examining my sexuality.

Sex work is almost always a mixture of some experiences that are empowering and others that are dehumanizing. In "Uses of the Erotic: The Erotic as Power," Audre Lorde defines sexuality as a source of personal power, making her one of the few positive models for queer Black women's sexuality. She also makes a distinction between two sexual modes: the erotic (an experience of deep feeling and power) and the pornographic (sensation without feeling), and describes how patriarchy and capitalism have limited our sexuality to the pornographic. Sex work seems like an obvious example of the pornographic: as a dancer, I performed a specific role on stage, the male fantasy of the sexually available naked girl, complete with makeup, a wig and heels. It was a cash transaction where customers dropped quarters in a slot to watch anonymous female bodies and I was paid to "meet the customers' needs." But sex work can also create openings for erotic empowerment. And in a society increasingly defined by the pornographic, we are all forced to look for the erotic in its cracks and boundaries.

For me, sex work became an entryway to understanding and controlling my sexuality, to fighting racism and to developing my own agency. The time I spent on stage was only one aspect of the experience, which included the relationships I developed with the other dancers, the working environment at the Lusty Lady and my own political activism. Dancing was a way to understand my own relationship to the pornographic as a Black bisexual woman who also happened to have an exhibitionistic streak. It enabled me to confront many of the negative experiences I'd had that taught me to repress my sexuality and desires. This was not a simple thing for me to do. Working at the Lusty Lady turned out to be the best opportunity I had to focus on gaining control of my sexuality.

Because of my background and who I am sexually, it was freeing to be in an environment where I was rewarded for being outwardly sexual and could explore that side of myself. I soon discovered that I loved showing off my body and flaunting my sexuality. I loved the stage and the theater's neon lights, dancing with the other women to familiar modern rock music, and looking at my body on stage. (I often looked at my vagina from all angles in the mirrors.) It felt incredibly empowering to have men and women pay money to see me. It brought up all the desires that I felt for the first time dancing naked as a teenager in my room— as a dancer, I finally had the chance to express some of that exhibitionism without fear.

Most importantly, though, my sexual self-esteem improved tremendously while working there. The theater was an environment where men both played out their fantasies and tried to proposition women for sex. But on stage, I was physically separated from the viewers by glass, and I was given set rules regarding contact with customers. The more experienced dancers were supportive and reminded us that when customers asked us to perform in specific ways we were never obligated to do it. In this environment, I soon learned how to assert myself sexually. Ironically, I found more freedom in the sex industry to show off my body and be sexually expressive without the threat of harassment. In the strip clubs where I've worked, guys usually know their place and nudity is already an expectation. They sit down, pay money and behave while a woman gives them a show—unlike when I'm walking down the street in a short skirt and twenty guys harass me because I dare to be sexual.

At first, this feeling of empowerment did not cross over racially. I had to deal with the racism of white customers, many of whom preferred to watch white dancers. There were windows surrounding the stage and sometimes the window near me would open and then close right away. Once a white customer even tried to wave me out the way. This affected my wages because the management would always watch the stage and the windows, and they would take note if windows were going down too quickly. All my life I had been afraid of being seen as a Black Jezebel—overly sexual. But in the sexual environment of a strip club, being Black marginalized me. Men were afraid of me and seemed to view me as less human than the white dancers. Perhaps since I was already sexualized by virtue of my Blackness, it meant less to these men to see me in a strip club. Once, on the way to the Lusty, two middle-aged white men called me a nigger for not responding to their cat calls, and that incident made it very hard for me to dance for white customers or interact with my white co-workers.

When the union drive took off in summer of 1996, I fought very hard to get more Black women and other women of color hired to counter the management's racist hiring practices. The management argued that white men would pay a quarter to see a Black woman on stage, but wouldn't pay more money to see a woman of color in a Private Pleasures booth—a private, more lucrative show. Beyond reinforcing the desirability of whiteness, this policy created an unfair pay scale. Since dancers were paid more for working in the Private Pleasures booths, and Black women were never scheduled to work in them, the Black dancers at the Lusty Lady could never make as much money as the white dancers.

During the union drive, I stopped wearing my wig and started wearing my dreadlocks on stage as a political gesture. This was a big deal because not many Black strippers have natural hairstyles. The management said my hair was too short, even though it was shoulder length, and said the customers wouldn't like it. (Some didn't, and would look past me, but many did seem to like it—especially the Black customers.) Soon another dancer also started dreads and wore hers on stage. We argued that some white dancers had short hair, so why couldn't we wear our dreads, short or long? We both felt more sexy and empowered in our natural hair. (Later I filed a racial discrimination complaint.) When we won the first union contract and more women of color were hired, we started bringing in rap CDs. I felt stronger in my own Black identity after the work I did for the union, and dancing to Ice Cube and Tupac Shakur countered the invisibility I had felt on stage as a Black dancer. It also forged political solidarity with the other Black dancers and created a bond with the customers of color who could relate to it.

The white beauty standard persists, and I think that sex work generally isn't as positive for women of color as it is for white women. It feels powerful to be an object of desire, to be in the position of satisfying others' sexual needs. But it's far less empowering if you lose too much of who you are either by performing a role or by being perceived as less than human. The negative things I internalized about my appearance and my sexuality as a Black woman were all confirmed by the reactions of various white customers. But because the experience also helped build my confidence and sexual self-esteem in other ways, I was able to respond to racism with political action and resistance.

Sex work isn't necessarily a way to get in touch with your own desires; you are supposed to be performing for the sake of the customer. After a while it could get boring, and I dreaded watching men come in and display women's underwear, or insert vegetables up their anuses, or look at the sex toys women used to get off. When I had sex in my personal life, I actually did not want to role play, use sex toys, or have phone sex. I just wanted intimacy, not performance. But I also truly enjoyed performing for the customers. In an environment where anything went, I found myself turned on to sexual behaviors that I normally would not be interested in—or even do—with a sexual partner. Sometimes men would do drugs in front of me or want to role-play. They would call me "dirty little bitch" or I would call them worthless scum. I got pleasure out of it—not because I hated the customers (usually), but because it was a fantasy world. I loved being in a place that had no limits on sexual expression, where dancing or fantasizing was just a job and carried no risk or consequences.

Sometimes, I would get turned on by the women of color who entered the Lusty Lady—especially some of the butch/femme ones—or by certain men. A few times, I was so turned on I had to masturbate after the show was over. This expanded my sense of my sexuality, but it was also just a beginning. I had to take what I'd learned about myself outside of the theater in order to truly understand and explore my own sexuality and desires.

I always knew I was queer—even before I had the language to describe my desire—but I started exploring my bisexuality for the first time while working at the Lusty. During middle and high school, I had found myself attracted to the boys everyone thought were gay. I loved Black and Latino boys who were into modern rock, had one earring, wore cologne and possessed other "feminine" traits. I never pursued any of these love interests, but I masturbated as I looked at their photos in the school yearbook. I'd also been attracted to the girls who made themselves up in the bathroom (wearing eyeliner, lipstick, nail polish), and I remember feeling embarrassed when my eyes drifted toward their fifteen-year-old breasts while putting on my own makeup. As I look back on my crushes, it makes perfect sense that I was attracted to "femme" guys because I am a femme and am also attracted to femme women. Now I feel that my attraction to feminine people of both sexes is a reflection of my love for my mother, and an appreciation for the feminine aspects of me. It is a way of reclaiming femininity as a sign of strength rather than a sign of weakness.

I felt out of place at lesbian clubs because I had mostly slept with men, and I never felt that I was really queer enough to be there. At the Lusty, I was able to explore the queer side of myself just by being among different queer women in a very intimate space. The awakening of my queer desires came not from my experience dancing, but from interacting with all the other dancers at the theater. It was nice to admire the different bodies of the other women who worked there, and not be considered strange for looking at someone's breasts, piercings, butt, hair, etc. It was safe and acceptable to be sexually expressive, open and honest. Queerness was normalized throughout the club and everyone supported queerness in one way or another, either by being queer or queer-friendly. Because it was a sexual environment, the other dancers often talked about their sexuality and sex lives. When I started viewing women as more and more sexual, I was finally ready to explore my own queer desires.

Even though I have come a long way, controlling my sexuality is something I am still dealing with and learning about. In a recent romantic encounter, my lover (a Black woman in another city) went down on me without a barrier. Only later did she tell me she had oral herpes—she had been embarrassed and didn't want to tell me right away. Luckily, she wasn't having an outbreak when we had sex, but up until that point I had always assumed oral sex was pretty safe, unless the person's gums were bleeding or they had obvious sores on their mouth. Aside from the fear and anger and powerlessness I felt learning that I had been at risk for an STD, this encounter also brought back many of my old internal conflicts about skin color and sexuality.

My lover was dark-skinned, a twenty-eight-year-old single parent, and an aspiring artist. Her daughter was light (part Latina). She'd had her daughter at seventeen, was a former welfare recipient and was attending a junior college. In so many ways, she and her daughter reminded me of my mother and me. We talked a lot about stereotypes and issues affecting teen parents. She is doing pretty well in the face of racism and sexism, and her daughter attends a good school and is an honor roll student. But because of my own background, there was still a part of me that viewed her as a failure and did not approve of her having a child in her teens. When she talked about how frustrating it was that it was taking her so long to get her BA, I couldn't help thinking that if she'd had an abortion at seventeen, then she would be farther along in her career as a photographer.

Essentially, I resented her for being everything I was socialized not to be: a teenage mother on welfare. Yet I also resented her for exploring sex and expressing her sexuality in ways that I was not allowed to. She'd had unprotected sex in her teens and twenties—and appeared not to have any shame about this as she told me of her favorite sexual positions. I had done all the "right" things: I didn't get pregnant, never got a permanent STD, graduated from college, became a published writer, moved out of the ghetto. I had looked the "right" way: tall, thin, light (but not too light). And after all this, I hadn't known how to protect myself this time, and I still didn't know what *my* favorite sexual position was—I still had a lot to learn about my sexuality. How dare she have this luxury, when I'd tried so hard to do all the "right" things, the things that would save me from being her?

When she sent me a letter telling me she had herpes, I ended up taking out all my own negative feelings on her—unfortunately in a mean way. I called her up, threatened to sue her (even though I knew I was fine) and told her in so many words that I thought she was a pathetic bitch with low self-esteem. I hung up on her, and even though I knew I was also in the wrong, I felt a sense of pleasure telling her that her life was a sociological statistic.

Later, we discussed what happened. We both apologized, and we departed amicably. I felt bad that this relationship had triggered all these issues for me. That she was a Black woman like me made it all the more intense. It's always more painful for me to be betrayed by a Black woman than by anyone else, because I love Black women so much and I always long for my relationships with Black women to work out. But it was a learning experience, just like everything in life concerning sex and relationships. I just thought I was done with all these old issues. But I am still healing and growing, negotiating sex, and learning about my sexuality, which is always changing.

No, Audre, sex work is not poetry. But it gave me the tools I needed to seek erotic empowerment. And at twenty-eight, I know that it will be a lifelong process.

BETTER LIVING THROUGH PORN

⭐ Abby Levine

I have always had a powerful fantasy life. My sexual fantasies began in childhood, and my sexuality is still driven by fantasy, by fictional, anonymous narratives of lust and sex. I am also unequivocally drawn to porn and have sought it out since I was old enough to read a magazine, the images and stories feeding my fantasies or picking up where my mind leaves off.

Fantasy #1. A high school dance. Our couple is on the edges of the crowd. She's thirty-something, a teacher, dressed conservatively. No one really looks twice when she dances with this student. He's skinny, short hair, long black trench coat. He doesn't want to get caught, but he can't stop himself from wanting her. You'd have to look closely to know that anything is going on, that they are too close, that in fact under his coat her hands are on his ass pulling him into her. She's in control. He wants to come and he knows he only has the length of this song to hold her. Anything else is up to her.

Fantasy #2. A father is punishing his son and daughter. He caught them fooling around. He'll make sure they never enjoy that again. He hauls his daughter over his lap and forces his son to enter her. Then he spanks his son. Every slap is also a thrust.

Fantasy #3. An older man, late forties maybe, sitting in a chair in a posh room, maybe the banquet room of a hotel. He is rich, powerful, established, etc. Sitting near him are two young boys, seventeen or so—inexperienced sexually and very eager to learn. A posh woman is standing next to the man. She has large breasts and a tight, fancy, sheer top on. The sitting man controls the entire situation. Everybody has to do what he says. He tells the boys they can have the woman, but they must only act as he tells them. He is controlling everyone's pleasure.

I am never in my sexual fantasies, nor is anybody real—they are a purely fictional world. The ones I make up usually involve at least three people: a doer, a done-to and an observer. The sexes of the roles change with my mood. I can feel the situation from any one of the three roles, and the stories almost always involve someone struggling—against their own desires, the constraints of the situation (what will the desperate boy do when the dance ends?) or an authority. Once in a while I have sexual daydreams about myself or other people I know, but they never go very far. If I want to turn on, I need a truly alternate world, and pornography brings it to me.

When I'm turning on, I can't just be, I don't know, in my body. I've tried. I've tried to be all body and sometimes, when the moment is full of its own story—taboo, first time, a public place—I'll be caught up in it, but that's rare. Most of the time I'm in my head, planning my next move, worrying about being heard by the neighbors, analyzing. Sometimes my critic analyzes every move—that finger thrust hurt, my lover just pinched too hard, I'm not wet enough. Sexual fantasies help drown out that chastising sardonic voice. I get much more turned on thinking about a police sergeant tweaking a new recruit's nipples, as my lover plays with my nipples, than I do thinking about my lover and myself. I need a narrative, and porn offers plenty.

For me, desire came first. I'm not a psychologist. I don't know if I was hardwired wanting to wear leather and date men or if it was a process of social construction, but I know by the time I started reading pornography, I was looking for words and images to retell the story I already knew.

When I was little, I created a school called PLEEVE. It stood for Penis Love [PL]EE Vagina, and I added an extra E because it didn't look right otherwise.

This is hard for me to write about, I don't know why. I feel like I'm betraying a very special story—not so much by writing it but by remembering it with an adult brain. PLEEVE was a school that trained young people in sex. Everyone had their own little room with a bed and a kitchenette. Everyone also had connecting doorways, and you couldn't always control who came in your door. One of the main tenets of this fantasy was the learners had no choice. They had to have sex with whomever was sent to them, and they had to go where they were told to go. There was a class where they watched people having sex, and sometimes they were called up to demonstrate. Sometimes they got tickled and were told when and when not to pee.

I would turn my electric blanket all the way up to nine. Then I would lie on top of it, hot coils separating my fingers from where they were pushing. I'd pile wool blankets on top. Comforters were no good—too light. My head smashed by old feather pillows, I felt trapped, could barely breathe, my face sticky with sweat and my fingers trapped down there too. That's when I would fantasize about a man and woman whose lips were Super Glued together. The person who glued them watched while the two struggled to separate but couldn't help but keep kissing.

At my grandmother's apartment, I took a nap in her large walk-in closet. I closed the door and lay on the floor overwhelmed by smells—leather, old plastic, dust. I imagined a man on top of a woman, pinning her down, her head turned just like mine was. I loved that warm, closed-in feeling.

My first porn-buying expedition was at age ten and it was utterly spontaneous. It was 1976. We were on our way to Philadelphia for our annual trip back East and had a layover at the airport. My body was only just starting to change: I didn't need a training bra, and I still slept with all my stuffed animals and had tea parties with my dolls. I went to the bookstore to look for magazines, gum, all those overpriced treats you never get anywhere else. The Playboy symbol was everywhere; even little girls noticed the magazines at the checkout stand, the fake wood barrier a tantalizing cover for the nude figure on the front. In front of me were *Playboy, Penthouse, Hustler, Forum, Playgirl*. I stared at the covers. Bold black headlines like "Ten Ways to Drive Women Wild" and "East Coast Coeds"—tall models, jutting out their breasts, or scrunching them together and leaning forward, sometimes you could see their nipples.

I remember the checkout person was a man, and he gave me this kind of funny look when I brought up a magazine. He asked me if I had my mother's permission. I said yes, which was true, and I bought a pack of Wrigley's and a *Playgirl*. What was his look? Amused, maybe even a little condescending. If this had been ten years later, he probably would have refused to sell it to me and sent my mother to jail. But this was the sexually swinging '70s. My mother was not a swinger, but she was a librarian; she supported free access to information.

I carried it back to our gate in a brown paper bag, feeling the thick, glossy paper slide under my fingers. I tried to show my sister, but she was busy coloring and didn't seem to care. My mom told me she was just eight and probably not interested yet. I felt a little smug being ready for something before her and a little scared, in unknown territory without her.

I think my mom told me not to look at it in public, to wait. I remember being disappointed when I finally looked. Yes, there were naked men. Bronzed men, lying on rocks with water dripping off their skin. Yes, there was pubic hair, testicles and penises much better and more real than in any *My Body Is Changing* book. But the penises just flopped to the side. They were languorous, boring. That was the first and last *Playgirl* I wasted my money on.

Three years later, another airport. I was thirteen. My body more developed. I wore a bra and had my period. I still had never been kissed. The books were on a shelf facing away from the front door. Women on the covers, backs arched, nipples showing through their T-shirts, heavy-lidded eyes. Books with titles like *Lust or Bust* and *Her Bodily Charm.* Open the book anywhere, find sentences like, "Louella, the sexy little rich girl, looked up at Judd, a sneer on her face. Then his lean body was over her, sitting lightly on her breasts, stroking his asshole over her nipples, while he freed his cock, fisted it and moved it towards her mouth." First the tension of looking at the covers and titles while pretending I was looking at the less explicit romance novels. Then, when I saw an intriguing title, quickly thumbing through. Did the plot fit with my fantasies? Was the story okay? Not making eye contact with anyone else. Bringing the book up to the counter and looking away or staring straight at the checker, daring them to comment in any way.

Buying porn is not socially acceptable. That first time, my mother with me, I felt safe. I remember she was a little embarrassed, a little amused, a little proud I knew what I wanted and was able to tell her, and probably hoping I'd outgrow this phase.

I didn't. I didn't outgrow my fantasy life, and I didn't outgrow my attraction to porn. After those early ventures, I loved going to airports because I could buy more porn books. I used to read them in the airport or on the plane, trying to hide the covers. Even now I have a Pavlovian reaction to airplanes—they make me horny.

Back then, I couldn't wait for my first kiss, the first time a boy would put his fingers in me. And it didn't happen for an excruciatingly long time. No one was interested when I was ten, and they still weren't knocking when I was fourteen.

I was a fat, smart weirdo; my mother hates it when I label myself this way, but let's face it, I was not Miss Hot Popularity. I was also more cautious and more of a good girl than my desire would have preferred; I was always home by dark. So porn, and my fingers, took care of me.

A lot of people might be shocked at the thought of a teen girl using porn (though dirty magazines are widely accepted as a rite of passage for teenage boys). But as a teenager, porn helped keep me safe from all sorts of real world complications. I didn't have to worry about STDs or pregnancy. My porn characters could fuck all night long and get up fresh for school the next morning. They didn't have to worry about a cement floor that was too cold and hard or the vermin that might be running around on it. They didn't get arrested for being naked on the bus, or if they did, the cop handcuffed them to the jail cell wall and fucked them blind.

I had a lusty sexual exploration in high school—lots of fingers and tongues—but I didn't fuck these boys. I didn't have orgasms with them and didn't want to. I did have some tender moments with high school partners, some sweet loving kisses and cuddles. When my high school boyfriend touched my breasts for the first time, we were both completely awed—I can still remember feeling like the world had lost its moorings. But I didn't love him or any of the others. I made it a point of honor and also a point of control to be responsible for my own sexuality. I never told these boys about the porn. It was my private world, my outlet, my safety net. It helped me stay in control of my sexuality, just like my mother telling me to make sure I had cab fare home.

I was so brazen about porn when I was little, buying it in public—hell, reading it in public. But, like most girls, I got much less confident in my teenage years, especially about sexuality. And I was fully aware that even knowing about porn could get me in trouble.

An image from senior year: On a river-rafting trip, Susan, cool-crowd stalwart, yelled from her raft to ours, "Who starred in *Deep Throat?*" After a brief pause, I yelled back, "Linda Lovelace." I was proud that I knew the answer and figured it was safe, the type of thing you could learn from mainstream culture. But it was a trick question. Susan replied, with that sneer she was so good at, "You would know." Events like this taught me to keep my mouth shut about porn. I cared more about my feelings than championing free speech. It might sound crazy, but just remembering this makes me want to cry. A sneer can be powerful.

I took that caution about pornography with me to college, and I left my porn books at home. And at school I encountered the mid-'80s feminist critique of pornography. My history of women's sexuality course met once a week in the women's center. We read *Pleasure and Danger, The Sadean Woman* and Foucault's *History of Sexuality*, but I never did catch all the undercurrents in that room. I really wanted to be talking about my sexuality and the role pornography played in it, but that didn't fit into the academic structure of the class. I actually masturbated to Foucault's opening scene about the village idiot getting the local girls to masturbate him; I don't think that's how I was supposed to be using those texts. I kept my mouth shut and tried to learn the party line. I admired the other women in my class, and my professor, and wanted their approval. I got the message that feminists don't build their fantasy worlds on the pornography mass-marketed to men; they picket that stuff.

So, I didn't tell anyone. I didn't bring my pornography to school, and I tried to sanitize all my fantasies. Peer pressure and feminist rhetoric managed to make me feel numb and ashamed, but it couldn't change what turned me on.

Of course, it's much more popular now to be pro-porn. Feminists are more likely to write porn than to protest it. No one thinks twice before calling herself "sex-positive"—after all, who wants to be anti-sex? Women may be heading out to feminist sex shops en masse in search of porn, but that doesn't mean they are really okay with hardcore porn that isn't "feminist"—porn that includes degradation, subservience and force. And I know that many "sex-positive" women would still find my fantasies and my taste in porn disturbing.

I'm now comfortable with the fact that porn lets me enjoy fantasies beyond the bounds of what I am willing or even want to do. I don't want to fuck children. Can I say that really loud? *I don't want to fuck children.* I care what happens to others. But fantasy lets me be a very bad girl. It lets me walk the streets. I get to fuck children, dogs, dead people.

Gang initiation. In a dark and dirty room, Sharon's got to take every member however they want. "Bitch," they hiss, "Get on it, bitch." One pins her arms behind her, yanking her shoulders. She's down on her knees, cum dripping from her, when the German Shepherd mounts and plunges in . . . The boarding school benefactor arrives to inspect. He takes three little girls back to his room. Have they really learned how to open wide? . . . The rich businessman drugs the secretary. She is out-of-her-mind horny. She doesn't object when the boss pushes her to her knees . . . The boy wants to skip gym class? He better bend over for the teacher. He's crying . . .

In college, the only way I could handle the contradiction between my fantasies and my belief system was to put my fantasies in one mental box, my beliefs in another. When I was out in the world, standing on my feminist soap box, I never let on, even to myself, that a part of me could imagine a woman tied up and raped with a gun. I wasn't hypocritical, I didn't rail against porn. I just didn't open the box marked sexual fantasy. When I was home, my door shut, the curtains pulled, I didn't worry about the dog's nails on the girl's back or get horrified at the teacher. I dimmed out the part of me that cared and let the fantasies run.

The feminism I was trying to follow made the boxes approach hard. I was willing to fight for the personal as political in so many other arenas and I felt I had to apply it to myself. But I couldn't find a philosophy that could hold my politics and sexuality. The whole erotic side of me shut down. It took a long time to convince myself that I wasn't doing anything wrong. I just couldn't explain why having violent fantasies didn't make me a bad person.

The relationship between desire, reality and fantasy is hard to pin down. My fantasy material comes from everything around me: newspaper reports, friends' stories, social inequities. But the desires that drive my fantasies are completely divorced from the real world. I don't know why my sexual energy is connected to stories of submission and servitude, why these are the stories that turn me on—especially when I have no desire to act on them in reality. Something about fantasy is already like domination: You are using the characters in the scene to get off, adapting the material to serve your own lust. In that sense, porn that uses submission as a theme is simply playing out the porn experience. But the impetus for that experience is unknowable. My fantasies, like dreams, come from a place inside me that is both separate from and immune to my conscious beliefs.

My big break came one night during college. I was in bed with a casual lover discussing whom we found attractive. He said he often fantasized about having sex with a woman down the hall. I realized that I never put myself in my fantasies. Abby never got raped. Abby never crawled in bed with her father. No one I knew was in these stories, not the man whose bed I was in, not a famous actor, not even a TV character. Lying next to him, I had a premature flash of holier-than-thouness. At least I kept my fantasies safely fictionalized, at least I didn't jeopardize my relationships by fantasizing about my friends and teachers, real people. I had pure fantasy. But of course, I—my feelings, my senses, my desires—*was* in all of the stories. I was the gangbanger, the girl getting raped. I was the dog. And of course it still would be just fiction, even if the character Abby grabbed a whip and started whaling on her brother. I wasn't holier than anyone, but I wasn't worse either. Realizing my fantasies only used fictional characters just made it easier to see that they took place in a completely separate world.

I also started a new relationship—not just a new person, but a new type of relationship. I shared more with John than I had with anyone else. I didn't hold back my interest in porn, and he met me, ready and willing. One night I pulled out the porn books and we read them to each other. Hearing the words out loud was shocking, like turning on a light in a room that is supposed to be and has always been dark. I was embarrassed for these words; they were so poorly put together, so pitiful after all. But I loved his voice, especially his reading voice, and to have it bring me these words that were mine alone, to share them with him, was incredibly intimate. It was also powerful to see how they turned him on too.

John gave me a copy of *Kensington Women's Home Erotica.* Even though I was hoping my feminist beliefs and sexual leanings could find a home together in this literature, the term "erotica" made me very nervous. It's got this sickly sweet connotation—porn is nasty, but erotica, candy with a little bite. As I suspected, the Kensington women were much too tame for me. The writing was so careful not to send the wrong message—women don't really want to be raped, you know, really—that it bogged me down in boredom. But even though I didn't like it, it was an important gift. John wasn't just entering my private world, he was helping me build it. And I don't remember any other gifts during those years, just this book and the one that came after it, Anaïs Nin.

Nin was my first encounter with feminist porn that immediately clicked for me. She writes about women so tortured with sexual fever they service an entire French opium den, and about an adopted son and daughter whose sexual energy rages through thirty pages. Seduction, rape, incest, exhibitionism and voyeurism—there is nothing politically correct about Nin. Such a strong feminist woman writing wild, taboo sex stories: I felt I had met a soulmate.

Soon I found other soulmates like Grace Zabriskie, Susie Bright and Carol Queen who got off on what I did, were proud to be feminists and wrote extremely well. Not that I've ever been to an orgy in Texas, but when Zabriskie wrote about "the game" and childhood rules, I felt like she'd been to PLEEVE. And with good feminist erotica, I can check my screening devices at the door; everybody at this party has been invited. I don't have to worry while I'm enjoying an incest fantasy that some bozo really thinks women want to do it with their daddies. The author is already clear on the concept. And the editor has gone on and on about the issue in the intro. Everybody's politics have been examined, and now we can all enjoy no-guilt fantasies.

Funny that during the conservative backlash of the '80s, more and more uncensored erotica emerged from feminists. I truly wanted feminist erotica to be the total answer for me. Nin, no question, met me on every level, but most were not that impressive. Even though these authors were in let-yourself-go space, many didn't. If a real feminist wouldn't make out with the boy stocking zucchini, this character wouldn't either. Furthermore, these stories were by good writers who wanted to flex their literary muscles. I admired the story about the woman who peeled blood oranges, and wrote the seventy-two names of God on her lover with menstrual blood, but it didn't excite me. Feminist erotica draws things out more, pays attentions to women's orgasms and is generally more honest about human emotions and how sex works than the fuck-a-page garbage I've got in my bedroom. I certainly read those erotica anthologies and enjoy them, but for mindless get-there-and-disappear, it's not what I need. Maybe I got so programmed to the smut I started out with that I became set in my ways.

But not so set in my ways that I couldn't jump ship to gay male porn. When queer friends introduced me to this pornographic genre it became the ideal solution to my conflicts about het hardcore porn. It's now my favorite source of material. With gay male porn, I discovered, I could truly leave my feminist baggage behind. I am perfectly comfortable with porn in which women are humiliated or forced into submission, because I know that it does not correspond to my perceptions about myself or any other women in reality. But I'm not convinced this is true for everyone who uses this material. For some people, there undoubtedly is a connection between porn use and misogyny. Singling out porn as the cause of the problem is absurd; but just knowing that there is a connection there, even a symptomatic one, makes me less enthusiastic about buying it. When men are humiliated and forced to submit on paper, I know that everyone knows that this is just a fantasy. Like most feminists, I also have reservations about the mainstream porn industry's treatment of its women workers. Just like I don't want to wear sneakers made in sweatshops, I don't want to support the oppression of women in the sex industry. When I'm using gay male porn, I'm pretty sure the men wanted to be there and got paid a decent wage.

Best of all, gay male porn charges my sexual energy. Lush descriptions of hard pecs and glossy cocks don't hurt. But with gay porn it's more than the glorification of male bodies; it's men together. Part of me gets off on a little payback: In my standard het fantasy, men make women open their mouths or spread their legs; now they're getting a taste. Ha! I think to the characters, Get down on your knees and like it! Part of me is in each of their bodies imagining my cock being sucked, my asshole twitching. I get to experience male lust, I get to be male from all angles. Detachment is already built into the structure of my fantasies: I am on the outside watching the scene, moving between the characters. When I enter gay male fantasies, I'm not even female. I get that much more distance and story from the experience.

More than anything, it's so deliciously dangerous to imagine men kissing, men being fucked, desire crashing through societal rules. One of my most precious memories is of being in a car with two men. I was making out with one in the front seat. I knew he was bi. He reached his hand back and stroked the cheek of the other man. That moment of tenderness, of letting go of all rules and following desire was breathtaking for me. Women and men together is a turn-on for me but normal, ordinary. Men together are creating a new world, a sacred space, and I get to visit.

Somehow, male/male characters and sexual energy can convey uninhibited lust better than anything else. I love being dropped into a world where the peeping Tom is eyeing the blond jock with great sacks, humpy guys grease their assholes every morning, just in case, and men want to drop to their knees and kiss the velvety tip. Gay male porn is a straight girl's ticket to true sexual freedom.

What's most striking to me now is how utterly normal, even wholesome, porn can be when it is removed from a socially stigmatized and sexist environment. I go to Toys in Babeland about twice a year—even though I'm glad to have smut at my fingertips, I still want it to be a treat. I usually get John a book for his birthday, and he gets me one for Christmas. It's the private present we open just together. And, since we are always flying to visit relatives over the holidays, I get mine on the airplane. My porn moved from a bag hidden in the top of the closet, to a few books in a bedside drawer, to an entire bookcase in the bedroom. They are just more books on the shelf, mixed in with some poetry and wedding planners, an integrated part of our lives.

ONLY SUCKING COCK

⊛ Jill Nagle

I was shocked to learn in college that fraternity brothers forced their pledges to run around in the snow in their underwear, stick their asses in the air, endure epithets like pussy, bitch, cunt and whore, wear makeup and—get ready for this—suck cock. Most shocked, perhaps, at the lack of irony in the older boys' approach. These guys were dead serious about killing the feminine, and in the process, got about as homoerotic as young "straight" men get.

What, then, of this pathetic pussy boy in a cub scout uniform, his ass getting whacked by a Leather Daddy in full regalia? "I want to see you choke on it, Pussy Boy!" shouts Daddy. "Take it, you little faggot!" Here, at this fag-dominated queer S/M party, my cub scout uniform and tit binder render me Boy, from which status I am then denigrated back to the girl I have disguised in the first place. If someone had described such a female-bodied being to me ten years ago, in my Birkenstock feminist days, and told me I would one day be her, I'm not sure I would have believed it. It took the petri dish of

331

San Francisco's gender-fucking, spiritually oriented sex-radical culture to grow me into the odd bird—or fish—I appear to have become.

This is where I learned to suck cock, or rather, to love it—here at Girlfriend's crotch, with her huge nine-inch schlong poking the back of my throat. The dick of my faggot girlfriend, fucking my faggot mouth. When she thrust too deeply, I would bite down, knowing I couldn't make a metaphor bleed, at least not with my teeth, but I could prevent it from choking me. Did the freedom to bite allow me to learn to love to suck?

Facing Girlfriend and murmuring to her, the Leather Daddy whacked and tormented the rest of me while Girlfriend's dick vacuum-packed my brain into oblivion. The fuck in my throat, the whack on my ass. Together, they took me elsewhere: a place without time, comfort or dignity. The balls of lint at Girlfriend's crotch became my visual universe, the smell of leather and latex my environ, the names they called me my surround-sound.

Hazing brings the initiate to the edge of death in the service of a higher dedication. Pledges weather humiliation and physical torture for admission to the fraternity house, and later to the golf course, the locker room, the men's club—sexy places where power passes through a handshake. Property boundaries shift, jobs appear and disappear, expensive women offer themselves without limits. It is for the key to these spaces that the pledges stick their asses in the air and get called bitch, faggot, pussy. Why do I?

Later that night, I face flesh and blood. My tongue flicks back and forth, just on the underside of Michael's cock, up the shaft from his cool, shaved balls. A glistening drop of pre-cum swells at the tip. Over dinner last night, Girlfriend's words: She knows of two people who've seroconverted in the last year who only sucked cock. Never let 'em cum in their mouth. Only sucked cock.

I lift Michael's engorged penis straight up so the crystal droplet stays contained in its own surface tension. My tongue comes closer to his glans, then down again. I want desperately to take it all in my mouth, to taste the salty slipperiness against sweet skin. I'm scared. I feel resentful. If I slip a condom on him, my cover will be blown—because, you see, there are rules for boys, and rules for girls. Girls—at least queer girls—put condoms on live dicks before sucking them at all. Boys don't. If you're a boy, you can go to any sex club in the city and get your dick sucked, 24/7, and if some guy puts a condom on you, well, he's a rare fool who doesn't understand that raw dick is the first food group. But girls—everyone knows girls care about these things too much today to let a naked cock slide past their lips. And not only do we care about ourselves, we care about each other. Even Pat Califia's nasty fiction has back-alley boys sliding condoms on their swordlike schlongs before fucking each other to shards. We try, in the most sexy ways imaginable, to eroticize the latex we believe may well save our own, and our brothers', lives. Smart bad girls know enough to be that good.

After the party, Girlfriend will ask, "Were you sucking Michael's dick?" "Well, yeah, sort of," I will reply. "I thought you weren't going to do that without a condom," she will say. "Well, I avoided the head," I will say, with a pang of guilt for considering doing otherwise, for playing that close to the edge. "And maybe sucking cock is okay from time to time," I will add, defensively. Faggy Girlfriend has turned suddenly female—confined—and I have just left the girl cage to dance with the real boys for but a brief moment.

But this act of pseudo-solidarity feels equivocal, misguided and dangerous. Especially since the Centers for Disease Control knows so little about how women contract the virus and what happens to our bodies once we have it. My mouth on Michael's dripping cock risks not only my body, but also Girlfriend's. Backed into a corner, I feel the smallness and squareness of this cage for girls, and want out— want to flex my muscles and move about the room. But do I dare face the danger?

Probably half the men in this room are HIV-positive. Some have HIV-POSITIVE tattooed on their skin, rendering their living bodies fierce declarations, walking defiances. How do I meet these bodies with my own girl-in-boy-drag body, to pleasure and consume them with my protected and watchful girl mouth?

And in it all, the quiet omnipresence of this angel of death, sliding in next to, between and among pairs and clumps of men seeking ecstasy and release in each other's arms. Within the pandemic we stumble upon spaces of peace and pleasure, making little hurricane eyes in the deathstorm. Like this gathering. Yet, within the bliss and peace, desperation erupts in painful blisters, often silently. Another drug experiment failed. Another KS outbreak. Near sweeps with death. And, just as quickly, flashes of hope. New treatment combinations. Undetectable viral loads. Immune systems inventing wildly improbable alternatives to decimated T-cells.

Some HIV-negative men have spoken of feeling outside the community's strongest bond, and even of waiting with impatience to get infected: survivor's guilt. Is sucking cock then the ultimate act of solidarity? I do not want to be thought a coward. I also do not want to join the ranks of the afflicted. Or do I?

Safety is never far from a well-trained girl's mind. Even the worst of the good girls don't flirt with Death, whose eros is taboo even on these edges. By death I don't mean frail, battered bodies skirting the abyss; we can talk about flesh-and-blood human beings struggling for their lives. I mean the parentheses of death around the moment, the special whispered attention to now, right now, what you want is here, that seduces and invites my mouth to swallow Michael's cock. For now is all that we may have, any of us, HIV-positive or not. And those with the virus remind me of my mortality, of the ephemerality of pleasure—of this pleasure, known better by no bodies than these.

It is, after all, the world of unfettered male hunger for male bodies that brought me here, to this space where few women have ventured. It is, after all, the sight of ropey muscles grabbing manly ass cheeks, steel cocks pumping jaws heavy with razor stubble, moving into realms of fuck and suck with little ado. It is, after all, the lack of such ado that makes this space boy.

It doesn't seem fair that I can't bring myself to take Michael's cock down my throat without a condom. I curse the tasteless latex that abuts my tongue for its impermeability. Not because of how badly I yearn to taste that salty tear, not because the latex dulls his sensations, but because naked mouth on raw cock is a rite of gay male passage. An act of self-love perhaps defined by having a cock in the first place. I can love you enough through a condom, I think to myself. I look up, into Michael's eyes. He looks back. Still and sad. Four of Michael's friends have died of AIDS in the last year and a half—and who knows how many others before. I do not know Michael's HIV status. I must assume that he is positive. I think of conversations with other men: If cocksucking were an effective way to transmit AIDS, they argue, then all the men who suck dick in San Francisco would be positive, not just half. But what about the two guys my girlfriend told me about?

Michael waves his dick in front of my face, grabbing the back of my head. "You owe me, boy," he says, referring back to our earlier conversation, in which we negotiated this scene while his hand fucked my pussy and his blindfold covered my eyes. Michael's sad eyes focus to gleaming lasers, and I feel his low growl in my belly. My cunt puckers inside. We've talked about fucking. I like the idea of being fucked in the ass by a gay man, but my pussy feels so much better. The ass still hurts. Dick too big. But not too big for my hungry mouth. My throat deepens for the kill.

What we swallow separates the boy fags from the girl fags. I smell his precum, the sweat of his balls. It's only sucking cock, I think, and this is where I become the boy who would please the man, who then gets reduced to a girl, a pussy. Always the failure, always outside, always an imitation passing. Except that now, I don't fear that I am girl; I know that I am girl. For this one moment, the cage protects rather than confines me.

Michael's cock is lubed and hard, and he's squeezing it at the base, forcing the blood down its shaft. I lick up his shaft with my naked tongue, taking care not to dislodge the condom hidden in my cheek. When I reach the top, I grab the base, displacing his hand, and with expert lips, easily slide the greasy glove around his warm head. Protected, I exhale and suck freely. And then fear. Fear all he'll feel is the latex. And, more horrifying, that I'm not for real. The cage contorts and cramps my body. It sucks. I hurt. I suck deeper. It hurts more.

My throat cramps. For a moment, I revisit the first time I felt a faggot's hard dick in my mouth. Then, as now, I became a vessel for receiving cock; a python with unhinged jaws who would absorb her prey but for the annoying flange of the rest of his body. Yet, I wanted the rest of his body, too, and at moments believed that I could become a toothless serpent sheath and engulf him completely. His whole body would alchemically become his cock, folding, slimming, squishing and spiraling into me, his obverse, the ultimate vagina.

I don't know whether Michael has noticed my sleight-of-mouth. His eyes are half closed, and my mouth is mostly covering the condom, which I roll down just enough to hug his head. "Take it, boy," he whispers hoarsely, fucking my throat as I unhinge my jaw even further. He fucks me harder and harder, and just when I think I have to stop him, he grabs the back of my head in two hands and cums with a low growl, fades into a moan, then whimpers off.

Minutes pass through his fingers in my hair. Michael strokes and scratches my head, like I'm his good son. My cheek warms against his tummy, rising and falling with his breath, and I'm tracing a bead of sweat into his navel with my pinky. Here, I forget I was ever a girl to begin with. Here, I revel in the freedom to enjoy sexual domination without everyday domination. Here is a man I could obey for a good long while and walk away from feeling full, exhilarated, high as a kite, with whom I will tomorrow enjoy dinner as a complete equal.

I couldn't imagine bottoming like this to a straight man. It would only reify his expectations of "women's" places. The Eros for me in serving Michael is in being seen as Boy, writhing in the airless space outside of rigid gender boxes where my boner floats and fucks. Having my playmate revel in the shared fiction of my shapeshifts makes them real. What greater disappointment to a child than when, after declaring, "Okay, I'm the bad guy and you're the princess," his playmate goes, "Huh?" Queer men see the boy in me who wants to suck their cocks; straight men miss the point entirely for their own standard girly fantasies. They go "Huh?" or worse, "Ew," to the Boy in me. Michael, on the other hand, gets it. He gets me. Outside of these scenes he is my friend. We hang out at the beach, do yoga, massage and potlucks.

Recently tested HIV-negative, I reaffirm my safety practices to myself, balancing girl and boy, dutiful daughter and slutty son. I spend a good long while perusing the intricacies of Michael's abdominal muscles, woozy with the moment, with envy, drinking in his beauty, which I'm finally allowed to gaze upon.

When I look up, a couple of young guys are gathering around with condoms in hand. "The trick was pretty cool," they say. They want me to show them how. Michael looks at them through half-lidded eyes, then back to me.

"Trick?"

KISSING HER

 Laurel Gilbert

She is not with me anymore.

But her kiss—the taste of her mouth, the scent of her body—her kiss stays in the spaces in my mind and creates part of my recollection of desire. The memory of her kiss is with me, still.

Yesterday, we went shopping together for my daughter's eleventh birthday. We met at the mall; I shuffled my feet and looked at the ground while she suggested stores where we could browse. We wandered through the mall considering and discarding appropriate present ideas. She finally suggested a large kite—more than six feet wide—with a rainbow motif.

"I love the rainbow flag thing," she said. "It seems sort of appropriate . . . she's just about old enough to be a baby-dyke." We laughed. She bought the kite and I bought some string.

"Can I come over and watch her open it?" she asked. An awkward question, since we'd lived together for six years and she'd moved out three months ago.

We endured a long moment of silence. I examined my shoes

again. There were so many subjects we couldn't cover and too many things we didn't dare talk about: The man I was now seeing, the woman she had left me for. We wanted so badly to be more than just friends, but less than the lovers we had been.

We bought some chai and a roll of bright frog wrapping paper and went back to her tiny apartment to wrap the kite. We sat on the floor and laughed (a first in months), talked about simple and inconsequential things. Dogs. Plants. The weather. Frog wrapping paper.

Eventually, I had to leave. Life is like that, I've learned. She hugged me, held me, put her small arms around my neck and I smelled her breath through my hair. I touched her back, her shoulder blades, her small rib cage. I knew exactly how she felt in my hands.

She is not with me anymore. I don't kiss her anymore . . . not her soft mouth, nor her long neck, nor her sweet breasts. Our kisses went beyond intertwined tongues and frenzied mouth gymnastics. Kissing her was all of sex. I kissed her with my fingertips, I kissed her with my eyes, I kissed her with my tongue. Once, I rolled her over and tasted the small of her back. Another time, I sucked on her toes. When I opened her legs and tasted between them, that was the finest kiss of all.

She is not with me anymore . . . but once, seven years ago, I stood by an October windowsill and watched the leaves fall underneath a silver slipper of a moon. I stood behind her with my hands on her shoulders and knew this was it, this was our moment to step into lovers. This was our first kiss. I buried my face in her neck at first, and then turned her face to me slowly, to taste a woman for the first time. Nervous, tied in knots, my heart leaping from my skull, I turned her around oh-so-slowly and nestled her face in my hands and I kissed her.

Later that night—in my huge brass bed and with the moon peeping through the window—I kissed her again and again and again. I tickled my tongue over every inch of her body. And when I lay down between her legs for the first time and parted those lips with my fingers, I was aroused by the wetness there. I lay my tongue against her clit. I licked like a cat, from deep within her up past the curly hair and back down again. I lapped at her like a thirsty animal. She moaned and writhed, her knees grasped around my shoulders, and she drew me inside, reached for me, thrust her body forward.

I thought, *I am kissing a woman. I am truly kissing her now.*

I learned that cool October night that a woman returns your kiss with her whole body. You begin sucking on her lower lip, you brush your tongue against hers, sometimes your teeth bump and you laugh. Then you continue, down, down over her body, your kisses continue and there is another mouth, also hungry and yearning for your kiss, reaching out to be filled and touched and nibbled and adored. When I put my fingers inside of her, I felt she was sucking on them. She returned my kisses . . . I could feel her throbbing and contracting, those hot muscles wanting to take me in, surround me with wetness. So like a kiss. If I had a penis, I would want so badly to put it inside a woman. I can only imagine what that might feel like, to be a man, to make love to her as a man.

Do men know this, I wonder? Do they understand what it means to kiss a woman's soul?

Before that cool October night, she had kissed other women. I had not. She was more experienced, but I seduced. I teased her to my bed. With my tongue, I held her there.

As a shy, fourteen-year-old girl, I had one of those *experimental* friends. Until her boyfriends did for her what I could not, she let me touch her, look at her, arouse her, but never, ever kiss her. My mouth was taboo. I was not, under any circumstances, to lick or suck any part of her body. Never, ever kiss. This thing called kissing was too intimate, too far beyond the *you pretend to be the boy now* games she was willing to play with me. My mouth, my tongue, my teeth, my lips—they could never trace shapes on her skin, never dive into her secret, dark, wet self.

Her body was beautiful; her skin was soft and smooth. Her breasts made me wet even before I knew why I would be wet. But her mouth, her breath, her taste . . . all of that was beyond my reach. My fingers could wander, but kisses were taboo, forbidden. That sort of intimacy would have made us different, made us not normal. If I'd have kissed her, the stakes would have been higher. Kissing might have put our hearts into the game.

That friend was not my first lover because I could not—did not—kiss her. She would not let me kiss her. Bodies are easily acquired, but a kiss . . . oh, a kiss! In many ways, fucking means so little. It's animal and impersonal. You don't have to look someone in the eye to fuck her, but to kiss her, to kiss her requires a truly face-to-face moment. A kiss is beyond intimate. Prostitutes and strippers know this truth; it isn't the zipless fuck that is cool and impersonal and safe . . . it is the kissless fuck.

Kissing is dangerous.

Right now, my only lover is a man—and we kiss. Sometimes, we kiss for hours, never-ending nibbling, searching, tasting, licking. Sometimes, his kisses are tender—more tender than I thought a man-kiss would be—and, at other times, they are deep and penetrating. He holds the back of my head, leaves me breathless.

He is my lover. And I love him. And he pleases me. He knows—better than anyone else, I think—how to pleasure me, how to leave me gasping and breathless and satiated.

But he is different. Once, with him, I was overwhelmed with desire to kiss *her,* not just my ex-girlfriend, but any *her;* I just wanted to taste a woman, to lick her, to kiss her, everywhere, all of her. I went down on him, but instead of taking his penis in my mouth and performing the standard *blowjob de jour,* I held the member out of my way and licked underneath it. I suckled the scrotum, I buried my tongue between his balls and searched for that wonderful hidden mouth. I lapped and sucked and imagined the penis was only a hugely engorged clitoris (which it essentially is). I pretended he was, in fact, *she* . . . and I kissed the her in him with all my might.

The "blowjob that wasn't" performed on my partner was ignoring the phallus itself to tease out the indirect pleasure that most men don't consider. Coming is criminally easy for most men. My activities with my lover that night showed him how elusive ecstasy can be for a woman. *Right there, no . . . here . . . no, up a bit, ahhh. There! There!* But the "there" of a woman's orgasm is fleeting and special and can't be pinned down and dissected. It must be coaxed and teased out of hiding. A woman's orgasm has to trust you.

That particular blowjob took hours.

Afterwards, as he held me, he said, "That was different . . . that was how I do it to you."

Yes. Yes it was. Thank you for noticing.

Yes, he is my lover, and I love him dearly. But I miss her, and I miss her body, and I miss her kisses. I long to bury my face in the musk and the warmth and to feel the depths and the pulsing and throbbing that draws me in and holds me there. I miss feeling enveloped and moist. I want to kiss. I want to be kissed . . . I want to be kissed by a woman whose body knows that depth and darkness.

She is not my lover now, but on that long ago October night, she became my lover, and I kissed her. She was my first woman-lover, because she was my first woman-kiss. As she turned in the window with the moonlight caressing us both, time was measured in heartbeats (and coffee spoons) and I touched her hair and leaned forward and I felt her breath on my face. Our lips touched and my soul hushed. Later, I laid her out across my bed and we kissed again and again, until I felt her come in my mouth.

She and I kissed many times over the years we were together. We unfortunately also refrained from many kisses, because of our fear and the world's hate. Each kiss recalled that first kiss, the first taste and smell and touch of each other, as lovers. Our kisses were a conversation. Sometimes, our kisses would say *Take care,* or *I'll see you later.* When we were alone, our kisses might say *I love you,* or *You are so beautiful.* Running my lips over the secret recesses of her body might mean *I want to caress your soul. I want to make you mad with desire. I want you to want this so bad you will die if I don't kiss you.*

I wanted very much to kiss her yesterday, in her small apartment, with the frog wrapping paper crumpled on the floor. I wanted to pull her small, still face close to mine and inhale, take in the scent of her that I remember in my very cells. I wouldn't have carried her to bed. I wouldn't have pressed my breasts against hers or plunged my fingers deep within her body. I wouldn't have made her come. I wouldn't have sought that most intimate kiss with a woman, where the mouth you kiss is soft and deep and dark and without teeth and doesn't speak except with desire.

I wouldn't have done any of that. But I might have put my lips to hers, as a reminder of the life we lived together and the love we had. I could have kissed her, as intimate and as wonderful as that might have been. My mouth misses it. Yearns for it. I want to kiss her again, I want to make her shiver. I could have just kissed her.

But the moment passed. Eventually, I had to leave. Life is like that, I've learned.

Confusion Is Sex

 magdalen

> *Names/details/events have been changed to protect the*
> *innocent/guilty/unindicted.*

I don't really know "Stephen." I'm not accustomed to having
sexual escapades with people I don't know well. But he's cute,
he's funny and, best of all, he's leaving the country in two
weeks. He became attracted to me while watching me kick a
drunken, violent madman out of the store where I work.
Stephen suggested coffee, I went and here we are a couple
days later, running around his house.

Literally running. I'm shrieking and laughing, he's lung-
ing for me and tickling me. Then he's wrenching me across
the room. I'm giggling but fighting hard. Then he—a stranger,
more or less—pins me facefirst against the wall. I hear the
click of handcuffs closing behind my back even before I feel
the cool metal. My legs go weak as he breathes on my neck
and drags me to the bed.

Later—both of us still giggling—he straps a belt around
my neck and connects it to my chained ankles so that if I
move, even a little bit, I'll choke instantly. Then he tortures
me with amazing little teases and strokes. Then this unknown

man, a serial killer for all I know, grins maniacally and pulls a Glock from his jacket pocket. He puts it to my head, and I, terrified yet delighted, come.

Okay, so maybe this bondage-'n'-handgun setup isn't everyone's ideal scenario. In fact, you may be thinking, "Dude, you're a freak!" I wouldn't blame you. Until I started exploring my sexuality and learning about others', I hadn't a clue that so many people have unusual sexual proclivities and indulge them. It's kind of like conspiracy theories and aliens: I used to know a few people who were really fascinated by all that, but it took the *X Files* to bring these ideas to the masses. Thanks to zines like Lily Burana's original punk/fetish *Taste of Latex* and online communities where participants feel safe enough to talk about these things in graphic detail, it wasn't very hard for me to come out of the bondage closet. Though I don't require it all the time, I have come to accept that I just happen to like the strange bliss of submission. For me, it's an act of trust and a relinquishing of all anxiety and control, an erotic version of getting on the back of someone's motorcycle for the first time and understanding that you're putting yourself in the hands of fate.

Many a psychologist would beg to differ, no doubt, especially once she heard that I also like blood-'n'-blades. Yes, bloodplay! Undoubtedly you've seen enough vampire fetishism in movies to understand this urge. It's taboo, it's beautiful and for whatever reasons, I'm one of those people who finds the sight of a well-honed razor aesthetically breathtaking. Add a drop—or a stream—of blood to this equation, and I'm very, very *there*. Some blood players make it part of actual sex or theatrical S/M games; for me it's either an act of ritual scarification or an intimate form of sharing with a friend or lover.

For better or for worse, we live in the kind of society where you actually can play with this stuff. Maybe you wouldn't want to tell your parents about these activities, and certainly not all your potential partners would appreciate them, but it doesn't have to be that difficult to accept your proclivities. Pick the right online community, live in a hip city or cool college town and you'll find lots of people who are into every imaginable type, version and style of sex and eroticism. My inclinations are pretty darned tame and normal compared to the vast selection of preferences out there.

So dude! Maybe I'm a freak, but I'm hardly alone. And whatever happens to turn *you* on might not float *my* boat. Let's just agree that we all have different things going on.

Which is where Stephen comes in. If everyone has such a wide variety of tastes and a conveniently yet confusingly post–sexual revolution society in which to indulge them, why's it so damned difficult to find someone you're sexually compatible with? And if you should find him or her, what are the chances that your non-sexual lives, traits and preferences will match up to any reasonable degree? And what about those wackier proclivities you may have—do you communicate them to your partner verbally, repress them or just ignore them because other parts of the relationship are oh-so-fabulous?

I didn't ask Stephen to do any of those things to and with me: that's part of why it worked so well. I had no cause to consider whether our non-sexual lives would fall in line. And since the Future involved only his inevitable departure, I (for the only time in my life) really didn't give a shit. Absolute freedom, a sense of danger, a guy who can find silliness sexy, someone who appreciates bondagey stuff but doesn't get all serious about it or talk about safewords. Instant recipe for amazing, weird sex.

But Stephen and I had enough time together for me to deduce that he wouldn't have been a long-term candidate, regardless of the bondage fun. He was into the malicious, gossipy soap operatics of a particular social group; I hate that kind of stuff. Though smart and funny, he seemed a bit artificial. We were both young and flaky, no doubt about that, and he especially seemed to lack groundedness. Just not my type of boyfriend. Not compatible. But that's just *one* time when Real Life incompatibility coincided with sexual compatibility, right?

Ha. As fucking if.

Train Wreck

When the combination of sexual compatibility with non-sexual incompatibility is less extreme, it can be more seductive, delusional and, eventually, painful. With "Bob," the vibe is there from the instant we meet. You know what I'm talking about. My tummy feels buzzy, and we talk about assorted off-the-wall interests that we share. Yes, we do have a few things in common! Yes, we take weeks and weeks to get to know each other before diving into the big, scary, vast world o' *s-e-x!* We're romantic and sweet to each other, too!

Handily enough, it transpires that Bob likes bondage as much as I do. When Bob and I hook up, I'm about 95 percent submissive or "bottom" (that word always makes me think of Bottom in *A Midsummer Night's Dream;* you know, the guy who gets turned into the donkey?) and he seems more 50/50—a "switch" (puns abound in Webster's BDSM Dictionary). We both like regular, vanilla sex too, and our playtime of riding crops, shackles, clamps and ropes seems a natural, intimate extension. It's as sensitive as it is rough. And oh, is it satisfying! Bob explores his "top" side, since he has this more-than-willing bottom to play with, and I occasionally top him. We're having a grand old time. He's a perfectionistic craftsman type and studies up on Japanese rope bondage—wow. I'm a magpie, and I get to pile up shiny objects for us to play with—whee.

But then there's that Real Life stuff. Bob likes living in Marin County, while I love my West Oakland warehouse. Bob's quiet. I'm loud. Bob's a vegan. I grew up raising cattle. Bob doesn't smoke, drink or do drugs, and never has. I smoke, drink, etc. Bob is hypersensitive, I'm obnoxious. Bob likes to keep his projects secret and reveal them only when they're finished. This drives me insane. Then again, I show people "manuscripts" scrawled in the dark on cocktail napkins. Bob likes to stay in or go to peaceful parks. I like to spend my evenings in noisy, smoke-filled bars with my friends. We agree to disagree: he stays at his house or hangs out in his photography studio; I play gigs with my band or watch my friends' bands play, or watch my friends' friends' bands play, all of which activities involve consuming booze, chainsmoking, gesticulating wildly and so on.

Bob likes home, and he likes to be with me a great deal of the time. I like to travel—by myself when possible. Bob likes action flicks. I like wannabe-arty indie films. Bob likes electronic music. I like singer-songwriters and punk rock. Bob is peanut butter, I'm chocolate. And in real life, this does not necessarily make for a perfect Reese's Peanut Butter Cup. Sometimes these common ingredients, inert when isolated, combine to create a spectacular train wreck.

In hindsight, a disastrous breakup was inevitable. But was I going to admit that to myself while I was in puppy love *and* getting the particular, peculiar kind of amazing sex I adore? Hell, no. Maybe we thought that Real Life would somehow fall in line with Sex Life. Maybe he convinced himself he could truly accept a chainsmoking, partying omnivore—despite the judgmental note he tried to fight out of his voice when discussing such things. Maybe I convinced myself I could be with someone who couldn't or wouldn't participate in large chunks of my social life, who didn't seem to share my lust for all sensory experience. Or maybe we thought a mutual interest in cuddling, 1920s literature and velvet corsets was an adequate basis for a relationship.

There's nothing new or different about my exs and breakups and miserable little stories. I know that. I've read the books, seen the movies and—much more important—heard hundreds of stories from friends and acquaintances who've gone through similar stuff. Maybe they don't drag out the sexual details for public display as an exhibitionistic writer does, but they do speak of the same basic elements: great sex, impossible relationship. They speak of it with agony, nostalgia and confusion, even years later. Justine's marriage to the alcoholic blues player: probably doomed, but earth-shattering sex right up to the day she rented a U-Haul and left him in New Orleans. Kay's relationship with the pathological liar who manipulated and insulted her: brilliant sex until she left and he stalked her. Jason's tempestuous affair with Elaine, who descended into pills and booze: Each of them was astounded, even glorified by the bedroom aspect of their relationship, before Real Life tore them to shreds.

It goes on and on. It's not just me. It doesn't just happen to people who have common unusual proclivities (bondage, spanking, anal sex, latex fetish) or more unusual ones (bloodplay, infantilism, sensory deprivation fetish). Even if you match up on most sexual matters, suppose your libidos happen to be wildly mismatched? I've known people who expected sex *daily* if they were seeing someone; others figure once a month is fine and dandy. I've experienced the subtle slackening of sex drive in a partner after we've been together for a year; his libido did a graceful, slow nosedive while mine just kept increasing. This particular setup, and the insidious erosion of self-esteem that accompanies it, had been described to me many times by other women. The more compatible they became with their men as housemates and companions, the more off-kilter their libidos grew. Let's not forget age, drugs, drink, pregnancy, menstrual cycles, medications, depression and high stress, all of which tend to alter one's libido radically. Obviously there's a lot of territory to explore regarding these dynamics, but on one level we're still looking at basic incompatibility: if one partner isn't getting laid enough, he or she is not going to be a happy camper!

While we all bring a complicated array of capital-I psychological Issues to the table with us, could all of our behavioral backgrounds be so similar? Is that what sets us up for this excruciating combination of sexual compatibility with non-sexual incompatibility? Or is it simply some sick joke perpetrated upon humanity by Nature with her pheremones, Evolution with its biological imperatives, God in His legendary mysterious ways or Fate with its demented sense of humor? Is it Gaia's way of promoting voluntary population control among *Homo sapiens sapiens?*

If you're waiting for me to supply the definitive answer to these questions, let out your breath before you turn blue. All I've got is more hypotheses: maybe it's an evolutionary thing, so that your Real Life–compatible mate won't turn you on too much, leaving you free to spend time and energy raising the young 'uns, putting food on the table, and otherwise seeing to the continuation of the species. It could be caused by a secret potion, dumped into water supplies by local freebie newspapers to ensure the ongoing popularity of their personal ads.

Or it could be that some of us spend our time either lulled into complacency by good relationships that lack the extra spark of spot-on sexual compatibility or unable to tear ourselves away from ecstatic sex with an otherwise incompatible partner . . . which just doesn't leave a lot of time for finding The One—that person who might, if you took things slowly enough, explored patiently, made reasonable compromises with but didn't sacrifice too much for, *might* help create the balance of extraordinary sex and compatible Real Lives.

Überslut

Shortly after walking away from the rubble on the train tracks that used to be me-'n'-Bob, I cry on the shoulder of my friend and bass player, Gerald. He's terribly sympathetic about my dissolved relationship and how awfully it ended. Gerald and I have lots in common: we're in the same band, we're compulsive media meta-commentators, we garden together . . . well, you know what happens next.

With Gerald, it seems as if all the elements come together, including lots of hot sex. Yeah! Hot *vanilla* sex, though. Which brings us to the question: what do you do about those odd proclivities? Can you even be certain they're odd? Are they worth sacrificing a whole relationship to satisfy?

Theoretically, communication is the key. Sounds wonderful, doesn't it? But there's something remarkably *blah* about telling someone every last detail of what you want and how you want it (especially if you're a masochist and submissive, desiring to *have things done to you*). Gerald, it turns out, is a sport about all this. He knows I like bondage and playing around; he's creative enough to make up his own way of doing it. It's great. Plus, I begin to explore my dom side a little more and discover I actually like it. Together, Gerald and I are fun, playful, exploring—until he says he's not into it. Oh. Well, at least he gave it a shot, right? And I figure it's a fair trade-off. I mean, I can live without bondage play and whips and such. It's not the end of the world. Right?

If I'd told Gerald that I absolutely required the wacky stuff, I bet he would've even gone along with it. But who wants to coerce a partner into doing stuff they don't really enjoy? Once the partner gives it the old school try, if they conclude they don't like it—here we are again, stuck in the land of incompatibility. What do you do? Ignore your burning inner desire, or leave your partner? (Gerald and I, incidentally, did not end in an actual train wreck. Our parting resembled the messy extraction of two viney plants whose tendrils had grown hopelessly intertwined. And I don't think bondage had anything to do with it.)

Navigating your proclivities is made even more awkward by the fact that what seems like a pretty straight-ahead bedtime preference to one person may seem incredibly embarrassing or bizarre to another. There's no way to gauge it until you're there, either. My friend "Kay" has been discovering this recently, dating the first guy since she broke up with "Dan." Having just suffered a breakup myself, I can relate: you don't realize how accustomed to one person you are until they're suddenly gone. Your perspective on what's okay in bed and what's weird or awkward disappears the more time you spend with a partner. You don't realize what a luxury it is to be open and free with someone until you're back to square one, getting to know some stranger. Personally, I can't deal with it at all and plan to spend the next several years with the fetish and hardcore porn on wasteland.com. But Kay's actually out there, bravely navigating the choppy waters of post-breakup sexuality.

Open verbal communication was a given between Kay and Dan, so she feels strange trying *not* to say so much about or during sex with her new paramour. "I had a difficult time not talking while fucking," she says. "What will he think of me if I tell him to tease my pussy? If I tell him I want him to finger-fuck my pussy, fast? Or if I tell him to touch my ass while he fucks me?"

Why can it be so damned hard to ask for what we want in bed? For Kay, it's fear of what Dan will think of her. "I'm afraid he will automatically think, 'she gets around.' Rather than that I am a woman who knows how she likes to be fucked." Wow, I'd never even thought of that. Perhaps the men I've had sex with thought I was a 'ho for telling them not to touch my clit too hard or asking them how they liked to be touched. And when they saw the handcuffs and the riding crop under the edge of the bed, or the arty black and white photographs of me doing scarification? Were they thinking, "Scary überslut"? Would I care if they were?

Squeal Like a Pig

Personally, I like it when a lover shows or tells me what he likes. But sometimes being able to ask for it and trying to deliver don't quite match up. Incompatibilities, you see, are everywhere. Even for me and "Stan" in our garden of earthly delights.

I'll spare you the details of Stanley's and my full relationship; suffice it to say we have a lot of good things going on. But I'm not a top, and Stan wants to be topped. I mean, a few little things here and there come naturally to me: I put clamps on his nipples and scrotum and tease him with my mouth, and then snap off the clamps right when he's ready to go. I tie him up and tease him; he does the same to me. When we're in bed, I grab the riding crop and turn him over, smacking his ass until the red stripes glow in the candlelight. But that's it. I don't really want to take it any further or do it any more often, lazy submissive that I am.

Stan has to come right out and ask for it. He wants to be topped, for realsies, and he wants to be fucked up the ass. Some people don't like blood and blades, some people don't like being tied down and blindfolded. They'd find these practices of mine weird or disgusting, or it may just not be part of their erotic reality. That's how I feel about the whole anal thing: it's an asshole, you take shits out of it and that's it. I've tried to find it erotic or titillating, but I just find it neutral to slightly gross. I even tried anal sex once; I yelled "ouch," he got out of there and that was the end of that.

But I'm a good sport, right? So I ask what feels good to him and sometimes put my latexed, lubricated finger inside him during sex, and he shows me how to put a dildo up him without hurting him. None of it turns me on, but I like that it turns him on. The night Stan approaches with his tasteful black rubber strap-on, I put it on. We lose some momentum because I find it very hilarious to have my own cock suddenly, and I have to run immaturely around the room, posing with it and such. That accomplished, we get down to the serious business at hand. Stan pleases me sexually, all the time, so I want to return the favor—even if it's new to me, or not quite my cup of tea. I may end up really liking it, too!

Once we've gotten through the tying up and teasing part, the whipping and towering over his prone frame on the bed part, I have to actually fuck him. I force him onto his hands and knees. He trembles in anticipation while I lube up my new penis. And I very carefully insert it in his anus. At first slowly, I begin to fuck him. He moans. I pump at him faster, a little cautious at first; he moans more. Something begins to turn over in my brain, something I don't like: I'm taking on a vicious quality as I fuck him harder and faster. His moans, instead of making me feel delighted to please my partner, make me feel contemptuous of him. I want to hurt him for all the wrong reasons. I pull out and draw back, contemplating what to do next. He immediately falls at my feet, practically crying yet looking insanely eager, and lies on his back with his legs pulled up to his shoulders, his posture begging for it.

I'm really not cut out for this. I'm beginning to hate Stan, squirming around beneath me. I want either to run from the room or to taunt "Squeal like a pig!" If I had a real cock right now, it would either be a raw, violent hard-on or it would fade pathetically and meekly withdraw from the whole situation. But I don't, and Stan seems ecstatic about the proceedings. So I finish fucking him with my black strap-on, eventually pulling him onto his knees, fucking him from behind again while manhandling his penis. After he comes and collapses against the wall, I realize not only that I can never do this again, but also that I can't ever look at Stan the same way.

Perhaps it was a symptom of some deeper incompatibility, or perhaps my negative response to being the fucker instead of the fuckee has some twisted psychological significance my therapist hasn't dragged up yet. Sometimes, people who've been raped or abused can't handle playing the dominant role in sexual situations, perhaps because they don't want to identify with their past assailants. Since I'm fortunate enough to have escaped the sexual abuse experienced by a large portion of the population, I don't have an explanation for my inability to cope with topping Stan that night. The vicious feeling had its appeal, but I didn't want to feel that way toward my lover: Could it mean that this was how I secretly viewed him? Was this how my lovers felt when topping me? They never *seemed* to, but hey, how could you ever know?

In any case, the attempt to fulfill Stan's desire just damaged us on some level. I also couldn't come out and tell him the full extent of what I had felt, either, and there's nothing more harmful to relationships than having to keep secrets. Eventually, the two trains ended up on the same track, coming from opposite directions, doing 120 mph.

End of the Line

Which brings us to the end of the line. I've suffered my share of train wrecks. I've explored enough public BDSM parties and clubs to conclude that "the scene" is definitely not for me. I have no interest in my sexual preferences becoming the defining factor either in my relationships or in my identity—something that easily happens within the gay, lesbian, bisexual, fetish and BDSM communities, all of which have been socially marginalized to various degrees and at different points in history. I'm not sure where to turn next.

I do want to see compatibility, sexual and non-sexual, all around me. Not just in my life, but in the lives of the couples I know, the old married people in the supermarket, my single compatriots. I believe we can achieve a delicately balanced state of sexual satisfaction and Real Life sharing, exploration and support. Is there some magic alchemical formula for it? If so, I hope someone gives me the recipe soon. Like they say on the *X Files,* I want to believe.

THE HIGH HOLY DAYS ARE NOT SEXY

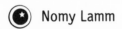 Nomy Lamm

The High Holy Days are not supposed to be sexy. We atone for our sins in temple, beating our chests, reciting the *Al Cheyt,* saying over and over: "For the sin which we have committed before you by unchastity, and for the sin which we have committed before you openly or secretly. For the sin which we have committed before you by spurning parents and teachers, and for the sin which we have committed before you in presumption or in error. For the sin which we have committed before you by idle gossip, and for the sin which we have committed before you with wanton looks . . . " Yom Kippur is about abstinence from everything—food, water, sex, even showering and brushing your teeth (supposedly). You focus your entire being on *Teshuvah,* the process of spiritual redemption, of returning to your highest self. You take a spiritual assessment of your life, look at the past year, make amends for wrongdoings and make plans to change destructive or counterproductive behavior in the coming year.

Call me a pervert, but all I could think about this year during High Holy Days services was sex. Don't get me wrong—I wasn't daydreaming to take my mind away from the task at hand. I was paying attention. I was seriously digging into my soul, trying to figure out exactly what I need to do in the coming year to make my life more spiritually fulfilling. And one of the major things that kept coming up for me was: more sex. More sex in more interesting contexts. More fulfillment of my own (and others') sexual needs, desires, fantasies and fetishes. As I recited my sins, "We have trespassed, we have dealt treacherously, we have robbed, we have spoken slander, we have acted perversely, and we have wrought wickedness," I secretly changed the words in my head to "I haven't acted perversely enough."

Let me give you some context. While a person's identity can never be boiled down to a few words, I would say that, in a nutshell, I am a twenty-three-year-old fat femme amputee Jew dyke. I am an anarchist, a freak and a queer. I believe in pushing boundaries and I believe that queer sexuality (in whatever form that takes—the freakier the better) is subversive and (duh) exciting.

I'm also a fairly religious Jew. I believe that I fit into the world in a kind of cosmic sense. I believe in God—what Michael Lerner (a Jewish writer, activist and rabbi) has called "the force in the universe that makes possible the transformation from what is to what should be." I believe that it's my duty and purpose as a Jew to work toward the healing and transformation of myself, my community and the planet, to work for justice and freedom from oppression on all levels and to make life as fulfilling and meaningful as it can possibly be.

I don't know how I feel about the concept of "sin," but if I did believe in it, I'd say that it's a sin for me not to make the most of my life, to stifle my sexuality out of fear and inhibition. It's not like I think that sexuality in itself is the key to revolution, but it is a part of it, and it's definitely part of being a whole, happy and fulfilled person.

Does it make more sense now, my fixation on sex as *Teshuvah?* I'm not interested in dividing my identity into different parts, like I'll be a pervy dyke but not a Jew when I go out dancing, and I'll be a devout Jew but not queer when I'm in *shul*. Being a Jew and a queer are entirely compatible, complementary even. I'm not saying that I recite a *Barucha* when I get off (although the *Shehecheyanu* might do nicely: "Blessed are you, Adonai our God, ruler of the universe, who has kept us alive and sustained us and allowed us to reach this moment"), I'm just saying that the philosophies and lifestyles make sense together.

But let's get back to the story. So I'm in temple, I'm beating my chest, I'm atoning, I'm thinking about fucking. I guess I feel a little bit naughty, worrying about what all the good Jews around me would think if they knew what was going on in my head. I'm thinking it's been a pretty dry year, and I find myself hoping and wishing for more and better sex in the coming year. Oy yoy yoy, I think, I may as well be asking God to send me a girlfriend.

The High Holy Days are not about hoping and wishing for things, and God isn't a big dude in a throne pointing a wand around and granting wishes. It's not enough just to hope for the forgiveness of those you have wronged. You go out and ask for it. You don't wish for more fulfilling relationships with your family and friends, you figure out what you need to do in order to build those relationships. You don't hope and wish for a just world, you make plans to go out and create it. Likewise, I can't sit around and say, "I want a big butch stud who will fuck me good and take all my cares away," like I'm wishing on a star or blowing out candles on a cake. If that's what I want, I gotta go out and find her. I have to make plans of action.

This is hard. It's no easy task to take control of your sexuality and your sex life, to figure out what you want and how you can get it. Namely because that involves telling people what you want, and asking them to be involved. That can be scary as hell, especially when you have been desexualized all your life, told by society as well as specific people that you are gross and ugly and don't deserve to be touched, not to mention that your desires are sick and depraved. I know that I am a major hot babe, I know that I deserve to get what I want, but I also know that a lot of the world thinks that people like me shouldn't even exist.

Even in my community of freaks and pervs, there are beauty standards. They may not be obvious, but you know that skinny girls still get the most dates. Truly freaky people still take the back seat to saucy little tarts and strapping young lads. This is a constant source of annoyance to me and my other fat dyke friends, who see a lot of lip service but not a lot of action, if you know what I'm saying. Especially for those of us who are femme, it's a constant struggle because we don't fit the one role that fat dykes are allowed to be sexy in—the big burly butch top.

My group of friends tends to be almost absurdly sex-focused. Our perversions and desires often make up the bulk of our conversation, sometimes to a point where I can't tell what's for real and what's just talk. It's confusing; when we are constantly talking about and simulating fucking each other but it never actually happens, what does that mean? Is it all just a joke? Should we get a move on and just do it? Sometimes being in a community that is so open about sex helps me to feel confident in my sexuality, but sometimes it really fucks with my self-esteem. I second-guess myself a lot when it comes to reading people's signals, and all the fakeout signals that are always flying around make it even more difficult for me when it comes to the real thing.

How many times have I stood next to somebody, feeling like there was chemistry, waiting for her to make the first move? Why do I always wait, kicking myself later on if nothing ends up happening? Why wasn't I able to just do something, say something, bust a move? Wouldn't it have been worth the risk of rejection?

Not necessarily. Sometimes that risk of rejection is terrifying. I know that most people have a lot of fucked-up ideas and feelings associated with fat people, regardless of their politics. Sure, they may say that they support fat liberation all the way, but that doesn't mean that they don't cringe at the thought of actually getting it on with a fat girl. If a thin person comes on to somebody who's not interested, it can be humiliating, but you know that it probably just boils down to a matter of personal preference. When you're fat, you always know there's a possibility that your crush is gonna think you're gross. Being a crip only adds to this: I don't think there's that same kind of general hatred and repulsion for people with disabilities as for fat people, but disabled people are generally seen as kind of pitiful, definitely not sexy.

In light of all this negative input, what's a pervy fat crip dyke to do? Well, draw strength and inspiration from Jewish tradition, of course. (I'm being facetious, in case you can't tell.) If God is defined as the power to heal and transform our lives and our world, then *Avenu Malkaynu* (translation: our parent, our ruler—i.e., God) is just as applicable in this situation as in any other: "*Avenu Malkaynu,* repeal the evil sentence that may be decreed against us; *Avenu Malkaynu,* inscribe us in the book of happy life; *Avenu Malkaynu* inscribe us in the book of freedom and salvation; *Avenu Malkaynu,* provide us with your abundant blessings . . . "

What is the book of freedom and salvation? What are the abundant blessings of God? What the hell does this have to do with sex? Maybe I'm getting a little too heavy, maybe a little too blasphemous, but you must see what I'm getting at here. I'm saying, fuck the evil sentence that may have been decreed against me, I'm going after the abundant blessings of God. In a world that exploits our passions and tries to keep us down, we are told to only expect so much from life, to play out our prescribed roles as best we can and die happy if we did a good job of meeting expectations. That doesn't work for me. The Christians may believe that they go on to a better world, but as a

Jew I believe that better world is now.

Talk, talk, talk. So, what is this plan I speak of? What am I gonna do to make my sex life more fulfilling? Well, it's not like I haven't done anything. I've done a lot in the past few years. I came out as a pervy femme dyke and found a community that respected and reflected that. I've learned to flirt and use body language to say what I'm often unable to say out loud. I've expanded my boundaries to include a lot of people and things that probably would have scared me away three years ago (S/M, genderfuck, role playing). I've read and experimented and talked about my desires with friends. I've even been known to make the first, if tentative, move a few times.

So what is my plan of action from here, and how will I find this butch stud? Of course there are the obvious cheesy channels—bars and personal ads. And I'm not above that. I've even been known to read my personal ad aloud at my spoken-word performances. But that's not really the issue. The problem isn't necessarily finding a person to fulfill my fantasies, it's letting her know what I want when I've found her, whether it's "I really want to kiss you," or "I want you to top me, fuck me hard and make me take it like a man."

The first step in being able to do this is for me to decide what I want. I have a pretty broad definition of sex, which includes a lot of theatrics. Not like it always has to be like that, but for me, the biggest turn-ons include power play, costumery and props. I like dressing up and applying makeup while being watched, pretending I'm the doll that you're playing with. I like acting out characters: I'm the boy, or you're the boy, or we're both teenage boys doin' it in the locker room, or we're both little kids, or you're the teacher and I'm the naughty student. I like experimenting with pain—biting, hair-pulling, spanking, clamps, electricity. I like the feeling of being covered, engulfed, cared for and protected.

Knowing all this, it's time I learned to ask for it. Yeah, it's scary for me to put myself on the line, and yeah, I worry about rejection, but I can get over it. Everyone knows that the sexiest, most appealing people are those who have no shame or inhibition, who know what they want and go after it. And a lot of times, the most important step in making something happen is just deciding that it's going to.

FAT ASS AND FREE!

23 YO Fat Freaky Femme ISO Boychick who will make me feel foxy. I am: one-legged Olympia dyke on the verge of being very bitter about my lack of options. I hate long walks on the beach, but I'm down for memorizing dance routines from Michael Jackson videos, vandalizing weight loss centers, writing stupid poetry, making rubber fetish gear, talking politics, dressing in drag, making a scene. I drink occasionally but it is not my main source of entertainment. You are: punk-ass gender deviant, lookin' for a good time but down for the heavy shit too . . . a good communicator who likes her women complicated—tough, sleazy, dorky and vulnerable. Not too much of a grown-up, but mature enough to be responsible for your actions. Body size/type unimportant, but you better be strong enough to hold me down. Leather pants a plus.

SEX AND THE SINGLE MOM

⊛ Spike Gillespie

Beginning of 1995: I break up with my last boyfriend and swear off men for a year. Within weeks, I meet Eddie, perfectly normal (unusual for me and therefore enticingly exotic) and definitely adorable. In my own silly way I woo him. When he is not around I dream of getting him in my bed. One night, I line up an SOP (that's sitter off premises). My four-year-old is gone for the entire evening. I've asked Eddie to meet me at a bar where I will be doing a poetry slam, my favorite art form at the time. Eddie says, "Maybe." My ears hear: "Yes, I will be there, I will sweep you off your feet, I will make slow passionate love to you, and when we are finished I will flat out fuck you. And when that is finished, we will sleep. For two hours. Then we will do it again."

Since this is what I hear, here is what I do. I cue up some Van Morrison on the stereo. I light the Christmas lights strung around my bedroom ceiling. I make sure cold imported beer and fancy gourmet snacks are tossed casually in the refrigerator amid the leftover macaroni and cheese and the

357

near-empty gallon jug of milk, as if it is standard for a single mother to have this combination of things lying about, as if her budget affords it.

Finishing touch—and yes, I know I might be jinxing myself—I remove the rubber sheet from its place under the regular sheet on my bed: A rubber sheet there not because I have an oooh-baby-I-wanna-piss-on-you fetish, but rather because my son still sleeps with me at night sometimes. And he doesn't always wake up in time to make it to the bathroom. I know that, should I get Eddie where I want him, the crinkle of plastic beneath us might not be, er, the aphrodisiac of champions.

Unbelievably, it goes almost as planned. Sure, Eddie almost doesn't show up at the club. But at the last minute he does. We drink ourselves silly. We make out like teenagers. Then we are home. On my couch. Then in my crinkleless bed, getting it on and on and on. At breakfast, I am giddy. I am back in my twenties for a few moments. I have a hangover and no responsibility. Eddie drives me back to my truck, which the night before I claimed I was too drunk to drive. We kiss once more. And then . . .

I am a mother again. I pick my son up from the SOP. I take him home and love on him. We play his favorite game, Bounce On Bed, in no way similar to Eddie's favorite game even though it involves the same main piece of equipment and could easily share the same name. My relationship (with Eddie, not Henry) lasts a few months. There are many babysitters and lots of sex. Then Eddie leaves me. I cry for a spell. And then I find myself another lover.

Henry is now nine. I was never married to his father, who split after a couple years. In the seven years since, I have had seven lovers and one husband, whom I divorced rather quickly (thank you, baby Jesus).

While I do get it on, so to speak, with my buddies Ben and Jerry rather regularly these days (yes, even smuggling them into my candlelit boudoir, lifting them up, up, up into my big delicious husband-free, four-poster, princess bed— a relic from a friend's divorce), I haven't had sex in well over a year. This has nothing to do with my morals, though I have plenty. This also has nothing to do with being a dedicated mother; I'm always a dedicated mother.

My current lack of sex has to do with just one thing: I've had no good offers.

But I have every intention of leaping at (and on) the next opportunity. And having the opportunity do me up, down, sideways and, should I so desire, on top of the goddamn refrigerator. I'm thirty-six, a year past my alleged sexual peak. I hear, though, that sex just keeps getting better. Not only am I hungry for it, I am, I'd say, about due some catching up.

Do I want permanent monogamy? Who, raised in our society, hasn't had it pounded into her head forever that a lifelong companion, *a soulmate*, is the ultimate golden ring, preferably symbolized by . . . a golden ring? Of course I'd love the mythological perfect man (gay in sensibility, straight in bed). And if he's that good, hell yes, I'd like him to stick around for a while. But will I wind up marrying the next guy who gets me off? *Highly* unlikely.

Excepting my foolish choice to hastily marry a nutcase Republican (who neglected to mention either of these characteristics pre-nups, who in fact feigned a sane, liberal and—no, really—*feminist* stance to woo me), I have managed to live the bulk of my adult life purposefully insulated by people like me. Genuine liberals. Genuine feminists. Or at least open-minded enough to differ in opinion and lifestyle without judgment. In which case, they still meet the main requirement: genuine.

Purposefully ensconced among this sort, some married some not, the stigma and pity and fear my single-mother status earns me among fans of Rush and Dr. Laura move to the background. Sometimes I get a little too comfy. I let the love and support that emanate from my inner sanctum flavor my take on society at large. I start to believe (so naive, so naive!) the entire world is letting down its guard, reaching the amazingly intellectual conclusion that (gasp!) single moms are not to be tossed in the nearest pond for the float/sink witch exam.

Days, sometimes weeks pass before some unfortunate reminder of *how it really is* smacks me in the head like a poorly tossed used condom thwacking wetly against the side of the wastebasket. At which point my personal search engine goes on an auto-jaunt calling forth all the times—blatant and subtle—I am differentiated because of my single status and the presence, nonetheless, of a son, nay, a *bastard*.

Now what could possibly piss these people off so much about the fact that I'm single? I'm a room mother. My kid gets straight As. I work at home, thus, I am always at home, waiting for him when he returns from any number of wholesome activities. I adopt stray animals. I do volunteer work. I give pep talks, sans engagement fees, to schoolchildren around the country. I fucking bake cookies, okay? What complaint could they possibly have?

Easy: The same patriarchy-driven lament that has held women hostage for years. Women who fuck men who aren't their husbands are bad. Mothers who fuck men who aren't their kid's father or at least a reasonable facsimile (to be determined by presence of aforementioned wedding band—you know, the second husband come to rescue the poor abandoned woman) are sick, sick, *sick*.

Redemption isn't impossible. If I'd just focus on raising my child, I might rank as a black sheep version of a widow in the '50s, the pathetic gal with no man and a brood running at her feet. But bad? No. See, *bad* only comes into play the same way it always has—when some allegedly pure conservative (think Jim

Bakker, icon of sexual morality) lets his filthy mind wander to the possibilities of what goes on in my bedroom. (And I bet any real-life action I've seen—and I confess I've seen quite a bit—could not hold a candle or any other phallic object to the fantasies these fellas conjure.)

May 1988: Theo is my new lover. It's crazy at my house. My French friend is visiting, along with her mother. In her seventies, the mother teeters on high-heeled espadrilles throughout my house, clad only in black lace lingerie topped with a sheer flowered blouse. The French have my room. I have the futon in the living room.

Because my affair is new, I cannot wait for my friends to depart. Sex is available and must be had. Half-joking and half-worrying I am a bad hostess, I ask my friend in hushed tones if it would be rude for me to have sex in the living room while her mother sleeps in my room; I promise to be quiet. My friend bursts out laughing and, to my horror, races to her mother. I do not understand French—I do not need to. Within moments the mother joins her daughter, laughter bordering on maniacal. These people were not born in a country founded on twisted Puritan morals. They expect me to have sex. They will be very disappointed if I don't.

A week later: The French depart, but not before my friend's mother has laughed some more and, in a low voice stained with near sixty years of smoking, chortled while pointing to the toaster shooting a piece of toast across the room, "Orgasm! Theo! Orgasm!" as if the the appliance were not malfunctioning but, in fact, experiencing joyous, empathetic ejaculation.

Now I have my room back but I am not alone. One night, Henry and his best friend are sleeping. Theo and I, once certain they are asleep, work our way through any number of positions. I drift off around 3:00 a.m. and awake before the alarm, set for 7:00 a.m.

Because I have not hit the point yet where I am bored with or despise Theo, I want, very much, to please him. It would, I believe, please him (very much) not to be awakened by the sound of Super-Poppin' Sugar Crunchies being gulped down at ten decibels by two squealing first graders. So I tiptoe into their bedroom, wake the boys softly and say the words that make them sit up and pay attention most: "I'll make you a deal."

The deal is this. If they will, more or less, get dressed in the car, I will take them to the BK Lounge for breakfast *and* . . . "And what?!" they demand. And I will let them make as much noise as they want, and not once will I tell them they have to shut up so I can focus on not crashing the car.

The deal is on. The boys are delighted. I've gotten up too early, and, even after Burger King, we have time to kill. I drive around and strike upon an idea.

I will go and buy a box of condoms with the children locked in the car. In the store, I discover that I am a teen boy trapped in a grown woman's body. I cannot just buy the condoms—*Why? Why?!*—so I must buy a "few" things—a gallon of milk, a gallon of OJ, a pound of coffee and so on and so on—to disguise my real purchase.

By the time I reach the car, the jubilant children are nearly peeing their pants. They've had enough time to invent a new noise. Yes. A new noise. They simultaneously rub their straws against the sides of their juice containers and blow into the juice, bringing me right to the edge of the edge. "Boys! Stop—"

They laugh. Juice shoots out of orifices—theirs or the straws'? "You promised not to say that!"

And so I did.

This is just one occasion where, to balance my life as a mother and my life as an independent human, I have to do double, sometimes triple duty. In some ways, Theo made this easy. He worked ridiculous hours and—due to his bizarre living arrangements that resembled a high-tech commune of Trekkies—preferred to come to my house rather than attempt to incorporate me into that fold, like some Marilyn to their Munsters (though I suspect it was *them* he wanted to shield from *me*).

We rarely went out, which was fine with me. I didn't like leaving Henry with a sitter and my days of wild clubbing had passed. We'd eat supper together, play games—penny-ante poker, Boggle—then Henry would sleep, and we'd stay up half the night, talking, watching movies, playing Scrabble and, yes, having sex, sex, sex and more sex.

Of course, I was the one left exhausted in all this. No matter how late I stayed up, the school did not push back the starting bell. I didn't care so much. Yes, weary and frustrated came into play. But, if there is something I want to do, I find a way. If having a kid and a job and sex means losing sleep, okay, I lose sleep. If an event called for no Henry, I'd go through my list of close friends and find someone—not just anyone, not some stranger babysitter—with whom he would be glad to hang out.

Though I am now distanced enough from Theo to see it was not a good relationship, at the time I was in love. I was having some of the best sex of my life, which was certainly a reason I didn't leave him sooner. Until the trade-offs were no longer worth the energy expended, I did whatever was necessary to maintain a closeness with the man.

In 1999, to help promote my memoir, *All the Wrong Men and One Perfect Boy* (which details my life as mother and as lover) an essay of mine was published in *Texas Monthly.* I opened that essay with the juice-noise incident. But I told the story a little differently. My editor informed me that his editor informed him that I was not allowed to use the words "lover" or "condom." I'd included the rubber sheet story in the original draft (the part of the pitch that got me the assignment to begin with), but it was flat-out cut. I protested, to no avail. The audience, I was told, would never, ever tolerate what it would consider to be my sluttish ways.

I fumed and thought the magazine woefully prudish. Come *on!* This was 1999!

Then the reader mail, on which I was cc'ed, began to arrive.

Readers were, to put it mildly, enraged. Several suggested that Child Protective Services be called in to take my son away from me due to my "promiscuity." "It is maddening to think this is what some children endure in today's increasingly amoral society," declared one. Another chastised, "Promiscuous females generally don't find lovers who stick around very long for sound evolutionary reasons." (Dare I guess this reader homeschools his children, preaching creationism?) More than a few demanded "Cancel my subscription!" One even insisted, "She's no mother, she's just a woman with a child." (Huh?) I think more than a few believe my epitaph should read: "Best Little Whore in Texas."

That was a triple shot of espresso waking me up from my dream that the world was becoming kinder, more accepting. I started toying with the idea of having a scarlet "A" tattooed to my breast. Can this be just a case of grasping for a scapegoat to hang all society's ills upon? If I get laid by more than one man over the course of my son's life, will he really grow up to abuse women (another friendly reader suggestion)?

Other criticisms creep in, unspoken, or spoken only by the voice in my head, or spoken when single mothers meet and compare notes. These judgments are smaller by comparison to the vitriolic mailbag, but sharp and accusing nonetheless. For example, at least one of my sisters told her kids I was married to Henry's father, despite the fact that honesty is otherwise upheld as the most virtuous of virtues in her house. Though you don't need the explanation, let me spell it out for you, to emphasize my point: Under no circumstances did my sister want her children to know that I had sex (or a child) without the "benefit" of marriage.

Here's another example. If Henry has an overnight guest (other than his best friend, another child with "freakishly liberal" parents—adopted dad gay and bio-mom bisexual), I most likely will not invite a lover to stay the same night, falling prey to the same sort of concern I claim to loathe. On some level, I am— despite my best efforts—cowing to the discomfort others feel when it comes to my choice to be single *and* a mom *and* have sex. I don't want to have to ask some kid's parents if they mind if I fuck while the kids are asleep. And "fuck" would be what they thought I meant if I said, "Would you be comfortable if my lover stayed the same night as your child?" (Okay, fuck probably would be what I was thinking, too.)

Why do I think I even have to ask? Because many people *do* care. Even those who sleep with lovers other than their own children's biological parent. By that I mean, if Joey's mom is doing the nasty with someone other than Joey's dad, but they're married, no problem is perceived. They don't ask permission to sleep together or decide to spend the night apart simply because kids are in the house. They're married, dammit, and marriage is the ideal.

But it will damage your son! He'll remember a parade of men. He'll remember his mother the slut who let men stick it in and walk away. He'll be embarrassed, tormented, go insane, knock off banks, murder animals, maybe people even. He'll tote illegal handguns (lifted from the pants left by mom's nodding junky sex slave!), run drugs and be too unfocused to read the classics because he'll be obsessed with dreaming of the day he is old enough to procure swastika tattoos and overpower old ladies and others: namely, all those who worked so hard to build and those who grew up in the "security" of a classic nuclear family.

They make it sound like I force my kid to videotape me taking it up the ass on the front lawn while the dog sucks on my toes.

You want to know how it really goes—me and Henry and the men we entertain? I already told you about poker and Boggle with Theo. For the shortest while, there were Monday nights when Theo would pick Hen up and take him to his place, to be among the Trekkies as they watched professional wrestling with religious zeal.

Early on, confusing the fact that Theo had an eight-year-old's social skills with the idea that he was a mature man who loved kids, I reveled in their bonding. Henry simply enjoyed the hell out of him. There was no romance, no other woman (yes, Theo was that type) to bog down *their* relationship.

Of course, ultimately these things did interfere. Because when I finally cut Theo loose, I had no intention of coming up with a mock custody arrangement. But I did not want to give my son the message that we simply discard others, seemingly without reason.

So we did the same as upon the departure of Eddie. And Barry. And Jerry. And Andy. And Lance (whom Henry never met, but heard much about). And Dickweed (that would be the ex-husband). We did what I fear too many parents don't do. We *talked about it.*

Sometimes, Henry will wonder aloud, whatever happened to someone. And

I'll remind him: Theo didn't tell the truth. And trust is the most important thing in life—you can't love without trust. Someone fails in that department, well, sorry, we can't afford to waste more time.

Mind you, they weren't all harsh breakups. Painful? Sure. Hateful. Nah. Henry still speaks of several fondly, as do I. We speak most fondly of all about his father, whom we both love and, who, if you think about it, was the first man I slept with as an unmarried mother.

I always have had a rule, once unspoken, now spoken: If a man has no interest in my son, he can take his interest in me and hit the road. I do not mean I am looking for a replacement father for my child. I am not and never have been. Long ago my close platonic male friends (and there are many) stepped forward, unasked, and took that role. But, with only one exception—the man I married, who voiced his jealousy of Henry—we have only allowed into our lives men who make him (and me) laugh.

Would it have been better for me to stay with my ex-husband, who restrained me, stalked me and now has a record on file down at the courthouse? Would it be best to teach my son to get married and stay married to and only have sex with one person, even if he is an addict and a liar?

When he is grown and looks back, will he remember the tears I shed for Theo, or will he remember that I walked away from pain, turned my attention elsewhere, became stronger for asserting my independence?

We'll just have to see.

Two months ago: Henry and I are hanging out. I've been thinking about this sex thing, and I have a question for my son. Though I act all self-assured about this "I'll have sex when and with whom I want" stance, the fact is, he's getting older, more aware. I wonder if, next time, he'll get uncomfortable. He knows what sex is, though he has requested I save the serious details for a later date. (If he asks a question, I answer it, on his level, and give him the option to stop me when he's had enough.) One reason I am wondering if I need to be more careful is because recently, I was in my room, getting changed, when he happened in. His eyes shot to my crotch, and I realized my ill-fitting underpants were exposing more than a little fuzz. Thick black pubic hair pointed what must've seemed like taunting or accusing fingers at him. I looked at him. "Do you want me to stop getting changed when you're around?"

"Yeah." He's not ready to think too much about sexuality—not mine or his.

"So, Hen, do you think if I get another boyfriend, you'll be uncomfortable if he sleeps over, like Theo used to?"

"Ooooohhhh," replies Henry, in his best sarcastic voice, "Henry's not supposed to know about that stuff!" Then he laughs and tells me of course he won't mind. I believe him. Maybe, when the time comes, I'll change my mind. Maybe he'll change his. We'll adapt. Henry first. I won't *not* have sex in my house, but I will use discretion as discretion is called for, which could mean sex while he's at school or sending him for a sleepover on nights I want to get it on all night.

I tell Henry a few days after that conversation that I am writing about sex again. I ask him how he feels; I check some of the quotations used in this story. At one point, he stops me. His eyes say, Wait a minute. "You've had sex?" he asks, surprised. I realize he has taken information he's been given and turned philosophical. Like so many children, he knows there is this sex thing, but the mechanics escape him, as they should.

"Of course I've had sex," I say, but I don't laugh or tease. "How do you think I got you?"

"I know that mom!" he replies, but he seems still at that stage of thinking his parents have had sex precisely as many times as there are children. Then he starts to ask if I've had sex with others. This question fascinates me, but of course a little child who knows his mother sleeps beside men thinks only: they are sleeping beside each other.

"How do you feel about me having sex again sometime?"

He thinks about this. "Well, it's fine if it's someone you know really well and love. Not the guy you just met down at the Texaco."

While I have hopped into relationships quickly, I have never in my son's life hooked up with "the guy down at the Texaco," though I have tried variations on that theme pre-motherhood. I think sometimes he takes the information I give him, mixes it in with the stuff he hears at school, on the radio, on the TV and comes up confused—a confusion he doesn't waste much time contemplating. Yet.

It'll catch up with him, sure. And when he's ready for the next level of knowledge, what will I tell him? I don't know, but I'm thinking, for starters, I'll say, "It's fine if it's someone you know really well and love. Not some guy or gal you just met down at the Texaco."

And yes, this information will contradict parts of the life I've lived thus far. But, you know, we all want better for our kids. Though I try to have no regrets (preferring to think of life as a series of lessons), I can look back on my life and clearly see moments of hurt. But on that list of pain, there is no mention of sex. The one-night stands? There were some good ones. The fuckbuddy period, with Thad, whom I never wanted for more than his friendship and his body? I still can say, thirteen years later, that that was one of the most fun years of my life.

What I regret, if I regret anything, is the lack of information I had for so long. As a child, I knew little more about my body than what was offered in a vague film in fifth grade thematically focused more on flowers than vaginas. In a house filled with nine daughters, my mother did not speak of periods. Two pamphlets appeared on my bed one day. My job: figure it out. Tampons were taboo. I still look at Tampax and remember the first box I bought, on the sly, brought home, struggled with, could not ask for help with.

No one taught me the basics of birth control. I had a Catholic, holy-rolling daddy who toted his kids around in a car with Abortion Is Killing Your Own Child painted in huge fluorescent letters across the back. I had to decipher that message and, when eventually I did, to take from it that choice was not an option. My first birth control pills—and whatever damage they did to me then and over the years I took them—came long after I gave up my virginity, drunk, to a sleazy bouncer years my senior and with a girlfriend.

When I got those pills, I felt like a sinner. Until I learned to appreciate them, and then to loathe them for the havoc they might be wreaking upon me. That cycle repeated for years. On the pill. Off the pill. On the diaphragm. Forget to put in the diaphragm. Get pregnant, three times. Lose one to miscarriage. Have one—my Henry. Abort one—not hard after all, a great relief in fact. Have men, upon being told of a late period, get angry at me for not having been more careful. Have myself think, "They have a point" (until that last scare, when finally, *finally* I said, "For god's sake, *you* could've dug out a condom").

I regret not being told I could be in control—not just chemically—but emotionally. That other me was so warped by the messages and silences that for years foreplay entailed getting drunk to take away all those stupid fears planted in childhood.

What turns my stomach most is that, somehow, I finally bought into the myth of marriage as a potential cure, and, consequently, I will spend the rest of my life watching my back, my child's back, fearing the man with whom I "did the right thing."

But the sex? When I wasn't drunk, when birth control was handy and used, when I was feeling it and loving it and laughing and sometimes crying with the joy of it? You won't hear regret when I recall those moments.

I am in control now. Of my body and my mind. I am waiting for sex because I want to wait. I know where I can get it if I want it fast; I don't want it fast anymore. Raging hormones be damned, that happens to be what I feel like doing. When that changes, I will find an opportunity, I will *be* an opportunity. And I will fuck whomever I want (okay, contingent on mutual agreement) whenever I want (contingent on schedules).

This is the knowledge I want my son to have. I want him to know his body, what it is capable of at its best and finest, its most random and sloppy. I don't want him stopping, mid-thrust, as his mother once did, to run to the bathroom and puke a drunken puke only to have his partner demand they finish. I don't want him to knock up some girl the first time they do it and then have to deal with making a choice.

But do I want him to wait? To save it? To marry and dedicate his life and body to just one?

Hardly.

At some point during our conversation, we touch on how sex feels. "It feels good," I say.

"It does?!"

"It does. But you know what? We can talk about this more another time. Now, it's time for you to go to camp and have fun. Okay?"

"Okay," he says, and already the conversation is drifting away as he thinks of more important matters at hand: Box hockey. Water fights. Summer.

CONTRIBUTORS

ASKHARI is coediting an anthology of prison writings entitled *Convictions* (www.askhari.com). She is the founder and moderator of an online writing workshop called de Griot Space (www.degriotspace.com) and currently resides somewhere out there.

@NONYMOUS remains at large.

BLACK ARTEMIS is the alter ego of one of thousands of activist writers in New York City. With her sun in Virgo, moon in Cancer and Leo rising, trust me, she's an interesting piece of work. She's cool though, getting her fingernails dirty with issues from police brutality to multicultural education. Under her real name, she holds degrees from—get this—Columbia University, and is developing numerous writing projects. I've threatened to become the dominant personality, however, if she doesn't allow me to create a website of feminist erotica for women of color, so I'll see y'all online.

JULIAN BELL is currently working on her master's degree in literature and performance studies in English. She has been published in *Synapse* and the *Evergreen Chronicles*.

HANNE BLANK is a writer, editor, educator, historian and musician. Author of *Big Big Love: A Sourcebook on Sex for People of Size and Those Who Love Them* and editor of *Zaftig: Well*

Rounded Erotica, she is the associate editor of *Scarlet Letters: A Journal of Femmerotica* (scarletletters.com). Her work has been published in the *Boston Phoenix, BBW Magazine, Black Sheets, Paramour* and *Radiance,* as well as in *Best Bisexual Erotica 2000* and *Best Women's Erotica 2000.* She lives in Boston with her intergendered life partner and two cats. Visit her at www.hanne.net.

SIOBHAN BROOKS was born and raised in the Sunnydale Housing Projects in San Francisco, and started school when she was eight years old. She is currently pursuing a master's in sociology at the New School for Social Research. Her writings have appeared in *Z* magazine, *Bitch,* the anthology *Whores and Other Feminists,* and she interviewed Professor Angela Y. Davis about race, feminism and pornography for the UC Hastings *Women's Law Journal.* She has lectured at various universities including UC Berkeley and Yale University. She is also working on a book about men and women sex workers of color.

KAREN BULLOCK-JORDAN has been a progressive activist and organizer for over a decade. Now at Haymarket People's Fund, she has worked at *Sojourner, OutWrite,* and the National Gay & Lesbian Task Force. In her "spare" time, she writes and gives workshops on sexuality—specifically S/M, women's sexuality, people of color's sexuality, gender identity and expression, radical sexual politics and various combinations thereof. She has presented at numerous universities and conferences and been published in various queer and feminist publications. A Black femme diva, she is a sacred whore by calling, a sexual adventurer by birth and a slut by practice.

CHELSEA CAIN lives in Portland, Oregon, where she works as a freelance writer. She is the author of *Dharma Girl: A Road Trip Across the American Generations,* and the editor of *Wild Child: Girlhoods in the Counterculture.* She also writes frequently for alternative weeklies and other small literary ventures. Currently, Chelsea is working on a novel. She enjoys confessional poetry, snowboarding and referring to herself in the third person.

BETHANY JEAN CLEMENT is a Seattle-based writer and editor who now attempts to act like an adult.

DIANA COURVANT is a trans, intersex, feminist, anti-violence, anti-racist, anti–domestic violence and disability rights activist. She is also currently the Programs Coordinator for the Survivor Project, the nonprofit agency dedicated to addressing the needs of intersex and trans survivors of domestic and sexual violence. In her spare (!) time she is busy working away at her novel, examining the subtle differences between Portland's best French fries, and acting as a personal grocery shopping consultant to her upstairs neighbors.

When she's not prying into the nooks and crannies of human relationships, MEG DALY is a writer and editor. She coedited *Letters of Intent: Women Cross the Generations to Talk About Family, Work, Sex, Love and the Future of Feminism.* She is also the editor of *Surface Tension: Love, Sex and Politics Between Lesbians and Straight Women.* Her writing has appeared in *Best of the Best Lesbian Erotica* and other anthologies, as well as the *Women's Review of Books, Newsday* and *Tikkun.* She lives in Portland, Oregon.

CHRISTY DAMIO, a confirmed—make that addicted—New Yorker, received her B.A. from Sarah Lawrence College in 1997 and immediately began to invade the Latin media world as a stealth *mulata.* Christy has lent her flair for the unusual and her pit-bull grip on American vernacular to some of the best-known Latin magazines in the U.S., including *Latingirl, Urban Latino,* and the much-celebrated *Mia.* She also recently appeared in *What About the Children?* AMP Productions' documentary on interracial couples. An award-winning poet, she lives in Queens and is currently writing a comic novel about eighties rock and the freaks that still love it.

LAUREL GILBERT is an author and artist who lives in the Midwest with her family. Her work has appeared in *Listen Up: Voices of the Next Feminist Generation,* and she is coauthor of *SurferGrrrls: Look, Ethel, an Internet Guide for Us!* She is currently working on her first novel.

SUSAN JANE GILMAN is the author of *Kiss My Tiara: How to Rule the World as a SmartMouth Goddess,* forthcoming from Warner Books. Her nonfiction has appeared in the anthology *Body Outlaws: Young Women Write About Body Image and Identity,* as well as in the *New York Times,* the *Los Angeles Times, Newsday, Ms., Us,* the *Utne Reader* and the *Village Voice,* among others. She is also a published fiction writer and former feminist humor columnist for the (sadly) now-defunct *HUES* magazine. A native New Yorker to the core, she lives in "rent exile" in Washington, D.C.

SPIKE GILLESPIE is the author of *All the Wrong Men and One Perfect Boy: A Memoir.* Her work has appeared in print in *GQ, Elle, Self, Playboy, Cosmo, Mademoiselle, BUST, HipMama, Minx, Texas Monthly,* the *Austin American Statesman* and the *Austin Chronicle,* among others. Online she has written for *Salon, Word, Tripod,*

Prodigy, Oxygen, and *Underwire.* More of her work can be found at www.spikeg.com. Currently, she is working on a novel about the laughingstock we call the Internet. She is single mother to The Amazing Henry. To the best of her recollection, she really, really likes sex.

ADRIEN-ALICE HANSEL was raised in upstate New York and Moorhead, Minnesota. After graduating from Smith College, she worked in the literary offices of Actors Theatre of Louisville and Seattle Repertory Theatre. A dramaturg, poet and playwright, she is currently studying dramatic criticism at Yale School of Drama, reading more than may be good for her and learning to write sentences with fewer clauses.

TARA HARDY is a femme dyke who lives and writes in Seattle. She is a member of the Seattle Slam! Team 2000, and her work can be found in *Vox Populi, Switched On Gutenberg,* and *Vs.,* her self-published chapbook. You can also find her at publishingonline.com, local stages around Seattle, and the dog park, where she frequently frolics with her chi-weiner, Lily.

DAISY HERNÁNDEZ is an essayist, poet and fiction writer. A contributor to *This Bridge Called My Back, Twenty Years Later* (forthcoming), she is currently a graduate student of journalism and Latin American and Caribbean studies at New York University focusing on language usage and race relations in Latina communities in the United States. She is working on a collection of essays, short stories and poems about the languages and experiences of immigrant Latinas and their U.S. born children. She also works with WILL (Women in Literature and Letters), a women of color–centric organization in NYC devoted to social and political change through writing, reading and publishing.

LISA JOHNSON lives in Georgia where she teaches freshman composition at the State University of West Georgia. She is the editor of a forthcoming collection of essays on sex and feminism, *Jane Sexes It Up,* to be published by Four Walls, Eight Windows in spring 2001.

SARA JOHNSTON, also known as Thirston W. Prescott, is a drag king looking for liberation through drag and other revolutionary acts. Sara would like to thank her girlfriend for making space to discover masculinity and for her never-ending support in learning how to celebrate genders.

MARA KAPLAN is a freelance writer in San Francisco.

Born in Chicago, ANNIE KOH grew up in New Hampshire, sulked in Connecticut and Ohio and now lives in San Francisco. Regardless of location, she has never made her bed, although now she does wash the sheets. She has written for various offline and online publications, including the *San Francisco Examiner* and her own zine *For Motion Discomfort*, and is a member of Kearny Street Workshop, the nation's oldest Asian-American community arts organization. Her next project is www.crankygirls.com.

NOMY LAMM is a fat freaky Jew dyke amputee from Olympia, Washington. Her writing has been published in anthologies and magazines including *Listen Up: Voices from the Next Feminist Generation, Body Outlaws: Young Women Write About Body Image and Identity, Ms., HUES* and *Seventeen.* She recently wrote and helped produce a punk rock opera, *The Transfused,* with Oly queer band The Need. She is also a drag performer, lecturer, community organizer, poet, show tune diva, and a Virgo.

J. KEIKO LANE is the fourth-generation Japanese-American daughter of an artist and a jazz musician. Her poetry and essays have appeared most recently in *Calyx, americas review, Harrington Lesbian Fiction Quarterly,* and the *Journal of the Nuclear Age Peace Foundation,* which awarded her the 1998 Barbara Mandigo Kelly Peace Poetry Award. She has recently completed *The Rememberers,* a manuscript of poems. She lives in Northern California where she writes and studies somatic psychology.

ABBY LEVINE has an M.A. in creative writing from the University of Minnesota. She lives in Seattle where she teaches writing at the local community colleges. Her poetry has appeared in *Calyx, Bridges* and *Paramour,* among others. She is eager to write for the sex industry.

BETH LISICK is a writer and performer. She is the author of *Monkey Girl* and has a band called The Beth Lisick Ordeal. In addition to writing a weekly column for the *San Francisco Chronicle*'s website, she has been published in *Best American Poetry 1997* and *American Poetry: The Next Generation.*

MAGDALEN and her assorted alter egos have been published in magazines including *BUST, Bookforum, SIGNUM* and *Wired,* as well as in several books.

MARY MARTONE is a Seattle-based writer who has penned the queer advice column "Big Tips" since 1994. She is also the former co-host (with Dan Savage) of the sex advice radio show *Savage Love Live*. She dreams of traveling around the country in an Airstream trailer, dispensing advice at sliding scale fees. In this dream, she is accompanied by her sweetheart Maura and their two nutty dogs, Kiera and Brenda.

Erika Mikkalo, the daughter of a pension actuary and a perfect mother, was born in Portland, Oregon. She studied literature and painting at Indiana University, and is currently an M.F.A. candidate at Columbia College in Chicago. Her story "Throwing Stones" received the 1998 Tobias Wolff award for short fiction by the *Bellingham Review*. She is decompressing from a bad marriage and is considering meeting people for coffee.

Geraldine Mitchell is a Brooklyn, New York–based writer.

Lisa Miya-Jervis is the editor and publisher of *Bitch: Feminist Response to Pop Culture*. Her work has also appeared in *Ms.*, the *San Francisco Chronicle*, the *Women's Review of Books*, *BUST*, *HUES*, *Girlfriends* and *Punk Planet*. She is currently at work on the forthcoming Seal Press anthology *Young Wives' Tales: Feminists on Love and Commitment* (with Jill Corral). She lives with her husband in Oakland, California.

Mary Anne Mohanraj (http://www.mamohanraj.com) is the author of *Torn Shapes of Desire*, editor of *Aqua Erotica* and consulting editor for *Herotica 7*. She has been published in a multitude of anthologies and magazines, including *Herotica 6*, *Best American Erotica 1999*, and *Best Women's Erotica 2000*. Mohanraj serves as editor-in-chief for the erotic webzine *Clean Sheets* (www.cleansheets.com). She also moderates the EROS Workshop, co-moderates the newsgroup soc.sexuality.general and is a graduate of Clarion West '97. She has received degrees in writing and English from Mills College and the University of Chicago; she now teaches writing at the University of Utah, where she is currently starting both a new speculative fiction magazine and a Ph.D. program.

Augusta Moore is a twenty-eight-year-old Ph.D. dropout who left the university with a master's degree and a better understanding of what matters. She works as a freelance writer, editor and magazine publisher on the West Coast.

Jill Nagle's most recent book, as associate editor, is *Male Lust: Pleasure, Power and Transformation*, with editor Kerwin Kay. Her work has appeared in such periodicals as *American Book Review*, *Moxie*, *Girlfriends*, *On Our Backs* and *Blue Food*, as well as in anthologies such as *Best Lesbian Erotica*, *Best Bisexual*

Erotica, Looking Queer and *Bisexual Politics.* She is currently working on a number of literary and screenwriting projects. Visit her web site at www.jillnagle.com.

Notorious M.E.G. was born in Detroit and spent her formative years there and in northern New Jersey. A cofounder of *Push,* a magazine by and for queer women, she currently lives in Seattle where she works as a freelance writer and an associate producer at a website. M.E.G. thanks all of her exes—she's learned something from every one of them—and also the late Biggie Smalls for the temporary use and bastardization of his name.

E. René Parker is a Southern writer who one day hopes to visit Savannah, Georgia, New Orleans, Louisiana and the Greek Isles.

Karleen Pendleton Jiménez is a mixed Chicana boydyke from Rosemead, California. She is a teacher and writer currently residing in Canada. She is the author of *Are You a Boy or a Girl?,* a kid's book published by Green Dragon Press, and hopes some day to get her novel *Not Everyone Turns Pink Under the Sun* into print. She is the former director and founder of San Diego's Queer Players and now writes with Lengua Latina of Toronto.

Carla Richmond is a black West Indian dyke social worker and a sometime-writer and avid reader of sci-fi and "erotica." Her work has appeared in *Ma-Ka: Diasporic Juks: Writing by Queers of African Descent* and in *The Bluelight Corner: Black Women Writing on Passion, Sex, and Romantic Love.* She was born in Jamaica, raised in the Bahamas and further nurtured in New York City. She currently lives in San Francisco—within walking distance of Good Vibrations—with her partner and (predictably) their two cats.

Karen Rosenberg grew up in New York City and currently makes her home in Seattle, Washington. She works at a domestic violence program and will be entering a graduate program in women's studies. Her writing has been published in several literary magazines, but this is the first time her work has appeared in a book. She's thrilled to be included in this anthology, though part of her wishes the subject matter were knitting or gardening instead of sex. Then there would be no doubt that she'd show it to her family . . .

Sara Seinberg just moved to providence, rhode island. she can't say enough about buddy cianci, the mayor who did some time in prison and got re-elected the minute they let him out. a great town. strange. way better than the tv show. she has toured with sister spit a few times, thinks often about carving out enormous debt for herself and returning to school, and really loves the color orange. she is a writer, performer and photographer living with gus, the cutest dog in all the land. gus is a taurus. in case you wondered.

CECILIA TAN writes about sex, baseball and other things from her cat-inhabited attic office in Cambridge, Massachusetts. She is active in local and national S/M-leather politics and an officer of the New England Leather Alliance. She is also the founder, editor and janitor of Circlet Press, pioneering publishers of cutting-edge erotica. Her collection of erotic short stories, *Black Feathers*, was published by HarperCollins in 1998, and her short stories have appeared everywhere from *Ms.* magazine to *Penthouse.* She is at work on an erotic "novel mosaic" entitled *The Book of Want.* Visit her at http://www.circlet.com/pub/u/ctan/home.html.

MICHELLE TEA is the cofounder of Sister Spit, a traveling girl-poetry road show, and the author of *The Passionate Mistakes and Intricate Corruption of One Girl in America* and *Valencia.* She lives in San Francisco.

KARY BARRETT WAYSON received her M.F.A. from the University of Washington in 1997, where she won the Joan Grayston prize upon graduation. She was a finalist for both the Randall Jarrell Poetry Prize and the Floating Bridge Press Chapbook Award in 1998, and she was a semi-finalist in the Altanta Review's first book contest in 1999. In October of 1999, she was chosen for a month-long writer's residency in Oysterville, Washington by the Willard Espy Literary Foundation. Her poems have been published in *Poetry Northwest,* the *Seattle Review, Pontoon #2* and *FIELD,* among others. She works as a waitress in Seattle, Washington.

MEG WEBER is a twenty-six-year-old polyamorous dyke living in Portland, Oregon with her partner Kelly and their stuffed wolf pup (named Wolfpup). A Portland native, Meg attended Central Catholic High School, where she learned to love writing by keeping a journal. She has a bachelor's degree in psychology, and is pursuing an M.A. in creative nonfiction from Portland State University. She works as a retail manager and graphic designer for a local artist who creates handmade greeting cards and journals. Meg strives for honesty in all aspects of her life to encourage authentic communication about sexuality, power, polyamory and desire.

About the Editor

LEE DAMSKY worked in independent publishing for four years as a publicist, production director and editor and is now a freelance writer and editor in New York City. Inspired by a natural curiosity about sex and a passion for the written word, she has long been a reader of sexual literature.

SELECTED SEAL PRESS TITLES

Body Outlaws: Young Women Write About Body Image and Identity, edited by Ophira Edut, foreword by Rebecca Walker. $14.95, 1-58005-043-3. Essays filled with honesty and humor by women who have chosen to ignore, subvert or redefine the dominant beauty standard.

Valencia by Michelle Tea. $13.00, 1-58005-035-2. The fast-paced account of one girl's search for love and high times in the dyke world of San Francisco. By turns poetic and frantic, *Valencia* is an edgy, visceral ride through the queer girl underground of the Mission District.

Cunt: A Declaration of Independence by Inga Muscio. $14.95, 1-58005-015-8. An ancient title of respect for women, "cunt" long ago veered off the path of honor and now careens toward the heart of every woman as an expletive. Muscio traces this winding road, giving women both the motivation and the tools to claim "cunt" as a positive and powerful force in the lives of all women.

The Mother Trip: Hip Mama's Guide to Staying Sane in the Chaos of Motherhood by Ariel Gore. $14.95, 1-58005-029-8. A witty, honest and empowering book for mothers who want to create their own road rules for the unpredictable and transforming trip that is motherhood.

Listen Up: Voices from the Next Feminist Generation edited by Barbara Findlen. $14.95, 1-878067-61-3. For the first time, the voices of today's young feminists, the "Third Wave," are brought together to explore and reveal their lives. Topics include racism, sexuality, identity, AIDS, revolution, abortion and much more.

Lap Dancing for Mommy: Tender Stories of Disgust, Blame and Inspiration by Erika Lopez. $14.00, 1-878067-96-6. Not for the faint of heart, this debut collection of comic narratives is shockingly incisive and offers reams of racy, raunchy and riotous appeal.

She's a Rebel: The History of Women in Rock & Roll by Gillian G. Gaar. $16.95, 1-878067-08-7. *She's a Rebel* tells the fascinating story of the women who have shaped rock and pop music for the last five decades.

Wild Child: Girlhoods in the Counterculture, edited by Chelsea Cain, foreword by Moon Zappa. $16.00, 1-58005-031-X. Daughters of the hippie generation reflect on the experience of a counter-culture childhod, presenting a fresh perspective on our current world as seen through the legacy of sixties ideals.

Seal Press publishes many books of fiction and nonfiction by women writers. If you are unable to obtain a Seal Press title from a bookstore, please order from us directly by calling 800-754-0271. Visit our website at www.sealpress.com.